P9-BTM-354

AUSCHWITZ:

BEGINNING OF A NEW ERA?

Reflections on the Holocaust

Papers given at the
International Symposium on the Holocaust
held at the Cathedral of Saint John the Divine,
New York City, June 3 to 6, 1974

AUSCHWITZ:

BEGINNING OF A NEW ERA?

Reflections on the Holocaust

edited by

Eva Fleischner

KTAV Publishing House, Inc.
The Cathedral Church of St. John the Divine
Anti-Defamation League of B'nai B'rith

© COPYRIGHT 1977
THE CATHEDRAL CHURCH OF ST. JOHN THE DIVINE

Library of Congress Cataloging in Publication Data

International Symposium on the Holocaust, Cathedral
of St. John the Divine, 1974.
Auschwitz, beginning of a new era?

Includes bibliographical references.
1. Holocaust (Jewish theology)—Congresses. 2. Christianity and antisemitism—Congresses. 3. Judaism—Relations — Christianity — Congresses. 4. Christianity and
other religions—Judaism—Congresses. I. Fleischner, Eva,
1925-   II. New York (City). Cathedral of St. John
the Divine. III. Title.
BM645.H6157   1974   296.3'87   76-53809
ISBN 0-87068-499-X

MANUFACTURED IN THE UNITED STATES OF AMERICA

Table of Contents

Contents

Contents

Introduction

On May 8, 1945 Germany laid down its arms. For the world at large this meant the end of the European phase of World War II. For a few thousand Jewish men, women, and children it marked the end of hell on earth, the end of the Holocaust. For many of the survivors of the death camps the gates to freedom opened too late. They were in such advanced stages of starvation and disease that even the best medical care could not save them. For the majority freedom marked the beginning of a slow and painful journey from the land of the dead to that of the living, an agonizing struggle from the infernal darkness of the Kingdom of Night back to the light of day. This is how one survivor, who had entered the camp as a child and, in his own words, left it as an old man, has described his moment of "liberation":

> Three days after the liberation of Buchenwald I became very ill with food poisoning. I was transferred to the hospital and spent two weeks between life and death.
>
> One day I was able to get up, after gathering all my strength. I wanted to see myself in the mirror hanging on the opposite wall. I had not seen myself since the ghetto.
>
> From the depths of the mirror, a corpse gazed back at me. The look in his eyes, as they stared into mine, has never left me. [Elie Wiesel, *Night*]

Some lacked the psychological strength to complete the journey. Others carry the burden of their haunting memories of the nightmare silently within themselves to this day. A few felt compelled eventually to speak out, to "tell the tale," for the sake of their dead Jewish brothers and sisters, so that the world might know and the six million not have died in vain. They did so at a cost none but they will ever be able to measure.

For their fellow Jews throughout the world, the revelation of the dimensions of the Holocaust brought the realization that one-third of the Jewish world population had been murdered, that Eastern European Jewry in particular, source of the richest aspects of Jewish life, was reduced to ashes, never to rise again. The trauma was too great to be faced. The Israeli poet Yehuda Amichai, in his novel *Not of This Time, Not of This Place,* writes that "most people in our time have the face of Lot's wife, turned toward the Holocaust yet always escaping."

Seeking to escape the reality that was the Holocaust—no wonder.

Few of us can muster the courage for the alternative—to confront it. But can we say that the non-Jewish world is even turned toward the Holocaust thirty years later? It was this question that eventually led to the Symposium of which the papers in this volume are the tangible outcome.

Although Auschwitz is a historical event now thirty years in the past, its repercussions are still felt today; and not only in the Jewish consciousness. Auschwitz forces upon us a radical reexamination of the very concepts of "culture" and "civilization." For if Hitler and some of his closest associates were men devoid of the rudiments of culture, many of the "technicians," those who saw to the smooth functioning of the machinery of death, were Ph.D's, lovers not only of Wagner, but of Goethe and Beethoven. Auschwitz rang the death knell for at least a certain kind of Western civilization.

The Symposium can be seen as one attempt to approach the Holocaust, to reflect upon it, from a variety of angles. The authors of the papers in this volume bring their own disciplines to bear upon this reflection. A multidisciplinary approach to the Holocaust is one of the distinguishing features of the Symposium.

Another characteristic is its joint undertaking by Jews and Christians. Jews and Christians each bear their own burden, yet they are willing to share it with each other—not so as to lessen it or place it upon the other's shoulders, but in the hope that the effort of common reflection may help us understand, assume the past for the sake of the future.

For Jews, even for those who did not live through the death camps, to approach the Holocaust is to risk being consumed by its flames. The event has traumatized Jewish experience and continues to traumatize it, both in the Diaspora and in the State of Israel. For some it calls into question the very concepts of God and of faith in Him. "Perhaps some day someone will explain how, on the level of man, Auschwitz was possible; but on the level of God, it will forever remain the most disturbing of mysteries" (Wiesel).

For Christians, the Holocaust necessitates a confrontation with certain fundamental aspects of Christian tradition and teaching that lead some speakers to raise the question, Can one still be a Christian after Auschwitz? Those who answer affirmatively are then faced with the further question of how; What can those who answer no offer the world in place of Christianity? A secularity, a humanism, a faith in man rather than God? Was Auschwitz, then, not the work of man? The dilemma is rendered particularly acute for the Christian. For however one assesses the role which Christian teaching, or the churches, or Pius XII, played in the Holocaust (a question frequently dealt with during the Symposium), none can claim dissociation from the event. In the face of the Holocaust neutrality becomes apathy, noninvolvement becomes guilt.

Hence the radical reassessment of Christian tradition as it bears upon Judaism, which is attempted by some Christian theologians and philosophers in this volume. Is Christian theology itself at stake? Is anti-Judaism endemic to the very nature of Christianity? Yet this very effort to examine the roots of Christian teaching and theology leads one historian to ask whether Jews can afford to wait while Christians engage in their intramural theologizing. Will a new Christian theology be any greater guarantee against anti-Semitism than the old?

A certain tension runs through the Symposium between the Holocaust as a uniquely Jewish phenomenon and as transcending Jewish experience. This raises several questions:

Can one come to grips with the full horror of Auschwitz without recognizing the "scandal" of Jewish particularity? For the non-Jew in particular, is there the temptation (as witness the de-Judaizing efforts carried out in Soviet Russia and Poland today with regard to Babi-Yar and Auschwitz) to lose sight of the fact that whereas non-Jews *could* become victims of Nazism, Jews were inevitably destined to be so, because they had become in Nazi ideology the paradigm for the "inferior race"?

At the same time, how does one explain the undeniable preoccupation with the Jewish dimensions of the Holocaust? Even to raise this question—at least on the part of non-Jews—may border on insensitivity. As Elie Wiesel has said, "One Jew was put to death in Jerusalem 2000 years ago and the non-Jewish world has not ceased to speak of his death. Do we [Jews] not have the right, the duty, to keep alive the memory of 6,000,000 dead?" Jewish experience has been profoundly shaped and reshaped across the centuries by historical experiences—of salvation above all, but also of destruction. A deep sense of identity and mission, coupled with the genius of telling tales, has preserved not only for Jews, but for the rest of the world that cares to hear them, root experiences of the Jewish people.

What of the preoccupation with the Jewish aspects of the Holocaust on the part of a growing number of non-Jews, especially Christians, which is so evident in this volume? We may well touch here that ambiguity which has marked the relationship between Jew and Christian across the centuries. In a certain manner the Christian is obsessed by

the Jew—an obsession which has all too often taken the form of persecution and hatred, as is amply documented in the Symposium. Yet to
speak of this only is too one-sided a picture. The question raised by
one speaker needs to be given serious consideration: Why was it that
the church, throughout the Middle Ages, saw to the survival of the
Jewish people? If one can indeed speak of a love-hate relationship between the two communities, is it perhaps because Christians perceive
Jews as the bearers of a universality, across their very particularity,
which Christianity has claimed for itself from the beginning, and still
dreams of realizing?

Another perspective for placing the Holocaust squarely within the
Jewish experience, and at the same time beyond it, may be provided by
studying it within the wider framework of cultural history. The Holocaust culminated in a total reversal of the most cherished values of the
West. For this very reason it should be studied not as a chapter in Jewish history only, but in the history of civilization which is reflected in
the history of the Jews. While such a perspective would not eliminate
or mitigate the role played by Christianity, greater attention might be
given than has generally been the case so far to the role played, not by
religion, but by its replacements through a "pseudoreligion," in which
the most basic concepts of God, redemption, sin, and revelation are
radically reversed, and their place is taken by the state, the party, the
race.

The Symposium represents a joint effort by Jews and Christians to
speak of the unspeakable. Readers of this volume will detect again and
again a certain ambiguity—an ambiguity that was evident already in
the initial planning stages of the meeting. To speak: Is it not to shatter
a silence which is more deafening than words; to fall into the danger of
explaining and analyzing a dimension of existence which, because it
reveals at one and the same time the depths of human depravity and
the heights of the human spirit, can only be approached in fear and
trembling?

Yet if speaking carries with it the danger of defilement and irrever-
ence, silence can lead to oblivion. In the words of the Baal Shem Tov,
"Forgetfulness leads to exile. Remembrance is the secret of redemption." To forget Auschwitz, to write history as though it had never occurred, or to make of it a mysterious, numinous event, is only to height-
en the ever-present danger that Auschwitz will recur, that millions will
have died in vain, that even the most fearful lessons of history have
taught us nothing. Auschwitz was the work of human hands, con-

ceived and executed by human beings. Therefore we, as human beings, must seek to come to grips with it.

The Origins of the Symposium

In June 1973 a group of some twelve Jewish and Christian scholars met at the Cathedral of Saint John the Divine in New York City, at the invitation of Dean James P. Morton, to discuss the possibility of holding an international Symposium on the Holocaust. We were a diverse lot, from different parts of the United States and Canada, laymen and women, rabbis, ministers, and priests, college professors, theologians. We shared a common concern for examining the implications of Auschwitz for our respective traditions and the relationship between them, but little else. Some felt that it was time to move on to present and future concerns. Others—particularly the Christians present— expressed the view that the very word "Holocaust" had not yet entered the vocabulary of millions of people. Out of a long day's discussion came several conclusions:

• Although an in-depth discussion of the Holocaust is taking place today here and there, large numbers of people are still almost totally unacquainted with this grim chapter of Western history. Hence the decision was made to hold the Symposium.

• Even when the subject is explored, this is done all too often in isolation, rather than in mutual contact between Jews and Christians. It was decided, therefore, to try and achieve interaction by inviting speakers and participants from both traditions. (The absence from the Symposium of Arab speakers, whether Christian or Muslim, and of more representatives of Eastern Christianity, is regrettable. See the Statement by Gabriel Habib, p. 417.)

• The Symposium would not be a closed scholars' conference, but would aim to attract the widest possible audience.

• It was considered important to explore Auschwitz and its repercussions not only through intellectual debate, but through artistic media as well. A collection of sculpture, paintings, and lithographs by contemporary artists was assembled by the Cathedral staff, and remained on display in the Cathedral throughout the meeting. (It provided a much needed space for quiet and meditation.) Two evenings were to be set aside for music and poetry. They proved to be among the high points of the Symposium, but did not save it from the charge of "intellectual overkill."

• Auschwitz was to be the focus and point of departure. The Symposium would also, however, explore problems facing Jews and Christians today, all of which have in one way or another been affected, or given a new visibility, by this watershed in twentieth-century history. Hence the inclusion in the program of topics such as Blacks and Jews, the New Left and Israel, Christian mission, the New Romanticism and biblical faith. Some of these topics make it clear from the start that, however deep our religious and theological concerns, other disciplines, such as psychology, history, and sociology, are needed to throw light on questions of faith. In a predominantly secular society, a purely theological approach is clearly inadequate and outdated.

• The Symposium was to be international in scope, drawing scholars from Israel and Europe, as well as Canada and the United States. Yet the fact that it was being held in the United States was never questioned, and is significant. For if the leading role of this country in world politics today is undeniable (however ambiguously it is regarded by many), it also has the largest Jewish community in the world, and more diverse and viable Christian groups than any other country. If the United States bears a special political responsibility toward the rest of the world today, this is no less true in the religious realm. Nowhere is this more evident than in the relations between Jew and Christian.

• While the program is not lacking in some of the well-known names among Jewish as well as Christian scholars, the decision was made to have less frequently heard voices as well. Hence the inclusion of some comparative latecomers to the arena of Jewish-Christian studies. This "new generation" owes its existence to the persevering and consistent work of pioneers, who patiently and courageously spoke out and wrote on the Holocaust and the State of Israel at a time when it was far from fashionable to do so in Christian circles (men such as Franklin Littell, A. Roy Eckardt, J. Coert Rylaarsdam, Edward Flannery—to mention only a few).

Out of the June 8 discussion a smaller Steering Committee was formed, which worked on the program in the ensuing months. Dean Morton put the entire resources of the Cathedral at our disposal. The lectures and discussions were to take place in Synod Hall rather than the cathedral, because it represented relatively neutral territory. (It is worth noting, however, that despite this effort at "neutrality," the close association with a Christian place of worship still proved painful for some Jewish participants. I had the difficult experience of being given a ride home one night by a Jewish couple who told me that if we had been really serious about wanting to reach Jews, we should have known better than to hold this meeting on Christian territory.)

On that sunny June day no one could have foreseen that a few months later another war in the Middle East would have broken out, and that much of the planning for the Symposium was to occur beneath the shadow of one of the most serious crises the State of Israel had yet faced in its brief existence. The tensions of the Yom Kippur War inevitably affected the preparatory work. The projected section on Israel now became "Reflections on the State of Israel in the Light of the Yom Kippur War." During the Symposium itself, the political situation in the Middle East was reflected in numerous discussions and dissensions, on the podium as well as the floor. While we lived through many painful moments, the constantly changing historical reality, which included within a short time the Egyptian cease-fire, as well as Kiryat-Shemona, Ma'alot, and the Syrian cease-fire, forced upon us a down-to-earth realism. We were reminded that even the most refined scholarly considerations are subject to the vicissitudes of history. Auschwitz was, and will remain, a historical event. The destinies of Jew and Christian, whether separately or in relationship, will be shaped by historical circumstances in the present and future as inevitably as they have been in the past.

Welcome

THE RIGHT REV. PAUL MOORE, JR., Episcopal Bishop of New York

It is a great joy for me to see this hall filled for the event which opens today. I cannot take credit for it, but I am very proud that our Cathedral is host to this Symposium, and especially of Dean James Morton, who has provided the principal leadership. I hope this will be more than a conference.

Although I am here only to say Welcome, and to invite you to enter fully into these days and enjoy the facilities of the Cathedral, as the chief rabbi I cannot help say a few words—it is an occupational disease.

It is good not to have only Episcopalians out there, but an audience other than our own.

I hesitate to speak tonight about the subject of the Symposium. It is one of such horror that, despite the fact it happened so many years ago, I believe we still turn away from it in horror; except for those brave poets, writers, artists, and musicians who have dared to look into its depths and depict the reality of Auschwitz. We turn away in horror not only from what happened then, but because, if we look into our own souls, we know that we too were there, at Auschwitz; that any one of us could, under certain circumstances, have committed those atrocities. We are terrified by the depth of depravity of which human beings are capable. I was not at Auschwitz, I was not in Europe during World War II, but I was in the war and I know what is within me. Allow me to be personal for a moment. I entered the Marine Corps as a rather decent, Christian American boy; I was trained to kill; and I did kill, I saw other people killed. I found my soul somehow so warped and immunized by the propaganda to which I was exposed that I could do these things without feeling, and could see others do them without feeling. I have had my Mylai in my own life, so that our Mylai did not surprise me when it came; and I think that perhaps any one of us could also have had his or her own Mylai, his or her own Auschwitz. That is why we draw back in horror at what is in us, and in our brothers and sisters.

At the same time, I believe that we tread on holy ground tonight. This too I hesitate to touch. I take off my shoes, lest walking on it I somehow destroy the fragility, the holiness, of that ground. I am refer-

ring to our sharing, as fellow human beings, the strange glory of innocent suffering, the strange glory of heroism which came out of the stories from Auschwitz. But even deeper, that mystical miracle which per-
vades creation all the way back from Auschwitz: the blood of all those
who have died for humanity, for justice or for peace, or for their God—
even the sad eyes described so well by Leon Blois in *The Woman Who
Was Poor,* the sad eyes of the beasts pacing back and forth in the pris-
ons of the zoos, the innocent suffering not only of adults and children,
but of God's animal creatures. This innocent suffering is a strange
thing in our creation, and Auschwitz may well be its greatest symbol.
Perhaps there is some mystery of atonement here. Perhaps this cosmic
power of the Holy Innocents can be a means by which we become one.
And so I bow down and worship before that innocent suffering and innocent death.

If this Symposium is to mean anything, it must release within us the
power generated by that sacrifice and innocence. It must somehow enable us, in the mystery of the power of God, or the mystery of being, to
apprehend it and make it part of our lives: so that we will dare to share
in that passion, that vicarious suffering, so that we will not only dare
believe that our own lives can be redeemed, but will dare seek to be
one through that blood, and continue to bear and make whatever sacrifices we can to be worthy to share—if only to a small degree—in this
suffering.

So, let it be. Let it be. Let us listen with our hearts and with our souls
to the cries of anguish. But let us also see with our eyes the clouds of
glory. Let those cries and let that vision not be wasted, and let us take it
up once more so that the very things which for so long have been barri-
ers between Christian and Jew, between brother and sister, may now
become means that bind us together. For the time is short, very short.

I am grateful to all those who in the days ahead will lift up for us
something of this vision.

Acknowledgments

Of the many people who helped make this Symposium possible, none played a more crucial role than Dean James Morton. He hosted and coordinated the many Steering Committee meetings during the year of preparation, saw to it that the program became a reality, and that innumerable details were attended to. During the Symposium itself all the facilities of the Cathedral were put at its disposal, participants and out-of-town guests were welcomed, housed, and fed by Dean Morton. Without his generosity and the support and cooperation of the entire Cathedral staff, the meeting could not have taken place.

Special thanks are due to a group of young musicians, the "Trees," in residence at the Cathedral, who provided a haunting evening of music. And to Muriel Rukeyser, who organized an evening of Holocaust poetry during which men and women, some of them survivors, read poems about the Holocaust—many of them their own—in the nave of the Cathedral.

I wish to express my personal gratitude to Dr. Edith Wyschogrod and Mrs. Helga Croner for their valuable editorial help, and to Mrs. Laura Oller for assisting me in the preparation of the manuscript. Thanks, finally, to all the contributors to this volume for their patience and cooperation in making possible its publication. Although I sought to achieve an overall consistency of style in preparing their contributions for publication, I occasionally thought it best to permit some contributors to retain their obvious preferences regarding the capitalization of certain significant religious terms.

PART I

*Theological Reflections
on the Holocaust*

Introduction

In the opening paper of the Symposium, *Irving Greenberg* raises questions that are taken up in one form or another by other speakers, Jewish and Christian alike, throughout the meeting.

Greenberg sees the Holocaust as an unprecedented challenge to Judaism and Christianity, because it radically contradicts the central affirmation of both faiths: that man is made in God's image and that human life is infinitely precious. How can faith in a redeeming God be maintained in light of the revelation of a hitherto unimaginable depth of cruelty and inhumanity?

For Christianity, this question is compounded by another: To what extent has the centuries-old Teaching of Contempt contributed to the Holocaust? Is there something inherent in Christian teaching that created a context for the unprecedented anti-Semitism and mass murder of the Holocaust? (Cf. the papers by Ruether, Pawlikowski, Baum, Huchet-Bishop). But the burden of guilt lies not on Christianity alone. All of modern culture (which climaxed in the gas chambers), the democracies (who were silent), even world Jewry—none are guiltless. The Holocaust forces a response upon all.

Greenberg outlines the main elements of such a response. We must be willing to reexamine our beliefs in the light of the Holocaust. He discusses some contemporary Jewish attempts to do this, those of Emil Fackenheim and Richard Rubenstein in particular. Both represent a genuine effort to grapple with monumental evil, but neither is satisfactory. For each seeks to cut the tension. It is precisely this tension, this dialectic of the Holocaust, which we must be willing to bear. Greenberg speaks of "moment faiths," the alternating rhythm between light and darkness, nihilism and redemption. After Auschwitz an untroubled, serene faith in God as Lord of History no longer seems possible to him. Instead, we must be willing to live with a "troubled theism."

To help us bear this dialectic Greenberg suggests three new "theological models": Job, the Suffering Servant, and chapter 3 of the Lamentations. In the case of Job, no attempt is made by God to justify his suffering. All he is granted is the experience of God's presence in the whirlwind. This gives him sufficient strength to wait for further revelations. For Christianity this image suggests a special challenge: Can it accept new revelations with regard to Judaism? Can it entertain the possibility that the State of Israel may be such a new revelation "out of the whirlwind"?

Chapter 3 of the Lamentations suggests another possible response. No attempt is here made to justify God. Rather, anger against God and struggle with him are the main themes. God is blamed in order that man may be justified. Again, Greenberg suggests a direct application for Christians: perhaps they must quarrel with the gospels themselves for being a source of anti-Semitism. The Word of God itself must be challenged, if need be, for the sake of a purer

3

faith. After Auschwitz neither an easy hope nor an easy faith is possible any longer, for Jew or Christian.

If the Holocaust is radical counter-testimony to the central affirmations of Jewish and Christian faith, it in turn elicits from us the affirmation of what it denies: witness to the dignity and preciousness of life. This is the central testimony that must be given in a post-Auschwitz world. For Jews after the Holocaust, the willingness to give birth to children and raise them as Jews is heroism; but it is not enough. We must also create a world where children will not be hungry, a world where the dignity of every human being is affirmed and the image of God in man restored. A deep commitment to humanity is part of the central witness that must be given in a post-Auschwitz world. It is incumbent upon Jew and non-Jew alike.

The Protestant theologian *Alan Davies* is more critical than Greenberg of Rubenstein's response to Auschwitz. If God is indeed dead, then the Holocaust becomes merely one more absurdity in the chain of human absurdities. Davies's main question to Greenberg, however, concerns the root experiences of Judaism and Christianity. He does not see history as playing the same role in both faiths. Whereas the orientating event for Judaism is the Exodus, for Christianity it is the cross-resurrection, an event that is both historical and transhistorical. This means that Christianity finds the ultimate meaning of history not within history itself, but beyond it.

Davies does not conclude that Christians should minimize history and its tragedies, least of all the scandal of the Holocaust; nor does he advocate an "untroubled theism," as though history does not matter. But if all of history is fragmentary, Christians will be on guard against interpreting it in unqualified theological terms. As a Christian, Davies can, and does, rejoice in the rebirth of Israel; but he is not sure that it can be to him "a sign received out of the whirlwind."

Davies agrees with Greenberg that Christian complicity in the Holocaust presents the Christian conscience with an unprecedented crisis. The same question which Greenberg raised Davies asks of himself: Is it morally possible to remain a Christian after Auschwitz? Regardless of the conclusion, the question must be asked. For the Holocaust can be said to have turned the age-old Christian statement, "Christ died on the cross," into "Christianity died at Auschwitz."

Alfred Kazin, author and lecturer, expresses deep disillusionment in his paper. For a short time, after the end of World War II, there was a moment when the world seemed to recognize the enormity of the Holocaust. But this moment has passed, and the endless flow of revolution and violence to which we have become accustomed has again led to indifference. A true understanding of Jewish fate, Kazin believes, can come only from a religious awareness. It alone is able to cut through the many hatreds of our time.

All of European history was the seedbed of the Holocaust. The Jews had remained an anomaly in the trend toward unity of modern Europe, just as they had remained outside the framework of medieval Christendom. Despite efforts at assimilation on their part they could not, in the long run, be absorbed by the cultures in which they lived. The contradictions so visible in Jewish existence puzzled and enraged non-Jews. When the catastrophe came, Stalin, the Papacy, the Allies, all alike ignored or minimized their plight. And the Jews themselves, who could neither believe nor understand the hatred directed against them, often reacted with confusion and passivity. Yet many also bore witness to their existence as Jews, whether in armed or nonviolent resistance.

As an American Jew Kazin asks, What of those Jews who were not there? Since Auschwitz is stamped on their souls too, they must seek to appropriate a historical experience that was not theirs, yet is central to Jewish existence. Just as all Jews came out of Egypt, so too all must bear witness to the Holocaust.

The contemporary situation leads Kazin to deep pessimism. He questions whether the war has ended for Jews. For the precariousness of Jewish existence, in Israel and in the Diaspora, has increased rather than diminished. Can this century of total revolution and ever-growing expansion still find any relevance in the people to whom God spoke, the people whom George Chapman called "the heart of the world"? The very seriousness of the crisis, I assume however, also gives Kazin some hope. For we cannot live without faith and hope. Jews must rediscover the meaning of their ancient history, and they can do so only with the help of Christians. The Christian involvement in the Symposium is to Kazin a sign of hope for the future, of the world as well as of the Jewish people.

Cloud of Smoke, Pillar of Fire: Judaism, Christianity, and Modernity after the Holocaust

IRVING GREENBERG

To the memory of my father,
Rabbi Eliyahu Chaim Greenberg,
1894–1975

I. Judaism and Christianity: Religions of Redemption and the Challenge of History

Both Judaism and Christianity are religions of redemption. Both religions come to this affirmation about human fate out of central events in history. For Jews, the basic orientating experience has been the Exodus. Out of the overwhelming experience of God's deliverance of His people came the judgment that the ultimate truth is not the fact that most humans live nameless and burdened lives and die in poverty and oppression. Rather, the decisive truth is that man is of infinite value and will be redeemed. Every act of life is to be lived by that realization.

For Christians, the great paradigm of this meaning is the life, death, and resurrection of Jesus Christ. By its implications, all of life is lived.

The central events of both religions occur and affect humans in history. The shocking contrast of the event of salvation come and the cruel realities of actual historical existence have tempted Christians to cut loose from earthly time. Yet both religions ultimately have stood by the

Work on this article was supported by a fellowship from The National Endowment for the Humanities in 1974–75 and research support from the Meinhardt Spielman Fund for the Department of Jewish Studies, City College, CUNY. The author wishes to thank Professor Alvin Rosenfeld of Indiana University for his most helpful close reading and extensive editorial comments on this text as well as for a series of conversations in Jerusalem which affected the final content of this essay.

7

claim that redemption will be realized in actual human history. This view has had enormous impact on the general Western and modern view that human liberation can and will be realized in the here and now.

Implicit in both religions is the realization that events happen in history which change our perception of human fate, events from which we draw the fundamental norms by which we act and interpret what happens to us. One such event is the Holocaust—the destruction of European Jewry from 1933 to 1945.

The Challenge of the Holocaust

Both religions have always sought to isolate their central events—Exodus and Easter—from further revelations or from the challenge of the demonic counter-experience of evil in history. By and large, both religions have continued since 1945 as if nothing had happened to change their central understanding. It is increasingly obvious that this is impossible, that the Holocaust cannot be ignored.

By its very nature, the Holocaust is obviously central for Jews. The destruction cut so deeply that it is a question whether the community can recover from it. When Adolf Eichmann went into hiding in 1945, he told his accomplice, Dieter Wisliceny, that if caught, he would leap into his grave laughing. He believed that although he had not completed the total destruction of Jewry, he had accomplished his basic goal—because the Jews could never recover from this devastation of their life center. Indeed, Eichmann had destroyed 90 percent of East European Jewry, the spiritual and biological vital center of prewar world Jewry. Six million Jews were killed—some 30 percent of the Jewish people in 1939; but among the dead were over 80 percent of the Jewish scholars, rabbis, full-time students and teachers of Torah alive in 1939.[1] Since there can be no covenant without the covenant people, the fundamental existence of Jews and Judaism is thrown into question by this genocide. For this reason alone, the trauma of the Holocaust cannot be overcome without some basic reorientation in light of it by the surviving Jewish community. Recent studies by Prof. Simon Herman, an Israeli social psychologist, have indicated that the perception of this event and its implications for the Jews' own fate has become a most widespread and powerful factor in individual Jewish consciousness and identity.[2]

The Holocaust as Radical Counter-Testimony
To Judaism and Christianity

For Christians, it is easier to continue living as if the event did not make any difference, as if the crime belongs to the history of another people and faith. But such a conclusion would be and is sheer self-deception. The magnitude of suffering and the manifest worthlessness of human life radically contradict the fundamental statements of human value and divine concern in both religions. Failure to confront and account for this evil, then, would turn both religions into empty, Pollyanna assertions, credible only because believers ignore the realities of human history. It would be comparable to preaching that this is the best of all possible worlds to a well-fed, smug congregation, while next door little children starve slowly to death.

Judaism and Christianity do not merely tell of God's love for man, but stand or fall on their fundamental claim that the human being is, therefore, of ultimate and absolute value. ("He who saves one life it is as if he saved an entire world"—B.T. Sanhedrin 37a; "God so loved the world that He gave His only begotten son"—John 3:16.) It is the contradiction of this intrinsic value and the reality of human suffering that validates the absolute centrality and necessity of redemption, of the Messianic hope. But speak of the value of human life and hear the testimony of S. Szmaglewska, a Polish guard at Auschwitz, about the summer of 1944. The passage (from the Nuremburg trial record) deserves commentary:

> WITNESS: . . . women carrying children were [always] sent with them to the crematorium. [Children were of no labor value so they were killed. The mothers were sent along, too, because separation might lead to panic, hysteria—which might slow up the destruction process, and this could not be afforded. It was simpler to condemn the mothers too and keep things quiet and smooth.] The children were then torn from their parents outside the crematorium and sent to the gas chambers separately. [At that point, crowding more people into the gas chambers became the most urgent consideration. Separating meant that more children could be packed in separately, or they could be thrown in over the heads of adults once the chamber was packed.] When the extermination of the Jews in the gas chambers was at its height, orders were issued that children were to be thrown straight into the crematorium furnaces, or into a pit near the crematorium, without being gassed first.
>
> SMIRNOV (Russian prosecutor): How am I to understand this? Did they throw them into the fire alive, or did they kill them first?

WITNESS: They threw them in alive. Their screams could be heard at the camp. It is difficult to say how many children were destroyed in this way.

SMIRNOV: Why did they do this?

WITNESS: It's very difficult to say. We don't know whether they wanted to economize on gas, or if it was because there was not enough room in the gas chambers.[3]

A word must be said on the decision to economize on gas. By the summer of 1944, the collapse of the Eastern front meant that the destruction of European Jewry might not be completed before the advancing Allied armies arrived. So Hungarian Jewry was killed at maximum speed—at the rate of up to ten thousand people a day. Priority was given to transports of death over trains with reinforcements and munitions needed for the Wehrmacht. There was no time for selections of the healthy, of young Jews for labor, or even for registering the number of victims. Entire trainloads were marched straight to the gas chambers.

The gas used—Zyklon B—causes death by internal asphyxiation, with damage to the centers of respiration, accompanied by feelings of fear, dizziness, and vomiting. In the chamber, when released, "the gas climbs gradually to the ceiling, forcing the victims to claw and trample upon one another in their struggle to reach upward. Those on the top are the last to succumb. . . . The corpses are piled one on top of another in an enormous heap. . . . at the bottom of the pile are babies and children, women and old people . . . . "[4]

The sheer volume of gas used in the summer of 1944 depleted the gas supply. In addition, the Nazis deemed the costs excessive. Therefore, in that summer, the dosage of gas was halved from twelve boxes to six per gassing. When the concentration of the gas is quite high, death occurs quickly. The decision to cut the dosage in half was to more than double the agony.

How much did it cost to kill a person? The Nazi killing machine was orderly and kept records. The gas was produced by the Deutsche Gesellschaft fur Schadlingsbekampfung m.b.H. (German Vermin-Combating Corporation, called DEGESCH for short). It was a highly profitable business, which paid dividends of 100 percent to 200 percent per year (100 percent in 1940 and 1941; 200 percent in 1942, 1943) to I. G. Farben, one of the three corporations which owned it.[5] The bills for Zyklon B came to 195 kilograms for 975 marks = 5 marks per kilogram. Approximately 5.5 kilograms were used on every chamber-load, about fifteen hundred people. This means 27.5 marks per fifteen hundred people. With the mark equal to 25 cents, this yields $6.75 per fifteen hundred people, or forty-five hundreths of a cent per person. In the summer of 1944, a Jewish child's life was not worth the two-fifths of a cent it would have cost to put it to death rather than burn it alive. There, in its starkest form, is the ultimate denial.

In short, the Holocaust poses the most radical counter-testimony to both Judaism and Christianity. Elie Wiesel has stated it most profoundly:

> Never shall I forget the little faces of the children, whose bodies I saw turned into wreaths of smoke beneath a silent blue sky.
> Never shall I forget those flames which consumed my faith forever.
> Never shall I forget that nocturnal silence which deprived me, for all eternity, of the desire to live.
> Never shall I forget those moments which murdered my God and my soul and turned my dreams to dust.
> Never shall I forget these things, even if I am condemned to live as long as God Himself. Never.[6]

The cruelty and the killing raise the question whether even those who believe after such an event dare talk about God who loves and cares without making a mockery of those who suffered.

Further Challenge of the Holocaust to Christianity

THE MORAL FAILURE AND COMPLICITY OF ANTI-SEMITISM. Unfortunately, however, the Holocaust poses a yet more devastating question to Christianity: What did Christianity contribute to make the Holocaust possible? The work of Jules Isaac, Norman Cohn, Raul Hilberg, Roy Eckardt, and others poses this question in a number of different ways. In 1942, the Nietra Rebbe went to Archbishop Kametko of Nietra to plead for Catholic intervention against the deportation of the Slovakian Jews. Tiso, the head of the Slovakian government, had been Kametko's secretary for many years, and the rebbe hoped that Kametko could persuade Tiso not to allow the deportations. Since the rebbe did not yet know of the gas chambers, he stressed the dangers of hunger and disease, especially for women, old people, and children. The archbishop replied: "It is not just a matter of deportation. You will not die there of hunger and disease. They will slaughter all of you there, old and young alike, women and children, at once—it is the punishment that you deserve for the death of our Lord and Redeemer, Jesus

Christ—you have only one solution. Come over to our religion and I will work to annul this decree."[7]

There are literally hundreds of similar anti-Semitic statements by individual people reported in the Holocaust literature. As late as March 1941—admittedly still before the full destruction was unleashed—Archbishop Grober (Germany), in a pastoral letter, blamed the Jews for the death of Christ and added that "the self-imposed curse of the Jews, 'His blood be upon us and upon our children' had come true terribly, until the present time, until today."[8] Similarly the Vatican responded to an inquiry from the Vichy government about the law of June 2, 1941, which isolated and deprived Jews of rights: "In principle, there is nothing in these measures which the Holy See would find to criticize."[9]

In general, there is an inverse ratio between the presence of a fundamentalist Christianity and the survival of Jews during the Holocaust period. This is particularly damning because the attitude of the local population toward the Nazi assault on the Jews seems to be a critical variable in Jewish survival. (If the local population disapproved of the genocide or sympathized with the Jews, they were more likely to hide or help Jews, resist or condemn the Nazis, which weakened the effectiveness of the killing process or the killer's will to carry it out.) We must allow for the other factors which operated against the Jews in the countries with a fundamentalist Christianity. These factors include Poland and the Baltic nations' lack of modernity (modernity = tolerance, ideological disapproval of mass murder, presence of Jews who can pass, etc.); the isolation and concentration of Jews in these countries, which made them easy to identify and destroy; the Nazis considered Slavs inferior and more freely used the death penalty for any help extended to Jews; the Nazis concentrated more of the governing power in their own hands in these countries. Yet even when all these allowances are made, it is clear that anti-Semitism played a role in the decision not to shield Jews—or to actually turn them in. If the Teaching of Contempt furnished an occasion—or presented stereotypes which brought the Nazis to focus on the Jews as the scapegoat in the first place; or created a residue of anti-Semitism in Europe which affected the local populations' attitudes toward Jews; or enabled some Christians to feel they were doing God's duty in helping kill Jews or in not stopping it—then Christianity may be hopelessly and fatally compromised. The fact is that during the Holocaust the church's protests were primarily on behalf of converted Jews. At the end of the war, the Vatican and circles close to it helped thousands of war criminals to escape, including Franz Stangl, the commandant of the most murderous of all the extermination camps, Treblinka, and other men of his ilk. Finally in 1948, the German Evangelical Conference at Darmstadt, meeting in the country which had only recently carried out this genocide, proclaimed that the terrible Jewish suffering in the Holocaust was a divine visitation and a call to the Jews to cease their rejection and ongoing crucifixion of Christ. May one morally be a Christian after this?[10]

EVEN SOME CHRISTIANS WHO RESISTED HITLER FAILED ON THE JEWISH QUESTION. Even the great Christians—who recognized the danger of idolatry, and resisted the Nazi government's takeover of the German Evangelical Church at great personal sacrifice and risk—did not speak out on the Jewish question.[11] All this suggests that something in Christian teaching supported or created a positive context for anti-Semitism, and even murder. Is not the faith of a gospel of love, then, fatally tainted with collaboration with genocide—conscious or unconscious? To put it another way: if the Holocaust challenges the fundamental religious claims of Christianity (and Judaism), then the penumbra of Christian complicity may challenge the credibility of Christianity to make these claims.

IS THE WAGER OF CHRISTIAN FAITH LOST? There is yet a third way in which this problem may be stated. In its origins, Christianity grew out of a wager of faith. Growing in the bosom of Judaism and its Messianic hope, Jesus (like others), could be seen either as a false Messiah or as a new unfolding of God's love, and a revelation of love and salvation for mankind. Those who followed Jesus as the Christ, in effect, staked their lives that the new orientation was neither an illusion nor an evil, but yet another stage in salvation and a vehicle of love for mankind. "The acceptance . . . of Jesus as the Messiah means beholding him as one who transforms and will transform the world."[12] As is the case with every vehicle, divine and human, the spiritual record of this wager has been mixed—comprising great inspiration for love given and great evils caused. The hope is that the good outweighs the evil. But the throwing into the scales of so massive a weight of evil and guilt raises the question whether the balance might now be broken, whether one must not decide that it were better that Jesus had not come, rather than that such scenes be enacted six million times over—and more. Has the wager of faith in Jesus been lost?

II.   The Challenge to Modern Culture

The Breaking of Limits

The same kinds of questions must be posed to modern culture as well. For the world, too, the Holocaust is an event which changes fundamental perceptions. Limits were broken, restraints shattered, that will never be recovered, and henceforth mankind must live with the dread of a world in which models for unlimited evil exist. Pre-modern man thought there were limits. But consider Einsatz Commando A, Strike Commando 3, which reported its daily activities as follows:[13] [Executions]

8/23/41	Panevezys	1312 Jewish men, 4602 Jewish women, 1609 Jewish children	7,523
8/18 to 22/41	Rasainiai District	466 Jewish men, 440 Jewish women, 1020 Jewish children	1,926
8/25/41	Obelisi	112 Jewish men, 627 Jewish women, 421 Jewish children	1,160
8/25 and 26/41	Seduva	230 Jewish men, 275 Jewish women, 159 Jewish children	664
8/26/41	Zarasai	767 Jewish men, 1113 Jewish women, 1 Russian communist woman, 1 Lithuanian communist, 687 Jewish children	2,569
8/26/41	Pasvalys	402 Jewish men, 738 Jewish women, 209 Jewish children	1,349
8/26/41	Kaisiadorys	All Jews (men, women and children)	1,911
8/27/41	Prienai	All Jews (men, women and children)	1,078
8/27/41	Dagda and Kraslawa	212 Jews, 4 Russian prisoners-of-war	216
8/27/41	Goniskis	47 Jewish men, 165 Jewish women, 143 Jewish children	355
8/28/41	Wilkia	76 Jewish men, 192 Jewish women, 134 Jewish children	402
8/28/41	Kedainiai	710 Jewish men, 767 Jewish women, 599 Jewish children	2,076
8/29/41	Rumsiskis and Ziezmariai	20 Jewish men, 567 Jewish women, 197 Jewish children	784
8/29/41	Utena and Moletai	582 Jewish men, 1731 Jewish women, 1469 Jewish children	3,782

9/1/41   Mariampole   1763 Jewish men, 1812 Jewish women,
                             1404 Jewish children, 109 mental patients,
                             1 female German national who was married
                             to a Jew, 1 Russian woman   5,090

The Demonic in the Modern World

In Zlutomir, Minsk, Firiatin, Mariampole, Nemirov, Stalinodorf, and Kiev among others, children were thrown alive into the killing pits or beaten over the head and dumped into the pits—to save bullets. In Berditchev the ground was turned into muck by the blood of the victims, and some wounded drowned in it. In Firiatin and Berditchev the ground settled and turned from the cries and writhings of those still alive and superficially buried.[14] No assessment of modern culture can ignore the fact that science and technology—the accepted flower and glory of modernity—now climaxed in the factories of death; the awareness that the unlimited, value-free use of knowledge and science, which we perceive as the great force for improving the human condition, had paved the way for the bureaucratic and scientific death campaign. There is the shock of recognition that the humanistic revolt, celebrated as the liberation of humankind in freeing man from centuries of dependence upon God and nature, is now revealed—at the very heart of the enterprise—to sustain a capacity for death and demonic evil.

Live through the Sabbath of the beginning of Elul 1942 with Rivka Yosselevscka in Zagrodski, Pinsk district.[15]

ATTORNEY-GENERAL: Yes. And what happened towards sunrise?

WITNESS, YOSSELEVSCKA: And thus the children screamed. They wanted food, water. This was not the first time. But we took nothing with us. We had no food and no water, and we did not know the reason. The children were hungry and thirsty. We were held this way for 24 hours while they were searching the houses all the time—searching for valuables. . . .

I had my daughter in my arms and ran after the truck. There were mothers who had two or three children and held them in their arms running after the truck. We ran all the way. There were those who fell—we were not allowed to help them rise. They were shot—right there—wherever they fell. . . . When we all reached the destination, the people from the truck were already down and they were undressed—all lined up. All my family was there—undressed, lined up. The people from the truck, those who arrived before us. . . .

When I came up to the place—we saw people naked lined up. But we were still hoping that this was only torture. Maybe there is hope—hope of living. . . One could not leave the line, but I wished to see—what are they doing on the hillock? Is there anyone down below? I turned my head and saw that some three or four rows were already killed—on the ground. There were some twelve people amongst the dead. I also want to mention what my child said while we were lined up in the Ghetto, she said, "Mother, why did you make me wear the Shabbat dress; we are going to be shot"; and when we stood near the dug-outs, near the grave, she said, "Mother, why are we waiting, let us run!" Some of the young people tried to run, but they were caught immediately, and they were shot right there. It was difficult to hold on to the children. We took all children, not ours, and we carried—we were anxious to get it all over—the suffering of the children was difficult; we all trudged along to come nearer to the place and to come nearer to the end of the torture of the children. The children were taking leave of their parents and parents of their elder people. . . .

We were driven; we were already undressed; the clothes were removed and taken away; our father did not want to undress; he remained in his underwear. We were driven up to the grave, this shallow. . . .

ATTORNEY-GENERAL: And these garments were torn off his body, weren't they?

A: When it came to our turn, our father was beaten. We prayed, we begged with my father to undress, but he would not undress, he wanted to keep his underclothes. He did not want to stand naked.

Q: And then they tore them off?

A: Then they tore off the clothing of the old man and he was shot. I saw it with my own eyes. And then they took my mother, and she said, let us go before her; but they caught mother and shot her too; and then there was my grandmother, my father's mother standing there; she was eighty years old and she had two children in her arms. And then there was my father's sister. She also had children in her arms and she was shot on the spot with the babies in her arms. . . .

And yet with my last strength I came up on top of the grave, and when I did, I did not know the place, so many bodies were lying all over, dead people; I wanted to see the end of this stretch of dead bodies but I could not. It was impossible. They were lying all over, all dying; suffering, not all of them dead, but in their last sufferings; naked; shot, but not dead. Children crying "Mother," "Father"; I could not stand on my feet. . . .

I was searching among the dead for my little girl, and I cried for her— Merkele was her name—Merkele! There were children crying "Mother!" "Father!"—but they were all smeared with blood and one could not recognize the children. I cried for my daughter. . . .

I was praying for death to come. I was praying for the grave to be opened and to swallow me alive. Blood was spurting from the grave in many places, like a well of water, and whenever I pass a spring now, I remember the blood which spurted from the ground, from that grave. I dug with my fingernails, but the grave would not open. I did not have enough strength. I cried out to my mother, to my father, "Why did they not kill me? What was my sin? I have no one to go to." I saw them all being killed. Why was I spared? Why was I not killed?

One of the most striking things about the Einsatzgruppen leadership makeup is the prevalence of educated people, professionals, especially lawyers, Ph.D.'s, and yes, even a clergyman.[16] How naive the nineteenth-century polemic with religion appears to be in retrospect; how simple Feuerbach, Nietzsche, and many others. The entire structure of autonomous logic and sovereign human reason now takes on a sinister character. It is like Hawthorne's pilgrims in "The Celestial Railroad," who speak so sweetly and convincingly of heavenly bliss, while all the time the barely stifled flames of hell rage in their breasts. For Germany was one of the most "advanced" Western countries—at the heart of the academic, scientific, and technological enterprise. All the talk in the world about "atavism" cannot obscure the way in which such behavior is the outgrowth of democratic and modern values, as well as the pagan gods.[17]

As Toynbee put it, "a Western nation, which for good or evil, has played so central a part in Western history . . . could hardly have committed these flagrant crimes had they not been festering foully beneath the surface of life in the Western world's non-German provinces. . . . If a twentieth-century German was a monster, then, by the same token a twentieth-century Western civilization was a Frankenstein guilty of having been the author of this German monster's being."[18] This responsibility must be shared not only by Christianity, but by the Enlightenment[19] and democratic cultures as well. Their apathy and encouragement strengthened the will and capacity of the murderers to carry out the genocide, even as moral resistance and condemnation weakened that capacity.

The Moral Failure and Complicity of Universalism

Would that liberalism, democracy, and internationalism had emerged looking morally better. But, in fact, the democracies closed their doors to millions of victims who could have been saved. America's record is one of a fumbling and feeble interest in the victims which allowed anti-Semites and provincial economic and patriotic concerns to rule the admission—or rather the nonadmission—of the refugees. Indeed, the ideology of universal human values did not even provide sufficient motivation to bomb the rail lines and the gas chambers of Auschwitz when these were operating at fullest capacity, and when disruption could have saved ten thousand lives a day. Thus the synthetic rubber factory at Buna in the Auschwitz complex was bombed, but the death factory did not merit such attention.[20] The ideology of universalism did have operational effects. It blocked specifying Jews as victims of Nazi atrocities, as in the Allied declaration of January 1942, when the Nazis were warned they would be held responsible for their cruel war on civilians. In this warning, the Jews were not mentioned by name on the grounds that they were after all humans, not Jews, and citizens of the countries in which they lived. The denial of Jewish particularity—in the face of the very specific Nazi war on the Jews—led to decisions to bomb industrial targets to win the war for democracy, but to exclude death factories—lest this be interpreted as a *Jewish* war! The very exclusion of specifying Jews from warnings and military objectives was interpreted by the Nazis as a signal that Jews were expendable. They may have read the signal correctly. In any event, liberalism and internationalism became cover beliefs—designed to weaken the victims' perception that they were threatened and to block the kind of action needed to save their lives.[21]

The very isolation and sense of the indifference of the world cowed the victims, and made them go more quietly to their deaths. In agonizing over why Warsaw Jewry had let the Nazis round up 300,000 Jews and send them to (what were discovered to be) the gas chambers of Treblinka, Alexander Donat later wrote:[22]

> In vain we looked at that cloudless September sky for some sign of God's wrath. The heavens were silent. In vain we waited to hear from the lips of the great ones of the world—the champion of light and justice, the Roosevelts, the Churchills, the Stalins—the words of thunder, the threat of massive retaliation that might have halted the executioner's axe. In vain we implored help from our Polish brothers with whom we had shared good and bad fortune alike for seven centuries, but they were utterly unmoved in our hour of anguish. They did not show even normal human compassion at our ordeal, let alone demonstrate Christian charity. They did not even let political good sense guide them; for after all we were objectively allies in a struggle against a common enemy. While we bled and died, their attitude was at best indifference, and all too often "friendly neutrality" to the Germans. "Let the Germans do this dirty work for us."

And there were far too many cases of willing, active, enthusiastic Polish assistance to the Nazi murderers. [p. 100]

Especially disastrous was the victims' faith in universalism and modern humanitarian values. It disarmed them.

> The basic factor in the Ghetto's lack of preparation for armed resistance was psychological; we did not at first believe the Resettlement Operation to be what in fact it was, systematic slaughter of the entire Jewish population. For generations East European Jews had looked to Berlin as the symbol of law, order, and culture. We could not now believe that the Third Reich was a government of gangsters embarked on a program of genocide "to solve the Jewish problem in Europe." We fell victim to our faith in mankind, our belief that humanity had set limits to the degradation and persecution of one's fellow man. [p. 103]

World Jewry Shares the Failure

Nor were Jews outside Europe models of overwhelming concern for their brothers and sisters. They were prepared neither to stop normal life nor to risk their standing in their own countries in order to pressure for top priority action to save European Jewry. While the historical balance sheet is not yet made, it is already clear that existing divisions and narrow organizational concerns ruled Jewish life to a great extent even in response to the ongoing Holocaust.[23] The absence of unity and special priority meant that attempts to save Jews were carried out in less unified and urgent ways than the destruction process.[24] Until the very end, the genocide received the highest priority and special consideration from the German authorities.

In retrospect, it is also clear that a major factor restricting the efforts of world Jewry was the paralyzing effect of the Jews' belief in, and burning passion to be fully accepted by the countries in which they lived. Organized Jewry felt bound by the principles of national loyalty and national interest, and feared to protest when that rubric was involved to justify only routine and restricted efforts by the national governments to save Jews. Here again the ideologies of liberalism, integration, and political equality played important roles in weakening the world Jewish capacity or will to maximally save (or pressure to save) their brothers and sisters. Part of this weakening lay within the Jewish psyche itself, where the strong consciousness of being an *American* Jew or *English* Jew, etc., meant that the community did not adequately see its fate as indivisible with that of the European Jews who were in Hitler's hands. Thus again, highly laudable values (secularist democracy, universalism, liberalism) are deeply implicated in creating the background for a relatively undisturbed pursuit of mass murder. The colossal human and moral failure needed to make possible such cruel slaughter has deeply tarnished the credibility and validity of all these values. In other words, no matter how valid a philosophy appears to be, no matter how internally convincing and autonomously persuasive it is, if it has the capacity to serve as a ground for unmitigated evil, then it must be challenged, shaken up, rethought—if it can survive at all. Failure to radically criticize and restructure means collaboration with the possibility of a repetition. Yet if there is any imperative at all that bursts forth from the hell of Auschwitz and Treblinka, if there is a flicker of human decency left in the observer, it surely must be: Never again!

III. The Holocaust as Orienting Event and Revelation

Not to Confront Is to Repeat

For both Judaism and Christianity (and other religions of salvation—both secular and sacred) there is no choice but to confront the Holocaust, because it happened, and because the first Holocaust is the hardest. The fact of the Holocaust makes a repetition more likely—a limit was broken, a control or awe is gone—and the murder procedure is now better laid out and understood. Failure to confront it makes repetition all the more likely. So evil is the Holocaust, and so powerful a challenge to all other norms, that it forces a response, willy-nilly; not to respond is to collaborate in its repetition. This irony of human history which is already at work, is intensified by the radical power of the Holocaust. Because the world has not made the Holocaust a central point of departure for moral and political policy, the survivors of the Holocaust and their people have lived continually under the direct threat of another Holocaust throughout the past thirty years. Muslims who feel that the event is a Western problem and that Christian guilt has been imposed on them have been tempted to try to stage a repeat performance. They lack the guilt and concern, and that in itself leads to guilt.

The nemesis of denial is culpability. Pope John XXIII, who tried strongly to save Jews in the Holocaust (he made representations and protests, issued false baptismal papers, helped Jews escape), felt guilty and deeply regretted the Catholic Church's past treatment of Jews. This pope did more than any other pope had ever done to remove the possibility of another destruction (through the Vatican II Declaration, revising Catholic instruction and liturgy with reference to the Jews, dialogue, etc.).* Pope Paul VI, who denied the complicity or guilt of Pius XII in the Holocaust, was tempted thereby into a set of policies (he watered down the Declaration, referred to Jews in the old Passion story terms, refused to recognize Israel's de jure political existence, maintained silence in the face of the threat of genocide), which brings the dreadful guilt of collaboration in genocide so much closer.

This principle applies to secular religions of salvation as well. Thus, the German Democratic Republic (East Germany) has denied any responsibility for the Holocaust, on the grounds that it was carried out by fascist and right-wing circles, whereas East Germany is socialist. As a result, it has allowed Nazis back into government with even more impunity than West Germany. Whereas West Germany has given back billions of dollars of Jewish money in the form of reparations (it is estimated that many more billions were directly stolen and spoiled), the GDR, having no guilty conscience, has yielded up none of the ill-gotten gains of mass murder. In fact, East Germany and its "socialist" allies have pursued policies which have kept the genocide of the Jewish people in Israel a live option to this day. Thus, failure to respond to the Holocaust turns a hallowed ideology of liberation into a cover for not returning robbed goods and for keeping alive the dream of another mass murder.

This is not to say that all-out support for Israel is the only way to avoid complicity in attempted genocide. The Communist world could have pursued a pro-Arab policy on its merits. Had they felt as guilty as they should have—as they actually were—they would have made a sine qua non the giving up of all genocidal hopes and talk by the Arabs. In

---

*Writing under a pseudonym, a priest who had served as ghost writer for Pope John published a report on Vatican II which stated that John had composed a prayer about the Jews. The text, to be read in all Catholic churches, said: "We are conscious today that many centuries of blindness have cloaked our eyes so that we can no longer see the beauty of Thy chosen people. . . . We realize that the mark of Cain stands on our foreheads. Across the centuries our Brother Abel has lain in blood which we drew, or shed tears we caused, forgetting Thy love. Forgive us for crucifying Thee a second time in their flesh. For we knew not what we did . . . "[25] While the prayer is apocryphal (no trace of it has been found in John's papers), widespread acceptance of its attribution reflects John's known regret and concern.

actual fact, the opposite occurred. Several times, when such extreme possibilities were about to be dropped by the Arab world, Russian intervention, with no such policy conditions attached (or with tacit encouragement of destructive goals), restored this abominable option.

The Holocaust cannot be used for triumphalism. Its moral challenge must also be applied to Jews. Those Jews who feel no guilt for the Holocaust are also tempted to moral apathy. Religious Jews who use the Holocaust to morally impugn every other religious group but their own are the ones who are tempted thereby into indifference at the Holocaust of others (cf. the general policy of the American Orthodox rabbinate on United States Vietnam policy). Those Israelis who place as much distance as possible between the weak, passive Diaspora victims and the "mighty Sabras" are tempted to use Israeli strength indiscriminately (i.e., beyond what is absolutely inescapable for self-defense and survival), which is to risk turning other people into victims of the Jews. Neither faith nor morality can function without serious twisting of perspective, even to the point of becoming demonic, unless they are illuminated by the fires of Auschwitz and Treblinka.

The Dialectical Revelation of the Holocaust

The Holocaust challenges the claims of all the standards that compete for modern man's loyalties. Nor does it give simple, clear answers or definitive solutions. To claim that it does is not to take burning children seriously. This surd will—and should—undercut the ultimate adequacy of any category, unless there were one (religious, political, intellectual) that consistently produced the proper response of resistance and horror at the Holocaust. No such category exists, to my knowledge. To use the catastrophe to uphold the univocal validity of any category is to turn it into grist for propaganda mills. The Nazis turned their Jewish victims into soap and fertilizer after they were dead. The same moral gorge rises at turning them into propaganda. The Holocaust offers us only dialectical moves and understandings— often moves that stretch our capacity to the limit and torment us with their irresolvable tensions. In a way, it is the only morally tenable way for survivors and those guilty of bystanding to live. Woe to those so at ease that they feel no guilt or tension. Often this is the sign of the death of the soul. I have met many Germans motivated by guilt who came to Israel on pilgrimages of repentance. I have been struck that frequently these were young people, too young to have participated in the genocide; or, more often, persons or the children of persons who had been

anti-Nazi or even imprisoned for resistance. I have yet to meet such a
penitent who was himself an SS man or even a train official who transported Jews. Living in the dialectic becomes one of the verification
principles for alternative theories after the Holocaust.

Let us offer, then, as working principle the following: No statement,
theological or otherwise, should be made that would not be credible in
the presence of the burning children. In his novel *The Accident*, Elie
Wiesel has written of the encounter of a survivor with Sarah, a prosti-
tute who is also a survivor. She began her career at twelve, when she
was separated from her parents and sent to a special barracks for the
camp officers' pleasure. Her life was spared because there were German officers who liked to make love to little girls her age. Every night
she reenacts the first drunken officer's use of a twelve-year-old girl. Yet
she lives on, with both life feeling and self-loathing. And she retains
enough feeling to offer herself to a shy survivor boy, without money.
"You are a saint," he says. "You are mad," she shrieks. He concludes,
"Whoever listens to Sarah and doesn't change, whoever enters Sarah's
world and doesn't invent new gods and new religions, deserves death
and destruction. Sarah alone has the right to decide what is good and
what is evil, the right to differentiate between what is true and what
usurps the appearance of truth."[26]

In this story Wiesel has given us an extraordinary phenomenology of
the dialectic in which we live after the Holocaust. Sarah's life of prosti-
tution, religiously and morally negative in classic terms, undergoes a
moral reversal of category. It is suffering sainthood in the context of
her life and her ongoing response to the Holocaust experience. Yet this
scene grants us no easy Sabbatianism, in which every act that can wrap
itself in the garment of the Holocaust is justified and the old categories
are no longer valid. The ultimate tension of the dialectic is maintained,
and the moral disgust which Sarah's life inspires in her (and Wiesel?
and us?) is not omitted either. The more we analyze the passage the
more it throws us from pole to pole in ceaseless tension. The very disgust may, in fact, be the outcome of Sarah's mistaken judgment; she
continues to judge herself by the categories in which she was raised before the event. This is suggested in the narrator's compassion and love
for her. Yet he himself is overcome by moral nausea—or is it pity?—or
protest?—until it is too late and Sarah is lost. There is no peace or sur-
cease and no lightly grasped guide to action in this world. To enter into
Sarah's world in fear and trembling, and to remain there before and in
acting and speech, is the essence of religious response today, as much
as when normative Judaism bids us enter into the Exodus, and Chris-

tianity asks we enter into Easter and remain there before and in acting or speaking. The classic normative experiences themselves are not dismissed by Wiesel. They are tested and reformulated—dialectically attacked and affirmed—as they pass through the fires of the new revelatory event.[27]

Resistance to New Revelation: Jewish and Christian

Much of classic Jewish and Christian tradition will resist the claim that there have been new revelatory events in our time. Judaism has remained faithful to the covenant of Sinai and rejected this claim when expressed in the life of Jesus as understood by St. Paul and the Christian church, or in the career of Sabbetai Zvi and others.[28] There are precedents for a reformulation of the covenant in the light of great events, such as the developments which followed the destruction of the Temple, especially the Second Temple.[29] It took, however, a major flowering of Judaism and extraordinary spiritual leadership to articulate and restructure the tradition, and it was a painful, soul-searching, and highly conflictual process.[30] The very quality of faithfulness to the covenant resists acceptance of new revelation—as it should. Human nature's love for the familiar conspires with faithfulness to keep new norms out. But no one said that the Holocaust should be simply assimilable. For traditional Jews to ignore or deny all significance to this event would be to repudiate the fundamental belief and affirmations of the Sinai covenant: that history is meaningful, and that ultimate liberation and relationship to God will take place in the realm of human events. Exodus-Sinai would be insulated from all contradictory events—at the cost of removing it from the realm of the real—the realm on which it staked its all—the realm of its origin and testimony. However much medieval Judaism was tempted to move redemption to the realm of eternal life, it never committed this sacrilege. It insisted that the Messianic Kingdom of God in this world was not fulfilled by the salvation of the world to come.[31] Even after the expulsion from Spain and the spread of Kabbalah, Messianic expectation was not totally spiritualized. There is an alternative for those whose faith can pass through the demonic, consuming flames of a crematorium: it is the willingness and ability to hear further revelation and reorient themselves. That is the way to wholeness. Rabbi Nachman of Bratzlav once said that there is no heart so whole as a broken heart. After Auschwitz, there is no faith so whole as a faith shattered—and re-fused—in the ovens.

Since this further revelation grows in the womb of Judaism, it may be asked whether it speaks only to Jews, or to Christians also. Classic Christianity is tempted to deny further revelation after Easter. Christianity testified and built itself on the finality of revelation in Christ's life and teaching. Yet, at its core, Christianity claims that God sent a second revelation, which grew out of the ground of acknowledged covenant, superseded the authority of the first revelation, and even supplied a new, higher understanding of the first event. Christian polemic has mocked and criticized the people of Israel for being so blinded by the possession of an earlier revelation and by pride in its finality that Israel did not recognize the time of its visitation. However unjust the polemic against Judaism was (as I believe it was), it ill behooves Christianity to rule out further revelation a priori— lest it be hoist by its own petard. Rather, it should trust its own faith that God is not owned by anyone and the spirit blows where it lists. They very anguish and harsh judgments which the Holocaust visits on Christianity (see above, pp. 11) open the possibility of freeing the Gospel of Love from the incubus of evil and hatred.

The desire to guarantee absolute salvation and understanding is an all too human need which both religions must resist as a snare and temptation. Just as refusal to encounter the Holocaust brings a nemesis of moral and religious ineffectiveness, openness and willingness to undergo the ordeal of reorienting by the event could well save or illuminate the treasure that is still contained in each tradition.

There are Jews who have sought to assimilate the Holocaust to certain unreconstructed traditional categories, to explain destruction as a visitation for evil.[32] To account for the Holocaust as God's punishment of Israel for its sins is to betray and mock the agony of the victims. Now that they have been cruelly tortured and killed, boiled into soap, their hair made into pillows and their bones into fertilizer, their unknown graves and the very fact of their death denied to them, the theologian would inflict on them the only indignity left: that is, insistence that it was done because of their sins. As Roy Eckardt wrote, this is the devil's work. God comforts the afflicted and afflicts the comforted, whereas the devil comforts the comforted and afflicts the afflicted.[33] A great Jewish scholar sought to account for the Holocaust in terms of Jewish sin. He was led by the logic of his position, first to blame the Zionists rather than the Nazis for the evil; then, to join the enemies of the Jewish state sworn to destroy the Jewish people in common ground of hatred and denunciation of Israel—in effect, collaborating in providing the setting for attempted genocide.[34] By the gracious irony of

God, this satanic denouement was happily frustrated by the strength
and exploits of those he maligned and excoriated. It is a sobering demonstration that failure to respect the dialectic of the Holocaust can dialectically turn faithfulness into demonism.

IV. Jewish Theological Responses to the Holocaust

A Critique

There have been some notable Jewish theological responses that
have correctly grasped the centrality of the Holocaust to Jewish
thought and faith. The two primary positions are polar. One witness
upholds the God of History. Emil Fackenheim has described the Commanding Voice of Auschwitz, which bids us not to hand Hitler any
posthumous victories, such as repudiating the covenant and retrospectively declaring Judaism to have been an illusion. Eliezer Berkovits
has stressed that Jewish survival testifies to the Lord of History. The
other witness affirms the death of God and the loss of all hope. Richard
Rubenstein has written: "We learned in the crisis that we were totally
and nakedly alone, that we could expect neither support nor succor
from God nor from our fellow creatures. Therefore, the world will forever remain a place of pain, suffering, alienation and ultimate
defeat."[35] These are genuine important responses to the Holocaust, but
they fall afoul of the dialectical principle. Both positions give a definitive interpretation of the Holocaust which subsumes it under known
classical categories. Neither classical theism nor atheism is adequate to
incorporate the incommensurability of the Holocaust; neither produced a consistently proper response; neither is credible alone—in the
presence of the burning children.

Rubenstein's definitiveness is part of this writer's disagreement with
him. Rubenstein concluded that "Jewish history has written the *final
chapter* in the terrible story of the God of History"; that "the world
will *forever* remain a place of pain . . . and *ultimate defeat,*" and that
the "pathetic hope (of coming to grips with Auschwitz through the
framework of traditional Judaism) *will never be realized*" (italics supplied).[36] After the Holocaust, there should be no final solutions, not
even theological ones. I could not be more sympathetic to Rubenstein's
positions, or more unsympathetic to his conclusions. That Auschwitz
and the rebirth of Israel are normative; that there are traditional positions which Auschwitz moves us to repudiate (such as "We were pun-

ished for our sins") is a profoundly, authentically Jewish response. To
declare that the destruction closes out hope forever is to claim divine
omniscience and to use the Holocaust for theological grist. Contra Rubenstein, I would argue that it is not so much that any affirmations (or
denials) cannot be made, but that they can be made authentically only
if they are made after working through the Holocaust experience. In
the same sense, however, the relationship to the God of the convenant
cannot be unaffected.

Dialectical Faith, or "Moment Faiths"

Faith is living life in the presence of the Redeemer, even when the
world is unredeemed. After Auschwitz, faith means there are times
when faith is overcome. Buber has spoken of "moment gods": God is
known only at the moment when Presence and awareness are fused in
vital life. This knowledge is interspersed with moments when only
natural, self-contained, routine existence is present. We now have to
speak of "moment faiths," moments when Redeemer and vision of redemption are present, interspersed with times when the flames and
smoke of the burning children blot out faith—though it flickers again.
Such a moment is described in an extraordinary passage of *Night,* as
the young boy sentenced to death but too light to hang struggles slowly
on the rope. Eliezer finally responds to the man asking, "Where is God
now?" by saying, "Here He is—He is hanging here on this gallows
. . ."[37]

This ends the easy dichotomy of atheist/theist, the confusion of faith
with doctrine or demonstration. It makes clear that faith is a life response of the whole person to the Presence in life and history. Like
life, this response ebbs and flows. The difference between the skeptic
and the believer is frequency of faith, and not certitude of position.
The rejection of the unbeliever by the believer is literally the denial or
attempted suppression of what is within oneself. The ability to live
with moment faith is the ability to live with pluralism and without the
self-flattering, ethnocentric solutions which warp religion, or make it a
source of hatred for the other.

Why Dialectical Faith Is Still Possible

THE PERSISTENCE OF EXODUS. Of course, the question may still be
asked: Why is it not a permanent destruction of faith to be in the presence of the murdered children?

One reason is that there are still moments when the reality of the Exodus is reenacted and present. There are moments when a member of the community of Israel shares the reality of the child who was to have been bricked into the wall but instead experienced the liberation and dignity of Exodus. (The reference here is to the rabbinic legend that in Egypt, Jewish children were bricked into a wall if their parents did not meet their daily quota of bricklaying.) This happens even to those who have both literally and figuratively lived through the Holocaust. Wiesel describes this moment for us in *The Gates of the Forest,* when Gregor "recites the Kaddish, the solemn affirmation . . . by which man returns to God his crown and his scepter."[38] Neither Exodus nor Easter wins out or is totally blotted out by Buchenwald, but we encounter both polar experiences; the life of faith is lived between them. And this dialectic opens new models of response to God, as we shall show below.

THE BREAKDOWN OF THE SECULAR ABSOLUTE. A second reason is that we do not stand in a vacuum when faith encounters the crematoria. In a real sense, we are always choosing between alternative faiths when we make a decision about ultimate meaning. In this culture the primary alternative to religion is secular man in a world closed off from any transcendence, or divine incursion. This world grows out of the intellectual framework of science, philosophy, and social science, of rationalism and human liberation, which created the enterprise of modernity. This value system was—and is—the major alternative faith which Jews and Christians joined in large numbers in the last two centuries, transferring allegiance from the Lord of History and Revelation to the Lord of Science and Humanism. In so many ways, the Holocaust is the direct fruit and will of this alternative. Modernity fostered the excessive rationalism and utilitarian relations which created the need for and susceptibility to totalitarian mass movements and the surrender of moral judgment. The secular city sustained the emphasis on value-free sciences and objectivity, which created unparalleled power but weakened its moral limits. (Surely it is no accident that so many members of the Einsatzgruppen were professionals.) Mass communication and universalization of values weakened resistance to centralized power, and served as a cover to deny the unique danger posted to particular, i.e. Jewish, existence.

In the light of Auschwitz, secular twentieth-century civilization is not worthy of this transfer of our ultimate loyalty. The victims ask that we not jump to a conclusion that retrospectively makes the covenant they lived an illusion and their death a gigantic travesty—a product of their illusions and Gentile jealousy of those pathetically mistaken claims.[39] It is not that emotional sympathy decides the validity or invalidity of philosophic positions. The truth is sometimes very unpleasant, and may contradict cherished beliefs or moral preferences. But the credibility of systems does rise or fall in the light of events which enhance or reduce the credibility of their claims.[40] A system associated with creating a framework for mass murder must be very persuasive before gaining intellectual assent. The burden of the proofs should be unquestionable. Nothing in the record of secular culture on the Holocaust justifies its authority claims. The victims ask us, above all, not to allow the creation of another matrix of values that might sustain another attempt at genocide. The absence of strong alternative value systems gives a moral monopoly to the wielders of power and authority. Secular authority unchecked becomes absolute. Relative values thus become the seedbed of absolute claims, and this is idolatry. This vacuum was a major factor in the Nazi ability to concentrate power and carry out the destruction without protest or resistance. (The primary sources of resistance were systems of absolute alternative values—the Barmen Conference in the Confessional Church, Jehovah's Witnesses, etc.)[41] After the Holocaust it is all the more urgent to resist this absolutization of the secular. As Emil Fackenheim has pointed out, the all-out celebration of the secular city by Harvey Cox reflected the assimilation of Christian values to a secular civilization given absolute status.[42] It is potential idolatry, an idolatry to which we more easily succumb if we have failed to look at the Holocaust.

If nothing else sufficed to undercut this absolute claim of nonaccessibility of the divine, it is the knowledge that the absence of limits or belief in a judge, and the belief that persons could therefore become God, underlay the structure of *l'univers concentrationnaire.* Mengele and other selectors of Auschwitz openly joked about this. I will argue below that the need to deny God leads directly to the assumption of omnipotent power over life and death. The desire to control people leads directly to crushing the image of God within them, so that the jailer becomes God. Then one cannot easily surrender to the temptation of being cut off from the transcendence, and must explore the alternatives. Surely it is no accident that in the past forty years language analysts like Wittgenstein, critics of value-free science and social sciences, existentialists, evangelical and counter-culture

movements alike, have fought to set limits to the absolute claims of
scientific knowledge and of reason, and to ensure the freedom for renewed encounter with the transcendental.

THE LOGIC OF POST-HOLOCAUST AND, THEREFORE, POST-MODERN
FAITH. A third reason to resist abandoning the divine is the moral urgency that grows out of the Holocaust and fights for the presence of the
Lord of History. Emil Fackenheim has articulated this position in
terms of not handing Hitler posthumous victories. I prefer an even
more traditional category, and would argue that the moral necessity of
a world to come, and even of resurrection, arises powerfully out of the
encounter with the Holocaust. Against this, Rubenstein and others
would maintain that the wish is not always father to the fact, and that
such an illusion may endanger even more lives. To this last point I
would reply that the proper belief will save, not cost, lives (see below).
It is true that moral appropriateness is not always a good guide to philosophic sufficiency; but the Holocaust experience insists that we best
err on the side of moral necessity. To put it more rationally, sometimes
we see the narrower logic of a specific argument rather than the deeper
logic of the historical moment or setting. This could make the narrower
logical grounds formally consistent and persuasive, yet utterly misleading, since they may start from and finish with the wrong assumptions.

Moral necessity validates the search for religious experience rather
than surrender to the immediate logic of nonbelief. Thus, if the Holocaust strikes at the credibility of faith, especially unreconstructed
faith, dialectically it also erodes the persuasiveness of the secular option. If someone is told that a line of argument leads to the conclusion
that he should not exist, not surprisingly the victim may argue that
there must be alternative philosophical frameworks. Insofar as the Holocaust grows out of Western civilization, then, at least for Jews, it is a
powerful incentive to guard against being overimpressed by this culture's intellectual assumptions and to seek other philosophical and historical frameworks. (cf. Wiesel's more mystical version of this argument—Gyula's comment in *The Accident:* "Lucidity is fate's victory,
not man's. It is an act of freedom that carries within itself the negation
of freedom. Man must keep moving, searching, weighing, holding out
his hand, offering himself, inventing himself."[43]

The point to keep in mind is that currents of thought and popular assumptions are so ubiquitous that they appear to be self-evident and
beyond cavil. It has been pointed out that the opposing positions with-

in one civilization (such as religion and secularity) may have more in common with each other than their presumed associated positions across civilizational lines. Thus modern religion and secularity may have more in common with each other than with their respective official analogues—medieval religion and secularity. The flaws, the hidden assumptions that turn out to be questionable, often do not become obvious until the whole climate of opinions and range of assumptions has changed as a new civilization emerges. The moral light shed by the Holocaust on the nature of Western culture validates skepticism toward contemporary claims—even before philosophic critiques emerge to justify the skepticism. It is enough that this civilization is the locus of the Holocaust. The Holocaust calls on Jews, Christians, and others to absolutely resist the total authority of this cultural moment. The experience frees them to respond to their own claim, which comes from outside the framework of this civilization, to relate to a divine other, who sets limits and judges the absolute claims of contemporary philosophic and scientific and human political systems. To follow this orientation is to be opened again to the possibilities of Exodus and immortality.

This is a crucial point. The Holocaust comes after two centuries of Emancipation's steadily growing domination of Judaism and the Jews. Rubenstein's self-perception as a radical breaking from the Jewish past is, I think, misleading. A more correct view would argue that he is repeating the repudiation of the God of History and the Chosen that was emphasized by the modernizing schools, such as Reconstructionism. This position had become the stuff of the values and views of the majority of Jews. "Being right with modernity" (defined by each group differently) has been the dominant value norm of a growing number of Jews since 1750, as well as Christians. Despite the rear-guard action of Orthodox Judaism and Roman Catholicism (until the 1960s) and of fundamentalist groups, the modern tide has steadily risen higher. The capacity to resist, criticize, or break away from these models is one of the litmus tests of the Holocaust as the new orienting experience of Jews, and an indication that a new era of Jewish civilization is under way. This new era will not turn its back on many aspects of modernity, but clearly it will be freer to reject some of its elements, and to take from the past (and future) much more fully.

THE REVELATION IN THE REDEMPTION OF ISRAEL. I have saved for last the most important reason why the moment of despair and disbelief in redemption cannot be final, at least in this generation's community of Israel. Another event has taken place in our lifetime which also has extraordinary scope and normative impact—the rebirth of the State of Israel. As difficult to absorb in its own way and, like the Holocaust, a scandal for many traditional Jewish and Christian categories, it is an inescapable part of the Jewish historical experience in our time. And while it is a continuation and outgrowth of certain responses to the Holocaust, it is at the same time a dialectical contradition to many of its implications. If the experience of Auschwitz symbolizes that we are cut off from God and hope, and that the covenant may be destroyed, then the experience of Jerusalem symbolizes that God's promises are faithful and His people live on. Burning children speak of the absence of all value—human and divine; the rehabilitation of one-half million Holocaust survivors in Israel speaks of the reclamation of tremendous human dignity and value. If Treblinka makes human hope an illusion, then the Western Wall asserts that human dreams are more real than force and facts. Israel's faith in the God of History demands that an unprecedented event of destruction be matched by an unprecedented act of redemption, and this has happened.[44]

This is not simply a question of the memories of Exodus versus the experience of Auschwitz. If it were a question of Exodus only, then those Jews already cut off from Exodus by the encounter with modern culture would be excluded and only "religious" Jews could still be believers.

But almost all Jews acknowledge this pheonomenon—the event of redemption and the event of catastrophe and their dialectical interrelationship—and it touches their lives. Studies show that the number of those who affirm this pheonomenon as central (even if in nontheological categories) has grown from year to year; that its impact is now almost universal among those who will acknowledge themselves as Jews, and that its force has overthrown some hierarchies of values that grew as modernity came to dominate Jewish life.[45] In fact, the religious situation is explosive and fermenting on a deeper level than anyone wishes to acknowledge at this point. The whole Jewish people is caught between immersion in nihilism and immersion in redemption—both are present in immediate experience, and not just historical memory. To deny either pole in our time is to be cut off from historical Jewish experience. In the incredible dialectical tension between the two we are fated to live. Biblical theology already suggested that the time would come when consciousness of God out of the restoration of Israel would outweigh consciousness of God out of the Exodus. In the words of Jeremiah: "The days will come, says the Lord, when it shall

no longer be said: 'as God lives who brought up the children of Israel
out of the land of Egypt' but 'as God lives who brought up the children
of Israel from the land of the north and from all the countries whither
He had driven them,' and I will bring them back into their land that I
gave to their fathers" (Jer. 16:14-15).

DESPITE REDEMPTION, FAITH REMAINS DIALECTICAL. But if Israel is
so redeeming, why then must faith be "moment faith," and why
should the experience of nothingness ever dominate?

The answer is that faith is living in the presence of the Redeemer,
and in the moment of utter chaos, of genocide, one does not live in His
presence. One must be faithful to the reality of the nothingness. Faith
is a moment truth, but there are moments when it is not true. This is
certainly demonstrable in dialectical truths, when invoking the truth at
the wrong moment is a lie. To let Auschwitz overwhelm Jerusalem is to
lie (i.e., to speak a truth out of its appropriate moment); and to let Jerusalem deny Auschwitz is to lie for the same reason.

The biblical witness is that a permanent repudiation of the covenant
would also have been a lie. "Behold, they say: our bones are dried up
and our hope is lost; we are cut off entirely" (Ezek. 37:11). There were
many who chose this answer, but their logic led to dissolution in the
pagan world around them. After losing hope in the Lord of History,
they were absorbed into idolatry—the faith of the gods of that moment.
In the resolution of the crisis of biblical faith, those who abandoned
hope ceased to testify. However persuasive the reaction may have been
at that time, every such decision in Israel's history—until Auschwitz—
has been premature, and even wrong. Yet in a striking talmudic interpretation, the rabbis say that Daniel and Jeremiah refused to speak of
God as awesome or powerful any longer in light of the destruction of
the Temple.[46] The line between the repudiation of the God of the covenant and the Daniel-Jeremiah reaction is so thin that repudiation must
be seen as an authentic reaction even if we reject it. There is a faithfulness in the rejection; serious theism must be troubled after such an
event.

This points to another flaw in interpreting the Holocaust through the
traditional response, which declares, "We were punished for our sins."
Blaming Israel is an attempt to be faithful to the Holocaust and to the
tradition, as well as the Exodus experience. But it lacks the combination of imagination and faithfulness of the rabbis and the honesty of
Daniel and Jeremiah. It justifies God, not man. Yet surely it is God who
did not keep His share of the covenant in defending His people in this

generation. It is the miracle of the people of Israel that they persist in faith. Surely it is they who should be justified. The Talmud teaches that if one suffers personally, it is meritorious to say, "I am suffering for my sins," and thereby be motivated to repentance. But if someone else is suffering and cannot help himself, and one tells him he is suffering for his sins, it is considered abuse with words. The Talmud calls it *onaat devarim,* literally, "to exploit or abuse with words." Since, in fact, even if the sufferer repented, he would continue to suffer, explanations of the agony that charge him with guilt are mockery and abuse.[47]

Moreover, summon up the principle that no statement should be made that could not be made in the presence of the burning children. On this rock, the traditionalist argument breaks. Tell the children in the pits they are burning for their sins. An honest man—better, a decent man—would spit at such a God rather than accept this rationale if it were true. If this justification is loyalty, then surely treason is the honorable choice. If this were the only choice, then surely God would prefer atheism. In this context, the Darmstadt Conference's statement that the Holocaust is God's call for a Jewish mea culpa which leads to Christ may have totally compromised the legitimacy of the cross as a religious symbol for any decent human being.

V. Explorations in Post-Holocaust Theological Models

Job and Renewed Divine Encounter

What, then, are the theological models that could come to the fore in a post-Holocaust interpretation of the relationship between God and man?

One is the model of Job, the righteous man from whom everything is taken: possessions, loved ones, health. It is interesting that his wife proposes that Job "curse God and die"; his friends propose that he is being punished for his sins. Job rejects both propositions. (At the end, God specifically rebukes the friends for their "answer.") The ending of the book, in which Job is restored and has a new wife and children, is of course unacceptable by our principle. Six million murdered Jews have not been and cannot be restored. But Job also offers us a different understanding. His suffering is not justified by God, nor is he consoled by the words about God's majesty and the grandeur of the universe surpassing man's understanding. Rather, what is meaningful in Job's experience is that in the whirlwind the contact with God is restored. That sense of Presence gives the strength to go on living in the contradiction.[48]

The theological implications of Job, then, are the rejection of easy pieties or denials and the dialectical response of looking for, expecting, further revelations of the Presence. This is the primary religious dimension of the reborn State of Israel for all religious people. When suffering had all but overwhelmed Jews and all but blocked out God's Presence, a sign out of the whirlwind gave us the strength to go on, and the right to speak authentically of God's Presence still.

Rabbi Joseph B. Soloveichik has presented a related image, "the knock on the door" of history. The image is taken from the Song of Songs. Shulamit has been taken to the king's court, is separated from her lover for so long that she begins to waver and to doubt the reality of her past love. Suddenly there is a knock on the door. It must be her beloved, but she hesitates to answer—she is too tired from the experience of separation and defeat. Then the emotional realization that it may be her lover fires her and she goes to the door. By the time she does open the door, he is not to be seen (Song of Songs 5:1 ff.). The entire episode is so ambiguous that it can be dismissed as the reaction of an overheated imagination, of romantic longing. But the knock has so keenly recrystallized her feelings for her beloved that she will not betray the relationship again.[49] As ambiguous as the secularity and flawed character of the reborn state is, it is enough to confirm the conviction not to "sell out to the court" and deny the past—or future—relationship with the beloved.

Israel's relationship to the Holocaust enormously intensifies the theological weight and testimony of both events. In turn, this deepens the irony of Jewish history and its dialectical impact on Christianity. Christian resistance to the possible new revelatory events in Judaism's history stems from the desire to be faithful to the finality of Christ. But inability to hear new revelation may be one of the signs of the death of the soul. (The phrase "may be one of the signs of the death of the soul" is used advisedly. It may be, in fact, that there is no revelation here. Those who deem it revelation may be mistaken, or it may be heard only by those for whom it is intended; those who do not hear it may not hear it because it is not addressed to them at all.)

One of the classic Christian self-validations has been the claim that the Old Covenant is finished; the old olive tree is blasted and bears no more fruit. New revelation in Judaism is perceived as incompatible with Christianity's superseding nature; the admission could destroy the structure of Christian authority. Yet confession by Christians of

Judaism's ongoing life and acceptance in gratitude of a new harvest of revelation would, at one stroke, undercut the whole Teaching of Contempt tradition in Christianity. This tradition has been a major sustainer of hatred within Christianity, and has made it the accomplice of many crimes that compromise its authority. Similarly, revelation in a time so secular and so closed to the transcendent restores the presence of God and sustains all faiths. In light of the Holocaust, classical Christianity "dies" to be reborn to new life; or it lives unaffected, to die to God and man.

The Suffering Servant and the Limits of Modernity

There is a second theological model that seems destined for a greater role in Jewish theology and, I dare say, for new meaning in Christianity: the Suffering Servant. Hitherto, this image has been played down by Jews because of its centrality in Christian theology. We are indebted to J. Coert Rylarsdaam for opening our eyes to this neglected model. Rylarsdaam once said that if being a Christian meant taking up the cross and being crucified for God, then the only practicing Christians were the Jews.

The Suffering Servant in Isaiah 53 sounds like a passage out of Holocaust literature. He is led as a sheep to slaughter (a term much and unfairly used in reference to the Holocaust). He is despised and forsaken of men. The term "despised" is repeated twice in verse 3. He is not only held in contempt, but there is a contempt-evoking element in him: he stinks. He is a man of pain and disease, with no comeliness. Men look away from him. (The chapter reads like an eyewitness description of the inmates of concentration camps after a month or two.) The Suffering Servant is smitten by God, but not for his sins. He is struck for the sins of all men. (In biblical language, in which all human actions have their source in God, it is stated: "The Lord hath made to light on him the iniquity of us all.")

Of course, the concept of vicarious suffering is not new to Jewish tradition. It is one of the great themes of the High Holy Day liturgy. Isaac's binding in particular is held up as a paradigm of suffering for others. "For the sake of the son who was bound, he will silence those who condemn us."

Karl Barth, Roy Eckardt, and Eliezer Berkovits have suggested that Israel suffers for the nations' anger at God. Because Israel is God's people, "other nations are constantly enraged by its existence, revolting against it, and wishing its destruction." Or, as Eckardt puts it: "In the existence of the Jewish people, we are confronted by God's electing grace, by His mercy as the only basis of human life. By our antagonism to Jews we show that we really do not like this fact."[50]

I would suggest another nuance, closer to Berkovits's emphasis on the Jew as witness. By its existence, Israel testifies to the God who promises ultimate redemption and perfection in an unredeemed world. Thus it arouses the anger of all who claim already to have found absolute perfection. Whenever there are Christian claims to absolute spiritual salvation, or Stalinist or Nazi claims to absolute social and political perfection, or capitalist or superpatriot claims to ultimate national loyalty, then Jews naturally become the object of suspicion and rejection. For this people's existence testifies: not yet. Beyond this point there are other civilizations and future perfections. Israel lays down this gauntlet whether or not it consciously testifies for God. How many times has the "non-Jewish Jew" testified, if not for God, then against idolatry, against the absolutizing of the relative current status quo.

Here I would suggest that a less mystical model of the Suffering Servant is crucial to our understanding. The treatment of the Suffering Servant is a kind of early warning system of the sins intrinsic in the culture but often not seen until later. Take the experience of Russia. The dangers of absolute power (even in the name of the proletariat) corrupting absolutely were not so apparent until the late period of Stalin. But the danger now broadcast aloud for all to see was foreshadowed earlier in the treatment of the Jews.

To borrow a homely metaphor: The old coal mines had no gas detectors. Instead, canaries and parakeets were kept in the mines. When coal gas escaped, it would poison the birds, for they were much more sensitive to it than humans. When the birds were poisoned, the miners knew it was time to go to another vein or move in a different direction.

The Holocaust was an advance warning of the demonic potential in modern culture. If one could conceive of Hitler coming to power not in 1933 but in 1963, after the invention of nuclear and hydrogen bombs, then the Holocaust would have been truly universal. It is a kind of last warning that if man will perceive and overcome the demonism unleashed in modern culture, the world may survive. Otherwise, the next Holocaust will embrace the whole world.

Unfortunately, the strain of evil is deeply embedded in the best potentials of modernity. The pollution is in the liberating technology; the uniformity in the powerful communication and cultural explosion; the mass murder in the efficient bureaucracy. This suggests a desperate need to delegitimatize the excessive authority claims of our culture. Yet some of its most attractive features may be the ones to lead us into the path of no return.

From this fact comes a call to Jews and Christians to resist the overwhelming attractions of the secular city even at its best. For as much as humanity needs immersion in the pluralism of its humanizing communications, and the freedom from fixed roles of its extraordinary options, and the liberating materialism of the city, it also needs groups to stay in spiritual tension with these same forces. The analogy may be to Ulysses, who must strap himself to the mast to make sure that, no matter how beautiful the siren song, he would not let himself be swept into the whirlpool of absolute commitment—and shipwreck. Christians and Jews are called upon to preserve their inner community and its testimony, out of the past and future. Their task is harder than Ulysses', for they are also called by the Holocaust to correct that very testimony's faults through participation in the new, open civilization. Let Gunter Lewy's and Gordon Zahn's studies of Catholics in Germany serve as warning.[51] The price of commitment to a *Kulturreligion* may be the inability to resist the worst moral possibilities in an otherwise good society. Once the center of loyalty is placed in that structure and there is absolute commitment to that society's values, then religion is powerless to check the excesses.

The Holocaust warns us that our current values breed their own nemesis of evil when unchecked—even as Nazi Germany grew in the matrix of modernity. To save ourselves from such error, we will have to draw on the warning of the experiences of the Suffering Servant. The Holocaust suggests a fundamental skepticism about all human movements, left and right, political and religious—even as we participate in them. Nothing dare evoke our absolute, unquestioning loyalty, not even our God, for this leads to possibilities of SS loyalties. SS Reichsführer Himmler could speak of "honor" and "decency" in carrying out the slaughter of millions. "By and large, however, we can say that we have performed this task in love of our people. And we have suffered no damage from it in our inner self, in our soul, in our character."[52]

At the same time, the Holocaust demands a reinterpretation of the Suffering Servant model, especially for Christians, who have tended to glorify this role. It is a warning that when suffering is overwhelming, then the servant may be driven to yield to evil. In *The Holocaust Kingdom* Alexander Donat tells of the experience of Sawek and his wife. When the expulsion of adults is ordered and they are included, they give their two-year-old Miriam a sedative and sling her in a knapsack over her father's shoulder. (Taking children along is prohibited, and in fact the children should have been taken by that time.) As they wait in line for processing, a baby which is being smuggled through ahead of them awakens and begins to cry. A Ukrainian guard goes over, bayonets the baby, and kills the father in front of them. All the blood drains from Sawek's face. "Take off the knapsack," his wife hissed. "As if in a trance, he did so . . . and carefully deposited the knapsack on the curb . . . then he went back to his original place, eyes vacant."[53]

There is also a conflict between the need for the promise of the sanctity of the Suffering Servant and of the world to come, and the danger of passivity at the fact of children burning now. The redemptive nature of suffering must be in absolute tension with the dialectical reality that it must be fought, cut down, eliminated. I once visited a great Christian, who had gone to India and devoted his life to a community caring in extraordinary sacrificial love for brain-damaged little children. Yet the community had never thought of bringing in a doctor to diagnose what treatment might be available to improve the condition of the children.

The Controversy with God—and with the Gospels

There is yet a third theological model which comes to the forefront after the Holocaust. I would call it the Lamentations 3 model (finding it in Chapter 3 of the Lamentations). It is the dominant theme in the writings of Elie Wiesel.

The early chapters of Lamentations are full of the "obvious" biblical solution: punishment for sins. Chapter 3 sounds a different note: "I am the man who has seen suffering." "God ate up my flesh and skin." "He [God] is a bear who stalks, and attacks me like a lion . . . " The agony is inflicted by God, but there is no note of sinfulness. There is only anger and pain. "And I said: my eternity and my hope from God has been lost." The climax is not guilt, but control, anger, and a feeling of being cut off from God.

Says Wiesel on Rosh Hashanah: "This day I had ceased to plead . . . on the contrary, I felt very strong. I was the accuser, God the accused . . . . I had ceased to be anything but ashes, yet I felt myself to be stronger than the Almighty . . . " Or again, "man is very strong, greater than God. When You were deceived by Adam and Eve, You drove them out of Paradise . . . . But there are men here whom

You have betrayed, whom You have allowed to be betrayed, gassed, burned; what do they do? They pray before You. They praise Your name!"[54]

In Lamentations, what pulls the narrator through is the sudden memory of past goodness. "This I recall to mind, therefore I have hope: the Lord's mercies, for they are not consumed." The Exodus memory is sustaining.

Wiesel teaches us that in the very anger and controversy itself is the first stage of a new relationship, perhaps the only kind of relationshp possible with God at this point in history. Could it be that the banal quality of prayer in our time is due to the fact that there are not enough prayers that, in our anger, we can say? Is it because we lack a prayer on the Holocaust that expresses the anger—that, at least, blames God? Anger is more compatible with love and involvement than pleasant niceties and old compliments.

Again, these are direct implications of this model. Centrally: it is to justify human beings, not God. It suggests a total and thoroughgoing self-criticism that would purge the emotional dependency and self-abasement of traditional religion and its false crutch of certainty and security. It involves a willingness to confess and clear up the violations of the image of God (of women, Jews, blacks, others) in our values, and a willingness to overcome the institutionalism that sacrifices God to self-interest. (One of the defenses of Pius XII's silence is that he felt he should not endanger the church and the faithful by stopping genocide.[55] If true faith means taking up the cross for God, then when will there ever be a truer time to be crucified, if necessary? Even if the attempt to help is doomed to failure, when will it ever be more appropriate to risk one's life or the church's life than to stop the crucifixion of children?) Justifying people means the fullest willingness, in both Judaism and Christianity, to defend the revolt against God and the faith that grows out of the desire to liberate man. Yet here too, the Holocaust demands a dialectical capacity from us. Rebels are not usually good at conserving; but if we simply validate the contemporary, we fall into idolatry and prepare the legitimization of another Holocaust.

In this model we find the source for one of the fundamental steps Christianity must take after the Holocaust: to quarrel with the Gospels themselves for being a source of anti-Semitism. For the devout Christian, the New Testament is the word of God. Yet even the word of God must be held to account for nourishing hatred, as well as for culpability in, or being an accessory to, the fact of genocide. Nothing less than a fundamental critique and purification of the Gospels themselves can begin to purify Christianity from being a source of hatred. The Holocaust reveals that Christianity has the stark choice of contrition, repentance, and self-purification, or the continual temptation to participate in genocide or pave the way for it. If Christianity has barely survived the first Holocaust, I do not believe that it can survive a second with any real moral capital at all. As painful as is the prospect, then, of a surrender of missionary enterprise to the Jew or a critique of the Gospels, this is possible out of a faith purged by the flames of the Holocaust. Ultimately it will be less painful than the alternative, of being accessory to the once and future fact of genocide. It will take extraordinary sacrificial effort to achieve this. But extraordinary catastrophes are not mastered by routine treatment or evasion. Only extraordinary outbursts of life or creativity can overcome them. To overwhelming death one must respond with overwhelming life.

Of course, none of these models can fully articulate the tensions of the relationship to God after the Holocaust. And it will take time to develop these models. This suggests that we are entering a period of silence in theology—a silence about God that corresponds to His silence. In this silence, God may be presence and hope, but no longer the simple deus ex machina.

VI. The Central Religious Testimony After the Holocaust

Recreating Human Life

In the silence of God and of theology, there is one fundamental testimony that can still be given—the testimony of human life itself. This was always the basic evidence, but after Auschwitz its import is incredibly heightened. In fact, it is the only testimony that can still be heard.

The vast number of dead and morally destroyed is the phenomenology of absurdity and radical evil, the continuing statement of human worthlessness and meaninglessness that shouts down all talk of God and human worth. The Holocaust is even model and pedagogy for future generations that genocide can be carried out with impunity—one need fear neither God nor man. There is one response to such overwhelming tragedy: the reaffirmation of meaningfulness, worth, and life—through acts of love and life-giving. The act of creating a life or enhancing its dignity is the counter-testimony to Auschwitz. To talk of love and of a God who cares in the presence of the burning children is obscene and incredible; to leap in and pull a child out of a pit, to clean its face and heal its body, is to make the most powerful statement—the only statement that counts.

In the first moment after the Flood, with its testimony of absurd and mass human death, Noah is given two instructions—the only two that can testify after such an event. "Be fruitful and multiply and replenish the earth" (Gen. 9:1–7), and "but your life blood I will hold you responsible for"—"who sheds man's blood, shall his blood be shed; for in the image of God made He man" (Gen. 9:5–6). Each act of creating a life, each act of enhancing or holding people responsible for human life, becomes multiplied in its resonance because it contradicts the mass graves of biblical Shinar—or Treblinka.

Recreating the Image of God

This becomes the critical religious act. Only a million or billion such acts can begin to right the balance of testimony so drastically shifted by the mass weight of six million dead. In an age when one is ashamed or embarrassed to talk about God in the presence of the burning children, the image of God, which points beyond itself to transcendence, is the only statement about God that one can make. And it is human life itself that makes the statement—words will not help.

Put it another way: the overwhelming testimony of the six million is so strong that it all but irretrievably closes out religious language. Therefore the religious enterprise after this event must see itself as a desperate attempt to create, save, and heal the image of God wherever it still exists—lest further evidence of meaninglessness finally tilt the scale irreversibly. Before this calling, all other "religious" activity is dwarfed.

But where does one find the strength to have a child after Auschwitz? Why bring a child into a world where Auschwitz is possible? Why expose it to such a risk again? The perspective of Auschwitz sheds new light on the nature of childrearing and faith. It takes enormous faith in ultimate redemption and meaningfulness to choose to create or even enhance life again. In fact, faith is revealed by this not to be a belief or even an emotion, but an ontological life-force that reaffirms creation and life in the teeth of overwhelming death. One must silently assume redemption in order to have the child—and having the child makes the statement of redemption.

There is a Jewish tradition that unashamedly traces the lineage of the

Messiah to Lot's two daughters (Gen. 19:30 ff.), the survivors of the brimstone-and-fire catastrophe of Sodom. Lot and the two daughters believed that they were the only survivors of another world catastrophe (ibid., v. 31). What is the point, then, of still conceiving? What possible meaning or value can there be to life? The answer to absurd death is unreasoning life; it is *chesed*—lovingkindness that seeks to create an object of its love, that sees that life and love can overcome the present reality, which points to and proves a new creation and final redemption. So the daughters stopped at nothing—getting their own father drunk, seducing him, committing drunken incest—yet conceiving the Messiah. (Jewish tradition traces the Messiah from Moab to Ruth, to David, to the final Redeemer.)[56] It is quite a contrast to the Immaculate Conception, but it is truer to human reality and redemption out of the human condition. In the welter of grubby human reality, with evil and death rampant, with mixed human motives and lusts, the Redeemer comes out of the ground of new creation and hope. "On the day the Temple was destroyed, the Messiah was born."[57] After the war, one of the highest birth-rates in the world prevailed in the displaced-persons camps, where survivors lived in their erstwhile concentration camps.

The reborn State of Israel is this fundamental act of life and meaning of the Jewish people after Auschwitz. To fail to grasp that inextricable connection and response is to utterly fail to comprehend the theological significance of Israel. The most bitterly secular atheist involved in Israel's upbuilding is the front line of the Messianic life-force struggling to give renewed testimony to the Exodus as ultimate reality. Israel was built by rehabilitating a half-million survivors of the Holocaust. Each one of those lives had to be rebuilt, given opportunity for trust restored. I have been told of an Israeli Youth Aliyah village settled by orphan children from the European camps, which suffered from an infestation of mice for a long time. There were children in this village who had lived through the shattering effect of the total uprooting and destruction of their reality, of the overnight transition from affluence to permanent hunger. Ten years after the Holocaust, some of these children would still sneak bread out of the dining room and hide it in their quarters. They could not believe that this fragile world of love would not again be shattered at any time. They were determined not to be caught without a supply of bread. And neither reassurances nor constant searches could uncover the bread; it was hidden in evermore clever caches—only to bring the mice. Yet these half a million—and the eight hundred thousand Jewish refugees from Arab countries—

were absorbed and given new opportunity and dignity. (They found enough strength to live under the shadow of another genocide aimed at themselves for more than twenty-five years.)

The Context of an Image of God

In a world of overpopulation and mass starvation and of zero population growth, something further must be said. I, for one, believe that in the light of the crematoria, the Jewish people are called to re-create life. Nor is such testimony easily given. One knows the risk to the children.

But it is not only the act of creating life that speaks. To bring a child into a world in which it will be hungry and diseased and neglected, is to torment and debase the image of God. We also face the challenge to create the conditions under which human beings will grow as an image of God; to build a world in which wealth and resources are created and distributed to provide the matrix for existence as an image of God.

We also face the urgent call to eliminate every stereotype discrimination that reduces—and denies—this image in the other. It was the ability to distinguish some people as human and others as not that enabled the Nazis to segregate and then destroy the "subhumans" (Jews, Gypsies, Slavs). The ability to differentiate the foreign Jews from French-born Jews paved the way for the deportation first of foreign-born, then of native, French Jews. This differentiation stilled conscience, stilled the church, stilled even some French Jews. The indivisibility of human dignity and equality becomes an essential bulwark against the repetition of another Holocaust. It is the command rising out of Auschwitz.

This means a vigorous self-criticism, and review of every cultural or religious framework that may sustain some devaluation or denial of the absolute and equal dignity of the other. This is the overriding command and the essential criterion for religious existence, to whoever walks by the light of the flames. Without this testimony and the creation of facts that give it persuasiveness, the act of the religious enterprise simply lacks credibility. To the extent that religion may extend or justify the evils of dignity denied, it becomes the devil's testimony. Whoever joins in the work of creation and rehabilitation of the image of God is, therefore, participating in "restoring to God his scepter and crown." Whoever does not support—or opposes—this process is seeking to complete the attack on God's presence in the world. These must be seen as the central religious acts. They shed a pitiless light on popes who deny brith control to starving millions because of a need to uphold the religious authority of the magisterium; or on rabbis who deny women's dignity out of loyalty to divinely given traditions.

VII. Religious and Secular after the Holocaust

THE END OF THE SECULAR-RELIGIOUS DICHOTOMY. This argument makes manifest an underlying thrust in this interpretation. The Holocaust has destroyed the meaning of the categories of "secular" and "religious." Illuminated by the light of the crematoria, these categories are dissolved and not infrequently turned inside out.

We must remember the many "religious" people who carried out the Holocaust. There were killers and murderers who continued to practice organized religion, including Christianity. There were many "good Christians," millions of respectable people, who turned in, rounded up, and transported millions of Jews. Some sympathized with or were apathetic to the murder process, while perceiving themselves as religiously observant and faithful—including those who did an extra measure of Jew-hunting or betrayal because they perceived it as an appropriate expression of Christian theology. Vast numbers of people practiced religion in this period, but saw no need to stand up to or resist the destruction process.

As Camus said:

> . . . I continue to struggle against this universe in which children suffer and die.
> . . . For a long time during those frightful years I waited for a great voice to speak up in Rome. I, an unbeliever? Precisely. For I knew that the spirit would be lost if it did not utter a cry of condemnation when faced with force. It seems that that voice did speak up. But I assure you that millions of men like me did not hear it and that at that time believers and unbelievers alike shared a solitude that continued to spread as the days went by and the executioners multiplied.
> It has been explained to me since that the condemnation was indeed voiced. But that it was in the style of the encyclicals, which is not at all clear. The condemnation was voiced and it was not understood! Who could fail to feel where the true conemnation lies in this case and to see that this example by itself gives part of the reply, perhaps the whole reply, that you ask of me.[58]

To add a final, more obscene note on the domestication of God and the denaturing of religion: Heinrich Himmler, overall head of the kingdom of death, told Felix Kersten, his masseur, "some higher Being . . . is behind Nature . . . If we refused to recognize that we should be no better than the Marxists. . . . I insist that members of the SS must believe in God."[59] (Whenever I reread this passage, I swear that the name of God must be hidden away in absolute silence and secrecy for so long that all the murderers and bystanders will have forgotten it. Only then can it be brought out and used again.)

IF "ALL IS PERMITTED," WHAT IS THE "FEAR OF GOD"? The Holocaust is overwhelming witness that "all is permitted." It showed that there are no limits of sacredness or dignity to stop the death process. There were no thunderbolts or divine curses to check mass murder or torture. The Holocaust also showed that one can literally get away with murder. After the war a handful of killers were punished, but the vast majority were not. Catholic priests supplied disguises and passports for mass murderers to help them escape punishment. German and Austrian officials cleared them of guilt—or imposed a few years of prison for killing tens of thousands. Men in charge of legally ostracizing Jews and clearing them for destruction became secretaries to cabinet ministers. Men who owned gas-producing companies, those who had built crematoria, were restored to their full ownership rights and wealth. Thirty years later, an anti-Nazi woman was imprisoned for seeking to kidnap and deliver for extradition a mass murderer, while he went free. Austrian juries acquitted the architects of the Auschwitz gas chambers. If all is permitted, why should anyone hold back from getting away with whatever one can? The prudential argument, that it is utilitarian not to do so, surely is outweighed by the reality that one can get away with so much. And the example of millions continually testifies against any sense of reverence or dignity to check potential evil.

I would propose that there is an explanation; a biblical category applies here. Whoever consistently holds back from murder or human exploitation when he could perpetrate it with immunity—or any person who unswervingly devotes himself to reverence, care, and protection of the divine image which is man, beyond that respect which can be coerced—reveals the presence within of a primordial awe—"fear of God"—which alone evokes such a response.

The biblical category suggests that fear of God is present where people simply cannot do certain things. It is, as it were, a field of force that prevents certain actions. The midwives feared God (Exod. 1:21), and therefore they simply could not kill newborn babies. When fear of God is not present, then there are no limits. Amalek could attack the weak and those who lagged behind because Amalek did not "fear God" (Deut. 25:18). A man can be killed in order to be robbed of his fair wife in a place where there is no fear of God (Gen. 20:11). We posit that this presence is a shield. This is why people cannot kill human beings in the "image of God" — they must first take them outside the pale of uniqueness and value before they can unleash murder. They must first be convinced that there is no divine limit. In the glare of the fires, by their piercing rays, we now can see clearly who has this fear of God and who does not.

It makes no difference whether the person admits the presence of God. From the biblical perspective, the power of the limit reveals that the divine presence's force is operating. (This is the meaning of Rabbi Akiva's statement in the Talmud, that in the moment that the thief steals, he is an atheist. Otherwise, how could be disobey the divine voice that says: Thou shalt not steal.)

RELIGIOUS AND SECULAR SELF-DEFINITION IN LIGHT OF AUSCHWITZ. Nor can we take self-definitions seriously. During the Holocaust, many (most?) of the church's protests were on behalf of Jews converted to Christianity. Consider what this means. It is not important to protest the murder of Jews; only if a person believes in Jesus Christ as Lord and Savior is there a moral need to protest his fate.[60] Can we take such self-definitions of religious people as reflection of belief in God?

When, in May and June 1967, it appeared that another Holocaust loomed, men of God remained silent. Pope Paul VI, moved by all sorts of legitimate or normal considerations (concern for Christian Arabs, concern for holy places, theological hang-ups about secular Israel) remained silent. A self-avowed atheist, root source of much of modern atheism, Jean-Paul Sartre, spoke out against potential genocide—even though he had to break with his own deepest political alliances and self-image in his links to Arabs and Third World figures to do so. He knew that there is one command: Never another Holocaust. Which is the man of God, which the atheist? By biblical perspective? By Auschwitz perspective? Are title, self-definition, official dress, public opinion—even sincere personal profession—more significant than action?

If someone were to begin to strangle you, all the while protesting loudly and sincerely: "I love you!" at what point would the perception of that person's sincerity change? At what point would you say, "Actions speak louder than words"? As you turn blue, you say, "Uh . . .

pardon me, are you sure that I am the person you had in mind . . . when you said, 'I love you'?"

One must fully respect the atheist's right to his own self-definition. But from the religious perspective, the action speaks for itself. The denial of faith has to be seen as the action of one determined to be a secret servant, giving up the advantages of acknowledged faith, because at such a time such advantages are blasphemous. Perhaps it reveals a deeper religious consciousness that knows there must be a silence about God—if faith in Him is not to be fatally destroyed in light of the Holocaust and of the abuse of faith in God expressed by a Himmler. Thus, the atheist who consistently shows reverence for the image of God, but denies that he does so because he is a believer in God, is revealed by the flames to be one of the thirty-six righteous—the hidden righteous, whom Jewish tradition asserts to be the most righteous, those for whose sake the world exists. Their faith is totally inward and they renounce the prerequisites of overt faith; and for their sake the world of evil is borne by God.[61]

THE STATE OF ISRAEL: A STUDY IN SECULARITY AND RELIGION AFTER AUSCHWITZ. By this standard, the "secular" State of Israel is revealed for the deeply religious state that it is. Both its officially nonreligious majority as well as its official and established religious minority are irrelevant to this judgment. The real point is that after Auschwitz, the existence of the Jew is a great affirmation and an act of faith. The re-creation of the body of the poeple, Israel, is renewed testimony to Exodus as ultimate reality, to God's continuing presence in history proven by the fact that his people, despite the attempt to annihilate them, still exist.

Moreover, who show that they know that God's covenant must be upheld by re-creating his people? Who heard this overriding claim and set aside personal comfort, cut personal living standards drastically, gave life, health, energy to the rehabilitation of the remnants of the covenant people? Who give their own lives repeatedly in war and/or guard duty to protect the remnant? Surely the secular Jews of Israel as much as, or more than, the religious Jew, or non-Jews anywhere.

The religious-secular paradox goes deeper still. Instead of choosing to flee at all costs from the terrible fate of exposure to genocide, instead of spending all their energy and money to hide and disappear, Jews all over the world—secular Jews included—renewed and intensified their Jewish existence and continued to have and raise Jewish children. Knowing of the fate to which this choice exposes them (a fate especially dramatically clear in Israel, where year after year the Arabs have preached extermination); aware of how little the world really cared, or cares, and that the first time is always the hardest—what is one to make of the faith of those who made this decision and who live it every day, especially in Israel? The answer has been given most clearly by Emil Fackenheim. To raise a Jewish child today is to bind the child and the child's child on the altar, even as father Abraham bound Isaac. Only, those who do so today know that there is no angel to stop the process and no ram to substitute for more than one and one-half million Jewish children in this lifetime. Such an act then, can only come out of resources of faith, of ultimate meaningfulness—of Exodus trust—on a par with, or superior to, father Abraham at the peak of his life as God's loved and covenanted follower. Before such faith, who shall categorize in easy categories the secular and the devout Israeli or Jew?

A classic revelation of the deeper levels can be found in the "Who is a Jew" controversy, and in the Israeli "Law of Return," which guarantees every Jew automatic admittance into Israel. This law has been used against Israel, in slogans of "racism," by those who say that if Israel only de-Zionizes and gives up this law she would have peace from her Arab neighbors, and by Christians and other non-Jews who then assess Israel as religiously discriminatory. All these judgments cost the secular Israelis a great deal—not least because any weakening of public support means a heightened prospect of genocide for themselves and their children. In turn, the secular Israeli is bitterly criticized by observant Jews for not simply following the traditional definition of who is a Jew. In 1974 this issue even disrupted attempts to form a government, at a time when life-and-death negotiations hung in the balance. Why, then, has the law been stubbornly upheld by the vast majority of secular Israelis?

It reveals the deepest recesses of their souls. They refuse to formally secularize the definition of "Israeli" and thereby cut the link between the covenant people of history and the political body of present Israel—despite their own inability to affirm, or even their vigorous denial of, the covenant! They see Auschwitz as revelatory and commanding, normative as great events in covenant history are, and they are determined to guarantee automatic admission to every Jew—knowing full well he is always exposed (by covenantal existence) to the possibility of another Holocaust with no place to flee. The lesson of Auschwitz is that no human being should lack a guaranteed place to flee again, just as the lesson of the Exodus was that no runaway slave should be turned back to his master (Deut. 23:16). (Needless to say, there is self-interest involved also—more Jews in Israel strengthen the security of Israel. But the admixture of self-interest is part of the reality in which religious imperatives are acted upon by all human beings.)

In light of this, Zionism, criticized by some devout Jews as secular revolt against religion and by other observant Jews for its failures to create a state that fully observes Jewish tradition, is carrying out the central religious actions of the Jewish people after Auschwitz. Irony piles upon irony! The re-creation of the state is the strongest suggestion that God's promises are still valid and reliable. Thus the secularist pheonomenon gives the central religious testimony of the Jewish people today. In the Holocaust many rabbis ruled that every Jew killed for being Jewish has died for the sanctification of the name of God. In death as in life, the religious-secular dichotomy is essentially ended.

Dialectical Reflections on the End of the Secular-Religious Difficulty

CONTRA HUMANISM. Once we establish the centrality of the reverence for the image of God and the erosion of the secular-religious dichotomy after Auschwitz, then the dialectic of the Holocaust becomes visible. Such views could easily become embodied in a simple humanism or a new universalist liberation that is totally absorbed in the current secular option. To collapse into this option would be to set up the possibility of another idolatry. True, it would be more likely a Stalinist rather than a fascist idolatry; but it reopens the possiblity of the concentration of power and legitimacy which could carry out another Holocaust. We are bidden to resist this temptation. Indeed, there is a general principle at work here. Every solution that is totally at ease with a dominant option is to be seen as an attempt to escape from the dialectical torment of living with the Holocaust. If you do escape, you open up the option that the Holocaust may recur. A radical self-critical humanism springing out of the Holocaust says no to the demons of Auschwitz; a celebration of the death of God or of secular man is collaboration with these demons.

CONTRA PROTEAN MAN. The fury of the Holocaust also undercuts the persuasiveness of another modern emphasis—the sense of option and choice of existence. This sense of widespread freedom to choose identity and of the weakening of biological or inhertied status is among the most pervasive values of contemporary culture. It clearly grows out of the quantum leap in human power and control through medicine and technology, backed by the development of democratic and universalist norms. It has generated a revolt against inherited disadvantage, and even genetic or biological limitations. The freedom of being almost protean is perceived as positive—the source of liberation and human dignity. In light of the Holocaust, we must grapple with the question anew. Is the breaking of organic relationships and deracination itself the source of the pathology which erupted at the heart of modernity? Erich Fromm has raised the issue in *Escape from Freedom.* Otto Ohlendorf—the head of D Einsatzgruppe, and one of the very few war criminals willing to admit frankly what he did and why—stressed the search for restored authority and rootedness (e.g., the failure to conserve the given as well as the freely chosen in modern culture) as a major factor in the scope and irrationality of the Nazis' murderous enterprise. Since the attack started against the people of Israel, but planned to go on to Slavs and other groups, it poses a fundamental question to the credibility of modern culture itself. There has not been enough testing and study of this possibility in the evidence of the Holocaust yet, but it warrants a serious study and an immediate reconsideration of the persuasiveness of the "freedom-of-being" option in modernity. The concept is profoundly challenged by the Jewish experience in the Holocaust.[62] For the demonic assault on the people of Israel recognized no such choice. Unlike the situation that prevailed in medieval persecutions, one could not cease to be a Jew through conversion. In retrospect, liberation turned out to be an illusion that weakened the victims' capacity to recognize their coming fate or the fact that the world would not save them—because they were Jews.

CONTRA THE SUPERIORITY OF THE SPIRIT OVER THE FLESH. This insight also reverses the historical, easy Christian polemic concerning the "Israel of the flesh" versus "Israel of the spirit." After all, is not Israel of the spirit a more universal and more committed category, a more spiritually meaningful state, than the status conferred by accident of birth? Yet the Holocaust teaches the reverse. When absolute power arose and claimed to be God, then Israel's existence was antithetical to its own. Israel of the flesh by its mere existence gives testimony, and therefore was "objectively" an enemy of the totalitarian state. By the same token neither commitment to secularism, atheism, or any other faith—nor even joining Christianity—could remove the intrinsic status of being Jewish, and being forced to stand and testify. Fackenheim, Berkovits, Rubenstein, and others have spoken of the denial of significance to the individual Jew by the fact that his fate was decided by his birth—whatever his personal preference. But classical Jewish commentators had a different interpretation. The mere fact that the Jew's existence denies the absolute claims of others means that the Jew is testifying. The act of living speaks louder than the denial of intention to testify, as I have suggested in my comments on fear of God above. During the Holocaust, rabbis began to quote a purported ruling by Maimonides that a Jew killed by bandits—who presumably feel freer to kill him because he is a Jew—has died for the sanctification of the Name, whether or not he was pressured before death to deny his Judaism and his God.[63] This testimony, voluntarily given or not, turns out to be the secret significance of "Israel of the flesh." A Jew's life is on the line and therefore every kind of Jew gives testimony at all times.

Israel of the spirit testifies against the same idolatry and evil. Indeed, there were sincere Christians who stood up for their principles, were recognized as threats, and sent to concentration camps. However, Israel of the spirit only has the choice of being silent; with this measure of collaboration, it can live safely and at ease. Not surprisingly, the vast majority chose to be safe. As Franklin Littell put it, when paganism is persecuting, Christians "can homogenize and become mere gentiles again; while the Jews, believing or secularized, remain representatives of another history, another providence."[64] It suggests that from now on one of the great keys to testimony in the face of the enormously powerful forces available to evil, will be to have given hostages, to be on the line because one is inextricably bound to this fate. The creation of a forced option should be one of the goals of moral pedagogy after the Holocaust. It is the meaning of chosenness in Jewish faith. The Christian analogy of this experience would be a surrender of the often self-deceiving universalist rhetoric of the church and a conception of itself as people of God—a distinct community of faith with some identification—that must testify to the world.

VIII. Final Dialectic: The Dialectic of Power

There is yet another dialectic we must confront. To do so we must encounter the Holocaust once more, in a scene from Tadeusz Borowski's account of life at Auschwitz. Says Borowski:

> They go, they vanish. Men, women, and children. Some of them know.
> Here is a woman—she walks quickly but tries to appear calm. A small child with a pink cherub's face runs after her and, unable to keep up, stretches out his little arms and cries: "Mama! Mama!"

"Pick up your child, woman!"

"It's not mine, sir, not mine!" she shouts hysterically and runs on, covering her face with her hands. She wants to hide, she wants to reach those who will not ride the trucks, those who will go on foot, those who will stay alive. She is young, healthy, good-looking, she wants to live.

But the child runs after her, wailing loudly: "Mama, mama, don't leave me!"

"It's not mine, not mine, no!"

Andrei, a sailor from Sevastopol, grabs hold of her. His eyes are glassy from vodka and the heat. With one powerful blow he knocks her off her feet, then, as she falls, takes her by the hair and pulls her up again. His face twitches with rage.

"Ah, you bloody Jewess! So you're running from your own child; I'll show you, you whore!" His huge hand chokes her, he lifts her in the air and heaves her on to the truck like a heavy sack of grain.

"Here! And take this with you, bitch!" and he throws the child at her feet.

"*Gut gemacht,* good work. That's the way to deal with degenerate mothers," says the S.S. man standing at the foot of the truck. "*Gut, gut, Russki.*"[65]

We have to comprehend that mother. We know from hundreds of accounts that Jews went to their death because they wanted to stay with their families. We know of mothers who gave themselves up to transport when their children were seized. We know of parents who declined to go to the forests or to the Aryan side because their children could not go. Imagine, then, this mother. She had voluntarily gone on the train to be with her child; she had declined to escape. She arrives at Auschwitz after a stupefying trip, described by another as follows:

When I climbed in, the carriage was half-full. The smell of chlorine hit my nose. The walls and the floor were white and everything was covered with disinfectant-powder. Immediately experienced a dryness and a queer burning in my mouth and throat. Thirst began to torture me. . . . The heat grew worse all the time. Moisture which had condensed from the vapours began to drip from the ceiling. People began to unbutton their coats to get relief from the heat and the stuffiness. . . . The heat in the carriage became worse every moment, and so did our state. We were dazed: half sane, half mad. The will-to-live became independent of the person and uncontrollable. . . . Manners and conventions which everyone observed up till now are no longer seen. They evaporate in the heat. The will-to-live has taken the floor. Women of all ages remove their coats. They tear their dresses from themselves. They stand half naked. Someone relieves himself. Everything is overturned and uprooted; a mist fogs one's consciousness.[66]

In this state, when she suddenly understood where she was, when she smelled the stench of the burning bodies— perhaps heard the cries of the living in the flames—she abandoned her child and ran.

Out of this wells up the cry: Surely here is where the cross is smashed. There has been a terrible misunderstanding of the symbol of the crucifixion. Surely, we understand now that the point of the account is the cry: "My lord, my lord, why have you abandoned me?" Never again should anyone be exposed to such one-sided power on the side of evil—for in such extremis not only does evil triumph, but the Suffering Servant now breaks and betrays herself. Out of the Holocaust experience comes the demand for redistribution of power. The principle is simple. No one should ever have to depend again on anyone else's goodwill or respect for their basic security and right to exist. The Jews of Europe needed that goodwill and these good offices desperately—and the democracies and the church and the Communists and their fellow-Jews failed them. No one should ever be equipped with less power than is necessary to assure one's dignity. To argue dependence on law, or human goodness, or universal equality is to join the ranks of those who would like to repeat the Holocaust. Anyone who wants to prevent a repetition must support a redistribution of power. Since this, in turn, raises a large number of issues and problems with regard to power, we will not analyze it here. But the analysis of the risks of power and the dialectic of its redistribution is a central ongoing task of religion and morality, and a vast pedagogical challenge to all who are committed to prevent a second Auschwitz.

IX. Living with the Dialectic

The dialectic I have outlined is incredibly difficult to live by. How can we reconcile such extraordinary human and moral tensions? The classical traditions of Judaism and Christianity suggest: by reenacting constantly the event which is normative and revelatory. Only those who experience the normative event in their bones—through the community of the faith—will live by it.[67] I would suggest, then, that in the decades and centuries to come, Jews and others who seek to orient themselves by the Holcaust will unfold another sacral round. Men and women will gather to eat the putrid bread of Auschwitz, the potato-peelings of Bergen-Belsen. They will tell of the children who went, the starvation and hunger of the ghettoes, the darkening of the light in the Mussulmen's eyes. To enable people to reenact and relive Auschwitz there are records, pictures, even films—some taken by the murderers, some by the victims. That this pain will be incorporated in the round of life we regret; yet we may hope that it will not destroy hope but rather strengthen responsibility, will, and faith.

After Auschwitz, one must beware of easy hope. Israel is a perfect symbol for this. On the one hand, it validates the right to hope and speak of life renewed after destruction. On the other hand, it has been threatened with genocide all along. At the moment it is at a low point— yet prospects for a peace also suddenly emerge. Any hope must be sober, and built on the sands of despair, free from illusions. Yet Jewish history affirms hope.

I dare to use another biblical image. The cloud of smoke of the bodies by day and the pillar of fire of the crematoria by night may yet guide humanity to a goal and a day when human beings are attached to each other; and have so much shared each other's pain, and have so purified and criticized themselves, that *never again will a Holocaust be possible.* Perhaps we can pray that out of the welter of blood and pain will come a chastened mankind and faith that may take some tentative and mutual steps toward redemption. Then truly will the Messiah be here among us. Perhaps then the silence will be broken. At the prospect of such hope, however, certainly in our time, it is more appropiate to fall silent.

Response to Irving Greenberg

ALAN T. DAVIES

If to speak of the Holocaust is painful for Jews, to speak of the Holocaust is also painful for Christians. Because the disaster erupted in Christian Europe, on soil fertilized for centuries by Christian ideas, because the Nazis, when not Christians themselves, were the baptized children of Christians, and because the German churches permitted themselves to be seduced too willingly by Nazi dreams and visions, the terrible question of Christian complicity is instantly ventilated. The subject is threatening, for the intrinsic worth of the Christian faith itself is brought under judgment. Generations of Christian theologians and preachers have proclaimed with assurance that Judaism "died on the cross"; now, ironically, the dictum can be reversed, for, with much greater justification, Jewish theologians are raising the possibility that Christianity died at Auschwitz! An awesome suggestion. One reads it, for example, in Eliezer Berkovits's polemical but powerful indictment of Christianity, *Faith after the Holocaust,* in which the Christian religion is charged with a total moral and spiritual bankruptcy, as the true source of the Nazi genocide. The fact that Berkovits almost certainly overstates his case by claiming that a direct rather than an indirect line extends from the Council of Nicaea to the death camps does not mitigate the agonizing crisis of conscience which the entire issue poses for the Christian churches. It is not without reason that Franklin Littell has described the Holocaust as a basic event in Christian history, "of the same order as the Exodus, Sinai and the fall of Rome,"[1] and therefore a serious challenge to Christian theology. Like Irving Greenberg, I approach the subject with fear and trembling.

In a profoundly moving fashion, Irving Greenberg has described the hideous crimes perpetrated by the SS, thereby raising implicitly the question as to whether such an event, so irrational in the radical absurdity of its evil, can be explained at all. I refer for the moment to its human dimensions, the incineration of living children in order to spare the two-fifths of a cent per child it would have cost to have gassed them first—rather than its transcendent dimensions. Whatever remains obscure about the role of God in the dark episode of which we speak, the role of man is not so obscure, even if Auschwitz represents, as Emil

Fackenheim believes, a new exercise in the diabolical possibilities of man's inhumanity to man, without any true counterpart in the "whole history of human depravity."[2] But the unique qualities of its radical evil are wholly consistent with the unique man who conceived the *Endlösung* in the first place. Anyone who has read Hitler's spiritual autobiography, *Mein Kampf,* cannot miss the intrinsically religious character of the author's adolescent identity-crisis, in which, in his own words, he was converted from a "weak-kneed cosmopolitanism" to a full-blooded anti-Semitism.[3] The illuminating vision in the Damascus journey of the young Hitler was his sudden glimpse of the Jew behind the hated Marxism of the Austrian Social Democratic party. Jean-Paul Sartre once pointed out that every anti-Semite is actually a dualist, specifically a Manichaean, who has organized his personal being around absolute symbols of good and evil, and imagines himself as an apostle of light at war with the powers of darkness.[4] Such was certainly the mind of Adolf Hitler. The religion to which he was converted could be described as a fanatical modern Manichaeism, in which the Jew suffered the incalculable misfortune of being cast as the evil demon whose eradication, for Hitler, became a sacred task: "By defending myself against the Jew," he wrote (presumably with complete sincerity), "I am fighting for the work of the Lord!" This, along with Hitler's relentless quest for power, was the one consistent theme of his life. His Manichaean universe, combined with his personal messianic complex and an unqualified faith in a pagan providence (*Vorsehung*), proves that nothing is as bad as bad religion; but a bad religion is nevertheless a real religion.

According to Sir Alan Bullock, the fate of the Jews was plotted in secret conversations between the Fuhrer and his chosen executioner, Heinrich Himmler: conversations to which no one else, except occasionally Martin Bormann, was ever admitted, and concerning which no records exist.[5] In its human dimension the Holocaust does not defy explanation. Its absurd and radical evil is wholly explicable in light of the religious world-view of the absurd but deadly serious man who was its chief architect. Irving Greenberg indicts modern civilization for creating a value-free atmosphere in which mass murder can flourish. To the extent that totalitarianism is the final logic of a wholly secularized and dehumanized society, I agree. But mass murder also occurs when the gutter comes to power, and Hitler, unmistakably, owed his origins to the most base and morally vulgar undercurrents of his age.

The transcendent dimensions of the Holocaust are more problematic. Here one encounters the ancient problem of theodicy, much confounded. Irving Greenberg's resolution of the religious and theological hesitations which have paralyzed Jewish reflection is dialectical: one responds with both faith and doubt, permitting neither Exodus-Sinai nor Auschwitz to submerge each other. The "death-of-God" conclusions of Richard Rubenstein, formulated as a result of a memorable conversation with Heinrich Grüber, dean of the Evangelical Church of East and West Berlin, are, in Greenberg's opinion, too absolutistic, although nevertheless authentic as one pole of the faith-doubt dialectic. I acknowledge that Rubenstein's negation of classical theism represents no ordinary form of atheism, but a sensitive and, in some sense, legitimate Jewish response to a situation in which not to question God would be deemed immoral. But I remain more critical than Greenberg of Rubenstein's theological "final solution" to problems of faith after the Holocaust.

Rubenstein, in my opinion, accepted too easily the rather simplistic version of the biblical notion of divine providence which he heard from the lips of Dean Gruber: *"Um deinetwillen werden wir getötet den ganzen Tag* . . . for Thy sake are we slaughtered all day long . . ."* (Ps. 44:22).[6] However much the great prophets of ancient Israel sought the origins of the afflictions of the covenant people in the will of the Lord, they "never gave this insight the systematic development which would have made every misfortune a punishment for sin. Men retained the simple perception that evil for which there was no further explanation was a part of life, and could not be linked up directly with moral judgments. . . . even the innocent may be surprised by a fearful end."[7] This suggests that the dialectic between faith and doubt is already present in the biblical tradition itself, so that the alternative to Dean Grüber's theological rationale for the Holocaust must surely be a more profound, and authentically biblical, interpretation of transcendent mystery, rather than a spurning of the God of traditional faith in favor of a neopaganism which finds the "gods of space" more congenial to the Jewish (or Christian) spirit than the Abrahamic "Lord of time" (Rosenzweig). Rubenstein, because he derives the anti-Semitic explosion of modern Germany from the mythical and magical potencies of Christianity rather than from paganism, seemingly fails to notice any affinities between his own celebration of Dionysian religion and the pietistic return of the Nazis to nature and the earth in their mystique of race, folk, and soil. In their new prometheanism, with its peculiar fusion of atavistic, romantic elements and the demonic techniques of modern scientific culture, the Nazis also affirmed the "death" of the biblical God.

Moreover, with the loss of God, and along with this the loss of transcendent meaning, the Holocaust itself seems to change its character, becoming a natural catastrophe rather than a monumental sin, or, in an absurd world, merely another absurdity. If cosmic law collapses in the universe, as it does if transcendence disappears, the moral condemnation of the Holocaust also loses its transcendent dimension as a cry against heaven—an appeal to "God against God"—and becomes instead not much more than a protest against the futility of human existence in a cosmos finally indifferent to man's fate. Paradoxically, in the end, one is driven back to ancient patterns of meaning, despite doubt. For who can believe that such inhuman crimes do not ultimately matter, or that the heavens contain no judgment!

One central challenge in Irving Greenberg's address—at least to a Christian respondent—is his question as to whether Christianity, long accustomed to relegating Judaism to a dead religious past, can now receive as a sign "out of the whirlwind" of God's continuing presence in Jewish history the momentous rebirth of the Jewish people in the modern State of Israel. Can Christianity acknowledge the reality of a new orientating event with revelatory meaning, or is the church as spiritually blind as it has always considered Judaism to be? Challenging Christian anti-Semitism, Greenberg wonders if Christians can overcome their old theological fixation with Jewish homelessness as a divine decree, a consequence of Israel's repudiation of Jesus. Can Christians, long accustomed to a Neoplatonic distinction between the spiritual Israel (identified with the church) and the carnal Israel (identified with postbiblical Judaism), overcome their antipathy toward a nation-state as a valid embodiment of Jewish aspirations and ideals? Can Christians enter sufficiently into Jewish self-understanding in order to grasp the significance of Israel as a resurrection symbol to a generation which barely escaped the jaws of total annihilation?

In challenging Christian anti-Semitism, however, Irving Greenberg has also raised another issue concerning faith itself and its possible meanings. Do the orientating (or root) experiences of Jewish and Christian faith teach the same lessons about the meaning of history in light of its cosmic setting? Providence, a more profound biblical idea than Rubenstein assumes, seems also a doctrine which Jews and Christians interpret with a nuance of difference. Eugene Borowitz writes that "history is the laboratory of Jewish theology,"[8] and Emil Fackenheim speaks of an indissoluble tie between God and history as the midrashic framework of Jewish belief, which, in spite of its meaningless character, even the Holocaust cannot finally destroy.[9] Greenberg has emphasized the significance of the Exodus as the great paradigmatic symbol, or orientating experience, of traditional Jewish faith, and it is obvious that a religion organized around such a symbol must regard God's providential presence in history as a crucial article of faith. The Holocaust, which threatens the midrashic framework, thus becomes a religious as well as a human crisis of unprecedented degree. "The whole Jewish people is caught between immersion in nihilism and immersion in redemption in immediate experience" (Greenberg). This explains, in part, why Rubenstein became an atheist. If God's presence in history is no longer discernible, or is seriously contradicted by the vicissitudes of man's experience, God seems no longer a possible idea. This also explains why Israel, its birth and survival, has been read in clear providential terms by Jewish theologians. Even secular Jews, according to Borowitz, were moved by the miraculous features of the June 1967 victory: "For a moment the tight naturalistic structure through which we secularized men see everything cracked open, and we saw him."[10]

For Christians, generally speaking, God's mode of relating to history is perceived somewhat differently. There is no midrashic framework of Christian belief. This is not because Christians have not as a matter of habit interpreted the Christian ages in terms of God's overarching design. On the contrary, ever since Lactantius regarded the triumph of the Christian church in the Roman *imperium* as a vindication of the true religion over its rivals, Christian thought has been colored by an ideological understanding of providence. Of late, with the disintegration of Christendom, most Christians are inclined to show much greater caution toward any attempt to decipher the presence of God in the events of history, a skepticism which, because of past distortions, is probably healthy. Even when the preoccupation with providence ran strong, however, those great theologians who dealt with the subject, such as Augustine, always operated from a different orientating experience than rabbinic Judaism: not the Exodus, but the birth, death, and resurrection of the Christ supplied the paradigmatic symbol. The cross, however (which includes the resurrection), unlike the Exodus, is both a historical and a transhistorical event. Its transhistorical significance has been described by Reinhold Niebuhr as a revelation of the "fragmentary and contradictory character of all historic reality,"[11] and a revelation of the fact that history will never succeed in making final sense of itself, but must finally be explained and fulfilled from beyond itself. If Niebuhr is correct, this means that Christians, wedded to a symbol which stands above history as well as in history, or perhaps at the margin of history, will typically have a different perspective on both the beneficent and tragic experiences of history than Jews. This difference, I believe, qualifies the extent to which Christian faith can accept new revelatory moments which, in some measure, are believed to overcome the contradictions of history, as Israel, to Jewish faith, becomes a sign out of the whirlwind that in some measure overcomes the Holocaust. What if the Holocaust stood alone, without Israel? Could Jewish theology retain its classical orientation?

One must, of course, be careful in stating this contrast between Judaism and Christianity. It would be abhorrent for a Christian to minimize historical tragedy, especially when Jews are involved, by an otherworldly appeal to transcendent symbols; nor would Niebuhr have intended or sanctioned this application of his doctrine of providence. Nor must the cross ever be employed by Christians in order to avoid the scandal of the Holocaust: a genuine temptation, reflected in any triumphalist theology of our age. Nor, I think, should Christians approach the subject as untroubled theists because, on this analysis, they are relieved of the necessity of scanning history for signs of God's continuing presence. All profound theistic (and biblical) faith embraces doubt as one of its elements. According to the New Testament, the death of Jesus was the death of a troubled theist who felt himself forsaken by God. Rather, the cross, itself a revelation of the scandalous nature of history, should reinforce for Christians their perception of the Holocaust as a hideous scandal which exposes, once again, the contradictory and seemingly meaningless character of historical reality. Interpreted in a Christian context, recent events should not, in my opinion, be organized into meaningful sequences in which the providential hand of God is unambiguously detected. As a Christian, I respond to Irving Greenberg's plea that Christians abandon their various forms of ideological prejudice against Israel, celebrating its birth and survival as a great human event of immense existential significance to both Christians and Jews. It is only when he asks me to receive the sign out of the whirlwind that I demur.

Christianity and Judaism perceive history in somewhat different terms; perhaps some critical theological decisions on the part of the two religious communities in the formative stages of their evolution have intensified the difference. Faced with the catastrophe of the Roman War, 66–70 C.E., rabbinic Judaism, under the aegis of Rabbi Yochanan ben Zakkai, accepted the destruction of the Second Temple without allowing this disaster to overwhelm the most treasured beliefs of Judaism and the continuation of Jewish life. Ancient Judaism elected a theology which came to terms with a transformed historical situation without appealing, as it might have done—and as some apocalyptically minded Jews wished it to do[12]—to a strategy of crisis-living in which history is effectively denied. Ancient Christianity, on the other hand, made the opposite choice. The church refused to settle down in a dying world, but concentrated instead on the imminent end of history and return of the Christ. A Jewish willingness to take history seriously has been one result of Rabbi Yochanan's choice, whereas Christianity, having purchased heaven at the expense of the earth, has had trouble with the latter ever since. Elsewhere, Greenberg has quite correctly pointed out the difficulties which the later church had with its own formative theology, mentioning that much modern Christian thought has sought to undo this option.[13] In another respect, however, the Christian emphasis on fulfillment beyond history rather than in history might be more relevant to the catastrophes of history than theologies which emphasize the presence of God in particular historical occurrences, since it eliminates the need for final explanation without paralyzing one's personal response.

Must faith require a sign out of the whirlwind before its response is possible? Or can the Gordian knot which the Holocaust poses remain unsevered, leaving us with fragmentary rather than final meanings, because history supplies no final meanings? Out of the Holocaust, which defies final explanation, there nevertheless emerge many fragments of meaning. Elie Wiesel, for example, has described with great poignancy the beauty and heroism of Jewish martyrs in the midst of death, and Berkovits has affirmed his faith in the future of man because of the extraordinary nobility of some of Hitler's victims. These fragments of meaning in a meaningless situation overcome, in part, the larger meaninglessness of the Holocaust. Given this fragmentary sense of meaning, it is, I think, possible to live without nihilism.

Irving Greenberg believes that the Suffering Servant imagery of Deutero-Isaiah is destined to acquire new significance in Jewish theology because of the suffering of the Jewish innocents in the twentieth century. This image, frequently stylized in Christian piety, acquires new significance also for the post-Holocaust Christian church. For what Christian today can truly look at the cross without seeing around it the fires of Auschwitz? Christians, of course, must be careful with such comparisons, which become obscene if the cross is employed by a triumphalist Christian theology to minimize the Holocaust, or deny it altogether. But perhaps it is legitimate for Christians to see in the Holocaust a more terrible revelation of the human condition, which, in

turn, adds a new dimension to the cross as a revelatory symbol linked
to evil and suffering. I would like some gifted Christian artist to paint a
crucifixion scene portraying Jesus as an Auschwitz Jew, including the
yellow badge *Jude* on his body, against the barbed wire of a death
camp.[14] In this sense, the religious meaning of the central symbol of
Christianity has been forever transformed and deepened for me, and
no theological response would be complete which does not recognize
this fact. At the same time, and for the same reason, I agree with Irving
Greenberg that it is more imperative than ever for Christians to struggle with the Christian sources of the Holocaust, the ideological roots of
anti-Semitism in the structures of classical Christian theology, and the
attitudes of historic Christendom. These painful realities have made
the Holocaust a basic event in Christian history and an unprecedented
crisis for the Christian conscience. They might raise the question, in
radical form, as to whether it is morally possible to remain a Christian
at all. To explore this problem seems to me the paramount theological
task of Christians of the post-Auschwitz generation.

The Heart of the World

ALFRED KAZIN

*But if God so beautifully dresses the wild grass, which is alive today
and is thrown into the furnace tomorrow, will he not much more surely
clothe you, you who have so little faith?*

Matt. 6:30 (Goodspeed trans.)

For us Jews the war never ends. As I write a school in northern Israel
has been seized by Arab terrorists, twenty-four youngsters have been
killed. We all know that this will not be condemned by most of the
principal powers and that it will be followed by more and more attacks
as well as by useless reprisals. The people of Israel are now all hostages. The same day, news comes from Austria of sudden press attacks
on the Jews, and of the most unrestrained Nazi vilification of Jews in
anonymous letters to the newspapers. It is reported that as many as 75
percent of the Austrians are still anti-Semitic.

There has never been a time since the war when Jews felt as isolated
as they do now. If the State of Israel had done nothing else but take in
the Jews cast out by other countries, it would have merited the admiration and sympathy of the world. But the resurrection of Israel is a miracle and a very great sign. It reminds us all that the Jews are a civilization, a very great tradition at once religious, philosophic, literary, that
kept itself alive in exile, that never died out even among the isolated
and unlettered Jews. Yet after four wars in twenty-five years, after so
many brilliant victories, after such heroic exertions, Israel is almost totally isolated on the international scene; the legitimacy of the nation is
constantly in question. While the nation struggles for the right to exist,
the people of Israel feel, as Jews have felt all through this century, that
to kill a Jew is regarded as a political virtue, where in the Middle Ages
it was a religious one.

There was a time after 1945 when "Auschwitz"—that word that says
so much more than can be taken in—somehow awakened a conscious
sympathy for Jews. There was, as the saying now goes, a kind of "gold-
en age" for Jews. Since America alone had come out of the war un-
scathed and rich, since Jews were now part of the mainstream, Ameri-

65

can Jews, at least, received some recognition of what the Jews of Europe had suffered during the war.

But by now the memory of Hitler's war has been succeeded by the experience of limitless change and revolution, especially in the Middle East, Asia, and Africa, countries that until 1939 were the preserves of Western imperialism. The acceleration of political change grows ever more violent. All races and all countries, it sometimes seems all generations, are simultaneously vying with each other. As Faulkner said in *Light in August,* "so much happens. Too much happens": the endless self-multiplication of technology and the shattering of traditions, the often meaningless flow of violence like the interminable succession of day and night! At such a moment it is very hard for a Jew to remember the beautiful saying of an old-fashioned American Protestant (John Jay Chapman) "the heart of the world is Jewish." Only a Christian brought up on the old biblical faith could have said that. But just as many Christians look on Jews as unconnected with biblical faith, Jewish *and* Christian, so there are many post-Christians who do not see the Jewish experience as spiritually relevant to anything. Here is a letter from a university professor, written to me out of the blue:

> What do you mean in your book *Contemporaries* when, talking of Freud, you say that "he could not have predicted the destruction of Western civilization at Auschwitz, Maidenek, Belsen"? Western civilization was not destroyed by that war; changed perhaps but it is still the dominant world model, for better or worse. Your claims are the narrow selfish ones of the Jew. Millions of non-Jews were murdered during that war. It is the claims to special righteousness that were responsible for that war, for the present war in the Middle East. . . . In this the Jews are the worst offenders; the chosen, the elect, the superior are the true enemies of peace.

It does not surprise me that Christian concern and solidarity with the people of the Bible have organized this moving occasion. Thank you for doing so. An understanding of Jewish fate in our time can come only from religious awareness, for the reality of our times is dominatingly secular, pseudoreligious, hysterical with hatred for races and classes whose existence is objectively intolerable. We live with a boundlessly vindictive spirit of revolution, on the right and on the left, fundamentally nationalistic, that cannot explain Jewish history and belief, that will not include Jews in its schemes to create the future in its own image.

I recognized this from the moment Hitler came to power in 1933, for the German working class, which was supposed to stop him, believed less in revolution than did the middle classes maddened by defeat and inflation. Ten years later, with Russia and America in the war, and with the whole continent seething against him, it was clear that Hitler could be beaten. But the Jews, though prime objects of Hitler's hatred, had somehow become a side issue for the world. In 1939 I had seen photographs of German army trains bearing soldiers to the attack on Poland. The soldiers had chalked on the trains: *We are going to Poland to hit Jews.* By 1943 I knew, as anyone could have known, that the Jews were being murdered from the Rhine to the Volga. Zygelboym, a Jewish labor leader in the Polish cabinet-in-exile, London, committed suicide in order to alert the world to the fate of his people. But it was clear that before Nazism went down to defeat it would first kill as many Jews as it could.

How did we know it? By the overwhelming logic of totalitarianism. All things and all people not absorbable into the sacred movement would have to be destroyed by the overmastering movement toward total domination, total control, that the Nazis had set up in Germany and now all over Europe under the banner of "national" revolution—of an "organic" revolution based on a total assimilation into the New Order of all existing institutions and on the pseudomythic sources of some ancient folk life, the true Germanic religion in race, blood, and soil that had succeeded Christianity.

The Nazis were revolutionaries. They were not concerned with the national majority any more than the Soviets have been concerned with the well-being of Russian workers and peasants. But they were maximum revolutionaries in the sense that the twentieth century was to make familiar from 1917 on. They were ruthless obliterators of people, institutions, other cultures—in the name of a monolithic future that represented the sheerest fantasy. We know how warmly the First World War was welcomed in 1914 by the generation that was to be slaughtered. As D. H. Lawrence said, 1914 was sensational delight posing as pious idealism. But this orgy of destruction could not be stopped, for national loyalties, national "regeneration," proved stronger than anything else, even when the savagery of the revolutionary new movements created a host of enemies dangerous to national survival itself. From the moment that revolutionary zeal became delightful not only to "advanced" elements in Europe but also to the embittered middle class, a spirit of blind action for action's sake, of nihilistic fury, seized millions of Germans. Those who may have dreamed of transforming Europe by other means discovered that nothing worked like the exercise of terror. Here were the foundations of the politico-sadism behind Hitlerism and Stalinism.

The revolutionary force of Nazism was its determination to move forward at any price, to arrogate to itself the power of all established institutions, to produce an atmosphere of constant aggression. Nazism sought above all to enlist total obedience from the masses, and by this to give them the illusion that through the rituals of obedience, vast popular demonstrations, and constant surveillance by "organs of the people," they were participating in a large political process whose demonic energy arose from renewal in the primitive forces of life. Here was revolution as virtue enraged against the sinfulness of enemies who could never change their spots, who were born evil, who were *ineradicably wrong* in the zoological scale of existence.

The Jews were *the* "enemy." Only those who hate Jews can ever satisfy themselves precisely *why* Jews as a group should be the "enemy." As Jacob Talmon noted in a magisterial essay, nothing less than all European history is "the seedbed of the Holocaust." The Jews embodied a contradiction that they could not explain and that even Christianity could not or would not resolve. They were an ancient civilization that had amazingly survived: a distinct people with their own religious cult who had somehow managed to perpetuate this ancient civilization while scattered among all the nations and (when allowed to) participating happily in the civic and cultural life of these countries. They were loyal to their past without being disloyal to their present obligations. Thus they were an anomaly to the unifying tendency of all modern thought, just as they had long been an anomaly to orthodox Christianity.

The Jews were assimilable as citizens, but somehow not altogether as a culture. By contrast with the dynamic, dramatizing stress on Christianity as personal salvation—which made possible the individual art and imaginative literature of the West—the Jews tended until very late in their history (only in our day), to discourage realistic fiction, drama, the art of painting. Religiously as well as culturally, the Jews tended to suspect everything that was not rooted in the life of the whole congregation, that did not express itself in special acts of remembrance and commemoration. By contrast with a Christian civilization in which they figured at worst as the murderers of God (a concept impossible for Jews to understand) and at best as eternal wanderers, the Jews seemed to deny and even to be in the way of the ceaseless elan, movement, purposive change, merciless political aggression, that the twentieth-century revolutions purported to represent. The Jews, as their wayward son Spinoza had said, explained everything by the will of God. God's mind explained all natural law, and for many many pious Jews, endlessly hypnotized by every jot and tittle of the Law, there was no law, no nature, no will in the universe but God's.

"The heart of the world is Jewish" and, said Pius XI, "spiritually we are Semites." But twentieth-century history represents the most violent inner convulsions and struggles on the part of all nations to accommodate themselves within national limits to the ambitions and conflicts unleashed by capitalism, imperialism, socialism. In a world increasingly conceived as the struggle between modern forces to release the hidden strength represented by the future, the Jews seemed to be entirely a people of the past, living in the past. Revolutions exist in order to perpetuate revolutions; a revolution that is really a revolution, necessarily totalitarian in its effects, cannot accommodate itself to what it cannot absorb, as we have seen with the Soviet leaders, who are nationalist, repressive, and reactionary in their values. The life of a revolution (as opposed to its ideal meaning in history) is purposive action, violent determination, power continually seizing more power in the name of a moral abstraction.

Given the Nazi fury of resurgent national power under the form of revolution, given the special drive to *create* a future for the domineering Germans in the name of primeval idols of blood, race, and soil—a revolution expedited by incessant propaganda, intimidation, and the self-multiplying forces of technology—the Jews were doomed by the forces of violence unleashed by World War II. These "great" wars are always the most terrible revolutions. The Jews of Europe were so vulnerable that one million of their children were to be exterminated. The process would go on and on, and it could be explained only by the murderers. The victims themselves could not understand or fully credit it. Although the Jews were hunted so obsessively that the Nazis actually weakened their forces at the second battle of Kharkov in order to round up Jews, the Russian Communists would not be able to explain why Jews were so deeply hated, and Marxists in general would not be able to explain the Holocaust any more than American liberalism could explain it.

The Jews were outside the law. The paradox of their existence in "revolutionary" times aroused their enemies and contributed to their destruction. They had inexplicably preserved their religion, their ancient culture, but as a people they were disorganized, powerless, intellectually divided. They cherished their own tradition, but as citizens looked for tolerance and safety to the Enlightenment and the "liberal" parties of Europe. The Jews of Eastern Europe, who had lived in little villages among a hostile peasantry, trusted only the intellectual leaders of these nations. Vast numbers of Romanians, Slovakians, Latvians, Ukrainians had a limitless hatred for Jews and assisted in their extermination. Russian Communism had never had any tolerance for Jews as Jews. Stalin and his cabal, who had gained and kept power over the bodies of their Jewish opponents in the Communist party, were venomously anti-Semitic and during World War II knew how to stoke national support by stirring up the age-old enmity to the Jew. The Papacy, afraid to alienate powerful Germany, was officially neutral. But there was evident satisfaction in some high church quarters that the obstinate disbelievers in Christ were getting their comeuppance. The indifference of the church extended at times even to Jewish converts, to priests and nuns who had been born Jews. Many individual priests were shining exceptions. But the silence from Rome and many Protestant churches, to say nothing of the many Nazi agents who called themselves good Christians, helps to explain the suffocating moral atmosphere that made the extermination of the Jews possible.

The Allies made no special effort to bomb the railroad tracks leading to Auschwitz, to support Jewish self-defense behind the Nazi lines, to provide a haven for the masses of refugees. The Jews were not a factor in the Allied plans for victory or the postwar scene. The Jews were simply a people *accused,* a people whose only occupation was to feel guilty. Here, without any relief, without suspension, any possiblility of conversion, the most powerful nation in Europe based the first article of legislation on the old theological infamy that a whole people should feel guilty throughout history, and continuously be made into a sacrifice.

The Jews reacted with all the confused submissiveness, misplaced trust, incredulity about their impending destruction, that one might expect of any powerless group totally cornered and set up for destruction. The Jews' real history, their true concerns, made it impossible for them even to reply to the accusations against them. To "understand" why they were being murdered, as a people, would have meant complicity in their own destruction. They did not comply. But they were helpless.

This is not the place to argue the rights and wrongs of Jewish behavior under Hitler. One who was not there will never fully understand the agonizing choices. Jewish civilization, religion, tradition, above all the weakness of the Jews in the face of the greatest army in Europe, made it impossible for the Jews fully to take in what was happening to them. They had simply become objects of obliteration.

What could the Jews do? What many did, in fact, do: in the face of death and on the verge of death, to bear witness, to give renewed meaning to their existence as Jews, to lift the curse from the word "Jew," to take up the word that was supposed to be the badge of their shame, the reason for their extermination, and to show that it was up to *them* to restore the historic meaning and sacredness of their historic continuity as Jews.

The real history of many Jews since 1945 has been to give Jews—not a "reason" for the Holocaust but an explanation in Jewish-historical terms. We who were not there, yet for whom Auschwitz is forever stamped on our minds, whose real life has been to restore the bond of sacredness to a history rooted in the bond of sacredness and meaningless without it—we have a historical experience that we did not live ourselves. It was a passion lived by our brothers and sisters. We live with the imagination of atrocity, with the picture of whole families locked in death, upright in the gas chambers, with the stench of the furnaces, with the bodies crucified on the electrified wire fence. This act of mourning, of memory, of devotion, this attempt to bear witness in the face of an indifferent and even hostile world—this stems not only from grief, but also because remembrance is the core of our religion. Every Jew, says the Passover service, should regard himself as having personally come out of Egypt. Many a Jew who was not in a death camp, many a Jew who, like the marvelous German poet Nelly Sachs, lived out the war in Sweden suffering every intimation of the Holocaust, many a Jew like Elie Wiesel and Pietro Levi, who were under the Nazi ax, recognizes the bond that unites us. We all bear witness to each other now.

At the core of our existence as Jews lies the *fact* of the Holocaust: a whole people, once called "God's people," condemned to death; the indifference to this, by which one really means the inability to take it in; the savage joy of the many who as foolishly believed that here was a "final solution" to the Jewish problem. Year by year these terrible events press themselves more tightly on our minds. The war has never ended. On a beautiful summer's day, the kind of day that Anne Frank described on her way to Belsen, an American couple, on their way to their honeymoon in Switzerland, encounters a Swiss businessman on the train. He boasts that the per capita wealth of the Swiss is greater than the per capita wealth of Americans, and explains, among other financial feats, that the Swiss sold passports at $25,000 each to the Jews fleeing from Europe, then took the passports back at the dock when the refugees had landed at Buenos Aires. A Latvian Nazi commander, accused of ordering executions and of killing many Jews himself, is found living in Queens. I think of the Germans in South America in 1945 who, informed that Germany had lost the war, said with simple sincerity to the French writer Roger Caillois, "At least we have made others suffer."

The war has never ended, nor has the moral nightmare which it set in motion. There are those who still place their faith in the inevitable progress of history. Isaac Deutscher wrote that once the "bloody fog" of the Nazi camps had rolled away, the Marxist revolutionary program would reassert itself as supremely logical and necessary. This specious universalism has always been characteristic of Jewish intellectuals; the Jews themselves were always the last item on their own agenda for the future. But the future, as announced by the "final solution" or even the "final conflict" propounded by Communism, is somehow already behind us. It is more to the point, as Jacob Talmon said, that the twentieth century will decide the fate of the Jews. The century of total revolution, of unlimited expansion into space, of aggressive conflict within and between so many races struggling for a piece of the earth—this century, growing ever more violent, may indeed not consider the ancient hopes and practices of the Jews to be a vital concern; let alone the people to whom God spoke: "the heart of the world," "the light of the world," "the salt of the earth."

But if that is so, then it is a problem for Christians as well as Jews. George Orwell said: "The real problem of our time is to restore the sense of absolute right and wrong when the belief that it used to rest on—that is the belief in personal immortality—has been destroyed. This demands faith, which is a different thing from credulity."

Where is faith? How can we possibly live without it? The secular mind had hope only in the name of progress. Now that too much "progress" seems to stand in the way of our environment, our health, our safety, our very lives, "progress" certainly offers no hope. And without hope, where are we and what are we? Without hope, Jewish history utterly nullifies itself, and the many-thousand-year history of our unworldliness, ended only in our day but certainly not for all Jews, becomes meaningless. Yet in some way our long, strange consistency through the ages argues that there is a greater meaning to our existence as Jews than we know. But as we try to discern its meaning it is hardly to ourselves alone that we look. Where there are no longer any Christians, Jews cannot explain *anything* about themselves.

PART II

*The History of
Christian Theology and
the Demonization of the Jews*

Introduction

The question of anti-Semitism recurred frequently during the Symposium. It is, perhaps, one of the signs of a radical change in our post-Auschwitz world that the Christian participants in the Symposium appeared at least as preoccupied with this subject as the Jewish scholars. For the Holocaust has raised as never before a painful question for Christians: In what manner and degree have Christian teachings about Jews and Judaism contributed to anti-Semitism, thus preparing the soil for the Nazi extermination of the Jews?

The main paper of this section pushes the question beyond Christian teaching to Christian theology and its very center—the Christology of the church. The responses do not so much challenge this thesis as raise further questions including the one whether theology—of whatever sort—can be the foundation for better relations between Jew and Christian.

What are the roots of the anti-Judaic tradition in the West, which goes back to the first century of Christianity? *Rosemary Ruether* believes that we must look for them elsewhere than in sociological conditions, or see them as mere byproducts of a more ancient pagan anti-Judaism. Rather, she locates them at the very heart of Christian theology—in the church's Christology.

This is the thesis which Ruether develops in her paper: anti-Semitism in the West is a direct outgrowth of Christian theological anti-Judaism. (Her full and detailed treatment of the subject can be found in her book *Faith and Fratricide* [Seabury, 1974]—not yet published at the time of the Symposium.)

Ruether sees anti-Judaism as the consequence of the claim that Jesus is the Christ. This claim inevitably pitted the church against the synagogue, since it saw itself as fulfilling and superseding Judaism. It led the church at a very early stage to develop an exegetical tradition that interpreted the Jewish Scriptures in Christological terms, and sought to prove that with the coming of Christ, and the failure of the Jewish people as a whole to recognize him, Judaism lost its status as people of God. Jews now came to be seen as obdurate, stiff-necked, perverse, and the loss of their land and consequent homelessness as divine punishment.

There is growing awareness and acknowledgment of this Teaching of Contempt among Christian theologians today. Ruether goes beyond many others, however, in at least two ways. First, she believes that the Teaching of Contempt was inevitable, given Christianity's claim that Christ is the sole way to salvation and its full manifestation. This is the meaning of her statement that anti-Judaism is "the left hand of Christology." In other words, anti-Judaism is endemic to Christianity, an inevitable consequence of the Christian kerygma. Secondly, she traces in detail how this hostility and teaching, religious in origin, were transformed into civil legislation once the church emerged from the catacombs and became identified with the power of the Roman Empire. Thus the theological *Adversos Judaeos* tradition resulted in the social and political degradation of the Jews, which lasted from the fourth century to the nineteenth, and under Hitler became transformed into genocide. Ruether maintains that to locate anti-Semitism in social conditions or ethnic factors is to bypass, or close one's eyes to, the heart of the matter: that its roots are religious, part and parcel not merely of Christian teaching and preaching, but of Christian dogma itself.

Is there, then, a way out of the impasse for the Christian? Can one hope to be a Christian without being an anti-Semite? Only a new Christology, Ruether believes, will offer such a way out: a Christology which attempts to rethink the ancient Christ-question in terms of a theology of hope. Ruether speaks of a "proleptic Christology," which sees the coming of the Kingdom not as a past and completed event, but as lying still largely ahead of us, "as a horizon of redemption that still eludes us both, Christian and Jew," and hence joins us in a common hope.

Walter Burghardt, a fellow Catholic theologian, has no basic disagreement with the history of anti-Semitism as sketched by Ruether, although he criticizes her presentation in some of its details. Because he agrees with Ruether that the source of Christian anti-Semitism is theological rather than social or political, Burghardt proposes a number of theological affirmations vis-à-vis Judaism which he hopes can serve to build a better future between Jews and Christians. While he considers these affirmations personal, they embody elements that are increasingly current among Catholic theologians since Vatican II: the enduring election and unique mission of the Jewish people, the rejection of any collective guilt of "the Jews" for Jesus' death, the incorporation of the Gentiles into God's covenant with Israel, which now becomes a universal covenant, the reaching of "a certain definitive term in Jesus" of God's promises, though a dimension of unfulfillment persists.

Burghardt does not go into the Christological question in any detail. It is here, however, that Ruether's central thesis raises for him a question: Does traditional Christology inevitably lead to anti-Semitism? His own tentative and brief answer is that it need not do so, and that we must distinguish between the faith in Jesus as the Christ, and the conclusions which some theologians have drawn from this faith.

Like Burghardt, *Yosef Yerushalmi* does not disagree with Ruether's basic thesis that anti-Semitism springs from theological anti-Judaism. He finds himself, however, confronted with questions that arise from what she left unsaid. These can be summed up for him in one central question: If such was Christian teaching, why did the church not destroy the Jews? Granted that we can explain their reprobation, how do we account for their preservation, for the fact that time and again throughout the Middle Ages, when Jew-hatred among the masses was at its height, popes and bishops intervened to protect Jews from popular outbursts of hatred? This, for Yerushalmi, is the unanswered and puzzling question. For it could—and logically should—have been otherwise. The church could have decreed the destruction of the Jews, as Hitler was indeed to do in the twentieth century. This decree, however, was the work of a secular power, and no parallels to it can be found anywhere in history at the level of official Christendom.

The answer to his question is not clear to Yerushalmi. None of the reasons sometimes given—the Jews' economic usefulness, the need for their preservation as a condition for the Second Coming—are really convincing to him. Had there been the determination to make the Jews disappear from history, he believes, a way would have been found—whether through forced conversion (never countenanced officially) or through extermination. He concludes that this determination was lacking in Christianity; but again the reason is not clear to him. He only hazards a guess: that the church could not bring itself to obliterate what remained in its consciousness, even if only subliminally, as the matrix out of which it was born. Was it the same intuition that led to the decision by the early church to retain the Jewish Scriptures in its own canon? Yerushalmi believes that all the damage done by traditional Christian exegesis does not compare to the harm that would have resulted if Marcion had been victorious.

Yerushalmi takes issue with Ruether with respect to her theory that modern anti-Semitism is a "transformation" of medieval anti-Semitism. His argument here is that when we come to the Holocaust we are confronted with the naked fact of genocide—a phenomenon which the church had consistently averted, for whatever reasons. However great the influence on modern anti-Semitism of traditional Christian teaching, the Holocaust was the work of a modern, pagan state. Yerushalmi sees Nazi Germany not as a transformation of earlier discrimination against the Jews, but as "a leap into a different dimension." Genocide became possible precisely when the medieval Christian world-order had ceased to exist. In this context he finds the silence of Pius XI and Pius XII as breaking with, rather than continuing, the tradition of the medieval papacy. Another puzzling—and unanswered—question.

In his concluding remarks Yerushalmi voices further doubts. Will the massive repentance of Christians for the sins of the past really guarantee a better future? He fears that the opposite may happen, and that "a collective mea culpa" may lead to new waves of hatred. He also questions whether we should stake our hope for a better relationship between Jews and Christians on theology. Granted that traditional theology vis-à-vis Judaism leaves much to be desired, what guarantee is there that a new theology, or even a new Christology, will produce better results? The time is urgent, Jews cannot afford to wait until Christians complete a new *Summa Theologica*. Can we not meanwhile build a better future on our common humanity?

Anti-Semitism and Christian Theology

ROSEMARY RADFORD RUETHER

The anti-Semitic legacy of Christian civilization cannot be dealt with as an accidental or peripheral element or as a product of purely socio-logical conflicts between the church and the synagogue. Neither can it be dismissed as a mere continuation of pagan anti-Jewishness or a transfer of ethnocentric attitudes from Judaism itself. Although elements from these two traditions feed into Christian anti-Judaic traditions, neither of these sources provides the main data or formative motivation for Christian anti-Judaism. The frequent efforts of Christian apologists to blame either or both of these sources, therefore, constitute an illicit refusal to examine the strictly Christian theological roots of anti-Semitism in Christianity.[1]

At its root anti-Semitism in Christian civilization springs directly from Christian theological anti-Judaism. It was Christian theology which developed the thesis of the eternal reprobate status of the Jew in history, and laid the foundation for the demonic view of the Jews which fanned the flames of popular hatred. This hatred was not only inculcated by Christian preaching and biblical exegesis, but it became incorporated into the structure of Christian canon law and the civil law formed under Christendom and expressed as early as the Code of Theodosius (438 A.D.) and Justinian (6th cent.). The anti-Judaic laws of the church and the Christian state laid the basis for the inferiorization of the civic and personal status of the Jews in Christian society from the time of Constantine until the emancipation of the Jews in the nineteenth century. In this essay I wish to summarize the central elements of this theological tradition and indicate briefly how it was translated into the social denigration of the Jews in Christendom.[2]

Anti-Judaism developed theologically in Christianity as the left hand of Christology. That is to say, anti-Judaism was the negative side of the Christian claim that Jesus was the Christ. Christianity saw itself

79

as the heir of Jewish Messianic hope, and believed that in Jesus that hope for the coming of the Messiah was fulfilled. But since the Jewish tradition rejected this claim, the church developed a polemic against the Jews and the Jewish religious tradition, to explain how the church could be the fulfillment of a Jewish religious tradition against Jewish rejection of this claim. At the root of this dispute lies a fundamentally different interpretation of the meaning of the word "Messiah" (Christ) in Christianity, which gradually separated it so radically from the meaning of this word in the Old Testament and Jewish tradition that the two traditions became incapable of communicating with each other.

Judaism looked to the coming of the Messiah as a public world-historical event unequivocally linked to a process that historically overthrows the forces of evil in the world and establishes the Kingdom of God. The Messiah is either the agent of this change or is established as the Davidic king after God has accomplished this transformation. Originally Christians also linked Jesus' Messianic role intimately to the final inauguration of the Kingdom of God. But as this event failed to materialize, Christianity pushed it off into an indefinite future. It became the "Second Coming," and Jesus' Messianic role was reinterpreted in an inward and personal way, or institutionalized in relation to the redemptive authority of the church. Such concepts bore little relation to what the Jewish tradition meant by the coming of the Messiah. Thus an impasse developed between Christianity and Judaism over the meaning of the Messianic advent.

The real differences between these two views have practically never been sorted out between Christianity and Judaism because, at the early stage of development, the increasing difference of meaning was accompanied by communal alienation and mutual polemic. Christianity developed an exegetical tradition which attempted to prove that its view of the Messianic coming was, in fact, the one predicted by the "Old Testament." (The very term "Old Testament" is itself a Christian anti-Judaic interpretation of the Jewish Scriptures.) In this same exegesis Christianity sought to prove that the Jews, even in Old Testament times, had ever been apostate from God and their spiritual leaders blind and hard of heart, in order to explain the rejection of the Christological interpretation of the Old Testament by the Jewish community and its teachers. Christian theology, in effect, set out to prove the rejected status of the Jewish community and the spiritual blindness of its traditions of exegesis and morality, in order to vindicate the correctness of its own exegesis and its claim to be the rightful heir of Israel's election.

This Christian polemic against Judaism did not stop merely with proving the special guilt of the religious leaders of the Jewish community for Jesus' death (today recognized as a dubious thesis).[3] Rather it quickly ramified out into arguments intended to prove the inability of the teachers of this community to read Scripture rightly, the discredited status of Jewish religious law, worship, and even its past history to Moses. In the Christian exegesis of the Old Testament, Jewish history becomes split down the middle. The dialectic of judgment and promise is rendered schizophrenic, applied not to one elect people, but to two peoples: the reprobate people, the Jews, and the future elect people of the promise, the church. One tries to show from the Old Testament itself that there always existed, in divine intentionality, two peoples; the true people of faith, who are the rightful heirs of the promise to Abraham, over against a fallen, disobedient people, who never obeyed God or heard the prophets. They, from the beginning, rejected and even killed the prophets and so could be expected to reject and kill the Messiah, the promised redeemer of the prophetic tradition, when He appeared. The rejection and murder of the Messiah is the logical climax of the evil history of the Jewish people. It is the church which is the true heir of the promise to Abraham. The church is the spiritual community of faith, foretold by the prophets, while "the Jews" (i.e., the religious community that still gathers around the temple and the synagogue, accepts the rabbinic leadership, and rejects the Christological exegesis of the church) are the heirs of this evil history of perfidy, apostasy, and murder.

As a result, the Jewish people have been cut off from their divine election. Divine wrath has been poured down on them in the destruction of the Temple and the national capital in Jerusalem. They have been driven into exile and reprobation until the end of time, when Jesus will return and the Jews will finally have to acknowledge their error. As Eusebius puts it:

> You can hear the wailing and lamentations of each of the prophets, wailing and lamenting characteristically over the calamities which will overtake the Jewish people because of their impiety to Him who had been foretold. How their Kingdom . . . would be utterly destroyed after their sin against Christ; how their Father's Law would be abrogated, they themselves deprived of their ancient worship, robbed of the independence of

their forefathers and made slaves of their enemies instead of free men.
How their royal metropolis would be burned with fire, their . . . holy altar undergo flames and extreme desolation, their city inhabited no longer
by its old possessors, but by races of other stock, while they would be dispersed among the Gentiles throughout the whole world with never a hope
of any cessation of evil or breathing space from troubles. [*Dem. Ev.* I,1]

These are the main outlines of the polemic against the Jews, as it developed in the exegetical tradition which underlies the New Testament
and hardened into a fixed form in the *Adversos Judaeos* tradition of the
church fathers.[4] Many of the basic themes of this tradition could be
found already in the New Testament: for example, the idea that the
Jewish people always killed the prophets and so will kill the Messiah
when He comes (Acts 7:51–52; 1 Thess. 2:14–16; Matt. 23:30–36). This
is seen as having been predicted by the prophets. The New Testament
also declares the worship and religious leaders of the Jewish community to be discredited. Their teachers are "blind guides"; their spirituality is hypocrisy and lacks the capacity to save. St. Paul in particular
develops the analogy between the Law and the Powers and Principali-
ties in such a way as to make the Law almost a demonic instrument. It
can only reveal sin, but has no positive relation to redemption (Rom.
7:7–24; Col. 2:8, 20; Gal. 4:3; 2 Cor. 3:7–18). Despite Paul's concept of
the "mystery" of Jewish reprobation, whereby the Jews' hearts are
hardened only until all the Gentiles are gathered in, and they will be
converted before the final coming of Christ, the view of both Paul and
the New Testament as a whole is that the Jews have lost their election.
The covenant with Moses has no power to save. The promise now resides solely in the church, and only by repenting and joining the
church can the Jews be saved (Acts 28:28; Rom. 9–11). The destruction
of Jerusalem is the sign of their present reprobate status (Matt.
23:36–24:2).

These themes, however, are greatly elaborated in the writings of the
church fathers in the period between the second and fifth centuries in a
way that hardened the lines between the two communities. The themes
of the patristic *Adversus Judaeos* tradition center around two major
theses: (1) the rejection of the Jews and the election of the Gentile
church, and (2) the abrogation of the Law.[5] As in the New Testament,
the Jewish rejection of the Messiah is read back into the Old Testament
as a heritage of evildoing that culminated in this final act of apostasy.
The Jews are said to have always rejected the prophets, refused to hear
their message of repentance, and even to have killed them. Moreover,

the Jews are condemned as inveterate idol worshippers. Beginning with the golden calf, the Jews ever turned away from God and worshipped idols. God sent the prophets to turn them from this idol worship, but to no avail. This view is derived from reading the prophets out of context, negating the fact that the very existence of the prophetic books in the Scriptures signified the acceptance of the prophetic message by the Jewish religious tradition. Even worse crimes are alleged, again using prophetic and psalmic texts out of context. The Jews are said to have been cannibals and to have sacrificed their children to idols. All manner of debauchery, lewdness, and immorality are also added to the list of crimes said to characterize the "Jews" (a favorite source for this is Ps. 106:34–40).

By the time we reach late-fourth-century Christian preachers, such as John Chrysostom, this picture of the Jews in Christian writing has taken on demonic proportions. The Jews are painted as preternatural demonic figures with a superhuman appetite for every depravity of flesh and spirit. The Mosaic Law is said to have been given the Jews, not as a mark of election and divine favor, but rather to curb their incorrigible appetite for idolatry and vice. As the fourth-century church historian Eusebius puts it: "Everything which the Law forbids, they had previously done without restraint" (*Dem. Ev.* 1) Some of the church fathers postulate a pre-Mosaic period before the Law, when patriarchal humanity obeyed God from the heart, guided only by the natural law implanted inwardly in the conscience. Christianity restores this patriarchal era of spiritual obedience. Mosaic religion is, therefore, painted as a fall. The giving of the Law comes to represent, not a special grace to the Jews, but a punitive restraint on the special viciousness of the Jews. This viciousness is attributed to bad habits learned in Egypt, when they sojourned among people noted for their proclivity for idolatry and unnatural vice.

The hermeneutical method for demonstrating this tale of evil Jewish history consists of splitting the right from the left hand of the prophetic message. All the negative descriptions, judgments, and threats are taken out of context and read monolithically as descriptive of "the Jews." The positive side of the prophetic message—the traits of repentance, faith, and promise—are applied to the future church. The heroes of the Old Testament become the forerunners of the church, while "the Jews" are regarded as a people "on probation," who have failed the test and are finally cast off by God. By splitting the left hand of prophetic judgment from the right hand of prophetic promise, applying one side to the Jews and the other to the church, one gains an unrelieved tale of apostasy supposedly characteristic of the Old Testament community, while depriving the church of the tradition of prophetic self-criticism. Anti-Judaism and ecclesial triumphalism arise as two sides of the same antithesis.

The climactic crime of this evil history is the killing of the Messiah. It was to give this "crime" a legacy and tradition that Christian apologetics read Jewish history in this manner. As Christology is heightened to the full doctrine of Christian faith, this comes to be seen not only as the killing of a prophet. It becomes the killing of God, the crime of "deicide"; a crime of treason and *lese majeste* against the Sovereign of the Universe Himself. For criminals of such a stamp, no vituperation can be too extreme. In the sermons of John Chrysostom the Jews are continuously spoken of as devils, their synagogues as brothels of the devil, and their very souls are declared to be dwelling places of demons.

For this final crime the election of the Jews has been revoked, and they have been exiled until the end of time. Their city has been destroyed; their Temple ravished, never to be rebuilt. All their former favor with God has been taken from them. They have been driven into captivity among their enemies, never to know any cessation of misery until the end of time. The fathers are fond of using the phrase "their back bend thou down always" (Ps. 69:24, mistranslated in the Septuagint), to represent this historical status of the Jews since the time of Jesus. The former captivities of the Jews are said to have had fixed limits. The restoration of the Jews from exile promised in the Scripture has already been fulfilled in these former restorations. But this final exile is to have no fixed limits and is intended by God to last until the end of time.

Christian theology took a dogmatic stance which denied the possibility that the Jewish people would ever be restored to their national homeland (a tradition not without significance for present Jewish-Christian misunderstandings over the State of Israel). According to the patristic tradition, the Jews are to remain in this status of exile and reprobation until Jesus returns in glory, when the Jews will get a final chance to acknowledge their mistake. Consequently, pressure on the Jewish community to convert to Christianity also took on an eschatological significance, since the mass conversion of the Jews was supposed to signal the imminent advent of Christ. Even circumcision is said to have been given to the Jews, not as a sign of election, but as a witness to their reprobation. By it they can be recognized as Jews and prevented from reentering Jerusalem, from which they were barred following the Bar Kochba revolt (A.D. 132–35). Circumcision thus comes to be interpreted by Christian theologians as a "mark of Cain," by which the Jews are to be preserved to the end of time as a wandering, reprobate people. The political overtones of this view are evident in the following passage from the fourth-century poet Prudentius:

> From place to place the homeless Jew wanders in ever shifting exile, since the time when he was torn from the abode of his fathers and has been suffering the penalty for murder and having stained his hands with the blood of Christ whom he denied, paying the price of sin. . . . This noble race [is] . . . scattered and enslaved. . . . It is in captivity under the younger faith. . . . a race that was formerly unfaithful confesses Christ [the gentiles] and triumphs. But that which denied Christ is conquered and subdued and has fallen into the hands of Masters who keep the faith. [*Apotheosis*, 541–50]

This anti-Judaic tradition grew into a fixed standpoint between the second and fourth centuries. It was repeated over and over again in every Christian sermon, biblical commentary, or theological treatise that touched on the Jews. Since the church claimed the Jewish Scriptures as its own foundation and understood itself as heir to the election of Israel, it was difficult to preach or teach without touching on the Jews in some way.

In the fourth century the church was transformed from a persecuted sect to the established religion of the empire. By A.D. 380 Orthodox Christianity had become the exclusive faith for all citizens of the Christian Roman *oecumene*. The faith and practice of pagans and heretics were proscribed by law. Their temples and churches were destroyed or confiscated. Toward the Jews, however, the attitude was more complicated. The Jews had gained the status of a protected national group under pagan Roman law. They were Roman citizens, and their right to worship and govern their own community internally by their own national laws and customs was guaranteed, even though some special disabilities were heaped upon them following the Jewish wars (such as a special tax, exclusion from Jerusalem, and laws against circumcising non-Jews). Moreover, although Christian theology decreed misery for the Jews, it did not decree extermination. In fact it demanded their ongoing existence, although in a status of reprobation, as the continuing witness to the triumph of the church and as the final witness to Christ at the end of time. The paradox of the church's attitude to the Jews was that it was simultaneously committed to their preservation, and to making them exhibit externally the marks of their reprobation. It was out of this contradiction that the tragic history of the Jews in Christian society was to flow.

By the fourth century the Christian view of the Jews began to be enacted into law by the Christian Roman emperors. The basic principle of this legislation was that the Jews should be allowed only the bare minimum of continued rights to worship and exist, but should have no honor in Christian society and should be deprived of any possibility of holding authority over Christians. The Jews were forbidden from circumcising, and later from owning, slaves (this was not part of any general denunciation of slavery, for Christians were not forbidden to own slaves). Since Jewish families incorporated their servants into the religious aspects of their households, this was intended to remove a potent source of proselytes to Judaism. The church itself had risen to some extent from the slave class. Severe laws were passed forbidding Jews from converting Christians to Judaism.

Jews also could not interfere in any way with the church's conversion of Jews to Christianity. Although Jews were allowed to worship, they were prohibited to build new synagogues or to repair old ones. By the fifth century the public recognition of the Jewish patriarch and his emissaries was withdrawn by the imperial government, a severe blow to the ability of Judaism to communicate decisions throughout the Diaspora. Jews were prohibited from holding civil or military office and barred from the *cursus honorum* of the state. They could not be judges or lawyers. The very idea that a Jew might hold authority over a Christian is termed in one law in the Theodosian Canon "an insult to our faith." The laws of this canon bristle with theologically loaded epithets which condemn the Jews as a vicious people. The synagogue is even referred to in one law as a "brothel" (*C.Th.* 16/8/1). Since agriculture and industry were carried out with slave labor, exclusion from slave-holding (and later, serfs) eliminated Jews from agriculture and large-scale industry.[6]

In addition to these civil laws, the church added laws condemning intermarriage or religious fraternizing of any kind between Jews and Christians. Marriage with Jews was classed as adultery. Christians were even forbidden to perform such services as lighting lamps for Jews in synagogues on the Sabbath. The church also accepted the civil anti-Judaic laws into its ecclesiastical codes, and so became the chief vehicle for passing these anti-Semitic laws down to the law codes of the new Germanic states and reviving them again in medieval law. The fourth Lateran Council of 1215, in particular, saw the church adding to these the medieval elaboration into codes of separate dress and segregated residence designed to create a visibly humiliating status for the Jew in Christian society.

By the late fourth century this official persecution of the Jews was supplemented by outbreaks of popular violence in the form of synagogue burnings, expulsions, and forced baptisms. The emperors tried to hold the line against these popular excesses, usually led by fanatical monks. But the bishops of the church often justified this violence and rebuked the emperor when he sought reparations for the Jewish community from the church. The most famous example of this was the confrontation between Ambrose of Milan and the Emperor Theodosius. The bishop threatened the emperor with excommunication unless he rescinded his decree of reparations to a Jewish community in Asia, whose synagogue had been burned by a fanatical Christian mob at the instigation of their bishop (see Ambrose, *Epistles* 40–41). Thus, through a combination of official inferiorization from the church and the Christian state and the hatred whipped up by popular preachers, who found the Jewish community an easy target for grievances which had their roots in the general economic breakdown of the empire, a status of apartheid was gradually shaped around the traditional ethnicity of the Jewish community, until such practices as the Jewish badge and the ghetto walls became institutions in the late Middle Ages. This status of the Jew as a person without honor or civil rights in Christian society was to last until modern times, and was swept away in Eastern Europe only by the Holocaust itself. All remnants of this tradition have by no means vanished in the Marxist states of Russia and Eastern Europe today.

The translation of theological vituperation into popular hatred was by no means automatic, however. Although popular pogroms took place in Syria and Alexandria in the fourth and fifth centuries, where old communal tensions between Jewish and native populations could be fanned into flames by the new theological teachings, other Christians continued to fraternize with the Jewish community and to regard Jewish observances as their own. Large groups of Judaizers in Antioch in the late fourth century continued to frequent the synagogue, especially on the High Holidays. This fact provided the occasion for John Chrysostom's eight vitriolic sermons against the Jews in the fall and spring of A.D. 386–87. In Byzantine society Jews were strictly reduced to a low social and economic status, and official clerical vituperation alternated with imperial decrees of forced conversion. But the tradition of intense popular anti-Semitism among the masses never developed. This seems to have been due to the fact that theological and legal anti-

Semitism were not translated into economic anti-Semitism in a society where the money economy and the apparatus of law and order remained intact.[7]

In the West, on the other hand, the city, the political structure of law, and the money economy failed. The fact that the Jews were the one group that could maintain trade contacts between the Christian West and the trade routes, in the hands of the Muslim East since the seventh century, meant that the Jews became the catalysts of Western economic revival. Jews also played a key role in the redevelopment of the money economy. But these roles, when combined with the church's view of the Jews as a reprobate, carnal people, and its attempt to confine them to a separate status without honor in Christian society, resulted in the structuring of the Jewish community into a peculiar economic role. The Jews were forbidden the normal range of economic activities. they could be neither farmers nor industrialists, since they were excluded from the guilds. Their role as merchants was largely expropriated by the Christians at the time of the Crusades. The Jews, officially defined as royal serfs, became the moneylenders for the Christian princes. This placed them in the position of living by their wits as economic innovators, while functioning simultaneously as the economic agents and the economic scapegoats for the European ruling class. Their financial success was transferred to the coffers of the princes, while the economic grievances generated by the princes' policies gave rise to a popular hatred that was focused on the Jews. It was this combination of theological demonization, legal-social inferiorization, and economic scapegoating that created the worsening image of the Jews in the later Middle Ages.[8]

At the time of the Crusades popular mass looting and massacres by crusading mobs broke out against the Jewish communities. These events taught the people that the Jewish community, although officially protected by the princes, was actually an easy mark for any mob. Once this lesson had been learned, popular violence against the Jews as a displacement of social crises never ceased. New myths, such as the story that the Jews killed Christian boys and drank their blood on Passover, violated Christain sacraments, and poisoned wells, were created to excuse these outbreaks and to foment new ones. By the late Middle Ages the Jew had been transformed into a full-blown devil in Christian popular mythology, complete with horns, a tail, and a peculiar stench.[9] But the actual Jewish communities had been economically broken, expelled from Western Europe and crowded into ghettos in Poland and

Eastern Europe, where the tradition of pogroms and expulsions was to continue down to the twentieth century.

Modern anti-Semitism is both a continuation and a transformation of the medieval theological and economic scapegoating of the Jews. But while the medieval tradition took its religious rationale from the Jewish refusal to accept Jesus as the Christ and enter the church, modern anti-Semitism builds on the medieval image of the Jew as a dangerous disease and demonic power precisely to resist both secularized and Christianized Jewish assimilation, and to blame the Jews for the secular trends that made such assimilation possible. The dress rehearsal for the modern anti-Semitism that arose in Europe in the latter half of the nineteenth century took place in fifteenth-century Spain. Spain, from the seventh to the eleventh century, had seen a unique society where Jew, Christian, and Muslim lived side by side in a country divided between the Catholic north and the Muslim south. With the final expulsion of the Muslims in the thirteenth century, the new Spanish monarchy could turn the zeal of holy war upon the Jews. Commanded to either convert or get out, large numbers of these assimilated Jews chose to convert, unlike their persecuted brethren in the German cities at the time of the Crusades, who had preferred martyrdom to baptism.

Spanish society woke up from this orgy with a startling new discovery. With their conversion, all the discriminatory laws against Jews had been automatically abrogated. Nothing now prevented Jews from advancing into the highest leadership positions of Spanish society, and many began to do so. Baptism proved insufficient to remove the image of negativity which had been stamped in the minds of Christians by a millennium and more of Christian anti-Jewish preaching. Within a generation new laws began to be enacted against these new Christians, excluding them from holding offices in Spanish society, but now on a purely racial basis. Like the laws of Nazi Germany, which copied those of Spain, the Spaniard must have his genealogy searched by the Inquisition to ascertain whether he had any Jewish ancestry.[10] These laws of "pure blood," which discriminated against Spaniards of Jewish descent who were all nominally Christians, and many of whom regarded themselves as the best of Catholics, remained on the books of such groups as the Jesuit Order until the Second Vatican Council.

Classical anti-Semitic politics, as it operated in Europe, played on the middle-man role of the Jews. To the right-wing clerical and feudal classes the Jew was the outsider, the impious threat to the Christian order and, later, the symbol and chief beneficiary of the forces of the new secular, industrial, and democratic society that was dissolving the power of the old ruling classes of Christendom. To the impoverished masses, on the other hand, the small Jewish pawnbroker, merchant, peddler, and tax collector represented the visible target for their rage against the invisible forces of economic exploitation that held them in a state of chronic poverty. The established classes encouraged this displacing of mob wrath onto the Jews and even allied with it, as a safe escape-valve for the real grievances of society, which they themselves were unwilling to remedy. It was this combination of right-wing reactionary, and left-wing popular anti-Semitism which made possible the rise of Nazism in Germany after the humiliation of the First World War.[11] A not dissimilar sort of anti-Semitic politics could develop in the contemporary United States, as the impoverished Black underclass in the ghettos vents its rage on the Jewish merchants, landlords, teachers, and social workers of the formerly Jewish neighborhoods into which the Southern-migrant Blacks have now moved. As Black militants are encouraged to vent Black rage on their former Jewish allies, the actual power slips to the right into the hands of reactionary WASP's.[12]

However, modern anti-Semitism does more than trade on a traditional diabolic image of the Jews, created by Christianity, to displace modern social tensions. It also takes its chief mythology directly from the Christian legacy. The myth of the Jewish world conspiracy had its earlier version in the Catholic myth of a Freemason conspiracy to explain the French Revolution, and the Protestant myth of a Jesuit conspiracy. But the Jews proved the ultimate carriers of the myth. The full-blown world-conspiracy myth, as fabricated by the Russian secret police in the era of late Czarist pogroms in the 1890s, drew on the ancient Christian idea that the Messiah whom the Jews expected was really the devil, and that a final age of the reign of the anti-Christ over the world signals the last breakdown of world history prior to the return of Christ. The fabricated *Protocols of the Elders of Zion* purports to be the minutes of meetings of a secret Jewish world government, in existence since the time of Christ, which plots to bring about this final reign of the anti-Christ in which the Jews, the agents of the devil, will rule the world. This myth, brought to Western Europe and America by Eastern Europeans fleeing the Communist victory after World War I, became a firmly established tool of Christian reactionaries in Europe and the United States.[13] Many people still remember the fulminations of the radio priest, Father Coughlin, in the thirties, against this mythical Jewish conspiracy. Despite the fact that the *Protocols* have been exposed many times as a fraud, their political power is by no means dead. In the form of the Communist world conspiracy they have shaped cold war American foreign policy. The racist Right can still use this document to lay the blame for racial unrest in this country at the door of the mythical Jewish-Communist conspiracy, of which Blacks are the willing minions. But the Left derives a similar myth of Jewish world conspiracy from the wide publication of this document by the Arab anti-Zionist press, and Black militants take up the cry to paint Jews as the archetypal capitalist exploiters of the world. Again, the classical attraction of anti-Semitic politics is this double bind, which allows a frustrated, impoverished class to vent its rage on the Jewish middleman, while the right wing simultaneously paints a picture of the Jews as the fomenters of left-wing plots against the established social order. When the pogrom is over, the Jewish merchant is dead and his store burned, but the real economic powers of society are more firmly entrenched than ever.

The politics of paranoia and displacement of judgment must be laid at the door, ultimately, of a psychology created by Christian theology itself. The Christian theological teaching that the Jew is reprobate in history until the end of time translated itself into a practice of social denigration, to demonstrate this state of divine reprobation through the outward evidence of dishonor and misery. This legal tradition of social inferiorization of the Jews, in turn, interacted with sociological and economic changes, until it became translated into what we must now recognize as a state of mass paranoia toward the Jewish community endemic to Christian popular culture. If the misery of the Jews is necessary to prove their reprobate status and the triumph of the church, then it tends to follow that any prospering of the Jews in Christian society, any power or success they gain among Christians, will be regarded as an affront to Christian society and an implicit challenge to the superiority of the Christian faith. It was this mass paranoia that flourished in the pogroms which began with the Crusades and lasted through the age of the ghetto into the twentieth century. In secular form, this politics of paranoia and displacement of judgment from one's own internal flaws upon some outside "insidious" enemy, typified by the Jews, has proven a potent instrument in modern social crises as well, ever revivable in new guises. The Jew, caught between the Christian ruling class and the impoverished masses, shuttling between the conservative politics of survival and the liberal politics of sympathy with the oppressed, becomes again and again the sacrificial victim for conflicts which he did not create and only marginally represents.

To bring this tragic history to an end will demand something like a massive repentant acceptance of responsibility by the Christian church, and a dramatic shift in the spirituality which it teaches. The Jewish community has traditionally taken evils that have befallen it upon its own shoulders. The Christian church, imbued with a self-image of infallible righteousness resulting from its doctrine of Messianic fulfillment, has typically displaced evil upon outside enemies, the unredeemed world and the godless forces without its walls, rather than take responsibility for its own sins. Displacement of unfulfillment upon the Jews has been the special archetype of this refusal to internalize self-judgment for its own sins. A repentant church was demanded already by the Protestant Reformation; but only with the Second Vatican Council has Catholicism begun to fashion a theology that incorporates self-judgment and breaks with the tradition of ecclesiastical triumphalism.

Ultimately such a shift in spirituality demands a reexamination of Christology, for this is the original root of theological anti-Judaism. A repentant Christianity is a Christianity which has turned from the theology of Messianic triumphalism to the theology of hope. This is possible only if we recognize that Messianic hope is not primarily behind us, as a fait accompli, but is ahead of us, as a horizon of redemption that still eludes us both, Christian and Jew. Christians, like Jews, must take responsibility for their sins in the still sinful world of which we too are a part. Both of us go forward, each on the basis of our different traditions and foretastes of salvation, to a future hope of redemption that transcends us both.

Response to Rosemary Reuther

WALTER BURGHARDT, s. j.

Professor Reuther's paper is at once profoundly discouraging and somewhat encouraging. It is discouraging because the history of Christian attitudes and actions is so cruel, so constant, so unchristian. It is encouraging, paradoxically, because the ultimate underlying motivation is not social or political or economic or personal; it is theological.

My brief critique comprises three elements: (1) some gentle discontent; (2) a pungent question; (3) a tentative theology.

First, a certain discontent. I am unhappy with some generalizations, e.g., "it was difficult to preach or teach without touching on the Jews in some way." I have read hundreds of patristic homilies that simply do not touch on the Jews. I am dissatisfied with unlimited affirmations where limitation of time and person and place is demanded, e.g., "Marriage with Jews was classified as adultery." I am distressed when isolated, uncommon Christian bigotry ("The Jews are said to have been cannibals") is given the same importance as more representative anti-Semitism. I regret the unrelieved blackness, a failure to balance the picture with the grays and whites of Christian-Jewish relations. I do not care for facile summaries of complex problems, e.g., Ambrose and the synagogue. I find puzzling a use of source material that does not distinguish literary genres, does not evaluate the comparative significance of the poet Prudentius, the preacher Chrysostom, the historian Eusebius. I look in vain for a distinction between "Christian theology" and Christian theologians, between theology and official church doctrine. And since Rosemary Reuther does project beyond the patristic period, I wonder why she makes no mention of contemporary Christian theology on the Jewish issue. Finally, I must challenge the bald affirmation that "the Christian church" does not "take responsibility for its own sins."

Second, a question. It is delicate, neuralgic, potentially irritating, but it must be put, because it is central to our concerns. Rosemary Reuther has called for "a reexamination of Christology, for this is the original root of theological anti-Judaism." I must ask her (as I must ask myself): Is traditional Christology inevitably a prelude to anti-Judaism, if not anti-Semitism? I do not believe it is; but perhaps I misunderstand what precise aspects of Christology are at issue here and call for reexamination. Is it the conviction that Jesus Christ is Messiah, God-man, Savior, Lord? Or is it the conclusions which some theologians, e.g., fathers of the church, have drawn from the basic conviction (e.g., that the Jews have been "rejected" by God)?

Third, a fresh "theology of the Jews," if only to indicate that the past is not necessarily programmatic for the future. It is indeed *my* theology—therefore in some sense personal; but it is more than individualistic, because it combines several traditional affirmations with a number of propositions that suggest the direction in which many Catholic theologians are heading. Here I can do little more than sketch the theology in a set of affirmations.

1. The Jews were chosen by God as His special people, His people of election. A covenant was made with Israel, with the Jewish people—a covenant guaranteeing that through this select segment of humanity would come to man, to the world, a unique message, a unique Scripture, a unique Messiah, a unique redemption.

2. Israel did not cease to be God's people after the death of Jesus. Israel is still God's first-born son, has God's presence, retains the covenant, a true worship of the priestly nation, the promises of God's grace and salvation; to Israel belong its ancestors in the true faith and the Christ.

3. As a Christian, with my own vision of God's promises, I must affirm that if it is true that Israel remains God's people, it is equally true that the Gentiles have been incorporated into God's people. From a rejected people, the Gentiles have been made into a chosen people. Not by any righteousness of ours; solely by God's free election. Israel has not been rejected; the covenant has become universal.

4. As a Christian, with my own vision of God's promises, I must affirm that God's promises reached a certain definitive term in Jesus. Here, of course, is the stumbling block, the scandal, the dividing line: on the one hand, the affirmation that Jesus is the eschatological event foretold by the prophets, that in him redemption has come, though it has not yet been definitively accomplished; on the other, the conviction that as yet there is no kingdom, no peace, no redemption.

5. "The Jews"—then, now, or at any time—cannot be called guilty of Jesus' death. There is no such thing as a collective responsibility of the Jews, then or now, in the crucifixion of Christ. Such responsibility is historically and theologically untenable. (Even the individual participation of Jews in Jesus' death is historically difficult, if not impossi-

ble, to reconstruct.) Such collective responsibility has been officially denied by the Second Vatican Council—not because the Jews needed somehow to be absolved of guilt, but because Catholics in untold measure needed to be told what genuine Catholic doctrine is and demands.

6. At various stages of its history the church has been responsible for injustice to the Jew that cries to heaven, perhaps not for vengeance, but surely for mercy. Not a collective responsibility; but the church has been responsible in the sense that so many Christians, high and low, have been responsible; because so many Christians in their attitude to the Jews are what St. Paul said of the godless: they are "ruthless, faithless, pitiless" (Rom. 1:31).

7. Israel has a God-given role to play in human history. Not simply the Jew who was, but the Jew who is and the Jew who will be. I do not think we are yet in a position to define that mission, especially in relation to Christianity. But it is possible even now to see *a* mission of the Jews on two levels: faith and life—age-old affirmation and centuries-old suffering—a unique witness to fidelity and love, to God and man, through all Israel's infidelities, through all her crucifixions.[1]

8. God continues to reveal Himself to and through the Jews, the here-and-now, twentieth-century Jews. Revelation has not been simply sealed and delivered. God is still revealing Himself. And in unique fashion He discloses Himself through a people that by all odds, by every human calculation, should have perished, a people that without arms, without violence, has survived every persecution and borne ceaseless witness to the Suffering Servant of Yahweh. God is here. He *is* here, and He *speaks* to and through the Jew, His Suffering Servant.

Response to Rosemary Ruether

YOSEF HAYIM YERUSHALMI

Professor Ruether's basic thesis that "at its root anti-Semitism in Christian civilization springs directly from Christian theological anti-Judaism" seems to me, in itself, unimpeachable. Insofar as the rest of her paper elaborates this point, it impresses me as a forceful statement informed by considerable moral passion. I could quibble with her about a few historical details, but within the framework of this conference it would be pedantic and irrelevant to do so. There are larger issues to be explored.

This is no ordinary scholarly symposium. It is a very contemporary discussion between Christians and Jews in the shadow of the murder of a third of the Jewish people a generation ago. Its title—"Auschwitz: Beginning of a New Era"—is ambiguous, even presumptuous, and some of its possible connotations trouble me.* Be that as it may, neither the conference nor the title have any raison d'etre unless they point forward. In the case of Rosemary Ruether's paper and, I assume, also in others to be presented, the historical record is invoked not merely as a post-mortem, but to help us all cope with the present and direct ourselves toward a future.

My reaction to Rosemary Ruether's historical summary has more to do with what she has left unsaid than with what she has actually narrated, though the one ultimately affects the other. It would be unfair, of course, to present this as a stricture. Her task has been to talk in brief compass about the impact of Christian theology upon the development of anti-Semitism, and she has done so with eloquence. There are, however, vital reasons for me to stress what she has left out.

Before I go on to explain what I mean, I must make one thing perfectly clear. I am obviously not a Christian apologist of the sort mentioned by Rosemary Ruether in her first paragraph, nor can I possibly be cast in any such role. I am, in fact, a Jewish historian. As it happens, my own work has been done largely out of the archives of the Inquisi-

---

*Editor's note: The question mark at the end of the title was inadvertently omitted from the material publicizing the Symposium.

tion in Spain, Portugal, and Italy. Concerning the reality and influence of Christian theological anti-Semitism through the ages I not only have no doubt; I could easily supplement Ruether's data at every stage with equally strong and more vivid materials. Nor is it for me, a Jew, to defend the church against Rosemary Ruether, a Christian, a notion as whimsical as it is absurd. Indeed, I am not at all concerned with the church per se, but only as it affects the fortunes of the Jewish people. And it is precisely for this reason that I find myself with a set of problems and emphases different from those of Rosemary Ruether.

Paradoxes

Throughout her summary of Christian theological anti-Semitism I could not help but ask: If such was the teaching, why did they not destroy the Jews?

Ruether touches briefly upon the issue when she states: "However, although Christian theology decreed misery for the Jews, it did not decree extermination." She then goes on to say: "The paradox of the church's attitude to the Jews was that it was simultaneously committed to their preservation and to making them exhibit externally the marks of their reprobation." The next sentence is, however, at least a partial non sequitur: "It was out of this contradiction that the tragic history of the Jews in Christian society was to flow." Surely Rosemary Ruether would agree that the tragedy flowed from only one side of the paradox; and that brings us to the heart of the matter.

The entire paper dwells exclusively on "reprobation." Of "preservation," except for this fleeting reference, we hear next to nothing. Yet both were present, and one can hardly understand the survival of the Jews in the midst of Christendom without taking both elements into serious account. That Christian theology "did not decree extermination" is, after all, not to be glossed over so lightly in a conference devoted to the Holocaust. In our time such restraint cannot be taken for granted. Nor, for that matter, was it self-evident in the past.

Speaking of the establishment of Christianity as the state religion of the Roman Empire, Ruether notes that "the faith and practice of pagans and heretics were proscribed by law. Their temples and churches were destroyed or confiscated." Yet whatever Judaism suffered, it did not suffer the same fate. Judaism, for Jews, continued to be a *religio licita*. Though technically no new synagogues were to be built (a rule obviously observed in the breach), existing synagogues were certainly protected by law. If, on occasion, that law was violated, such cases represent departures from the norm. That Jews are to be tolerated in the midst of Christendom, that they have the right to regulate their internal affairs according to their law, that they are entitled to a basic protection of life, property, and the free exercise of their religion so long as it does not directly interfere with the dominant faith—these principles remained constant in Christian law down through the Middle Ages. Had it not been so, I would not be here today.

It could easily have been otherwise. The church could have dealt with the Jews as it did with the Samaritans and declared Judaism a heresy. The penalty for heresy was death.

No, what happened is not obvious, at least not to me, and the problem as I see it is the reverse of that which preoccupies Rosemary Ruether. Perhaps I take a dimmer view of human nature, and so, for example, I am more baffled by the Danish rescue of Jews during the Holocaust than I am by the collaboration of other subject peoples in destroying them. Perhaps, also, I have a lower threshold of expectation from the past. I do not have any great difficulty in understanding the Christian animus against Judaism (to understand is not to condone). That is to say, I am not really surprised that the need of nascent Christianity to establish its legitimacy bred a violent hatred for those whose birthright it usurped. The problem is not why the Jews were derogated, but rather—why were they not wiped out?

Similarly when we come to the inferior status of the Jews under Christendom, which Rosemary Ruether has so ably documented. What are our expectations? In ages when religious truth was considered absolute and its possession exclusive, is it to be anticipated that *no* visible distinctions would be sought between believer and infidel? Islam, whose case against Judaism did not even rest upon an accusation of deicide, did the same, and indeed such symbols of reprobation as the Jewish badge had their origin there. But again, this is not where the real problem lies. Granted the hostility, and given the desire to objectify the theological inferiority of Judaism in the socioeconomic sphere, why did Christian theology not call at least for the actual enslavement of the Jews? In Visigothic Spain the attempt was actually made, but once again, this is an exceptional case which sets the norm into relief. Reprobate as they may have been, the Jews were not enslaved under Christendom. Contrary to the depiction by Rosemary Ruether of the "status of the Jew as a person without honor or civil rights," the Jews were never rightless in Christian society. Indeed, medieval Jewry has an entire gamut of well-defined rights which, on the whole, made the socioeconomic status of the Jews superior to that of the Christian peasantry who often constituted the bulk of the population.

The same problematics reveal themselves also with regard to conversion. Why did the church not decree the forced conversion of the Jews? The forced baptisms which did occur in the Middle Ages should not obscure the fact that conversion by force, however tempting, did not represent official church policy. To be sure, the papacy in the thirteenth century did narrow the definition of what constitutes "force," and once baptized the Jew was barred from reverting to his former faith. The often tragic consequences of such equivocations for Jewish history are manifest. But how much greater would the tragedy have been if the church had not followed the basic policy of Gregory the Great in disavowing force as a legitimate means for the conversion of Jews. That the church chose to take its stand on an *eschatological* rather than immediate conversion of the Jews was yet another factor of inestimable importance for the survival of Jewry, and, like the others, it is obvious only in retrospect. At the outset, it could well have been otherwise.

The explanations advanced for these phenomena are important, I think, yet inadequate. Historically, there was some momentum deriving from the tolerated status of the Jews in pagan Roman law. In the economic sphere, the Jews often proved themselves useful. Theologically, various reasons could be found, and were indeed proposed, for the preservation of the Jews. And yet somehow it all strikes one as insufficient. The theological arguments, especially, seem more like post-factum rationalizations than initial motives. Yes, the Jews preserve the Scriptures, and Christ himself asked mercy for them, and they testify by their degraded presence to the triumph of Christianity, and the prophecies forecast their ultimate conversion, so that they must be preserved until the Second Coming. It is all very neat, but is it really convincing? Had there been a real will to make Judaism disappear from history, whether by universal genocide or forced conversion, would these arguments have sufficed to prevent it, or would not some other theological rationale have arisen to condone it? As an example of what could be argued even within the accepted framework, consider Duns Scotus' strong advocacy of forced conversion. Anticipating the objection that the Jews must be preserved until the Second Coming so that the prophecies may be fulfilled, he observes that for this purpose it would suffice merely to leave a small band of Jews on some island until that time should come. Fortunately, however, this medieval "Madagascar Plan" remained a minority view.

In short, there must have been deeper, inner reasons for the preservation of the Jews than those thrown up on the surface. As to what these may have been I have no ready answer, and as a Jew I can only speculate. If the church did not decree the physical or spiritual extinction of Jewry, it must have been either because it could not bring itself to do so, or because it was vital to it not to do so. Perhaps it was both. Somehow, though there is no way of proving it, I think that the awareness of its Jewish matrix was, even if subliminal, sufficiently strong to inhibit the church from obliterating it. It is here that the real paradox resides and, upon examination, it turns out to be no paradox at all. The peculiar ferocity of the abuse of children for a mother is common enough; actual matricide is another matter. Be that as it may, I feel on firmer ground with regard to the "vital interest of the church." The decision to preserve the Jews has always appeared to me linked to an even more primal decision made in the early centuries, one which involved an intense inner struggle whose outcome was long in doubt. It was the decision to retain the Jewish Scriptures in the Christian canon, and to posit a direct continuity between the two. However adversely the exegesis which this decision entailed may have affected the image of the Jews, it is as nothing compared to what might have followed otherwise. One shudders to contemplate what might have been the fate of the Jews had Marcion been victorious.

Variables

I should like now to approach some other aspects of the paper.

The church, as Rosemary Ruether knows better than I, has never been a monolith. And yet, in relation to the Jews, she discusses the church in a curiously monolithic way. As a matter of fact, medieval Jews themselves knew very well how to distinguish among the constellation of forces surrounding them. In his analysis of Jewish historical catastrophe entitled *Shebet Yehudah*, the Spanish exile Solomon Ibn Verga observes that in the church it is generally the lower clergy who are the true enemies of the Jews, while the episcopate and the papacy are their protectors. Now while there is an obvious oversimplification here, there is also a core of truth which corresponds to the realities of medieval Jewish life. For all its pejorative references to Jews, the *Constitutio pro Judaeis* was a basic formulation of papal policy committed to the protection of Jewish life and property. In times of crisis the pope could be appealed to for a bull condemning the excesses. The blood libel was never condoned by the popes; on the contrary, it was condemned in many official pronouncements. To be sure, the very popes who periodically renewed the *Constitutio pro Judaeis* were not necessarily pro-Jewish. They could also call for the strict enforcement of the harshest canonical regulations concerning the Jews. Nor were papal condemnations of physical violence against Jews always prompt or effective. But that is not the point. One has only to consider the alternative. In what might otherwise have been for the Jews an anarchic jungle, the king, on the one hand, and the pope, on the other, were at least committed to the rule of law, and were thus pillars of whatever stability the Jews enjoyed.

As the church is not a monolith, so are people not theological automatons. All the bishops of the Rhineland during the First Crusade had studied the same theology, yet it was John of Speyer alone who made a genuine effort to protect his Jews. Bernard of Clairvaux was a theological anti-Semite, yet he issued a ringing and influential call against the massacre of Jews during the Second Crusade. Theology can be analyzed. The human variable still eludes us.

Into Modern Times

Coming to modern times, Rosemary Ruether states that "modern anti-Semitism is both a continuation and a transformation of the medieval theological and economic scapegoating of the Jews." Few, I think, would deny that medieval anti-Semitism survives into the modern age both in its original and in certain secularized forms, and that there is a continuum between the two. The crucial word is "transformation," and it is this which raises more complex questions.

Is modern anti-Semitism *merely* a metamorphosed medieval Christian anti-Semitism? Through what conduits and channels did the transformation occur? If, as has been proposed by some, it was through the French Enlightenment, then one must obviously take into account its non-Christian sources as well. But this is not the time to discuss such purely historical matters. More important, what is the nature of the transformation itself, and what are the consequences thereof? What happens along the way in the shift from religious to secular, theological to racial, anti-Semitism? Here, it seems to me, Ruether's formulation explains little and glosses over much.

The issue is physical extermination. Not reprobation, discrimination, or any variety of opprobrium, but—*genocide*. From Rosemary Ruether we gather that genocide against the Jews was an inexorable consequence of Christian theological teaching. I do not think that is quite the case. If it were, genocide should have come upon the Jews in the Middle Ages. By this I do not in any way intend to exonerate the church of its real and palpable guilt. There is no question but that Christian anti-Semitism through the ages helped create the climate and mentality in which genocide, once conceived, could be achieved with little or no opposition. But even if we grant that Christian teaching was a necessary cause leading to the Holocaust, it was surely not a sufficient one. The crucial problem in the shift from medieval to modern anti-Semitism is that while the Christian tradition of "reprobation" continued into the modern era, the Christian tradition of "preservation" fell by the wayside and was no longer operative. To state only that modern anti-Semitism is a "transformed" medieval anti-Semitism is to skirt this central issue. Surely there must be some significance in the fact that the Holocaust took place in our secular century, and *not* in the Middle Ages. Moreover, medieval anti-Jewish massacres were the work of the mob and the rabble. State-inspired pogroms of the type that took place in Czarist Russia, state-instigated genocide of the Nazi type—these are entirely modern phenomena. The climactic anti-Jewish measure of which the medieval Christian state was capable was always expulsion and, on rare occasions, forced conversion. The Holocaust was the work of a thoroughly modern, neopagan state.

To see how both of the classical strands in the Christian tradition concerning the Jews united in the medieval state one has only to consider the paradigmatic definition of the status of the Jews in the *Siete Partidas* of Alfonso the Wise of Castile. In this famous thirteenth-century legal code we read:

> Jews are a people who, although they do not believe in the religion of our Lord Jesus Christ, yet the great Christian sovereigns have always permitted them to live among them . . . .
>
> We intend here to speak of the Jews, who insult His [God's] name and deny the marvelous and holy acts which He performed when He sent His Son, our Lord Jesus Christ into the world to save sinners. . . .
>
> The reason that the church, emperors, kings, and princes permitted the Jews to dwell among them and with Christians, is because they always lived, as it were, in captivity, as it was constantly in the minds of men that they were descended from those who crucified our Lord Jesus Christ . . .

No, the terminology is not exactly flattering, and the clauses that follow are hardly the terms under which I should personally choose to live. *But there is no death here,* and at the court of Alfonso the Wise Jewish courtiers, scholars, and mathematicians moved with ease. The

Siete Partidas knows at least that "a synagogue is a place where the Jews pray . . . . And for the reason that a synagogue is a place where the name of God is praised, we forbid any Christian to deface it, or remove anything from it, or take anything out of it by force." European Jewry from 1933 to 1945 could have lived under the formulations of the *Siete Partidas*. Between this and Nazi Germany lies not merely a "transformation" but a leap into a different dimension. The slaughter of Jews by the state was not part of the medieval Christian world-order. It became possible with the breakdown of that order.

An example of a different kind may heighten our awareness of the problem. It concerns the behavior of the papacy during the Nazi era. My bill of particulars concerning Pius XII does not postulate a continuum to his medieval predecessors. On the contrary, my private *J'accuse* is based on the fact that he *broke*, in essence, with the tradition of the medieval popes. It is precisely because the medieval papacy managed to speak out for the Jews *in extremis* that the silence of the Vatican during World War II is all the more deafening. The same is true in other aspects of papal reactions. Rosemary Ruether has called attention to the statutes of purity of blood in Spain (which were not "copied" by the Nazis, though there are phenomenological parallels). What she fails to note is that when the first such statute was drawn up in Toledo in 1449, it was immediately denounced by Pope Nicholas V, and its perpetrators were excommunicated. No protest was heard from Pius XI when, in 1935, Germany promulgated its own infamous statutes of racial purity in the Nuremberg Laws. When we turn, finally, to Italy itself, the contrast is even more striking. Because it was the seat of the popes, Rome was the one great city of Europe from which the Jews were never expelled, and where they had the longest unbroken history. The roundup of Jews by the Nazis began in Rome in the fall of 1943. On October 18, over one thousand Roman Jews, more than two-thirds of them women and children, were deported from the Eternal City to Auschwitz. On October 28 the German ambassador, Ernst Heinrich von Weizsacker, reported to Berlin: "Although under pressure from all sides, the pope [Pius XII] has not let himself be drawn into any demonstrative censure of the deportation of Jews from Rome." Are we confronted here by a medieval or a modern phenomenon?

Toward a Future

Rosemary Ruether ends her paper with an incipient vision of a new relationship between Christian and Jew, sharing a future hope of re-

demption which, even for Christians, is still unachieved. In order for
this to be accomplished, she calls for a repentant church. Involved are
a "massive repentant acceptance of responsibility" for what Christendom has done to Jews, a new Christology, and an end to ecclesiastical
and Messianic triumphalism.

As a Jew, how can I not endorse such aspirations? Even in a secular
world the church still exerts an influence over millions. A forthright repudiation of anti-Jewish teachings, both in theory and in school cur-
ricula, would certainly help clear the air. Though there is no possibility of rewriting the text of the Gospels, a more historical exegesis
would also have an impact. As for a more future-oriented Christian
messianism—such a reassertion of Jewish prophetic emphasis would
obviously have wider reverberations.

But in the final analysis I am still troubled by two aspects of this paper, and since I am not even a Jewish theologian, I speak only for myself.

I do not think that I err in my impression that while Ruether's sincere and profound involvement in the fate of the Jews is abundantly
clear, the problem of the Jews must necessarily appear to her as part of
a larger problem—that of the church itself. She herself says so, in
effect, when she speaks of the displacement of evil upon the Jews as
"the special archetype of this refusal [by the church] to internalize
self-judgment for its own sins," and when she invokes Vatican II as the
beginning of a break with "ecclesiastical triumphalism." That is not
only her prerogative, it is entirely natural. And when she places the
dawn of a new attitude toward the Jews within the context of an obvious hope for a total regeneration of the church, she may well be correct,
for on a certain level the one may well depend upon the other.

And yet, it seems to me, on another plane the two must be separated.
Historically, reformist tendencies and movements within the church
have not necessarily led to a positive reevaluation of the Jews. Indeed,
they have often been accompanied by an even more virulent anti-
Semitism. The Cluniac reform, where it took cognizance of the Jews,
was hostile to them. Not even the most anti-Jewish popes of the Middle
Ages advocated such measures as expulsion, the destruction of synagogues, or the prohibition of rabbinic teaching, as did Martin Luther.
In Calvin's Geneva, not in papal Rome, Jews were forbidden to reside.
Nor was hostility to Jews limited to triumphalist official theologies.
Those who revolted against the church—Catharists, Flagellants, Mil-
lenarians of all sorts—were most often just as hostile, and sometimes
far less restrained. Rosemary Ruether will therefore forgive me if I am
initially somewhat skeptical that the reformist and revolutionary ten-

dencies within the Catholic Church today will necessarily engender pro-Jewish attitudes.

My last point concerns Ruether's presentation as a whole. If what she has related here is a summary of the history of Christianity vis-a-vis the Jews, then I see my own hopes dwindling. If the entire theological and historical tradition forged by Christianity is one of anti-Semitism, then the only hope lies in the radical erosion of Christianity itself. It would mean that in order to achieve a more positive relationship to Jews and Judaism Christians must, in effect, repudiate their entire heritage. But that, in turn, does not impress me as a very realistic expectation. It is partly for that reason that I have felt it important to argue that the historical record is more varied and complex than can be anticipated from this account.

Rosemary Ruether calls at the end for "massive repentance." I am not certain that this is what is required. There is something about the phrase that worries me. Knowledge and acknowledgment of what has been done to the Jews in the name of a crucified Messiah, yes. But no more. I do not welcome a collective mea culpa from Christendom. It tends toward a kind of masochism, behind which may lurk an eventual sadism. I do not want Christians to brood on the guilt of their forebears and to keep apologizing for it. I do not want to encounter Christians as confessor and penitent, just as when I go to the Spanish archives I don't expect the archivists to plead guilty for the Inquisition or the Expulsion of 1492.

Theology? In 1974, after all that has happened, do we still have to await a reformulation of Christian theology before the voice of Jewish blood can be heard crying from the earth? Is our common humanity not sufficient? In any case, Christian theology is an internal affair for Christians alone. Perhaps my trouble is that I am more oriented toward history than toward theology, more to what Unamuno called "the man of flesh and bone" than to the theologian in him. My fundamental problem has not been solved, and perhaps it is insoluble. I want to know why Rosemary Ruether is my friend, and one of the *hasiday 'umot ha-'olam*, the righteous among the nations. Her theology alone does not explain it, for there are others who share all her theological concerns and reformist causes, but who do not speak for the Jews as she does.

To Christians generally I should like to say: I hope that the condition for our dialogue is not our mutual secularization (though at times it certainly seems so). You do not have to repudiate everything in the Christian past concerning the Jews. Much of the record is dark. There were also patches of light. There was "reprobation" and there was "preservation," and each has to be understood in its historical context. It is up to you to choose that with which you will identify. If it is important to you, integrate and reinterpret what you cull from the past into your theology, as you will. Be it known to you, however, that not by your ancestors, but by your actions, will you be judged. For my people, now as in the past, is in grave peril of its life. And it simply cannot wait until you have completed a new *Summa Theologica*.

PART III

Christian Mission in Crisis

Introduction

The discussion begun in the previous chapter continues. How far must the church go in reexamining and reformulating its message? If Christian mission is no longer conceived in terms of conversion, what questions does this raise for the claims to universality of the Christian church? Can genuine religious pluralism coexist with a universal Christian message?

The church's attitude toward the Jewish people with regard to its missionary enterprise has also changed since Auschwitz. Conversion is no longer the avowed goal, but has been replaced by a spirit of service and cooperation. Why, asks *Gregory Baum* of the University of Toronto, has this changed attitude not yet affected the majority of Christians? He finds the answer in some of the symbols that are built into the very fabric of the Christian faith. The power of religious symbols is so great that it persists even in a post-Christian society. Baum distinguishes between utopian and ideological symbols, and shows how subtle the shift from one to the other can be. Thus, the absolutist claim of the early church, part of the utopian survival language of a persecuted minority, became imperialistic ideology once the church acceded to political power.

This is part of the ambiguity inherent not only in Christianity, but in all religions. All have a dark, unredeemed side to them; all must wrestle with this, especially those religions which have become culturally successful. The frequently made distinction between an essence, which is pure, and the periphery, which is impure, is not valid. There is no such thing as a "pure core" in any faith. For all religions are rooted in history, subject to its vicissitudes. The task for us is to become aware of our own ambiguity. For this we need to be in dialogue with others. Mission now becomes a two-way street. The church needs the other in order to be truly church.

Christian theologians today are asking themselves how the church's mission can be formulated without any trace of triumphalism. If Christianity renounces its imperialistic claims and perceives mission in terms of dialogue, service, and compassion, what are the implications of this new stance? Clearly, for Baum, religious pluralism is not a temporary necessity, but a precious gift from God. Judaism and other world religions are not merely provisional, destined to last until such time as the whole world will be Christian.

This does not mean, however, that the church renounces its universal mission. Its witness is universal, not because it is destined to embrace all peoples, but because it offers the world a universal message—of God's ultimate triumph over evil—in a particular form. This victory lies still in the future. Like Ruether, Baum believes that a reinterpretation of Christology is necessary, and that the church must recover the eschatological tension in its life. In Jesus Christ the future of humanity has taken visible shape; in the life of the church it is still fragmentary and unfinished.

Johannes Hoekendijk of Union Theological Seminary voices certain reservations with regard to Baum's paper. The crisis of mission in his view is as old as

Christianity. The first Christian missionaries were not white, Western imperialists, but a small powerless minority, frequently persecuted by those among whom they went. Only gradually was a cultural and ideological component added to the Christian faith. Hoekendijk rejects this "Christendom-complex" out of hand, and subscribes to the concept of mission as service and dialogue as described by Baum. While he passionately repudiates the distortions of the Christian message, the message itself, for him, does not require reexamination.

The Lutheran theologian *Aarne Siirala* is in basic agreement with Baum, in particular regarding the dangerous power and easy misuse of the basic Christian symbols. He presents some reflections on anti-Judaism in the Protestant tradition, thereby establishing a somewhat different perspective from that of the Catholic Baum. Despite this different approach he arrives basically at the same conclusions.

Siirala's starting point is Luther's treatise "On the Jews and Their Lies," which has only recently become available in a popular English edition. While clearly aware of the risks involved in publishing such a virulently anti-Semitic work, the editor does not go beyond Luther's own framework and fails to point out the ambiguity inherent in his theological claims of absolutism. Siirala sees this as evidence that Lutherans today still do not perceive the problem at its root. He finds a deep-seated resistance among them to confront "the cancerous element" in their tradition. Luther's outbursts are frequently deplored, but nowhere do we find a critique of his theological argumentation. Instead, there is the tendency to excuse his anti-Judaism in the name of his passion for God's Word, love of Christ, etc.

This leads Siirala to wonder, along with Baum, whether the negation of Judaism is not built into the very heart of Christian symbols. Western thought in general has resisted facing the basic ambiguities in human existence, tending instead to think in terms of dichotomies (God and the devil, life and death, mind and body, etc.). This results in our perceiving those who differ from us as enemies who must be mastered and overcome—what some scholars today call the "Faustian trend" in Western civilization. This has led to extraordinary technological achievements, but also to structures of persecution and exploitation of those who do not fit the accepted norms—ultimately to the Holocaust. One of the most dangerous manifestations of this mentality is the triumphalistic, ideological Messianism that runs through Western history, in which Christian symbols have been used repeatedly to bolster imperialistic crusades. Like Baum, Siirala sees these symbols so deeply ingrained in Christianity that it is not easy to perceive the shift from utopian to ideological use. Luther's anti-Jewish writings are a classical instance of a dynamic Christology that has become a rigid ideological block. For Luther, belief in Jesus as Messiah is not a matter of choice. Not only Jews but the whole world is "obliged" to know that God sent his Son as Redeemer. The Jews' refusal to know puts them beyond the pale of God's mercy. We see here the lengths to which an ideological use of religious symbols can lead, and how thoroughly it has shaped Christian consciousness.

Rethinking the Church's Mission after Auschwitz

GREGORY BAUM

I

After Auschwitz the Christian churches no longer wish to convert the Jews. While they may not be sure of the theological grounds that dispense them from this mission, the churches have become aware that asking the Jews to become Christians is a spiritual way of blotting them out of existence and thus only reinforces the effects of the Holocaust. The churches, moreover, realize the deadly irony implicit in a Christian plea for the conversion of the Jews; for after Auschwitz and the participation of the nations, it is the Christian world that is in need of conversion. The major churches have come to repudiate mission to the Jews, even if they have not justified this by adequate doctrinal explanations. We have here a case, frequently found in church history, where a practical decision on the part of the churches, in response to a significant event, precedes dogmatic reflection and in fact becomes the guide to future doctrinal development.[1] Moved by a sense of shame over the doctrinal formulations that negate Jewish existence, the churches have come to recognize Judaism as an authentic religion before God, with independent value and meaning, not as a stage on the way to Christianity.

A significant sign of the new approach is the churches' effort to create an institutional separation of the Christian approach to the Jews from Christian missionary action. At the World Council of Churches, the approach to the Jewish people, at one time connected with the International Missionary Council, was handed over to a newly created Committee on the Church and the Jewish People, which publishes its studies and documents in a special newsletter.[2] The *International Journal of Mission,* the organ of the Missionary Council, no longer deals with the relation of Christians and Jews. Similarly, at Vatican II, the Commission on Missionary Activity had nothing whatever to do with the Christian approach to the Jews. Pope John XXIII had asked the Secretariat for Christian Unity to prepare a special document on Jewish-Christian relations, which eventually became part of the Declaration on the Church's Attitude to Non-Christian religions.[3]

These institutional changes at the WCC and at Vatican II are significant signs that the churches no longer include the Jews in their missionary activity. Vatican II was even more specific. In the above-mentioned declaration, the council recognized Judaism as an authentic biblical religion in which God's Word is alive, a religion that deserves the brotherly respect and admiration of Christians.[4] Calling upon Catholics to enter into dialogue and cooperation with Jews, the Catholic church repudiated the traditional missionary stance. Salvation is present in Israel. What counts for the church at this time is to purify its teaching and language from the expressions of contempt and the spiritual negations of Jewish faith.

At the same time, other political events of world history have made the churches reconsider the meaning of their missionary activity or evangelization. They have been made to see how closely their missions have been associated with the extension of Western power and Western culture. The protesting voices from the Third World and the social critics in the West have convinced many churchmen that the doctrine of the church's mission has legitimated the invasion of the continents by the Christian nations. For many centuries, the church regarded the expansion of the white man as part of God's providential design. The missionary followed the soldier and merchant. The confidence with which whites gained power over the continents, drew the peoples of the world into institutional structures the centers of which were in the West, and organized the resources of the earth so as to make by far the greater share available to the Christian nations, cannot be separated from the Christian claim that the church is the unique instument of salvation and that it is destined to embrace all the peoples of the world. We do not suggest, of course, that the Christian church was the acting cause behind the expansion of the Western nationals. What we do claim is that the imperialistic invasion and appropriation of the continents, caused by a variety of economic, political, and cultural factors, was sanctioned by the church's understanding of world history, with the Christian commonwealth at the center and the non-Christian peoples on the periphery, destined to become Christian in due time.

Thanks to a keener social conscience, the churches have become sensitive to the political meaning implicit in their missionary action. The hidden implication of their claim to unlimited universality is the spiritual suppression of all other religions and of the various cultures that have been nourished by these religions.

In recent years the churches have modified their official stance toward the world religions, even if the dogmatic basis for doing this remained unclear. They have begun to acknowledge religious pluralism as a divinely given reality. Again, Vatican II is a significant example. In the Declaration of the Church's Attitude to Non-Christian Religions, which also contains the statement on Jewish-Christian relations, the council recognized the world religions of East and West as spiritual traditions in which the divine Word is operative, and while affirming that this same Word is fully present only in Jesus Christ, the council recommends that the Christian community enter into dialogue with members of other religions. This dialogue is not an effort to convert them. It is, rather, an attempt, through conversation and cooperation, to intensify the bonds that unite the human family and expand the values held in common. A special secretariat was created at the Vatican, whose task it is to promote dialogue of Christians with the followers of other religions. When Pope Paul VI visited the far East a few years ago, he met on one occasion with religious leaders of the Eastern religions and joined in a common prayer service with them. However weak the theological foundation of this new approach, the change of ecclesiastical policy is significant.

Needless to say, the new approach to the world religions demands a rethinking of the church's mission. Today missionary theology has become a highly controversial field of inquiry. Characteristic of this uncertainty is the teaching of Vatican II on the church's mission, which proposes three distinct approaches, without attempting to reconcile them with one another.

The Decree on Missionary Activity promulgated by Vatican II endorses the inherited understanding of the church's mission. The church is called and empowered to embrace in the unity of faith and sacrament the entire human family. This document, it should be mentioned, clearly acknowledged that divine grace is operative in the whole of mankind and that salvation is offered to people wherever they are—a doctrine that is more clearly stated in other conciliar documents.[5] Yet the divine grace acting among the peoples of the world destines them to the full enjoyment of God's presence in the Christian church.

The Declaration of the Church's Attitude to Non-Christian Religions proposes that the church's mission is to enter into dialogue with them.[6] The purpose of this dialogue, in which Christians speak clearly of their faith in Jesus Christ, is to promote love and unity in a divided humanity and to protect and foster the spiritual and cultural values of the world religions. The conciliar teaching clearly implies that this dialogue serves the presence of the Spirit and the action of the Word within these religious traditions and in humanity as a whole.

A third understanding of mission is found in the Pastoral Constitution on the Church in the Modern World. In this document the church declares itself in solidarity with the human family, especially with the underprivileged and dispossessed, and regards it as its mission to cooperate with all men and women in the building of a more just and more humane society.[7] The document implies that this mission of service is not a purely humanitarian effort, for by wrestling with others against the structures of oppression and for the humanization of social life, the church, obedient to Christ's call, prepares the way for God's kingdom and exercises a properly redemptive function.

The last two views of mission—mission as dialogue and mission as service—go together very well. They are based on a common trinitarian faith in the presence of the spirit in the human family, in the Word summoning all people to new life, and in the ultimate horizon of love and reconciliation to which broken and divided humanity is destined. These two views of mission are based on the church's solidarity with the entire human family. It is not easy, however, to reconcile this new understanding of mission with the more traditional understanding of evangelization. We acknowledge, of course, that if the church were deeply involved in missionary activity in terms of dialogue and service, the image of Christian life would become so attractive and Christian witness so powerful that many people would become Christians and join the community of believers. In other words, the new understanding of mission does not neglect the church's continuity, extension, and vitality.

The new openness to Jewish faith and the emergence of a new understanding of mission reflect the response of the Christian conscience to the voice of the Holocaust and, less directly, to the protest of the Third World. The churches believe that they have been addressed by God's Word through these events: they have placed themselves under God's judgment. Even without elaborating an adequate dogmatic basis, they have made significant public declarations and changed their public policy in remarkable ways. Christian theologians have reflected on the new trends and tried to establish their doctrinal foundation. Christian educators have begun to rewrite catechisms and schoolbooks. Many missionary congregations and Christian-action groups have abandoned their former ideal of evangelization and adopted a new policy, according to which missionaries enter into solidarity with the people in whose midst they serve, bear the burdens of life with them, and promote the self-discovery and humanization taking place in their midst. In particular the churches have renounced the desire to convert the Jews; they have begun to call them brothers and sisters.

While these changes have taken place on the highest ecclesiastical level, in official circles and among Christians intensely involved in the problems of contemporary life, the effect of the new policy on the great majority of Christians is negligible. Most Christians have not even begun to reflect on these issues. The contemporary success of the more conservative Christian groups, evangelical movements, and even various sects of "Jesus people," who firmly endorse the traditional negation of Jewish existence and restrict salvation within narrow bounds, is a sign of how little the great number of Christians have become aware of the sociopolitical implications of their piety. The reason why the new policies adopted by the churches have so little power and influence among Christians is that the negation of Judaism and other religions seems to be built into the central Christian symbols. The corrections made on the margin hardly affect the central teaching. Since Christian teaching confesses Jesus as the one mediator between God and man, and the church as the true Israel, the unique vehicle of salvation, in whom the peoples of the world will find forgiveness and new life, the dangerous social trends against which the new ecclesiastical policies have reacted continue to affect the Christian understanding of history. Unless people are well informed and belong to a religious elite, the traditional language continues to shape their outlook and attitude. What is demanded, therefore, is that the churches interpret the central Christian doctrine, in obedience to God's call, in a more socially responsible way and find a sound dogmatic basis for their new policies. But before we turn to a reinterpretation of ecclesiology, we must understand more clearly the power of religious symbols, for good and for evil, in the creation of culture.

II

In this section I wish to turn to sociological theory to bring out more clearly the power of religious symbols.[8] In the highly rational theologies that we have inherited, symbols were regarded as weak realities. Symbols were signs addressed to people's memory and imagination to elicit feelings and insinuate ideas. For sociologists, however, the symbols through which people understand their world are powerful society-building realities. Symbols, in this sociological perspective, are the framework of the mind, through which people perceive the world they encounter and respond to it: symbols enter into the process of world-building and create the orientation of life and action. Symbols are religious when they interpret the whole of reality, invest this interpretation with a sense of ultimacy, and produce a corresponding commitment of the heart.[9] Religious symbols, therefore, mediate the self-understanding of the community and affect its cultural and societal self-expression. For the sociologist, then, the human world is not a given; it has a history, it has been made by people through the symbolization of their lives. People have created their world through symbols which direct their action, guide their imagination, and find expression in their institutions.

One example of the power of religious symbols is the growing effect which the negation of Jewish existence has had on the history of Western civilization. Early Christian preaching refuted the Jewish interpretation of the ancient Scriptures by various sets of arguments and eventually negated Judaism as a way of life.[10] Judaism was a way of bondage. Later Christian writers elaborated this negation by making the Jews the symbols of all that was evil and opposed to divine redemption. The Jews were blind, carnal, stubborn, unfaithful; they were the enemies of God and the seat of darkness in the world. Because of their infidelities, we were then told, God had abrogated the ancient covenant with them and made a new one with the nations of the world, whereby the church was substituted in the place of Israel. This religious world-interpretation found its first expression in Christian literature, worship, and discipline. This was the first level of institutionalizing the symbols. When the Christian faith was adopted as the state religion of the Roman Empire, the same religious symbolism was translated into secular legislation. The Jews were excluded from society, they were pushed to the margin beyond the reach of justice; they were made a nonpeople. This was the second, the secular, institutionalization of the original negation of Jewish existence in the structures of society, and through them it created the consciousness of Western civilization.

Occasionally Christian theologians suggest, as a defense of the original language of negation, that the Christian message invalidated Judaism only as a *spiritual* reality, and that, since the same message summoned Christians to love their neighbor, the translation of the spiritual negation into social and political fact cannot be attributed to the power of the Christian symbolism. These theologians hold the view that if Christians have enough charity, the church's claim of exclusiveness and universality does not become a source of domination and imperialism. This view, alas, underestimates the objective power of symbols belonging to a religion that has become culturally successful. The power of symbols that have been institutionalized in language, custom, and law is so massive that personal virtue cannot overcome it. A particularly sensitive person, who for reasons of personal history stands somewhat outside the system, and hence is able to see through the devastating consequences produced by certain symbols of negation, may well be able to resist the power in his own personal life; but by himself he is quite unable to mitigate the objective power of these symbols in his culture.

Even when the religious inspiration of Western civilization broke down in the period of the Enlightenment, the symbols negating Jewish existence were carried forward by the cultural institutions. The French philosophers of the Enlightenment regarded the Jews as the symbol of all that was reactionary and hostile to reason. For the German Enlightenment, Judaism symbolized alienating and alienated religion. While the Enlightenment contributed to the liberation of Jews from political oppression and the cultural exclusion from Western society, it was unable to stem the tide of anti-Jewish sentiment created by the symbolic negation of Jewish existence built into the cultural tradition. Various forms of social alienation, either among the upper classes or in the lower middle class, led to virulent anti-Semitic movements that revived the traditional picture of the Jews as the evildoers, the carnal men, the betrayers, the unfaithful ones. It was the institutionalization of this ancient symbolism that enabled Hitler to make the Jews the scapegoat of his political paranoia and to become the demonic executor of the ancient death-wish.[11]

The exclusiveness of the Christian church is another symbol that has acquired great power through the cultural success of Christianity. To become a follower of Christ was a crucial decision in the early centuries of the church. This meant the repudiation not only of the Jewish option but also, and especially, of mystery religions, cultured philosophies, gnostic groups, and the official worship practiced in the Roman Empire. There was no salvation apart from Jesus; the church was the unique vehicle of salvation. When the Christian Church became the official religion of the Roman Empire, it regarded itself as the catholic, or universal, community, spread through the civilized world, destined to embrace all the peoples belonging to this cultural sphere. The church understood itself as situated at the center of the known world, as the one community offering salvation to the entire civilized world. This church-centered understanding of history remained operative in Christian culture even after the breakdown of the empire. Identified with the rebuilding of the Christian West, the church affirmed the language of universality and exclusiveness with new vigor against the groups that challenged it from within, and against the Muslims, who attacked Western society from without. At the time when the unity of the church was torn apart in Europe, the churches renewed their claims to absolute truth. The Catholic church, in particular, affirmed its universal mission and exclusiveness in the face of other churches, other civilizations, and other continents. This understanding of the church's mission, as we mentioned above, legitimated the invasion of the continents on the part of Christian nations and the colonial ties to which the West subjected the peoples of the world. The symbols of Church-centeredness, at first expressed in purely religious terms, became institutionalized in the secular order and thus gained objective power; and despite the goodwill and the scruples of many a saint, it sanctioned the creation of a colonialized world under the imperial dominance of the West.

It is precisely because of the objective power of these religious symbols, even in a secularized society, that the changes adopted by the churches in their approach to the Jews and to other religions are not enough, unless they deal in a new way with the central symbols of the Gospel, i.e., unless they qualify the Christian claims to exclusiveness and universality.

In culturally successful religions, we have shown, religious symbols achieve objective power. The meaning and force of religious statements depend on the sociocultural situation in which they are uttered. Theologians tend to be satisfied with a conceptual analysis of religious statements without paying sufficient attention to the *Sitz im Leben*, to the sociology of knowledge, which clarifies its meaning. It can be shown, in particular, that the symbols proclaiming the absoluteness of Christianity have had a variety of meanings. It is for *this* reason that we turn to the useful distinction made by the sociologist Karl Mannheim between ideology and utopia, which sheds light on the church's claim to ultimate and universal truth.[12] By "ideology" Mannheim meant a symbol system or an idea that legitimates the existing power relation and thereby reinforces the present social and political institutions: by "utopia" he referred to symbols or ideas that weaken the dominant ideals of society, depict the present system as threatened by God's judgment or its own inner contradictions, and anticipate the breakdown of the existing order. It is Mannheim's contention that the meaning of a symbol varies depending on whether it is an ideological or a utopian statement.

The song "We Shall Overcome" is a utopian statement. It was sung by people devoid of power who proclaimed their trust that the present order was about to be changed. I call this a language of survival and self-identity. If the government and its police force had adopted the song "We Shall Overcome" as their own motto, the song would have become an ideological statement. For then those who have access to power and the means of defending the present social order would have declared that they shall make use of this power to prevent the weakening of the present system. The same song would have given rise to a language of aggression and domination. Since the meaning of the identical statement or symbol changes in accordance with the sociopolitical situation of the groups that utter it, the songs and slogans of liberation movements, and of groups, religious or secular, that struggle for survival and self-identity, acquire a different meaning when these movements are successful and the struggling groups attain to power and prestige. Then the same songs and slogans, unless significantly modified, become a language of aggression and domination.

The absolute claim of the early church was utopian language of survival and identity. Having moved dramatically out of the Jewish world, surrounded by mystery cults, rational philosophies, and imperial religion, the Christian church affirmed itself as the one community of salvation. More than that: facing a hostile synagogue as well as the much more threatening opposition of the empire with its machinery of persecution, the church had reasons to fear for its future. It affirmed its survival in reliance on the promises of God's victory at the end of time. The church's self-definition in absolute terms had eschatological significance. The only guarantee it had for its earthly future was God's eschatological promise, the absolute on the horizon of human history. When the church's survival became eventually guaranteed by its institutional place in the dominant society, its faith in the Parousia became less important. As the church moved out of the situation of oppression and established itself as a significant power in the world, it lost its eschatological reference, and its absolute claims acquired an ideological meaning. The language claiming absolute truth remained the same, but its meaning changed. It now became an ideology protecting the ecclesiastical structure as the final and definitive work of God, and situating the church at the center of world history as the one source of light and salvation.

These are the sociological sources of the church's ideological language. Ideology, in the sense of Mannheim (and Marx), stands here for the deformation of truth for the sake of social interest.

It must be said, however, that the intense anti-Jewish rhetoric of the church throughout the ages cannot be wholly accounted for by such a sociological analysis. What was operative here was a pathology that by far surpassed any deformation that could serve the church's worldly interests. The church's ongoing demonization of the Jewish people, even when there were hardly any Jews left in the culture, was the product of several illnesses deeply rooted in the church's life, which unhappily converged in the hate-projection against a single people. There was the church's inability to leave behind the negation of the mother religion whence it came; there was the need to project the church's own dark self-image, which as God's "holy people" it refused to acknowledge onto another historical community; there was the compulsive effort of the Christian community to disguise its own doubts and lack of faith by vilifying and oppressing the Jewish community, which symbolized an alternative to the Christian option. This multiple sickness developed and grew strong because the sociologically induced ideology prevented the church from coming to an honest self-knowledge, from seeing itself in proper, finite, human proportions, from discovering how expressions that originally proclaimed God's final victory had become statements of institutional power and domination.

Today the Christian church has wrestled against these various illnesses and refuses to project its own dark history on the people of Israel. Still, it is necessary to deal with the ideological understanding of the church's claim to absoluteness. For it is this symbol that has achieved objective power in our culture, even if some of its sickening effects have been mitigated. We have shown in the first section of this paper how far the contemporary church has gone in rectifying its attitude toward Judaism and the world religions, and how ready the churches are, at least in certain places, to reinterpret their missionary task in terms of dialogue, service, and cooperation. Yet we also noted that the dogmatic basis for these changes of attitude is not too clear. Can the meaning of these central Christian symbols be changed? Is it possible to revive the eschatological reference of the church and its message and recover the utopian character of the good news?

III

In the first section we have shown that the churches, in particular the Catholic church, have modified their approach to the Jewish people and their attitude to the world religions, even if the doctrinal basis on which these modifications were made has not been clarified. The changed stance of the Christian church has theological significance. Why? Because it is not a compromise with, or an adaptation to, a self-centered and power-hungry world, but an authentic response in faith to a challenge addressed to Christians in the contemporary age. In this

section I want to reflect on the theological implications of the new ecclesiastical stance.

The church has been able to adopt a positive attitude to other religions because it regards them as dispensations of divine grace. A
clearer awareness of God's redemptive presence in the whole of human history has developed in some schools of Protestant theology
since Friedrich Hegel, and in Catholic theology since Maurice Blondel.[13] Karl Rahner has made the universality of divine grace a central
theme of his theology.[14] This general trend has been acknowledged in
the teaching of Vatican II.[15] Admittedly, for some theologians—and
some conciliar texts—the grace granted by God outside the church is
oriented by its own inner structure toward fulfillment in the church,
and thus the world religions are "implicit Christianities" on the way
to explicitation. Other theologians, however, regard the world religions, including Judaism, as authentic religious traditions in their
own right, as divine dispensations, and not simply as provisional
structures destined to disappear under the impact of the Gospel.[16]

Even Karl Rahner, who speaks of non-Christians touched by divine
grace as "anonymous Christians," acknowledges that the world religions are dispensations of grace, and that it would be wrong for the
church to persuade the followers of such a religion, living in their own
environment, to leave their religion and become Christians.[17] For
Rahner, the gift of grace is social as well as personal; while an intimate
dimension of personal life, grace is nonetheless mediated through the
social and/or cultural fabric to which a person belongs. While a conversion to Christianity may have great power and meaning to persons
who, for a variety of reasons, have become detached from their community and are free to be integrated into a Christian church, individual
conversions cannot be the goal of the church's mission.

Since theologians like Karl Rahner, who acknowledge the working
of grace in the world religions, usually leave open the question whether these religions, like Israel, are ultimately, in a distant or not so distant future, to give way to the higher dispensation of Christianity, I regard it as important to say clearly and emphatically that Judaism and
the other world religions are in no way provisional. They are not stages
on the way to Christianity. The church recognizes them as dispensations of grace. Religious pluralism is, therefore, no anomaly, no regrettable state of affairs that reflects the broken and unredeemed nature of
human history: religious pluralism is a sign of God's manifold and inexhaustible richness. Religious pluralism is not to be grudgingly acknowledged, but welcomed with gratitude.

Does such an affirmation lead to the relativism of truth? Are we unfaithful to the biblical teaching that the church is God's chosen community called from the darkness of the world into the light of god's kingdom? I defend the position that despite the acknowledgement of religious pluralism, the Christian community holds that Jesus Christ saves it from sin, blindness, and the triviality of the world. Since the social and economic institutions impose alienation and false consciousness on people, inflict on them games of competition and conquest, and often push them into a life of emptiness and superficiality, the Christian community confidently believes that it has been called, elected, and elevated to be the source of truth and salvation in the midst of darkness. If "the world" in biblical literature refers to the Roman Empire and the structures of domination erected by it—and to the contemporary equivalents of such systems of oppression—then we must repeat the biblical message that there is no salvation in the world. Christians are called out of this darkness into the light of truth. But this message of hope does not imply that people are called to become Christians out of the great world religions. The church's claim to be the unique source of saving truth is a judgment on the systems of the world, not on the great world religions.

Religions, we note, are ambiguous. By this I mean that they consist of trends that make them more subject to "the world," and of countertrends that open them to the call of grace, mediated by the best in their own tradition and making them powerful instruments of salvation for their followers. This ambiguity, it is necessary to add, also qualifies Christianity.

Before we clarify in greater detail what is meant by the uniqueness of the Christian Church, we must face more squarely the unredeemed side of the Christian religion. Religion is always ambiguous. Believers must always distinguish within their religion a variety of trends and commit themselves to the trends that foster redemption and new life. Every religion must wrestle against the magical trends operative in it. Every religion must wrestle against the subtle forms of enslavement which it places on people. Every religion must fight against the trends within it that promote dependency and infantilism. Every religion must wrestle against the ideological deformations of its original message that elevate the believing community above others, and legitimate the dominant culture and its structures of domination. Every religion must wrestle against the paranoid tendencies that make it reject without discrimination great values existing in traditions different from its own. Especially a religion that has become culturally successful, such as Christianity, must wrestle against the power plays implicit in its language of absolute commitment and ultimate truth.

Usually theologians do not attend to the ambiguity of religion. They try to make a neat distinction between the abuses operative in a religion and its essential core, and then claim that their reflection on the Christian religion deals with its essential and unchanging core. What this approach forgets, however, is that the essence of Christianity (or any religion) cannot be defined apart from its history, and that the conceptual analysis of dogmatic statements does not reveal what these statements mean in the actual situations of history. Especially if religion has become identified with a successful culture, its teachings, even when dealing with the presumed core, assume an ideological character and may have to be reformulated in order to remain faithful to the original message. The self-identity and continuity of the Christian religion is not guaranteed by clinging to an unchangeable dogma. It is assured, rather, through the Spirit operative in the church, the Spirit who summons the believing community to a critique of the inherited religious forms and doctrinal formulations and to a creative response in faith to the challenge of the present age.

The typically Catholic language of infallibility and the trend to attribute almost divine prerogatives to the church easily become an ideological device to exempt church authority and its teaching from honest critique, and hence to legitimize its power and position in the community. But this same language could also have a utopian meaning, referring to the advent of the kingdom and the presence of the Spirit in the community. It is this Spirit that enables the believers to discern the ambiguity in which their community lives, to respond creatively, in faith, to the demands of the present situation, and in this way to go on creating the self-identity of the Gospel in history.

Religion, including the Christian religion, is ambiguous. I propose that through dialogue and common action religions are drawn into a process that delivers them from the inherited ideologies and pathological deformations. When Vatican II proposed an understanding of the church's mission in terms of dialogue and solidarity, it mentioned only the redeeming effects which such a mission would have on other religions and the wider human community. It did not mention the significant point, without which this understanding of mission would be incomplete: that the church itself is being transformed by the dialogue in which the Gospel is sounded, and by the cooperative action which raises its consciousness. The church needs the other religions and other cultural traditions to become truly church! It must be obedient to God's word uttered in the whole of history and addressing it in the present. The church is engaged in mission to be freed from its own ideological trends and become more authentically itself.

The theologians who fear that the acknowledgement of other religions leads to a relativism of truth have too conceptual an understanding of religious truth. The understanding of the church's mission in terms of dialogue does not promote indifferentism, or a passive taking-for-granted of the various religions as they are. On the contrary, dialogue initiates the believers into a new spiritual awareness which commits them to the transformation of their religious tradition. This understanding of mission leads the church to a more authentic appropriation of its original message. While this new approach acknowledges religious pluralism, it does not promote indifferentism. On the contrary, it reveals the need for commitment and critique in each religious tradition so that the faithful are able to be in touch with the saving truth offered to them. To say that one religion is as good as another is a misleading formulation. It obscures the fact that in each religion truth is not on the surface but in the depth, and it disguises the uniqueness of each religion, including that of Christianity.

If the church acknowledges other religions as dispensations of grace, how can we go on saying that the Christian church is universal? To answer this question I wish to distinguish between two ways of understanding universality. Universality-A is the vocation of the church eventually to embrace all peoples, to replace Judaism and the other world religions, or at least to embody in explicit form the hidden presence of divine grace in the human family. Traditional Christian theology has affirmed the church's universality in this sense. Contemporary theologians have moved, cautiously and tentatively, to another view of universality, more in keeping with the church's new stance toward other religions. Universality-B, then, is defined as the vocation of the church to offer a witness that has universal significance, and yet to remain a particular religious tradition surrounded by others. The church enjoying universality-B remains a particular tradition, for the witness it offers can be followed and obeyed by people wherever they are, in any spiritual tradition. Here the church in no sense expects to replace the world religions, nor does it understand itself as the embodiment of all God's gracious action in the world. It accepts religious pluralism as a characteristic of God's universe. The church is open, of course, to the possibility that its witness may move some individuals to become Christians and even lead an entire culture to find its truest self-expression in the Christian faith; but it in no way prejudges the movement of history. The church is faithful to its divine vocation when it understands itself as one religion among others as long as it is deeply involved, through word and action, in offering its witness of universal relevance. This is the church's universal vocation. This defines the specific nature of the church's mission; to render present to all peoples, through dialogue and common action, the specifically Christian witness.

What is this Christian witness with universal relevance? I suppose there are various ways of formulating this testimony. Since we have shown that the church's return to an eschatological perspective delivers it from the ideological trends operative in its teaching, I propose that the church's witness with universal meaning and power is the message of God's approaching kingdom.[18] Jesus Christ is the unique instrument and servant of this kingdom, and through his humiliation and glory we have been assured of God's ultimate victory over evil, already pressing in upon us now. The kingdom of God is at hand. What is upon us, in whatever religion or whatever culture, is the divine judgment revealing the ideological deformation of truth, the power games, the structures of domination, the institutional pathologies, the workings of sin that oppose life in its fullness. What is equally upon us is God's life-giving grace, which enables us as persons and as peoples to sever ourselves from a destructive past and move creatively into the future. This judgment and this grace are offered wherever people are; and the Christian witness, offered to them in word and action, facilitates the discernment of the divine language. The church's eschatological witness constitutes its universal vocation.

If the Christian community itself were faithful to this witness, then its own life and its own structures would be a judgment on the powers of domination that oppress the world, and its own forms of interaction would anticipate the redeemed human existence promised for the kingdom. The church, in other words, ought to anticipate in its own life the future form of reconciled humanity. The division of the human family into castes, classes, and other opposing groups ought to be overcome in the church. In its social life, there ought to exist types of leadership, male and female, that transcend the worldly powers of domination.

The Jewish people, too, understand themselves as a particular tradition called to give a witness of universal meaning. Many Jewish thinkers understand this universal witness as a judgment on all forms of idolatry. But while the Jewish faith is largely tied to the continuity of a single people, the Christian religion identified itself with the ancient culture of the Mediterranean, embracing a great variety of peoples, and later became the matrix of Western culture and produced an extended Christian East, again including many nations. Where Christianity will move from here is quite uncertain. It may become a much smaller religion, a gathered community, a diaspora church, less identified with a culture, but with a witness that is all the more visible. Or it may remain identified with Western culture and its uncertain future. Or it may again move into new cultures, which find their deepest aspirations realized in the Christian faith. The future is quite open, and nothing in the church's self-understanding commits it to any particular view of history. But whatever the future of the church, the Christian religion regards itself as one particular religious tradition surrounded by others.

Only as the church recovers the eschatological tension in which it was created is it able to reconcile Christian dogma with the recognition of religious pluralism as part of divine dispensation. This means that whatever the future of the church, Christians are meant to be a restless people, never totally at home in the world, never fully identified with their culture, always eager for the reform of life and the deliverance from the structures of domination. Christianity has inherited an ardent Messianic hope for the future. Every day Christians call upon God that his kingdom come and that his will, which is justice and love, be done on earth, i.e., in human history. This eschatological turn will affect the church's reading of Christology. In Jesus Christ, humanity's ultimate future has taken visible shape. In his suffering and exaltation the church holds the assurance of God's victory over all the enemies of life. When the church prays, "Come, Lord Jesus, come!" it acknowledges the fragmentary and unfinished character of present redemption and confesses its eager hope in the approaching liberation. The church's absolutes are valid only in this eschatologic perspective.

These theological reflections show that the church's recognition of religious pluralism is in keeping with the Gospel if its eschatological dimension is recovered. Then the church is able to recite its ancient creed and speak firmly of the absolute revealed in Jesus, without falling into ideology. In this perspective the traditional Christian symbols give expression to a utopian message. What is necessary, of course, is that this turn to eschatology become incarnate in the church's critical witness, its public action, and its visible, institutional approach to the social and political realities of history. A new formulation of the Christian message alone is unable to free the church from its ideological trends. What is needed is a new involvement of the church, side by side with other religions and secular groups, in the liberation and humanization of human life.

Response to Gregory Baum

JOHANNES HOEKENDIJK

Auschwitz and Ma'alot, and all the crimes in between, perhaps more to come. Let us agree at the outset that we do not discuss "tragedies" in the classical sense. Our parents, sisters, brothers, and children were not simply caught in a demonic system of anonymous powers, they were not merely the victims of fate. As we all try to live by the *Tanakh,* we should know that the Holy One, "throned in heaven, . . . ridicules all these pseudo-powers" (Ps. 2:8). They are still abroad, but cut down to their proper size: little pharaohs heading for the Sea of Reeds.

He (or, why not? She) knows people by their first names. Those who were chosen to be His/Her own possession (Exod. 19:2), and the others, who had the audacity to "touch the apple of His eye" (Zech. 2:8). And even *we* remember the names: Rosah and David Eichmann, and Nayef Hawatmeh—and so many others.[1]

Are we anno Auschwitz 30 in a *New Era?* That is what the theme of our colloquium suggests. Colloquium—not just stunned silence. We keep the In-Memoriams in our hearts, and dare to speak—even with our unspeakable pain. The Holy One did not die, together with His people.[2] He is alive in grand old style: the Exodus-God, Liberator, and the Eisodos-God, who brings his children home. After Auschwitz: the State of Israel—a New Era.

So,

> Sing to the Holy One a new song,
> bless His name.
> Tell of His salvation day after day. . . .

> For He comes
> He comes to judge the earth.
> He will judge the world with righteousness,
> and His people with His truth. [Ps. 96]

In case you are wondering: this is not a pious preface, a kind of *captatio benevolentiae.* That would not be the correct thing to do even in

Dr. Hoekendijk died on June 25, 1975, before his paper was prepared for publication. Some of the notes were supplied by Dr. Letty Russell Hoekendijk.

an Anglican cathedral, where all the walls around us have heard these texts, and echo the Tanakh's language. I am already *in medias res:* talking with Gregory Baum.

I have had the privilege of meeting him before. In some odd places: a small village in Switzerland, Rome, Kansas City, with New York in between. I have heard his rage expressed against the incredible arrogance of Christians and their ethnocentricity. I vividly remember him saying in a workshop for Christian ministers last year, "All the people you keep talking about—Jesus, Marx, Freud—were Jews!" I suspect that for him, as for so many others (present or absent), this Christian arrogance has been, and still is, grotesquely manifested in what we call Christian missions. And here I am, a missionary; even worse, a second-generation missionary!

If you will graciously allow me, I prefer not to go into an explicit argumentation—picking out a paragraph here or a phrase yonder, where to the best of my knowledge my partner (to use a Scottish phrase) seems to me to be "a stranger to the truth." We have had more than enough of this kind of pseudo-dialogue. I prefer to share my own perspective. I shall try to be as brief as possible and then, in a second part, attempt to be more specific.

Christian Mission in Crisis: that is nothing new. Mission and crisis have been as inseparable as Siamese twins. We are not talking about a recent phenomenon. Right from the outset, at the beginning of the common era, this crisis has been amply documented (in the New Testament, for instance). The early messengers of the good news were not "white"; they certainly had no power; in many cases they did not even know that they were "missionaries." Their ecology has been described as "persecutions (by Jews, Romans, and others) and catacombs." At the first ecumenical council (at Nicaea in 325), the large majority of the bishops present were Asians and Africans. Out of approximately three hundred participants, there were no more than four from the Latin West. At that time there were already well-established Christian communities in different parts of Asia (Arabia, India) and Africa (Egypt, Ethiopia). When we search for the first state- or folk-churches, we should not look to Germany and Britain; they can be found in Edessa, Georgia, Armenia—not white man's country.

Parallel to this expansion of the Christian faith went the Jewish efforts at group proselytism: successful in the Black Sea region (the Khazars) and probably (as the Jewish historian Marcel Simon hypothesized) among the Berbers in North Africa.[3]

Before the Christian message made any significant impact on north-western Europe, Nestorian monks in the Middle East had set out to plant churches across the Eurasian heartland, as far as China.

In case this may appear to some as anachronistic data, please remember the thousands of missionaries from the Third World who are at present involved in missionary work in other parts of the globe: non-white, not protected by imperialist powers. They share the crisis-situation of their Euramerican brothers and sisters. Perhaps this is the crisis of the cross.

What I am trying to suggest, or request, is that we not blow up our private, always partial, sentiments into global statements. Gregory Baum urges us to stay away from this kind of "ideology." So let us do just that and be skeptical of all the ecumenical tourists, who went on a trip to Latin America, Africa, and Asia, and came back as "experts." Let us rather try, however briefly, to analyze this ideological complex that contributed to the present crisis of Christian missions. It is a long and complex history, difficult to summarize in a few paragraphs.

At the outset the missionary agent understood itself as *church:* the apostolic church, doing what the apostles were called to do. The *others* were identified as "all human groupings, the whole world, all of creation," everyone outside. After the disastrous schism between the Older and Younger Brothers (80–120 A.D.), the Jews were considered to be among those outsiders.

The interaction between the two groups can be summarized as "the Gospel, or proclaiming the Gospel" (evangelization). The hoped-for response is conversion, in the twofold meaning of turning-away-from whatever people considered before to be "the ground of their being" (*epistrephein*), and a change of heart and mind (*metanoia*).

As the church became more and more hellenized, it had to use the idiom of Hellenistic civilization ("becoming to the Greeks as a Greek"). Among many other things, it adopted the Greek-Hellenistic world-view: humanity was divided into two main categories, the civilized (Greek, of course), and the sub-barbarians.[4] Some Christians did not hesitate to call Abraham and other saints in Israel "barbarians"; the Tanakh was sometimes referred to as "Barbarian Scripture."

Evangelization was now understood as getting out the good news *plus,* or as culturation/humanization. The response hoped for became conversion *plus,* understood as cultural assimilation. In the subsequent romanization of this complex—church plus culture—a new dimension was added. Christianity became an ideological component of the empire. The *others* were regarded, and treated, as enemies. "Missionary activity" was now understood as conversion plus enculturation plus subjection. Those outside were expected to surrender or die.

I suggest that:

> Church plus culture plus empire was known as Christendom.
> Non-Christians plus barbarians plus enemies were identified as pagans.
> Evangelization plus civilization plus "pacification" was regarded to be Christianization.
> Conversion plus cultural assimilation plus submission is proselytism.

This may appear to be too schematic, too bookish an analysis. In the texts we find, however, ample evidence of this horrendous ideological configuration. To quote only one instance: "When the Lord King Charles [Charlemagne] had happily reigned for four years [in Christendom] the Saxon people were still [!] savage [barbarian] and most hostile [enemy] in any way and wholly given over to heathen [gentile] practices. So he brought together a great army [of soldiers and priests] to cause this people to take upon them the mild and gentle yoke of Christ."[5] That is only one typical instance. The many medieval prayers *contra paganos* tell a similar story.

This complex ideology has been with us for at least twelve centuries (from the fifth to the eighteenth century) and, even now, is still very much alive. Of course, there have been significant breakthroughs (e.g., the thirteenth and sixteenth centuries). But only around 1700 did people begin to challenge this monstrous syndrome. The Christendom-complex was no longer a meaningful symbol to be taken for granted.

For generations people lived through a crisis of missions. The conventional landmarks were no longer trustworthy. How does one behave, authentically, in a post-Christendom era? No more coercion, subtle or not so subtle, no more propaganda (defined as "creating other persons in our own image and likeness") or proselytism (defined as "trying to make repetitions—*Wiederholungen*—of what we are ourselves").

Since the beginning of the nineteenth century a "science of missions" (missiology) has emerged as a theological discipline; it was an attempt to use the same criteria as in any other scientific investigation. Check, with intellectual integrity (critical, consistent, documented), the gossip, such as "missionaries walk in the footsteps of soldiers and businessmen" (not true for Africa in the nineteenth century); or another very popular rumor: "They are part and parcel of the Western colonialist enterprise" (in many cases the colonialists have been the most fervent saboteurs of missionary work).

I am not trying to be apologetic; but I simply wonder how people with intellectual integrity dare to speak out on Christian missions when they are so blatantly ignorant. A current expression in missiology is "humble agnosticism." I am not in a position to judge the degree of humility; but the agnosticism is so evident that one need not worry about that part.

Let me now be more explicit. To facilitate the discussion I will present six very brief statements, putting my body on the line.

1. I trust it is evident to everyone that I reject the whole Christendom ideology. It is a version of Baalism, with the Jews on the other side of the fence. They were gentilized, barbarized, and hostilized. The sordid story of the Crusades, the pogroms, the constant humiliations of our older brothers and sisters in God's covenant, is found here. It would be bad taste indeed to point to exceptions, in order to get Christians off the hook. So, first of all, *mea culpa maxima est.*

2. I am very skeptical of all the attempts made in Germany today to prove that the Hitler gang had to eliminate the Jews in order to break the backbone of the Christian Church. The Nazis were not such good theologians!

3. What Gregory Baum suggested at the end of his paper is, I think, what we are trying to do in present missiology: *diakonia and dialogue.* I admit that there are many mavericks. To change the words of Joshua of Nazareth somewhat, "these mavericks you will always have with you." But I do not dare to monopolize; they can perhaps be found also in other communities.

4. If and when our older brothers and sisters still want to communicate at all, it will not be a *colloquium salutis,*[6] a dialogue about salvation. It will rather be a *colloquium caritatis,* a colloquy of mutual respect, honoring each other's *kabod,* and, hopefully, love.

5. I should like to exegete Gregory Baum's category of utopia in terms of promise and hope. The Holy One has gracefully put "His utopia for us at our disposal."[7] This is so much better than our own dreams and fantasies.

6. Let me conclude by quoting some phrases from dialogues. I refer on purpose to German texts:

The year 1913, Rosenzweig to Rosenstock:

> ROSENZWEIG: You Christians are all right in stating that "nobody can come to the Father, except through Jesus." Tell the story. We are already with the Father.

After World War I, Walter Rathenau writing to a Christian friend:

> Do you realize why we Jews arrived on the scene of history? To call everybody to Sinai. You do not want to go when I call you? Then Karl Marx will, or if that is not heard, Spinoza will. If you are still reluctant to go, Jesus will call you.

The year 1933, Martin Buber to K.L. Schmidt:

> BUBER: There is no center [*Mitte*] in history, there is a telos [*Ziel*], *the end of the ways of our Lord.*

The common theme in these dialogues is that the Jewish partners acknowledged the missionary task of Christians to non-Jews.

Perhaps even after Auschwitz and Ma'alot we can begin something new:

> The Lord will make his face shine upon us
> and be gracious unto us,
> and give us *shalom.* [Num. 6:25 f.]

Reflections from a
Lutheran Perspective

AARNE SIIRALA

Perhaps the most shattering inner earthquake I have experienced was my becoming aware, in the 1940s, of the Jewish Holocaust in the midst of Western Christendom. At that time I had finished my theological studies, but they had not prepared me at all to cope with this shocking realization. There was in me a totally blind spot in terms of the history of Christian anti-Jewishness. Over the years, as I have studied the background of these incomprehensible events and the Holocaust itself, I have become convinced that in our generation, one decisive element in our being a community of repentance and faith will be the way in which the often suppressed facts of the history of the persecution and discrimination against the Jews are brought into Christian consciousness. Therefore I deeply appreciate the concerns of those who have arranged this Symposium. There are few forums where this issue can be discussed seriously.

The remarks that follow can hardly be called a critique of Gregory Baum's paper. I agree too thoroughly with him even to raise any fruitful questions for our discussion. I have chosen, instead, to share with you some results of my studies of the Protestant anti-Jewish tradition, some reflections I have prepared in connection with the recent publication of Martin Luther's anti-Jewish writings in the American edition of his works. In this way I hope to establish a somewhat different perspective from that of Gregory Baum, who spoke primarily as a Roman Catholic theologian.

The American publication of Luther's treatise "On the Jews and Their Lies" (1543)[1] illustrates concretely the depth of the crisis we are discussing. This event has quite specific significance because it presents for the first time to a wide English-speaking audience that aspect of Luther's thought which has played—as the editors state—"so fateful a role in the development of anti-Semitism in Western culture."

The publishers are rightly concerned that the publication of this material should not be understood as endorsing "the distorted views of

135

Jewish faith and practise or the defamation of the Jewish people which
this treatise contains."[2] The Jews have suffered immensely because of
this treatise, and because of the centuries-long tradition of Christian
teaching and preaching it embodies. From Rabbi Josel of Rosheim, the
noble advocate of his oppressed people against Luther and the other
oppressors, to modern Jewish scholars, one finds expressions of deep
disgust at Luther's treatise. Josel of Rosheim, in his petition to the
magistrates of Strassburg asking that the circulation of the treatise be
forbidden, complained that "never before has a *Gelehrter,* a scholar,
advocated such tyrannical and outrageous treatment of poor people,"
and characterized it as "a coarse and inhuman [*grob unmenschlich*]
book." Modern Jewish students of the Reformation articulate similar
reactions. "Nothing written in the Middle Ages surpassed in calumny,
hatred and violence Luther's last pamphlets on the Jews."[3] Luther is
responsible for the most bitterly anti-Jewish statement "in all Christian literature."[4] Luther remains as a definite obstacle to any dialogue
between Jews and Lutherans.[5] When the publication of this treatise in
the American edition of Luther's works was discussed in a symposium
arranged by the National Conference of Christians and Jews last
spring in Philadelphia, one Jewish scholar expressed a deep dismay
and claimed that its publication contains great risks for the Jews: it
may strengthen anti-Semitic attitudes.

   The risk is real, and the Jewish objections should be taken seriously.
It is obvious that the editor wrote the introduction with this risk in
mind. The introduction is written with a deep awareness "of the possible misuse of this material" (p. 123). It presents a careful analysis of
the historical context and background of the treatise. It shows how
fully Luther shared the medieval prejudices against the Jews. It also
shows how Luther's approach to the Jews is an integral part of his
theology:

> Wilhelm Maurer has demonstrated in fact, that Luther's earliest lec-
> tures—those on the psalms, delivered in 1513–1515—already contained in
> essence the whole burden of his later charges against the Jews. The Jews,
> Luther asserts in these lectures, suffer continually under God's wrath; they
> are paying the penalty for their rejection of Christ. [pp. 126–27]

   The introduction claims that the question at issue in large portions
of the treatise is:

> Whose interpretation of the Sacred Scriptures—that of the Jews or that
> of the Christians—is correct? For Luther, the Scriptures' proper meaning

is Christological. But this has raised for him—as it had for earlier participants in the age-old Jewish-Christian—controversy—the question of who
should be regarded as the legitimate heirs of ancient Israel: the Christian
Church, or post-biblical Judaism. Has the new covenant so entirely replaced the old that the Jews no longer have any claim to the title "people
of God"?

What is shocking in this analysis is that it continues to discuss the issue in Luther's terms, without asking whether such alternatives are
theologically tenable.

The fact that the treatise is published without going into a serious
analysis of this question may compromise the publishers' intention to
prevent a misuse of the material by the way it is edited. The introduction
and the footnoting retain, in this respect, the same kind of ambivalence
that the mainstream Lutheran theological tradition has demonstrated in
its dealing with Luther's approach to the Jews. This ambivalence expresses itself especially in the concluding remarks: "These questions
have remained under discussion between Jews and Christians down to
our day although since the unspeakable sufferings visited upon the Jews
in the twentieth century in the midst of a 'Christian civilization,' Christians are perhaps less inclined to press their claims of superiority in an
uncritical manner" (p. 132). If the "claim of superiority" is not challenged at its roots, if one only seeks a more critical attitude in presenting
the claim, the blind spots revealed by Luther's approach remain.

It is shocking that the theological claims of this treatise, which contains in a nutshell the predominant theological approach toward the
Jews in our Western Christian tradition, have raised only a random interest in modern theological discussions. Even though Luther's treatise has played a fatal role in the process that led to the Holocaust, it
has not become a central issue in the post-Auschwitz Lutheran world.
World conferences of Luther research have never touched this issue,
and it was twenty years after the Holocaust, and thirty years from the
time Hitler publicly announced in *Mein Kampf* his determination to
exterminate the Jews, before Lutherans as a world body reacted to this
issue. The Løgumkloster Consultation in 1964 raised high expectations that we Lutherans would finally begin to deal with this cancerous
element in our tradition. The report on the consultation stated: "As
Lutherans we confess our own peculiar guilt, and we lament with
shame the responsibility our church and her people bear for this sin
[anti-Semitism]." Nevertheless, the following decade saw a relapse
into the earlier ambivalence and indifference. In the light of the material analyzed here, I could hardly say, as Gregory Baum does in his

context: "The churches believe that they have been addressed by
God's Word through these events: they have placed themselves under
God's judgment."

Some glimpses at traditional Lutheran reactions to Luther's approach to the Jews may help us understand how deeply rooted in our
tradition is the resistance against facing this issue. When the treatise
"On the Jews and Their Lies" was published in the scholarly, reputa-
ble Munich edition of Luther's works in 1936, a Lutheran theologian
of stature introduced it as a work to which Luther owes his reputation
as a leading anti-Semite. It can, the editor claims, be called the arsenal
from which anti-Semitism has drawn its weapons. And then the theologian continues: "To understand Luther's argument one has to keep in
mind that Luther's heart beat for the Word of God alone. The Word of
God set the Jewish question before him." During the same period, one
of the top Luther scholars characterized Luther's approach to Jews by
saying that for Luther the Jewish question was first and last the Christ
question. Even one of the leading theologians of the Confessional
front against Nazism stated that the Jews have been punished for two
thousand years because they "brought the Christ of God to the cross."
His protest in terms of the Jews remained—to say the least—vague:
"There is no charter which would empower us to supplement God's
curse with our hatred. Even Cain receives God's mark, that no one may
kill him."

There is no radical change in this respect when one moves to post-
Holocaust Lutheran theology. Most of it around this issue is carried on
in the spirit of a Luther cult where some form of apology for Luther becomes manifest. It is true that almost all studies touching this issue—
they are not numerous—deplore Luther's harsh language and condemn
his suggestions for practical measures against the Jews; yet they continuously emphasize that Luther's basic concern was "religious," that
his deepest commitment was to be obedient to the Word of God, that
he was totally committed to the mission of the Gospel. The monstrosi-
ties of his treatise are claimed to be there because he was "a child of his
time," or by nature a fighter, or because of the ailments of his old age,
or because of his deep disappointment at his failure to convert the
Jews.

In the Lutheran postwar encyclopedias (e.g., *Evangelisches Kirchen
Lexikon* and the *Encyclopedia of the Lutheran Church*) the same basic
pattern is discernible. This material creates a very vague interest and is
dealt with in a highly apologetic way. Luther's theological argument is
not analyzed. The same is true of most Lutheran studies of church his-

tory. To mention one example: in his presentation of the road of the church through two thousand years, Hans Preuss mentions the Jews four times.[6] The Jews are present in church history first in the Old Testament figures depicted in the catacombs, then as the persecutors of Christians, e.g., the old Polycarp was a victim of a mob, inspired by the Jews (*wobei namentlich Juden hetzen*). They are mentioned again when Delitzsch is presented as an example of the deep concern Christians have shown for the lost sheep of Israel. Finally the Jews are present in the concluding statistics: fourteen millions. No mention is made of the reason why the number is not higher.

When one goes through this kind of material one begins to wonder whether—as Gregory Baum puts it—the negation of Judaism and other religions is not built into the traditional, central Christian symbols. Even the most penetrating studies of Luther's anti-Jewish writings seem to become paralyzed with the power of some fixed web of symbols. One illustration of this can be found in Wilhelm Maurer's article on the Reformation in the *Handbook of the History of Christians and Jews*,[7] which presents the best theological scholarship in the post-Holocaust Christian world. Maurer's article articulates perhaps the most penetrating analysis of this controversial material in the Lutheran theological tradition. It is not possible to do justice to its content here. From the point of view of our theme, the puzzling thing is that Maurer, after his penetrating and radical critique of Luther's approach in this treatise, states that it expresses Luther's basic theological position, and that this position is biblical and basically the same as that of the apostle Paul.[8] Without any criticism of Luther in this respect, Maurer states that for Luther the Jewish refusal to accept Jesus as the Messiah is the central point of the Holy Scriptures and also of postbiblical history. Maurer insists that Luther's argument in this treatise is based on biblical evidence, without analyzing how Luther's exegesis destroys the spirit of the texts he uses. Maurer describes how, according to Luther, the Jews are subjected to divine punishment because they have refused to accept God's *Heilsangebot*, without showing how arbitrary and disastrous such an argument is. Though Maurer radically criticizes Luther's inhuman suggestions concerning the Jews, he fails to deal with the violence in Luther's theological argument.

It has been one of the basic weaknesses of the Western theological tradition—a weakness it shares with most of Western philosophy—to ignore the connection between ideologies and violence. It is not surprising, therefore, that the Holocaust has been considered predominantly as irrational outbursts of subhuman violence. Reinhold Niebuhr claimed in his book *Faith and History* that a culture like ours, which is "rooted in historical optimism, naturally turns first of all to concepts of 'retrogression' and 'reversion' to explain its present experience. Thus Nazism is interpreted as a 'reversion to barbarism,' or even as a 'reversion to the cruelty of the Middle Ages'."

This kind of consciousness, which refuses to connect the "ideal" and the "monstrous" with each other, makes it difficult to admit that the brilliant accomplishments of our culture and its long history of incredible violence are integrally related. The American political scientists Stillmann and Pfaff, claim, in their analysis of the sources of twentieth-century conflict,[9] that the ideological and technological achievements of our culture and the manifestations of excessive violence in its history are two sides of one coin; the best and the worst in a cultural tradition are inseparable.

The basic patterns of thought in our Western tradition have escaped reevaluation, despite the violence which the predominant ideologies have been used to rationalize. Western consciousness seems to have resisted facing the basic ambiguities of human existence. In his book *God Within*,[10] Rene Dubos gives a penetrating analysis of the ecological crisis of our Western world, and refers to the "distressing fact, that the Faustus legend is the only important one created by Western civilization." He says it symbolizes our restlessness and eagerness to achieve mastery over men and the external world, irrespective of long-range consequences. Stillmann and Pfaff also characterize the basic trend in the Western ideological tradition as a Faustian one.

This anthropological and ecological arrogance, which is impatient with all limits, is related to the tendency of the Western mind to think in terms of dichotomies, of splits, of mutually exclusive opposites: God and devil, life and death, health and illness, eternity and time, mind and body, etc. Man, then, sees himself surrounded by enemies he has to kill before they catch him. Deviants, illnesses, and death are considered as hostile aggressors from outside, as enemies that must be conquered.

The Faustian trend has had a double outcome. On the one hand, it has made possible the technological achievements of our Western world. On the other, it has lead to the Holocaust and to the ecological crisis. It has created systems of thought and action that have enabled modern Western societies to function—yet it has led to a persecution of deviants, to an exploitation of other societies, to concentration camps, ghettos, the Holocaust, and to the mass production of instruments of killing. When Adolf Eichmann was on trial in Jerusalem for his participation in the Holocaust, he summarized his defense by saying: *Ich war ein Idealist*—I was an idealist. This incident illustrates the deep ambiguities of the Faustian spirit.

This Faustian approach has reached cosmic dimensions in connection with a triumphalistic Messianism. Our Western tradition seems to have been, in a quite specific way, haunted with self-styled Messiahs who have promised to save mankind from its enemies. Innumerable movements with Messianic pretensions and delusions have promised to create a totally new world. The universal Messianic complex in human beings—the expectation that some "one" saves the world, the individual, and the collective, from itself and from its external enemies—has played an exceptionally strong role in our Western history. Messianic pretensions and delusions have tended to replace the Messianic hope.

After the Holocaust, the impact of an ideological Messianism in the history of Christian thought and action can no longer be ignored. Gregory Baum states rightly, in his "Jews, Faith and Ideology,"[11] that we Christians must ask seriously,

> how it was possible, that the Christian Church professing love as the highest value, could generate a profound bias against certain people, embody this conception in its teaching and promote unjust social practices. . . . The discovery of the anti-Jewish trends in Christian preaching has profound consequences for the Church's own self-understanding. We have come to realize . . . that the Christian Church is subject to ideology. Ideology, in the sense in which the term is used in the sociology of knowledge, refers to a set of teachings or symbols unconsciously generated by a society to protect itself against others, legitimate its power, and defend its privileges.

Studies of the socio-psycho-dynamics of the Western tradition in the conscious-unconscious dimension have created an awareness of the power of what could be called ideological blocks. Robert Bellah, in his book *Beyond Belief*,[12] describes this phenomenon in the following way: "Men are not oppressed by armies and unfair economic systems alone. They are also oppressed by dead ideologies which can be locked into personalities and societies and program them on a course of fatal disaster, often in the name of 'realism' and 'necessity.'" One such ideological block, which has created fatal blind spots in the development of the Western consciousness, is the combination of Faustian ideology and the Christian confession that Jesus is the Messiah. Christian symbolism has been often used to support a Faustian ideology. Gregory

Baum refers to this when he says that "the churches have been made to see how closely their missions have been associated with the extension of Western power and Western culture." Christian churches and theologies have often used biblical symbolism to rationalize Faustian crusades. The most violent examples are the Inquisition and the persecution of the Jews. The Holocaust in the midst of Christendom proclaims in harsh language the power of triumphalistic Messianism in our Western Christian heritage.

The triumphalistic Messianic characteristics of this ideological block become manifest in Luther's treatise. The crucial point in his theological argument is that the Old Testament prophesies, the New Testament reveals, the subsequent history confirms that Jesus is the Messiah. Luther claims the Jews are "forced to confess that the Messiah has come, and that he is our Jesus" (p. 139). The "fact" that the Jews have refused to accept God's Messiah is the turning point of all human history. The whole Bible and postbiblical history bear witness to this "fact." In this treatise Luther's rich and dynamic Christology has become a rigid ideological block. His treatise raises the question whether the traditional theological arguments against the Jews do not reveal an utterly destructive trend of ideological Messianism in our Christian tradition. Luther's argument here seems to follow a pattern that could be characterized as an idolatry of Jesus. It is not too different from the patterns of a cult of a hero-deliverer.

Luther claims again and again that the crucial difference between Christians and Jews is that we Christians confess Jesus to be the Messiah and the Jews are "asking God for the Messiah" (p. 176). "We do have the true Messiah, who surely came and appeared at the time Herod took away the scepter of Judah . . ." (p. 206). The Jews resist this because "their breath stinks with lust for the Gentiles' gold and silver . . . so they comfort themselves that when the Messiah comes he will take the gold and silver of the whole world and divide it among them" (p. 211). The Jews cannot endure to hear or see that the "Goyim should glory in the Messiah" (p. 217). The Jews and the Gentiles represent the "two seeds, the serpent's and the woman's. It [the Scripture] says that these are enemies and that God and the devil are at variance with each other." This enmity reaches its peak in the crucifixion of the Messiah (p. 226).

The idolatrous Messianism in Luther's approach becomes most clearly visible in the conclusion of his treatise. There Luther repudiates the claim that Jews cannot be judged by their attitude toward Jesus because so many Jews are not familiar with the New Testament and hardly know anything of Jesus. Luther argues that it is not a question of what you know or what you wish to know, but what you are obliged to know. "As it happens, not only the Jew but all the world is obliged to know that the New Testament is God the Father's book about his son Jesus Christ. Whoever does not accept and honor that book does not accept and honor the Father himself" (p. 281).

The cold logic of Luther's ideological Messianism is expressed most bluntly in the paraphrasing of a New Testament parable he presents as the final evidence of his argument:

> It is as if a king were to instate his only son in his place and command the country to regard him as their sovereign (although he would be entitled to this by right of natural inheritance), and the country as a whole readily accepted him. A few, however, band together in opposition, alleging that they know nothing about this, despite the fact that the king had in confirmation of his will issued a seal and letters and other testimony; they still insist that they do not want to know or respect it. The king would be obliged to take these people by the nape of the neck and throw them into dungeon and entrust them to Master Hans, who would teach them to say: We are willing to learn it.
>
> This is what God, too, has done. He established his Son Jesus Christ in Jerusalem in his place and commanded that he be paid homage, according to Psalm 2(11): "Serve the Son, lest he be angry, and you perish in the way." Some of the Jews would not hear this. God bore witness by the various tongues of the apostles and by all sorts of miraculous signs. However, they did then what they still do now—they were obstinate, and absolutely refused to give ear to it. Then came Master Hans—the Romans—who destroyed Jerusalem, took the villains by the nape of the neck and cast them into the dungeon of exile which they still inhabit and in which they will remain forever, or until they say, "We are willing to learn it."
>
> God surely did not do this secretly or in some corner, so that the Jews would have an excuse for disregarding the New Testament without sin. . . . He gave a reliable sign through the patriarch Jacob . . . that they could confidently expect the Messiah. . . . He also informed them through Isaiah that when they would hear a voice in the wilderness . . . then they should be certain that the Messiah had come. . . . Shortly thereafter the Messiah himself appeared on the scene. . . . If such signs did not move the Jews of that time, what can we expect of these degenerate Jews . . . ?

The material from Luther's treatise has been presented here in such length and detail to demonstrate what was said earlier about ideological blocks. Theologians seem to underestimate the influence of an ideological use of religious symbolism in our tradition. The cheaply rationalistic use of central biblical symbolism in Luther's treatise, and in most of traditional Christian teaching about the Jews, is absurd from both the historical and logical points of view. Nevertheless, it has been accepted by most churches for centuries as an expression of a biblical and Christian understanding of Jewish existence and faith. The history of Christian messianistic anti-Jewish ideologies seems to confirm Bellah's claim that ideologies can be locked into personalities and societies and program them on a course of disaster. Gregory Baum makes the same claim when he states that "the traditional negation of Jewish existence . . . is a sign of how little the great number of Christians have become aware of the sociopolitical implications of their piety," and when he speaks of the power of religious symbols institutionalized in language, custom, and law as being so massive that "personal virtue cannot overcome it."

However, biblical symbolism has also been one of the main channels to the liberating and healing resources latent in the transpersonal web of the human unconscious. In numerous ways, the biblical symbols and myths have sparked liberation from the prison of ideological blocks, from individual and collective self-deception. In the contexts of both the Jewish and the Christian traditions, the biblical archetypes and symbols express the power of the mythopoetic core of human life—to use Paul Riceour's phrase—defending man against the power of ideological blocks.

This defense is what I understand Gregory Baum to be doing in his paper. He develops what he calls a "utopian" understanding of the central Christian symbolism over against an "ideological" one. In the light of the material I have analyzed here, this approach seems methodologically promising and fruitful. There is, however, one element in the symbolism he uses that I wish to discuss further, again in the light of Luther's approach, but this time using the "utopian," nonideological trends of his approach. The element I have in mind is Baum's use of the church as a symbol. He rightly emphasizes the need for a reinterpretation of ecclesiology, but his way of doing it raises for me the question whether he does not remain too church-centered in his approach. He asks whether the acceptance of religious pluralism as a sign of God's manifold and inexhaustible richness leads to the "relativism of truth." "Are we unfaithful to the biblical teaching that the church is God's chosen community called from the darkness of the world into the light of God's kingdom?"

Even if Baum develops his reinterpretation of ecclesiology in terms of the church being a partner in the manifold divine humanization of life, he seems to give to the symbol "church" such a central place in Christian symbolism that it seems to lead to inner contradictions. I find it difficult to reconcile "ecclesiology" and "humanization" in his approach. If we Protestants tend to make the Bible into such a central symbol that it gives us an artificial identity over against others, and helps us to escape facing the reality of religious pluralism in our tradition, the Roman Catholic tradition seems to be doing the same with the symbol "church."

In my opinion church symbolism, when it occupies the center in the web of Christian symbols, has an inevitable tendency to create Messianic pretensions and delusions. I experienced this concretely at the Løgumkloster Consultation in 1964, where for the first time after the Holocaust Lutherans seriously discussed their responsibility. Its general theme was "The Church and the Jews." One would have expected that in that situation the pathologies and ambiguities of concrete church communities would become the focus of attention. Yet again and again the discussion steered away from coming to grips with the ideological violence in Lutheran churches and teachings. Instead it remained on the level of explaining the biblical view of the church and its bearing upon the relation between the Christian church and Judaism. Rabbi Gilbert—the only Jewish participant at the Consultation— repeatedly expressed his bewilderment over the way we Christian theologians speak about the church: in speaking about the Jews we speak about people, but in referring to Christians we use the term "church." We admit that individual Christians may have strayed into acts of violence, but in the same breath we declare that the church has always promoted love and righteousness and opposed all persecution. Jews are considered to be people who have taken the position of opposing divine election and revelation, while Christians are the church which represents the divine revelation. The Jewish people are confronted not by Christian people, but by the church. The message of violence in the common history of Jews and Christians is blocked from consciousness with discussion of the principles of the church in dealing with the Jewish question.[13]

When Luther criticized the ecclesiastical, church-centered theology of his tradition, he characterized it as a *theologia gloriae,* a theology of glory in which the church speaks of reality as if it could examine it from a divine point of view. It is this kind of ideological theology he articulates in the name of the Bible over against the Jews. In his struggle with the ideological blocks of his Church tradition, he tries to develop what he calls *theologia crucis,* a theology of the cross. Luther de-

scribes man's basic condition as crucifixion. With its tendency to ab-
solutize its knowledge of good and evil, humankind is crucifying itself. The cruciform shape of human existence is demonstrated in the
crucified Jesus. Intersecting each other in him are the knowledge of
good and evil, which suppresses life, and the grace which brings forth
new life out of death, sin, law, and wrath. Every person experiences
this cross in his own being. Luther stresses in his *theologia crucis* that
the divine will is encountered as the cross which breaks the hold of the
blocks and powers that suppress the growth of life. Divine humanness
breaks forth to expose the pretensions of human godliness, which as-
pires to be the judge and determiner of life. The theology of the cross is
an exercise in thinking according to the rhythm of crucifixion and resurrection, the death of the old and the springing forth of the new.
Therefore, in such contexts he does not view the church as a tradition
spreading gradually through mankind, a legacy to be preserved for
posterity. He views it as the new humanity that is to come, the promised land toward which mankind, liberated from bondage, is traveling.
Christianity is not, then, conceived primarily as the church, a community, born out of the influence of Jesus and his apostles gradually
extending over the whole earth. Luther prefers to use such expressions
as Christian folk or Christendom. He speaks of it as a net enclosing all
generations and all mankind from one end of the earth to the other, an
interlacing of human life which heralds the appearance of true humanity.[14]

In his theology of the cross, Luther is deeply aware of what Gregory
Baum characterizes as an ambiguity of all religious experience. "Our
good is hidden, and so profoundly that it is hidden under its opposite.
Thus our life is under death, love of ourselves under the hate of ourselves, glory under ignominy, salvation under perdition, justice under
sin, strength under infirmity, and universally every one of our affirmations under its negation."[15] Luther characterizes man as *simul iustus et
peccator,* as a being who is simultaneously just and sinner. There is at
work in the ambiguous human nature an unambiguous divine spirit, a
divine summons and word, which creates a constant tumult and meta-
morphosis in a world that is constantly under the threat of dehumanization. When Luther insisted that the church of his tradition had not
only neglected but actually opposed the Word of God, his basic intention was to articulate that the Scriptures proclaim the presence of the
divine Word in the midst of man's ambiguous experience. Luther uses
then the symbol "the Word of God" to designate the soil and atmosphere in which life grows, where the ambiguities of human existence

are broken and humanization takes place. All human life is bound together by the divine Word, which molds the experiences of the ages into the history of mankind and structures men into one humanity. God himself speaks and hears in man, *qui in nobis loquitur et audiat.* Men are to each other the means of divine grace, servants and ministers of the word of unambiguous life in the midst of its ambiguities. "If you wish to know, see, and reach for God, then see and attend to your-selves. For you are God's work and his work is in you, mutually through you in you."[16]

When Luther accuses his church of exercising tyranny over human life and claims that it violates the nature of man, he does not refer merely to some specific abuses in its life. He challenges the whole Church-centered approach. He charges that the main thrust of its work and teaching breaks down the basic unities of life, and severs the ties of mutual basic respect and trust, which bind men together, when it claims to be the embodiment of divine love and truth. If any structure, ecclesiastical or secular, sets itself up as the channel and mediator of divine authority, it is opposing the Word of God, which uses every per-son as its minister. Luther accuses both the spiritual and secular au-thorities of his time of destroying the fundamental web of life. He calls both to become guardians of the basic unities of life, in family and so-ciety. He claims that people encounter in the basic "life-communities" (*Gemeine, Gemeinschaft*) the spirit and power of the giver of life. *Gott stehet in der Gemeine*—God stands in the basic unities of life. Luther sees the divine will and revelation confronting man as communion, not as abstract laws and ideas. The divine spirit creates a web of human re-lationships where the dehumanizing blocks are continuously broken.[17]

The Word of God is the mother both of the Scriptures and of the churches. They both ought to point toward the basic texture of life, to-ward the divine Word which creates true humanness, toward the one church of God. Neither the Holy Scriptures nor the churches should be considered as specific realms of experience representing the divine. In his critique of Erasmus' church- and Bible-centered approach, Luther says:

> And who has given you the power or committed to you the right to bind Christian doctrine to places, persons, times, and causes, when Christ wishes it to be proclaimed and to reign most freely throughout the world? The word of God is not bound, says Paul, and is Erasmus now to bind it? Nor did God give us the word that it should be had with respect to places, persons, or times. As Christ says, "Go into all the world," not go into this

place and not into that. To bind the word of God and to stand in the way of the life of men.[18]

Faith means to Luther above all that basic human situation in which a person, such as she or he is, is addressed by the word of life. To live as a human being is to live by faith. Becoming a human being takes place in a situation in which an individual, so to speak, gives birth to her or his own humanness. This basic situation summons us to grow into a person; *fides facit personam,* faith makes a person. To become human is a matter of divine creation. Humanness is not born automatically, but is the result of divine creative activity: *creatures procedunt ex deo libere et voluntarie et non naturaliter*—creatures come forth from God freely and voluntarily, not naturally.[19]

To summarize:

The utopian elements in Luther's ideological theology express a Messianic hope that is in deep conflict with the Messianic pretensions and delusions of his anti-Jewish writings. The material analyzed here confirms basically what Gregory Baum presented in his paper. It raises, however, a caution against the use of the symbol "church," spelled with capital C, and calls for an awareness of, and respect for, the whole body of mankind as a temple of the divine spirit. As Baum puts it, Christian communities and movements should realize that within themselves "religious pluralism is not to be grudgingly acknowledged, but welcomed with gratitude."

PART IV
Judaism and Christian Education

Introduction

Given the strongly negative view of Judaism in Christian theology, it is somewhat surprising that these attitudes were never nailed down in dogmatic definitions or treatises. The positive aspect of this puzzling phenomenon is that there are no dogmatic roadblocks to impede new theological developments. We must not lose sight of the fact, however, that the mere absence of ecclesiastical formulations and documents does not guarantee right teaching. In the shaping of a religious mentality and outlook, it is teaching, preaching from the pulpit, and the liturgy itself that play the strongest formative role. The persistent anti-Judaism among the great majority of Christians through the centuries is in large measure due to traditional Christian teaching and preaching.

In the main paper of this section, The Catholic theologian *John Pawlikowski* examines the two areas of teaching and liturgy with respect to the image of Judaism they have traditionally conveyed. What are the deep roots of the Teaching of Contempt? Is it at last a thing of the past? If so, what has taken its place in the way of giving the Christian people a positive image of Judaism?

The phrase "Teaching of Contempt" refers to an age-old phenomenon in Christian history, the basic elements of which were developed already by the second century. Pawlikowski sums them up under three main headings: (1) The dispersion of the Jews since the late first Christian century was regarded as divine punishment for the crucifixion. (2) Judaism at the time of Christ was said to have been in a state of spiritual degeneracy. (3) The Jews were held responsible for having killed God.

Through a careful examination of both Protestant and Catholic textbooks that were in use as late as the 1950s, Pawlikowski concludes that both traditions share a common tragic patrimony of having distorted Judaism. The Teaching of Contempt appears repeatedly in the themes of Jewish homelessness as a divine curse, collective Jewish guilt for the crucifixion, and the stereotype of the Pharisees as hypocrites.

In addition to these strongly negative elements, the textbook study reveals important omissions. Judaism is equated with biblical Judaism; its riches are stressed, but primarily insofar as they have passed over into Christianity. Could this be due, Pawlikowski asks, to the "fulfillment" theology of Christianity? Like Ruether and Baum, he does not believe that a view of history that perceives the Messianic promises as having been fulfilled once and for all in the coming of Christ can give anything but tolerance at best, and condemnation at worst, to Judaism, which rejects this fulfillment.

Since the late fifties and early sixties, the textbook scene has considerably improved. The main elements of the Teaching of Contempt have largely been eliminated. Some striking omissions are, however, apparent: the Holocaust, Zionism, and the State of Israel are simply passed over in silence. Since these are central factors in shaping the consciousness of Jews today, Pawlikowski concludes that Christians still do not take into account Jewish self-understanding.

The central problem for Christian teaching as he perceives it is: How can we teach Jesus' message and the New Covenant without at least implicitly degrading the First Covenant? Is this possible as long as Christianity adheres to its traditionally absolutist stance and claims to be and have the full and definitive revelation? Is redemption, he asks, a fait accompli that happened in the coming of Christ, and has given Christians a prerogative on the total and complete truth ever since?

When we come to Christian liturgy the problems are compounded. For the inherent difficulties presented by many New Testament texts (e.g., the repeated use of "the Jews" in John's Gospel) are heightened when placed within the solemn liturgical context, which is perceived as a sacred event not to be tampered with. Holy Week presents a special problem, because of the great drama of the Holy Week liturgy and the centrality it occupies in Christianity. There is no easy solution.

If we succeed in achieving a genuine dialogue between Christian and Jew, the results will go far beyond this dialogue itself. We live in a time when our individual religious and cultural ghettos are breaking down, forcing upon us a reexamination of our traditional values. Christian-Jewish dialogue can become a powerful catalyst in broadening our consciousness of other religious viewpoints, in a world where religious pluralism is rapidly becoming the norm.

Claire Huchet-Bishop is in basic agreement with Pawlikowski's assessment of the religious-education and liturgical scenes. As a long-time coworker of Jules Isaac and the editor of his works, she is intimately acquainted not only with the situation in the United States, but with that pertaining in France, Italy, and Spain. Basically, her findings are the same: a distorted picture of Judaism, especially the Pharisees; and silence with regard to the Holocaust and the State of Israel. We tend to want for forget that which embarrasses us. Moreover, both Auschwitz and the State of Israel force the church to rethink its theology about Judaism.

While Mrs. Bishop concedes some progress, she warns against equating a more enlightened understanding of Judaism on the part of a small elite with that of the masses. Anti-Semitism is protean by its very nature, reappearing now here, now there, always in new disguises.

Mrs. Bishop is in agreement with Pawlikowski, also, as to the reason why postbiblical Judaism is still, by and large, ignored. She, too, sees this as symptomatic of fulfillment theology. If, with Christ's coming, Israel no longer plays a role in redemptive history (or only a negative role at best), Judaism ceases to exist as a viable faith, and becomes a puzzling anomaly in the Christian perspective.

Despite a generally pessimistic view, Mrs. Bishop sees signs of hope for a better relation between Judaism and Christianity. One such sign is the Statement on Judaism issued by the French bishops in April 1973, in which the unique and enduring vocation of the Jewish people is strongly affirmed. Reeducation is possible—did it not take centuries, after all, for the Teaching of Contempt to be inculcated? Given today's mass media, the trend can be reversed—provided only that the church seriously wishes it. Nothing less than consistent desire and effort will be able to remove the stain which the church incurred by remaining silent during the Holocaust. Because it did so it has indeed justly been said that "Christianity died at Auschwitz." And not only Christianity, but the most cherished spiritual and moral values of the West, so that it, too, can be said to have died there. Had the church spoken out it would, in all probability, have been persecuted, but it would have lived up to its prophetic role and upheld the spiritual heritage of the West.

It is not too late yet. The attitude toward the Jews is, as it were, the litmus test whereby the health of any human group, culture, or church can be gauged. If Christians face up to Auschwitz and its myriad masks, they may find the energy and will to help usher in a new dawn of reconciliation.

The second respondent, *Thomas Hopko,* speaks for Orthodox Christianity. In some respects his statement stands in marked contrast both to Pawlikowski and Claire Huchet-Bishop. While agreeing with their description and condemnation of a centuries-old anti-Judaism, Hopko is more optimistic concerning the teaching materials currently used in Orthodox Christianity. He finds them free from invective and sensitive to Judaism, especially to the Jewish origins of the church. Hopko considers anti-Semitism the result of social, political, and economic factors, rather than of the church's religious teaching.

Hopko's main disagreement with Pawlikowski, and obviously a very painful one to him, comes at another level: that of Christology. To him the concept of Christ as the fulfillment of all of God's promises is at the very heart of the Christian faith, and its abandonment or modification would destroy the latter. The solution lies not in the redefinition or reinterpretation of traditional Christology, but rather in its full acceptance, and living out, without the disastrous accompanying phenomena of prejudice and anti-Semitism.

The belief that the Christian fulfillment claim will, of its very nature, lead to contempt of non-Christians raises for Hopko the question whether there can be any universal religious or philosophical view of man and the world which does not, by its very nature, foster contempt for others. This would deprive us of our right to hold universally valid views, and leads to a dangerous relativism which makes serious religious dialogue meaningless. Such relativism claims for itself a universality which in turn breeds contempt for those who reject it.

Hopko advocates a standing by, and for, our deep religious convictions. Let us discover what unites us and admit our differences and divisions in openness, seeking to explain, listen, and understand. He believes that we are indeed entering upon a new era, an era when intolerance and persecution are—or can be—a thing of the past, and when meaningful debate about the ultimate purpose of life and the universe has become possible as never before.

The concerns voiced by Thomas Hopko point up, as nothing else in the Symposium has done thus far, several crucial points of difference among Christian theologians today: Must Christians maintain the traditional claim of Christianity to be the possessor, in Christ, of all truth, the total fulfillment of God's promises? Are there aspects of Christian belief which, by their very formulation, lend themselves to misinterpretation, feelings of superiority over others, and acts of injustice? Or will the Christian message, if only it is properly taught and understood, indeed lead to a better world? While debate over such questions may be dismissed by some Jews as "intramural quarreling," its repercussions are bound to have important consequences for Christian-Jewish dialogue.

The Teaching of Contempt: Judaism in Christian Education and Liturgy

Introduction

The title of this presentation, this paper itself, is a personal tribute to a man who has made a great difference in the Christian community's understanding of the anti-Judaism inherent in its theological traditions, its catechetics, its biblical interpretation, and its liturgy. That man is Jules Isaac. It may be said that no one person was more influential in preparing the way for the Declaration on the Church and the Jewish People adopted at the Second Vatican Council. And it was through a reading of Isaac's *The Teaching of Contempt: Christian Roots of Anti-Semitism*[1] while in the seminary that I first became alerted to the very serious distortion of Judaism central to Christian theology. In short, I probably would not be making this presentation today if it were not for Jules Isaac.

The seeds planted by Professor Isaac have borne considerable fruit in both the Protestant and Catholic communities. (I cannot speak with great authority about the Orthodox Christian community. I trust that Thomas Hopko's critique will fill in the picture with respect to his segment of Christianity.) Since my work has been largely in the area of prejudice in Catholic catechetics, I will focus primarily on my own tradition in the remarks that follow. But my contact with the Protestant denominations, and my reading of such works as Bernhard E. Olson's *Faith and Prejudice*,[2] which records the results of the Yale University study on prejudice in Protestant curricular materials, as well as Gerald Strober's recent update of the Olson research entitled *Portrait of the Elder Brother*,[3] leads me to the conviction that Catholicism shares a tragic common patrimony with the Protestant churches in its distortions of Judaism, and that the changes I propose for my own tradition are generally applicable to Christianity across the board.

155

Limiting myself still further, my analysis will concentrate only on the American Catholic scene. But both Jules Isaac's work and Catholic textbook studies on the image of the Jews conducted in other parts of the world bear great resemblance in their conclusions to those obtained in this country. A 1969 study on religion textbooks used in the world's French-speaking areas (France, Belgium, Switzerland, and Canada) under the direction of Canon François Houtart at Louvain University's Center for Socio-Religious Research, in cooperation with the University's Center for Catechetical Studies, found a basically pejorative image of Jews and Judaism in the examined materials. "The heart of the problem of the presentation of Jews in catechetical teaching," the study concluded, is that "Jews still remain as typical examples of nonbelievers of bad faith. They are examples not to be followed, serving as a foil contrasting with a Christian attitude."[4]

Judaism and Christian Education

Jules Isaac zeroes in on three main themes in *The Teaching of Contempt* (amplified more fully in his other major volume on the subject, *Jesus and Israel*):[5] (1) the dispersion of the Jews, seen by Christian writers as a providential punishment for the crucifixion; (2) the Christian portrait of Judaism as degenerate at the time of Jesus; and (3) the deicide charge. The concrete presence in Catholic education of the three themes brought out in Isaac's writings is attested to by the results obtained in the classic St. Louis University studies on prejudice, which I recently published with an interpretation and contemporary evaluation in my volume *Catechetics and Prejudice.*[6]

Inaugurated in the late fifties and continuing into the early sixties, the St. Louis University project, sponsored by the Institute of Human Relations of the American Jewish Committee as part of a tri-faith textbook self-study (Catholic, Protestant, Jewish), was coordinated by the university's sociology department. The research was done by a three-member research team consisting of Sisters Linus Gleason, Rita Mudd, and Rose Thering, who conducted a detailed analysis of all the major textbooks used in Catholic educational programs in the fields of literature, social studies, and religion. Overall direction of the project was in the hands of Fr. Trafford P. Maher, S.J., of the university's sociology department. The researchers utilized the most advanced instruments and techniques for attitudinal surveys available at the time. It is interesting to note that the study of religion textbooks came last. This was deliberate. The project directors were afraid at the time that criticism of religion texts, which in Sister Thering's words have achieved a kind of "sanctity by association," might outrage many Catholics. Hence the decision was made to concentrate first on the literature and social studies units. That such fears sound strange to us in 1974 is a clear indication of how much Vatican II has done to open up the Catholic mind, and how far we have advanced through the courageous work of such people as Sisters Mudd, Gleason, and Thering.

The St. Louis textbook studies did not examine only the picture of Jewish groups in Catholic materials, but of all "outgroups," including Native Americans, Blacks, Spanish-speaking, Orientals, etc. While the results attained for all the groups forced Catholics to revise their textbooks, the findings with regard to Jews were especially enlightening.

There is very little to report from the literature study with respect to the image of the Jews. Sister Gleason did not designate the Jewish group as a separate category. But the vast majority of visibility scores for the non-Christian group in the four sets of textbooks that were examined stood below 3 percent. Hence it is evident that students had little or no exposure to characters clearly identifiable as Jews. Whether this is due to the textbook compilers or simply reflects the literary scene from which the compilers had to select material is open to question. What is not open to question, however, is the discouraging nature of the results.

The social studies findings revealed only a minimal presence of materials dealing with Judaism. Jewish exposure ranked lowest among the seven ethnic-racial groups. What materials were used generally provided a favorable presentation of Judaism. Yet scores for the Jewish group stood considerably below those achieved by the racial-ethnic groups. In addition, most references to Judaism in the social studies units pertained primarily to Jews of the biblical period. This represents another manifestation of a clear tendency in Catholicism: to focus almost exclusively on biblical forms of Judaism. Even if such presentations are largely positive in tone, they leave the impression that there is not much worthwhile about present forms of Judaism. Yet the Jews with whom Catholics must live in harmony today are not the Jews of ancient times. Could this phenomenon be due, at least in part, to the "fulfillment" theology of Christianity? I personally suspect it is, but I have no concrete means of proving this hypothesis.

Also of significance in the results of the social studies analysis is the total exclusion of any material on the development of Zionism and the modern State of Israel, which have become so central to Jewish existence today even in the Diaspora. This omission is probably due, in great part, to the excessive preoccupation in this country with American and Western European history. It severely cripples the ability of Catholic students to relate to their Jewish brothers and sisters in a meaningful way, since Israel has become so pivotal to the self-identity of the American Jew.

The religion texts reversed the trend with regard to the appearance of Jews in the content of the units under examination. For in all of the textbook series, without exception, the Jewish group predominated in visibility among outgroups. This is not a totally unexpected finding, since it is virtually impossible to treat Christianity without significant reference to the Jews.

The majority of the positive textual references to Jews deal with the Jewish heritage of Christianity. A disturbing implication, however, is sometimes evident even in the seemingly positive passages. While stressing, on the one hand, the spiritual and cultural wealth of Judaism and its rich contribution to early Christianity, the inference is that its riches were absorbed by Christianity (and hence modern Judaism is shallow when compared to Christianity), and the textbooks' praise is reserved chiefly for those Jews who found it in their hearts to accept the teachings of Jesus.

The overwhelming majority of negative references concerning Jews focused around the following themes: (1) the Jewish rejection of Christianity and the consequent divine curse inflicted on the people; (2) the Jewish role in the crucifixion; and (3) comments regarding the Pharisees. In their treatment of the death of Jesus, the textbook authors often made reference to the responsibility that all men and women, including Christians, shared for this act. Nonetheless, this universalistic outlook seldom appeared in considerations of the specific events which led up to the crucifixion. Thus, even though the Catholic student may be told that the "sins of all men" were responsible for Christ's sufferings, this theological principle will remain an abstract notion unless it is meaningfully applied to the description of specific historical events. In representative excerpts from the religion materials we find the accusation of unique and collective Jewish culpability for the sufferings and death of Christ, rather than the incorporation of a more universalistic notion of responsibility. Such accusations become even more serious when the term "the Jews" is used to denote the enemies of Jesus, without the corrective information that a limited number of individuals, and not the entire Jewish population of Palestine, is in question.

The third negative theme in the materials concerned with Judaism is in many ways the worst of all. Passages referring to the Pharisees were among the most vile encountered in the textbooks. One basic series depicted the Pharisees in such a distorted fashion that the student would find it virtually impossible to sense any human identification with them, or to believe that they acted out of human motivation.

It is necessary at this point to stress that the textbook series that provided the data for the St. Louis studies are no longer in general use. Improvement has generally taken place. In fact, Sister Rose Thering, who worked on the religion study during the days of the council, already noticed an improvement in the textbooks which were appearing at that time. Most Catholic textbook publishers now have members of the Jewish community read through manuscripts prior to publication. Rabbi Edward Zerin, for example, served in such a capacity for some five years, and recorded his impressions in an article in the *CCAR Journal..*[7] He discovered much unevenness among Catholic ecumenical endeavors in this regard: some represent positive, creative efforts, which in his opinion should be welcomed and "both complimented and complemented." He cites as an example the following statement, which now forms part of a chapter on pluralism in the *Live in Christ* series (vol. I):

> But you must realize that being Catholic does not necessarily make you better than anyone else . . . There are many Protestants, Jewish persons and non-believers who are more faithful to their consciences than some Catholics are to theirs . . . We must beware of a Catholic superiority complex, not only as private individuals, but as a group . . . While we believe our *doctrines* are true, we must admit that our *customs* may not always be the best way to express our doctrines. [pp. 97–98] So we live today in what is called a *pluralistic* society, that is, one which is based on many ("plural") beliefs, rather than just one way of thinking. [p.95]

Nonetheless, according to Rabbi Zerin, other texts prepared by Catholic authors but not published "still exhibit the hand of the medieval artisan." He offers the following example:

> We differ in this: We Catholics believe that "a partial blindness only has befallen Israel" (Rom. 11:25). We believe that, because most Jews do not accept Jesus as the Messiah, we who are wild alive branches have been grafted into the cultivated tree of God's choice. We believe that, because they do not believe in Jesus as the Messiah, the Jewish people are temporarily cut off from the tree to which they belong by a right prior to ours.

The process of textbook analysis by Catholics as a means of rooting out vestiges of prejudicial teaching did not end with the St. Louis effort. The Archdiocese of Atlanta, for example, commissioned such an investigation in 1969.[8] A joint Catholic-Jewish study team there discovered considerable improvement in post–Vatican II textbooks in comparison to preconciliar materials. But even in these improved texts some anti-Jewish passages were still found.

The last major survey of Catholic education relative to its portrayal of Judaism and the Jewish people was undertaken jointly by the staffs of the national office of the American Jewish Committee and the Institute of Judaeo-Christian Studies, for presentation to the participants in the Convocation marking the fifth anniversary of the conciliar statement on the Jews, held at Seton Hall University in October 1970.[9] For the Catholic portion of this study, surveys were sent to a representative nationwide sampling of four key groups: Catholic seminaries (100 with 31 replies), Catholic colleges and universities (227 with 149 replies), Catholic high schools (500 with 170 replies), and offices of superintendents of diocesan schools (152 with 46 replies). The conclusions from the survey ran as follows: Very few of the Catholic institutions (zero percent of the seminaries) have departments of Jewish studies. Nearly half of the institutions provide separate courses in Judaism. Roughly 70 percent of the responding colleges indicated they have Scripture and/or theology offerings which specifically deal with the relationship of Christianity to Judaism. About 15 percent of these colleges also list courses covering the intertestamental period, while close to 50 percent of the Catholic seminaries handle this subject. Of the Catholic high schools, 55.3 percent teach the rabbinic background of the New Testament in religion classes.

On the question of the Nazi Holocaust and the history and theological significance of Israel, the figures drop markedly. The responses to the question as to whether the Holocaust was dealt with ranged as follows: Catholic colleges = 1.3 percent; Catholic high schools = 23.2 percent in religion courses, 13.6 percent in church history courses; Catholic seminaries = 6.8 percent. Regarding the question of courses on the history of Israel, 10.3 percent of the Catholic seminaries, 5.4 percent of the Catholic colleges, and 19.6 percent of the Catholic high schools said yes. Courses dealing with the theological significance of the State of Israel were presented in 1.3 percent of the Catholic colleges, 10.3 percent of the seminaries, and 25.5 percent of the Catholic high schools. On the question of whether Jewish scholars are teaching courses in their institutions, the Catholic response produced these figures: 7 percent for the Catholic seminaries, 42.5 percent for the Catholic colleges, 5.3 percent for the Catholic high schools (although almost 70 percent responded that they invite a local rabbi to join their classes when specifically Jewish subjects are being discussed). Over 50 percent of the high schools said their students visit neighboring synagogues for added lectures or Sabbath services. The high school response appears to be supported by the responses from the diocesan school superintendents: 50 percent of them responded that the treatment of present-day Judaism is covered in their schools; 56.5 percent indicated their belief that their religion textbooks convey an adequate and positive treatment of Judaism and its relationship to Christianity; 49 percent said that the theology of Judaism was part of the curriculum of their secondary schools, and 18 percent stated that the schools deal with the theological significance of the State of Israel.

From one point of view, the above results seem rather meager. Placed over against the situation a decade ago, however, there is room for guarded optimism. I would concur with the conclusion put forward by the compilers of this report that

> one possible conclusion is that the two most decisive events which forged the consciousness of contemporary Jews—the Nazi Holocaust and the rebirth of Israel—are relatively ignored in . . . Catholic . . . seminaries and colleges. It can also be surmised from the responses that Judaism is taught essentially as a "religion" . . . and probably most specifically as background for, or prelude to, Christianity. Of course this does not mean that Judaism must necessarily be presented in a negative light. But it does seem appropriate to question whether certain aspects of Judaism which are critical to Jews as they understand themselves receive full exploration, such as Jewish historical continuity, the strong sense of Jewish peoplehood, and Jewish religious development in the post-biblical period as reflected in the oral law and the opinions and decisions of the Talmudic and rabbinic scholars and teachers. In other words, even a sympathetic treatment of "Old Testament" Judaism in Christian educational institutions will not likely prepare students for an adequate understanding of contemporary Jews and Judaism.

Our picture of the state of the Jewish portrait in contemporary Catholic materials will hopefully become even clearer with the completion of the study now in process by Eugene Fischer, a doctoral student in the School of Education of New York University.

To summarize the textbook situation I would make the following assertions: (1) Overt denigration of Judaism and the Jewish people has virtually disappeared from all major Catholic textbook series. (2) The accusation of collective Jewish guilt for the death of Jesus, and the consequent notion that the Jews were to be punished for this by becoming perpetual wanderers among the nations with no homeland of their own, has been virtually eliminated. (3) While the worst denunciations of the Pharisees found in the texts analyzed by Sister Thering have generally vanished (though not to the same degree as the deicide accusation), little that is positive has been added to neutralize the highly negative picture of "the Pharisees" that emerges from the pages of the New Testament. (4) Some attempts have been made to introduce Catholic students to the positive values inherent in contemporary forms of Judaism. Virtually nothing, however, has been included about Zionism, the State of Israel, or the Holocaust, three core elements of the modern Jewish soul. In short, the principal result of the textbook studies thus far has been the elimination of denigrating portraits of Judaism. There has also been some inclusion of positive material on Judaism, especially background material on biblical Judaism and on Jewish liturgy. What continues to be omitted are materials dealing with the Holocaust and the State of Israel, which happen to be the two central experiences of Jewish life in the twentieth century. Sister Rose Thering, in follow-up research on textbooks released by Catholic publishers in the 1960s, found no mention of the State of Israel.[10] This same lack showed up in Protestant materials according to Rev. Strober. He claims that his update on the Olson study discerned a pattern in Protestant teaching on Jews and Judaism which "begins with a theological anti-Judaism, moves to an inability to come to grips with the Holocaust and the twin tragedies of its effect upon Jewish life and the Christian conditioning which aided its development, and concludes with serious misapprehensions concerning the meaning of the State of Israel to Jewish life."[11]

There is another trend in the educational area that further complicates the problem of improving the image of Jews and Judaism among Catholic students. This is the movement away from the reliance on standardized textbooks in the teaching of religion. I generally applaud this trend, but it does create a new set of problems. To begin with, merely changing textbooks becomes much less significant than it would have been a decade ago. There are so many different texts in use, and no one can be sure to what extent a teacher will utilize a particular text, even if it has been selected for his or her class. This means that the proper training of teachers is becoming more and more crucial. Many of the teachers, depending on their age, were presented with a more or less distorted picture of Judaism in their own training programs. With the new classroom freedom teachers now enjoy, they tend to fall back more and more on their personal resources. In addition, with the burden of choosing classroom materials more squarely on their shoulders, the positive presentation of Judaism will probably not find a place in their program unless they have been sensitized to the problems. Even those teachers with goodwill have expressed puzzlement on some occasions as to what they should do here. A few years ago a questionnaire was distributed to participants in a Catholic teachers' institute on Judaism which Sister Rose Thering and I directed for the Catholic Adult Education Center in Chicago. The replies indicated a serious confusion on an important point. On the one hand, the teachers were aware of Vatican II's Declaration of the Church's Relationship to the Jewish People and were in sympathy with it; but they simply did not know how to square the conciliar statement with the negative comments about Jews contained in the New Testament. This dilemma illustrates the amount of spadework that is required in teacher training in Judaism throughout the country. Chicago has had several such institutes under the sponsorship of the Catholic Adult Education Center, the ADL, the AJC, and the Catholic Archdiocese. The Institute of Judaeo-Christian Studies, in collaboration with the ADL, has organized intensive institutes for the past few summers, including one in Israel in June 1972. Another institute, directed by Sister Rose Thering for the School of Education of Seton Hall University, is at this time completing its sessions in Israel. There have also been intensive summer programs at Wheeling College, a Jesuit-run institution in West Virginia. Furthermore, the ADL television series has been shown to teachers in New York and Chicago. All these programs have been good, but so far they have touched only a handful of teachers. The only answer is to continue to increase the number of institutes. They are essential, to my mind, because of the recent changes in classroom methodology.

There are two other trends currently afloat which, I believe, could pose a serious challenge to improvement of the portrait of Judaism in Catholic teaching materials, and in fact might set the ecumenical clock back considerably. In the first place, we are presently witnessing within Catholicism a trend to "tighten up" the basic explanations of the Gospel message. While there is nothing wrong with this in principle, it could get out of hand and weaken our commitment to Vatican II's statements on religious liberty and on the church's relationship to the Jewish people. These two documents stand as the most important contribution made by the American church to the council; hence I feel

American Catholics have a special mandate to protect the thrust of both documents and to incorporate their basic spirit and message into our curricula. In addition, the growing trend toward evangelism in American Christianity, highlighted by the Key '73 movement, represents a real challenge to the maintenance of the historical spirit of American religious pluralism and the conciliar documents on religious liberty and on Judaism. I believe that the St. Louis textbook studies, in their recently published form, can help to counter both these trends and insure that "our last state is not worse than our first."

At this point let me examine in somewhat greater detail the specific issues raised by Jules Isaac and by the results from the textbook studies. Turning first of all to the interrelated questions of the deicide charge and the consequent perpetual wandering theology raised by both Isaac and the St. Louis studies, we can say with both great certainty and relief that these teachings have been stricken from mainline Christian materials. This has been the greatest single achievement resulting from the work of Isaac, the St. Louis research, and ultimately the decree of Vatican II.

This does not mean however, that all problems have been solved here, even though the deicide charge represents history that is now behind us. For the more traditional accounts of responsibility for the death of Jesus have not totally vanished from popular culture and piety.

New Testament scholars have come to virtual agreement that Jesus was put to death by the Roman government on a political charge, with perhaps some collaboration by the priestly elite in the Jerusalem Temple (who are hardly beloved figures in the Jewish tradition and with whom the masses of Jews at the time scarcely identified). Christian educational materials have generally incorporated this scholarly viewpoint into their presentations.

On the other hand, *Jesus Christ Superstar*, seen by millions of Christian young people and perhaps more influential on their thinking than a hundred new textbooks, has the Jewish populace shout "Crucify him, crucify him," over and over again. I grant there is a difficulty in scientifically assessing the direct connection between such a stage production–film and the development of concrete anti-Semitic attitudes among young people. Nor am I necessarily decrying the style of the production as such. But one must admit, at the least, that the potential for anti-Semitic attitudes is there, and that our children are being fed a highly distorted picture of Jesus' relationship to the Jewish people of his time. This is all the more tragic at a time when the new scholarly research is available for the asking, research that could have transformed a production of this type into one that would have contributed to the education of the Gentile world about Jesus and the Judaism of his day. A golden opportunity was lost to do something constructive in the realm of popular culture and mass education. We see here that there still frequently remains a gap between the theological-catechetical presentation and the popular consciousness which deserves our attention. Let us not fall into the trap of thinking that Vatican II has spoken the final word here.

We still have not reached the situation where the majority (or even a fair-sized minority) of Christians clearly sees that a large part of the Jewish population of the day would have endorsed Jesus' struggle against the Romans and the corrupt Temple authorities. Most Christians still see Jesus and themselves over against the Jews; in actuality it was a case of Jesus, his followers (with whom we Christians most directly identify), and, at least in spirit, the bulk of the Jewish population of the period over against the Romans and the leadership of the Jerusalem priesthood. The Passion story (apart from its later theological interpretations) should, in reality, serve as a focal point of unity between Jews and Christians, not a source of division and separation. The Jewish scholar Ellis Rivkin puts this fact succinctly when he writes:

> The question of "Who crucified Jesus?" should therefore be replaced by the question "What crucified Jesus?" What crucified Jesus was the destruction of human rights, Roman imperialism, selfish collaboration. What crucified Jesus was a type of regime which, throughout history, is forever crucifying those who would bring human freedom, insight, or a new way of looking at man's relationship to man. Domination, tyranny, dictatorship, power and disregard for the life of others were what crucified Jesus. If there were among them Jews who abetted such a regime, then they too shared the responsibility.
>
> The mass of Jews, however, who were so bitterly suffering under Roman domination that they were to revolt in but a few years against its tyranny, can hardly be said to have crucified Jesus. In the crucifixion, their own plight of helplessness, humiliation and subjection was clearly written on the cross itself. By nailing to the cross one who claimed to be the messiah to free human beings, Rome and its collaborators indicated their attitude towards human freedom.[12]

It is this sort of attitude that continues to be missing from a *Jesus Christ Superstar* and from our Christian textbooks. It should be one of our top priorities in any further textbook revisions. The great difficulty is, however, that such an attitude cannot be easily inculcated from a simple reliance on the Gospel narratives of the death of Jesus. Use of background material from modern scholarship is essentil if the historical situation is ever to be presented accurately.

It is also important that Christian students clearly understand what was intended in Vatican II's Declaration on the Jewish People. While the old charges against the Jews have been removed from Christian teaching materials, the reason behind their removal should be clearly explained; otherwise the action of the council will not have its full impact. Too often Christians still have the impression that the council "exonerated" the Jewish people for the death of Jesus. Lowell D. Streiker put the problem well when he wrote sometime ago:

> The only remedy for Christian anti-Semitism is a reform of Christian education which both corrects the villainous teachings of contempt and presents the ancient people of God in proper perspective. (It is sad that the American news media have chosen to describe the Vatican Decree on non-Christian religions as an acquittal of the Jews rather than as a condemnation of unChristian teachings about the Jews. I hope that some tribunal will "exonerate" the *New York Times* and other leading publications—as well as much of the Jewish press—for their guilt in this respect.) There is no need to "exonerate" the Jews of a crime of which they have never been guilty; something else is required. Unless Christian education carefully interprets the historical and theological ties which bind the two convenants, Christian anti-Semites will turn their energies to the production of new anti-Jewish calumnies to replace old, discredited myths.[13]

Educational materials need to state clearly why the Vatican Council discarded the traditional Christian teaching about Jewish responsibility for the death of Jesus, and should not simply presume that students understand it was in no sense an exoneration. Anything less will be to leave the gates open for new anti-Jewish calumnies, as Lowell Streicker suggests.

Also of high priority on the educational agenda must be the removal of the distorted image of the Pharisees in Christian teaching and preaching. Who of us has not heard a sermon denouncing the Pharisees, or used them in a classroom as a model of hypocrisy, as the antithesis of everything that Jesus stood for? Which of our students has not seen this same stereotyped image presented in graphic form in *Godspell*? The recent literature on the Pharisees by Christian and Jewish scholars must begin to be fed into our curriculum.[14] With the virtual removal of the deicide charge from text materials, I would assert that the negative image of the Pharisees stands as the single most important source of Christian distortions of Judaism in New Testament times. This becomes doubly important when we recognize that all modern forms of Judaism, despite their many differences, basically owe their existence to the Pharisaic-rabbinic movement, which produced a revolution within Second Temple Judaism. To attack Pharisaism, therefore, is in a real way to attack the validity of modern Judaism.

Even apart from the interreligious point of view, it is crucial that Christian students become better acquainted with Pharisaism. For this movement formed the context (not merely the background) of the teachings of Jesus and the early church in such key areas as ethics, the notion of God, liturgy, ministry, and church structure. The prominent Scripture scholar Dr. Norman Perrin of the University of Chicago once asserted that there exist only a handful of good New Testament scholars in the world today because only a handful are conversant with Jewish materials. For a proper appreciation and understanding of the New Testament, it is essential that Christian students have a grasp of Pharisaic-rabbinic Judaism. While the increased interest in and use of the Hebrew Scriptures is welcome, profound developments took place in Judaism after the canonical Hebrew Scriptures had been completed. It was these developments in the Second Temple period (which Christians erroneously call the "intertestamental" period) that most directly influenced Jesus and early Christianity. On the question of the image of the Pharisees we have hardly moved forward from the time of the St. Louis studies.

Christian students also need to become acquainted with the two issues that most Jews see as central to their identity in our time: the Holocaust and the State of Israel. As was pointed out earlier, even the best of contemporary Christian educational materials dealing with the image of the Jews totally bypass these issues. Yet there is no way Christian students can truly relate to real-life Jews in our time unless they understand how profoundly the Holocaust and the State of Israel have affected them.

With respect to the Holocaust I want to repeat the comment of Franklin Littell, who said recently at an informal meeting that from one perspective the Holocaust is something that happened to us Christians rather than to the Jews. We have been afraid to probe the significance of this catastrophe for our own Christian self-understanding. Certainly it will be trying for Catholics to face this serious challenge to the traditional notion of the church's basic moral integrity. But in spite of the inevitable pain, face it we must. Our credibility as religious people depends on it. As the Catholic philosopher Friedrich Heer of the University of Vienna has put it in his book *God's First Love*,[15] our failure to confront the Holocaust is symptomatic of how Catholicism has confronted all other evils, especially war and the potential of a nuclear holocaust. The neglect of the Holocaust by both traditional and liberal Catholics reveals one of the basic gaps that exists in the current Jewish-Catholic dialogue. When the issue surfaced a few years ago in connection with the play *The Deputy*, the overwhelming response of the Catholic community was to bury rather than to probe. The continuation of such an attitude can only widen the gulf between Jews and Catholics, given the central role the Holocaust has assumed in current Jewish thought.

With respect to the State of Israel, it is necessary to deal with the Vatican's generally hostile attitude to Zionism (originally rooted in the belief that the Jews were destined to be perpetual wanderers upon the earth for murdering the Messiah), the history of the Jewish people's struggle in the twentieth century to establish a national homeland, the centrality of Israel to the self-identity of American Jews, how the theology of the land has functioned in biblical Judaism and its meaning to Jews today, and why and how one Jewish speaker could recently say, in addressing a Christian audience, that "Israel is our Jesus."

Some attention needs to be given to the distorted image of the Jew that can easily result from statements in the Gospels and Epistles, especially when such texts are used in the liturgy, where they acquire a kind of halo. I will return to this issue later. The solution of this problem is not easy and lies beyond the scope of the average educator. One thing teachers can do, however, is to be on the lookout for such texts when they are about to appear in the liturgy, and to discuss them with their students beforehand.

Students also need to be initiated into the current thinking of Christian theologians on how Christianity's message about Christ and the New Covenant can be explained without implying that Judaism's covenant is outdated or inferior. This was the third major source of distortion with respect to Judaism that emerged from the St. Louis studies. The pioneering work of writers such as James Parkes,[16] Gregory Baum,[17] Monika Hellwig,[18] Rosemary Ruether,[19] Peter Chirico,[20] J. Coert Rylaarsdam,[21] and others should be brought to the attention of students in a form appropriate to their age level. While the views of these theologians must be viewed as provisional, they are beginning a process that will profoundly alter Christianity's self-definition and make possible a more realistic relationship to Judaism and to all other non-Christian religions. This process is especially necessary, but will also prove particularly unnerving for Catholicism, in view of its long-standing claim to be the full and totally complete revelation. What the scholars mentioned are generally saying is that Christianity must reexamine its belief that the Messianic age, the time of fulfillment, took place at the coming of Christ. However we may eventually come to explain the uniqueness and mystery of the Christ event, it has become obvious to these writers and to me that we can no longer simply say that the Jewish notion of the Messianic age, far more important to Judaism than the idea of a personal Messiah, was realized in the death-resurrection of Christ. We may still call Jesus the Messiah, but we shall have to radically reshape our definition of this term.

This process of redefinition requires much work and research. The task of Christian educators at present is simply to acquaint themselves with the writings in this area, to inculcate in their students the realization that Christianity in and by itself does not contain in their fullness all the ideas necessary for a complete understanding of man's religious dimension, and to help them appreciate that only through interfaith sharing can a person even begin to approach such an understanding. All this must be done now even though we cannot as yet articulate in any complete fashion a new definition of Christianity's role vis-a-vis Judaism and the other world religions. Humble acknowledgement that our past viewpoint was shortsighted is the imperative of the hour.

Students also require some exposure to the cruel history of anti-Semitism. On the whole, the accounts of the Christian persecution of the Jews have been simply torn out of Christian textbooks. Jews are painfully aware of this history. Until Christians achieve the same awareness, our conversations will, of necessity, be strained. They should also be acquainted with modern and contemporary Jewish thought. Too often even those sentitive to the positive Jewish influence on the New Testament leave the impression that Judaism's creative period ended in biblical times. Modern and contemporary Jewish thought has much to offer Christians today.

Finally, teachers must never forget that Jews are not only a faith community, but also a social group. Hence students need familiarity with Jews and Judaism in social studies and literature materials as well. I consider literature an area of special import. The virtual absence of Jewish characters in the literature materials examined by the St. Louis studies poses a real problem. Teachers obviously must apply good literary standards as their primary criterion for the selection of curricular materials. No one would advocate choosing inferior literature simply because it has a high intergroup orientation. None-theless, given the social tension of our day and the powerful effect literature can have on the attitudes of students, the intergroup aspects cannot be totally ignored in the selection of materials. Special efforts must be made to locate materials that have literary merit as well as expose the student in a positive way to characters clearly identifiable as Jewish. This is especially necessary since so much of Judaism's cultural life and theology have been presented in literature.

At the primary and secondary levels literature courses must be viewed within the broader context of the total curriculum, whose aim is the socialization of the student. Hence the goal of precollege literature classes is somewhat different from the goal of a literature course on the college level. The primary and secondary student is usually more confined in his or her contacts. As a result, literary characters may be the closest he or she will come to meeting in a positive way members of minority groups such as Jews. While no precise guidelines can be laid down, it is imperative that educators in primary and secondary schools be sensitive to the problem of intergroup relations and the special contribution literature can make in presenting "living" minority characters. The picture emerging from the St. Louis studies is rather bleak.

The acquaintance with Jews through social-studies on the part of Catholic students is especially important today, when so many Gentile Americans simply assume that Jews are no longer an oppressed minority in this country. Certainly the situation has improved greatly in the last few decades. But anti-Semitism still exists in subtle and in more overt forms. There are hundreds of thousands of Jewish poor, Jewish workers, and Jewish students who are suffering various forms of discrimination, because the larger society has too easily assumed that Jews have made it in our nation.

Some remarks are in order at this point about the problem of Judaism and the Catholic seminary curriculum. This issue was first brought to a head when the ADL, in cooperation with Loyola University and the University of Chicago, sponsored a two-day consultation on the subject in 1965.[22] The discussions held during this consultation opened the eyes of many Christian seminary professors and administrators to the extensive neglect and stereotyping of Judaism in Christian seminaries. Follow-up programs tried to rectify this situation. The ADL, in collaboration with the Chicago-area seminaries, set up a program in Judaism for Christian seminary students. Secondly, many seminaries, both Catholic and Protestant, added rabbis to their teaching staffs.

Another symposium, sponsored by the North American Academy of Ecumenists and the National Conference of Christians and Jews held in Philadelphia in March 1973, tried to further the process of change.[23]

Despite such advances, the surface has as yet barely been scratched. The basic problem is that whatever positive input on Judaism into the Christian seminary curriculum there has been so far has remained on the periphery, with little or no effect on the core curriculum (with the exception that the worst accusations and theological excesses about Jews and Judaism from the past have been eliminated). Until the core curriculum of the seminary is infused with the new attitudes toward Judaism, there is little hope for any substantial change. Such infusion will not come easily, however, and the reasons are not rooted entirely in some form of anti-Judaism. We are faced with the problem that in a theological seminary, a graduate institution, professors are very conscious of their academic freedom. They do not like to be told what they should and should not teach, nor are they easily convinced that they are seriously deficient in some area. All this makes the necessary professional retraining very difficult. The national office of the ADL has been particularly interested in this problem of late.[24] They have found that trying to get a school to alter its core curriculum and individual teachers to change their syllabi is indeed a formidable task. Further attempts must be made along this line. If it is to be successful at all, however, the impetus must come from the seminary professors' own peers and not directly from agencies, whether Christian or Jewish.

A further problem at the seminary level is due to the loss of interest in "formal ecumenism" typical of Vatican II among many of the more liberal professors. They have tended to turn to issues such as the church's role and responsibility in the Third World, and its dealings with minorities in this country. In such a perspective Jews are usually included among the "haves"; therefore specifically Jewish questions are met with indifference, and in a few cases even with open hostility (complicated by the Middle East political situation and the frequent identification of the Palestinians with the oppressed peoples of the Third World). On the strictly theological-liturgical level these professors tend to have a fascination with other world religions. For one reason or another Judaism is usually not included in this category. Could this be due to a lingering belief that Christianity has subsumed whatever there is of value in Judaism?

One part of the Christian seminary program that illustrates how far we have to go is the teaching of Scripture. While there has undeniably been an intensification of interest in, and appreciation of, the Hebrew

Bible, the vast majority of Christian Scripture professors utilize none of the Jewish interpretations of individual books of the Hebrew Bible as resource material, but tend to rely exclusively on Christian exegetes. I cannot pinpoint the cause of this phenomenon scientifically. It seems to me that a residue of the traditional scientifically Christian viewpoint, which insisted that the true meaning of the Hebrew Bible could only be found through the eyes of the New Testament, is at least partially the basis of this neglect. This is one area where improvement could be made without excessively altering the curriculum. The same might be said for at least a consideration of Jewish commentators on the New Testament, such as Samuel Sandmel, David Flusser, and Asher Finkel. Such inclusion of Jewish resource material, both primary and secondary, could have a significant impact on core Christian teachings.

Judaism and Christian Liturgy

Several areas of concern emerge once we embark upon an investigation of Judaism and Christian liturgy, especially the Roman Catholic liturgical tradition. Permit me to comment briefly on some of these.

In the first place we have the problem of certain New Testament passages, which, when read without any commentary or background information, appear to defame Jews and Judaism. This problem was brought to light in a dramatic way during Pope Paul VI's visit to the United States, when, during the course of the nationally televised Eucharistic celebration from Yankee Stadium, the Gospel text was read which speaks of the disciples hiding in the upper room after Jesus' death "for fear of the Jews."

While this problem goes beyond the strict liturgical context, it takes on a special nature in that setting. First of all, background information cannot always be easily provided, nor can corrective information be supplied in the homily (unlike classroom use, where this can be done more easily). In addition, their use in the liturgy gives these texts a kind of "halo" quality, which intensifies their impact. The liturgy is perceived to be a sacred event, and the average worshipper assumes that what is said within such a setting must have a certain validity and authority.

The solution to this problem is not an easy one. Professor Michael Zeik of Marymount College suggested several years ago, in a *Commonweal* article, that we should retranslate anti-Semitic-sounding texts or phrases in the Gospels.[25] In principle this sounds like the right approach. Very quickly, however, one encounters serious methodological problems. On what basis does one tamper with ancient texts? Obviously this could be done only if there were virtual unanimity among respectable scholars about the inaccuracy of a certain present translation. But such consensus is highly unlikely to occur, and in fact does not presently exist for any of the crucial problem texts in the New Testament. Take, for example the use of the term "the Jews" in the Fourth Gospel. Although a vast majority of scholars agree that the term was probably not intended in a global sense (some interpreters who see a basic anti-Judaism at the heart of this Gospel would not concur), there is no similar agreement on what should replace "the Jews": "Jewish leaders," "Judeans"? I sincerely doubt there will be sufficient agreement to convince ecclesiastical authorities to approve a change in the major translations now available, especially in the text used in the liturgy. In a few instances a different translation might be possible, based on an interpretation of Greek verb forms; but on the whole this approach offers little hope, in my judgment, for a resolution of our basic difficulty.

The Secretariat for Catholic-Jewish Relations of the National Conference of Catholic Bishops has commissioned a study group of biblical scholars and theologians to look into the question. Its current chairperson is Fr. Richard Kugelman of St. John's University in New York. Thus far the group has been bogged down because of the methodological problem, though all recognize the seriousness of the issue and would like to take steps to improve the situation. At the moment the prevailing approach of the group, one that I personally share, leans toward the elimination of certain texts, or parts of texts, from the lectionary. This avoids the methodological difficulty, and there already exists precedent for such a selective use of the Scriptures in a liturgical context. Rather than risk feeding people false historicizations of the Gospel by the use of substitute phrases or titles that might sound better, but would violate other important exegetical canons, let us simply ask whether such passages are really appropriate for public use when they are offered without commentary to those incapable of understanding the biblical text by itself in its proper perspective. One member of the group seriously questions whether the substitution approach is not an attempt to evade history or redirect it by means of unhistorical translations. While recognizing the delicacy of the problem, he feels that if we are incapable of putting such texts in a proper context and explaining them, we should do nothing at all rather than falsify the materials.

"Either use the biblical text as it really is or get rid of it and use something else." This seems to me the only approach that offers any hope at all for an improvement in this area within the foreseeable future.

A second major difficulty that arises in connection with the image of Judaism in the liturgy has to do with the "fulfillment" theme spoken of earlier in connection with Christian education. For a long time the primary presentation of Christology in Catholic theological manuals focused on showing that Jesus, in his life and ministry, fulfilled the Messianic prophecies of the Old Testament, and hence inaugurated the Messianic age. But such a direct connection between the Old Testament prophecies and the interpretation of Christology has generally vanished from contemporary Christian theology. Some prominent theologians and Scripture scholars, as we have seen above, have explicitly challenged the "fulfillment" concept as basically inaccurate—the Messianic age in the Jewish sense is not yet here. The ranking Scripture scholar W. D. Davies of Duke University said, in a paper delivered at a conference on Judaism and the Christian seminary curriculum, held in Philadelphia in March 1973, that even using the traditional fulfillment-of-Old-Testament-prophecies approach we must recognize that to say Christ fulfilled Jewish aspirations is inaccurate. Davies showed that the New Testament writers were highly selective in the prophecies they utilized, leaving aside many important ones which could not have been used with any credibility in explaining the meaning of the Christ event.

A close look at the Scripture readings used during Advent and Lent, and at the text of the fourth Canon of the Mass, will quickly show us that while the fulfillment-of-Old-Testament-prophecies approach may be dead or dying in theological circles, it is very much alive and well in current Catholic liturgy. The readings from the Hebrew Scriptures used throughout Advent, the Scripture readings and text of the great Exultet proclamation, which are central to the Paschal Vigil service, and the words "Father, you so loved the world that in fullness of time you sent your only Son to be our Savior" from Canon IV clearly play upon this theme.

A solution to this problem is difficult. Obviously, the provisional theological views put forward by the Baums, the Ruethers, the Hellwigs, and even the Pawlikowskis do not yet enjoy the widespread acceptance needed to serve as the basis of liturgical texts. However, given the widespread questioning of the simple "fulfillment" explanation of Christianty's relationship to Judaism, and cognizant of how important liturgy can be as a vehicle of instruction for the Christian masses, I feel that liturgists must make some adjustment that will downplay this fulfillment theme. The Scripture readings for Advent and the Paschal Vigil can be changed and the text of the fourth Canon can be modified, even though we do not yet possess any fully articulated and widely accepted new positive explanation of the Jewish-Christian relationship.

A reference must also be made to the Holy Week liturgy in general, in addition to the problem with the Paschal Vigil already mentioned. The growing tendency to dramatize the presentation of the Passion narratives on Palm Sunday, Holy Thursday, and Good Friday carries with it the same dangerous potential inherent in Passion plays for denigrating Jews and Judaism and thinking them responsible for the death of Jesus. The whitewashing of Pilate that has taken place in most of the Gospel accounts only intensifies the apparent guilt of the Jews. I see no really adequate solution to the problem without adding background materials to the actual Gospel text. If we are really serious about improving the image of Judaism, then I think we must set up commissions of liturgists and theologians sensitive to Jewish-Christian relations who could produce such materials for popular use. If this is left up to each individual parish or liturgical center, I am not optimistic that the sensitivity, knowledge, or creativity will be found to effect the required adaptations.

One final word about Holy Week. In many Christian circles it is now popular to celebrate a Seder supper on Holy Thursday. Such efforts are usually well intentioned and sponsored by groups that are open to Judaism. But frequently the Seder supper uses texts that contain a heavily Christological interpretation of all its basic symbols. Unwittingly such suppers produce a continuation of the old fulfillment theology. Why cannot we Christians celebrate a Seder meal using the Jewish symbols, without giving a Christological significance to everything? I suggest that the most moving and best experience for Christians is to participate in a Jewish-led Seder.

One liturgical aid in the minds of many for improving the view of Judaism is the recent inclusion of readings from the Hebrew Bible in the Sunday Eucharistic celebrations. While I do not wish to downplay this as a step in the right direction, my actual experience is that the texts frequently selected contain a list of strange names and places which leave nothing but blank stares on the faces of the average parishioners. Readings from Jewish writers such as Abraham Heschel and Martin Buber within the liturgy could do more, I am convinced, to instill a positive feeling for Judaism among our Christian people than a hundred readings from the Hebrew Bible. Here I am betraying my strong conviction that—not only to improve the image of Judaism, but the quality and meaning of our liturgy generally—we urgently need to break the limits of Scripture readings and incorporate texts that would forcefully express the major themes of the Scriptures in a contemporary idiom and setting.

At times a negative view of Judaism has been conveyed in connection with liturgy through supplementary materials. I recall sometime ago waiting to begin a Eucharist in a Chicago parish while the commentator read from prepared "commentator" material that is marketed across the country. The material presented one of the worst denunciations of the Pharisees I have ever heard, equal to the most vile descriptions discovered in the St. Louis studies and carrying on the theme of the bankruptcy of Judaism in Jesus' day. I immediately discarded my prepared homily to make a corrective presentation on the Pharisees. But I doubt that many other priests would have been in a position to do this on the spot. Some efforts should be undertaken to scrutinize commentaries prior to publication, perhaps including Jewish representation on an evaluative team, in the same manner as is now the case with textbook publication. This vehicle might be transformed into a positive source for improving the image of Judaism, serving perhaps as one foil for the effects of the problem New Testament texts pose as long as these remain in use.

Mention should be made here of two positive ways within the liturgical context to foster among Christians a deeper appreciation of Judaism and our troubled brotherhood. The first opportunity comes in the liturgy of Good Friday. Pope John XXIII's removal of the term "perfidious" from the prayer for the Jewish people was a great step forward. No one quite knew what the word meant, but it sounded bad. More importantly, Pope John's action opened the door to a whole new spirit which still has not been fully seized. The present prayer for Jews on Good Friday, while more positive in tone, still bears a conversionist ring. Why could we not alter the prayer so that in the first place it would humbly ask forgiveness for the centuries of persecution of the Jews and the weight the church thereby added to the cross of Christ, and secondly, that God give strength to the church in order that it might renew itself by sharing in the spiritual richness of Judaism?

Another liturgical possibility is closely connected to the theme of this Conference—the Holocaust. A number of years ago the chief rabbinate of Israel designated the twenty-seventh day of the Hebrew month of Nissan as "Yom Hasho'ah," Holocaust Day, to perpetuate the memory of the six million who perished at the hands of the Nazis. Slowly the observance is spreading in Jewish circles. Why cannot it also be liturgically commemorated in the Christian community, either separately, or jointly with a local Jewish community? As Franklin Littell's comment mentioned earlier makes plain to us, the Holocaust is our experience as well. At a conference on "The Holocaust and the Contemporary Religious Condition," sponsored by the ADL and the United Methodist Church in Chicago in October 1972, it was suggested that Sunday church services closest to Holocaust Day integrate appropriate readings, music, and audiovisual materials into the worship service and religious school programs. Sermons could also deal with this topic. Recommended materials for developing such a service in a Christian setting are available upon request from the ADL.[26]

Finally, let me make some remarks about the use of psalms as Christian prayers, particularly in the breviary. Frequently the problem lies more in the accompaning commentary than in the psalms themselves. Many that allude to Israel's failings as a people and the prophetic call for the chosen people's repentance can leave the Christian with the basic impression that Israel was totally unfaithful in her mission and therefore the church had to replace her as the New Israel. Msgr. John Oesterreicher exposes one example of this in his pamphlet *Shalom: The Encounter Of Christians And Jews And The Catholic Educator.*[27] He quotes from the notes accompanying the Latin-English version of the breviary published by the Liturgical Press in 1964. The notes are those of the late Canon Pius Parsch, a giant in the field of liturgical renewal. Parsch says, in introducing Friday Matins: "The Matins Psalms present a history of the Jewish People which is at the same time a history of falling away from God. It is an unbroken chain of sin, infidelity, ingratitude; and its final, logical link is the greatest crime of all: the murder of the Messiah."[28] Oesterreicher shows how Parsch annotates a number of psalms in which he finds the history of Israel's infidelities retold. In commenting on Psalm 80 that the Lord of the Covenant offers the people of Israel this choice, Parsch writes: "In yours hands lie death and life; choose: life, if you obey—death, if you are faithless like your fathers." He goes on: "Christ's death on the cross shows that the Jews chose death and final rejection."[29]

"That the sacred writers so freely confess the sins of Israel—of people, priests, and princes, multitude as well as elite—is to Israel's great credit," says Oesterreicher. "To my knowledge, there is no history of the church that is written with the same candor, the same openness, the same humility."[30] One might add that this judgment could even be made of the first history of the church—the New Testament. That a center of renewal and creative change such as the Liturgical Press could have reprinted such comments by Parsch toward the close of the council shows how deep the problem of reconciliation between Jews and Christians really is. We must continue to be on our guard against such unfortunate commentaries whenever the psalms are used as prayer texts. For the potential for distortion remains great.

Closing Remarks

This ends our examination of the image of Jews and Judaism in Christian education and liturgy. Before closing, however, I should like to emphasize the importance of the task I have outlined for Christian teachers and liturgists. Let me relate a Jewish folktale of a Jew who grew up in a small shtetl in Poland. There were some fifty Jewish families in the town and two Gentile families. Observant Jews are forbidden to do certain things on the Sabbath. One of the ways they avoided this was to use what is called a *Shabbes Goy* —a Gentile who came in on the Sabbath and did the work prohibited to Jews. One day this Jew from the village went to Warsaw. He was overwhelmed by the immensity of the city and finally asked a native Warsaw Jew, "Tell me, how many Jews are there here in Warsaw?" "About half a million," was the answer. "My God," said the shtetl Jew, "and how many Gentiles?" "About four million," was the response. "My God," he exclaimed, "what do you need so many *Shabbes Goyim* for?" For many Christians, as well as Jews, the last few decades have shattered their system and their limited, small world. Many accepted values and supposed realities have been undercut. Many Christians and Jews have made the trip from the shtetl to Warsaw in our day, with the resulting cultural shock. There is an attempt afoot today to begin a major reconstruction of values. Religion should and can have a part in this value reconstruction. This is in no sense, however, a mere return to the previous dominance of one religious tradition over another, or even a return to the dominance of religion over society at large. If religion is to have a voice in this reconstruction process, this voice will have to be interreligious in nature. The Jewish-Christian dialogue in its educational phase, then, whether it be formal education or the education that takes place in a liturgical context, assumes an importance far beyond the limited scope of the dialogue. If carried out along the lines suggested above, the dialogue through education will alter and universalize the consciousness of our people, helping them to become creative and productive members of a new world striving to be born, in which the great religions and humanitarian traditions of the world will help build a society in which "justice and peace can finally kiss."

Response to John Pawlikowski

CLAIRE HUCHET-BISHOP

Father John Pawlikowski's excellent presentation of the image of Jews and Judaism in Christian education and liturgy has brought to my mind a number of reflections which I would like to share with you.

Father Pawlikowski's presence here, as well as his courageous work on behalf of Jewish-Christian relations, is all the more remarkable in that he is a priest with a Polish name; we cannot help remembering that Catholic Poland has been the land of endemic pogroms, even in this century. Was it just by chance that Hitler chose Polish territory for his most infamous death camp? Father Pawlikowski's attitude is a source of deep encouragement to those of an older question who have known years of solitude in their fight against Christian anti-Semitism.

He has underlined the progress made for the last thirty years, and especially during the last decade, in the Church's attitude toward Jews. He has also emphasized how much remains to be done.

Personally, though I readily acknowledge whatever improvement there is—and it is very real—at the same time I cannot help but view it as meager in the face of nearly two thousand years of persecutions culminating at Auschwitz.

Auschwitz: the beginning of a new era? Yes, to a certain extent; and this we owe to a Jew, Professor Jules Isaac, who in 1948 sounded the alarm in his book *Jesus et Israel*,[1] which rocked the complacency of European Christians and pointed to their blindness. The Ten Points of Seelisberg came out of that,[2] as did also the first analysis of French catechisms.[3]

Would we have had the beginning of a new era without the decisive meeting of Professor Isaac with John XXIII in 1960? It was my privilege to hear about that memorable private audience from Jules Isaac himself, as we sat in his lovely garden at Aix-en-Provence. He told me: "As I waited in the anteroom of the pope's private library, where the audience was to be held, I felt weighed down by my responsibility. How to convey to the pope, within a few minutes, nearly two thousand years of Jewish suffering at Christian hands? I felt all the martyrs of the past ages present in that room, and also the six million victims of Hitler." The victims, as we know, included Isaac's wife, daughter, and son-in-law.

179

Out of that audience came the creation of a committee within the Second Vatican Council for the reevaluation of Christian teaching regarding the Jews. Out of it too, eventually, came the council's Declaration on the Jews, which, though unsatisfactory in many ways, yet gave us Catholics an opening toward a new attitude regarding the Jewish people. I am particularly grateful to John Pawlikowski for his moving personal tribute to Jules Isaac, distinguished scholar, gallant Jewish fighter for truth,[4] and noble human being.

As is glaringly apparent throughout John Pawlikowski's report, eleven years after Jules Isaac's death we are still plodding along, not even quite sure sometimes whether the few points gained are for the good. "What Christian teaching has done, it has to undo; and it will take a long time," Jules Isaac used to tell me. How true!

Social Studies

Before dealing with religion textbooks, I should like to comment briefly on social studies. John Pawlikowski tells us there are but minimal materials dealing with Judaism in Catholic writings on the subject. I am not sure I deplore the lack as he does; at least we are spared derogatory comments such as those revealed in the textbooks analysis carried out by Pro Deo at the International University of Social Studies in Rome and by the Centre de Recherches Socio-Religieuses at the Catholic University of Louvain, as well as in the latter's concomitant public-opinion survey. As I reported in *How Catholics Look at Jews*,[5] four-fifths of the respondents perceived the Jew as a businessman, mostly a smart, canny operator, more or less of an exploiter. This persistent image is the result of church history. The church forced the Jews into the role of financier, thereby creating a reality to match its prejudice. As Jean-Paul Sartre once said, "The right question to ask Christians is, What have *you* made of the Jews?"[6] But they would not understand it. And yet it is not farfetched, unfortunately, to relate a certain kind of criticism aimed at the State of Israel to the centuries-old Christian line that the Jew is an exploiter.

Religion Textbooks and Christian Conscience

Turning now to the religious context proper, I wish to point out that the French-language books examined in the Louvain study are free in toto from invectives and, in the main, from the deicide charge; even before Vatican II, owing to Jules Isaac's work. The same is not true of Italian and Spanish texts, as the Pro Deo research demonstrated. There-fore much, very much, remains to be done.

Moreover, as John Pawlikowski makes clear, there is a gap every-where between the attitude of the elite and that of the masses toward Jews. What a Christian minority has learned since Auschwitz has not yet reached the popular mind, least of all its emotive levels of being. Last year, in a memorable declaration, the French Bishops' Committee for Relations with Judaism referred to "The slow course of the Chris-tian conscience."[7] Rightly, John Pawlikowski explains how false and even injurious it is to speak of the Vatican II statement as exonerating the Jews. Indeed, it appears that Christians must be—not exonerated but exorcised, and not of a devil conveniently projected as an outsider, in order to change their attitude toward Jews.

The Pharisees

John Pawlikowski notes the overwhelmingly disparaging treatment of the Pharisees. I reported the same gross error in my book. In spite of the numerous scholarly studies published within the last decade on the Pharisees, showing that they did not oppose Jesus totally and that much of Jesus' teaching was in the best Pharisaic tradition, we do not find one positive statement about them in the texts reviewed by the Pro Deo and Louvain researchers.

The Holocaust

And now I come to what, in John Pawlikowski's all too true remark, the Catholic community prefers "to bury rather than to probe": the slaughter of one-third of the world's Jews during World War II. The near absence of any mention of the Holocaust in Catholic school cur-ricula is paralleled by the absence of any mention of it in Italian, Span-ish, and French religious textbooks, and this in materials published af-ter Auschwitz, between 1945 and 1966. Six million of the people to whom we owe Christianity were murdered, and Christian religious teaching ignores the fact! Catholic young people who still receive Christian teaching are taught nothing about the Holocaust; it is as if this genocidal catastrophe had never happened.

We know that it is impossible to speak, to write about it, adequately. The monstrosity is such that it remains beyond human grasp. Besides, each generation forgets what happened before it; human memory is short. Were it not so, we could not survive under the weight of past human abominations. However, since for nearly two thousand years the Christian church managed to keep alive the spurious tradition of the Jewish people's responsibility for Jesus' crucifixion, there are no excuses for ignoring the Holocaust today under the pretext that it is past history. Of course, to mention the Holocaust might bring back to mind other misdeeds, such as, the Crusades, the Inquisition, the burning of the Talmud, the pogroms, etc. and the church is in the habit of forgetting what might embarrass it. Yet young Christians have to be told that Auschwitz would not have been possible had not the Christian world been conditioned by nineteen centuries of the Teaching of Contempt for Jews.[8] Had Rome asked forgiveness from the Jews as it did from the Protestants, the road toward authentic friendship would be clear. As it is, we are confronted with an attitude of "charity" without justice, which is offensive to many Jews and perpetuates Christian arrogance. It is up to us, Catholic writers, teachers, parents, priests, and religious, to storm into the crack in the door opened by the Conciliar Statement on the Jews and "to prepare the way of the Lord, make his paths straight."[9] If we persist in our silence about the Holocaust, any effort toward Jewish-Christian reconciliation is a sham.

I am well aware that the difficulty in teaching the Holocaust is twofold. First, we are hampered by the tradition which not only places the responsibility for the crucifixion on the Jewish people, but also pronounces them cursed by God and therefore subject to never-ending persecutions. To begin with, there is no such thing as an accursed people. Morever, it is high time for Christians to understand that, as the French Bishops' Committee on Relations with Judaism declared, "On the contrary, according to the testimony of the Scriptures (Isaiah 53:2–4), to be subjected to persecution is often an effect and a reminder of the prophetic condition."[10]

The second reason for the Catholic reluctance to so much as mention the Holocaust is, as previously indicated, the church's complicity in it. However, as John Pawlikowski aptly says, "Our credibility as a religious people depends on our confronting this issue." It has been said that "Christianity died at Auschwitz."[11] It did: the Christianity we have known, Constantinian Christianity, seventeen hundred years old, the Christianity allied to power, rendering unto Caesar what is due to God, culminating in the only instance in history of genocide carried out as a concerted government policy, with the whole machinery of the state mobilized for the purpose and with the indifference of the institutional church to the fate of the Jews making it possible—an indifference directly due to the traditional anti-Semitism propagated for centuries.

Western Culture

This Christian teaching has permeated our Western culture so thoroughly that even people wholly detached from the church, including atheists, are no longer unbiased in their reactions toward Jews, though they may think they are. It is true that the religious factor obtains less and less in our hostility to Jews because we are living in a desacralized society, as Canon François Houtart and his research team demonstrated in the Louvain survey of French-speaking Catholics. This does not mean, however, that the long-lasting, emotion-charged indoctrination of anti-Semitism has ceased to affect people who have severed all ties with the Christian religion. That they give other than religion reasons for their hostility—sometimes superficially commendable ones, such as a humanitarian concern for the Third World—must not be allowed to obscure the fact that in our Western culture the image of the Jew has been created by the church. This derogatory image thrived for nearly twenty centuries; given the human psyche, it is not going to vanish overnight, the belief of some that they are free from prejudice notwithstanding.

Protean Anti-Semitism

Such a belief is a delusion because anti-Semitism is protean; it never presents itself twice in quite the same garb. The pogroms of 1881 in Russia were triggered by an accusation against the Jews of having engineered the assassination of Czar Alexander II. In 1894, Captain Dreyfus was accused of treason in France. Hitler declared the Jews responsible for the defeat of the Central Powers and the downfall of Germany in World War I. The Soviet Union finds it intolerable that some Jews want to leave the "best country in the world." Today, everywhere, liberals rightly concerned with the plight of the Palestinians and the general misery of the Third World, make the discovery anew that the responsibility for all ills rests on the Jews—call them this time the State of Israel. The Jew is always "that bald pate, that mangy creature who is the root of all evil," like the poor donkey stigmatized by the more powerful animals in La Fontaine's famous fable, "The Animals Sick from the Plague." And everyone always protests, "I am *not* anti-

Semitic, but . . ." The Arabs also proclaim that they are anti-Zionist and not anti-Semitic, that is, anti-Jewish, but they flood Africa and South America with copies of the spurious *Protocols of the Elders of Zion*. Given this perennial character of anti-Semitism, to ignore the Holocaust is to invite its repetition under another name, such as the liquidation of the State of Israel.

The State of Israel

This is the other ominous silence registered by John Pawlikowski: about the State of Israel the church is also mute. Silence is likewise to be found in Italian, Spanish, and French textbooks. While all Jews today throughout the world are deeply involved in the existence of the State of Israel, their one hope after Auschwitz, the church averts its eyes. No one expects it to approve everything the State of Israel does, but why be silent about its existence? Because the church does not know what to do with an event which contradicts its traditional teaching. Were not the Jews condemned to wander in exile on account of the crucifixion until the end of time, when they would recognize Jesus Christ? This is a silence that follows with implacable logic on its silence about Auschwitz. Auschwitz and the State of Israel necessitate a new theology about Jews, and the church does not yet have one, although thirty years have passed since the events. It retreats into what it claims to be Christian impartiality. In fact, the church uses a double standard: it takes great care not to offend the Arabs, but does not appear to be sensitive to the Jewish plight. Its so-called neutrality does not help those Arabs who are willing to sit down with the Israelis; it favors those who actually make use of its own deadly cliches in their propaganda—the Jew as avaricious, ruthless, hypocritical, apostate.

Judaism

The silence in religion textbooks regarding the State of Israel widens the gap between the Christians and Jews of today, a gap already made by the fact that the texts follow the recurrent church practice of treating only pre-Jesus Judaism as meritorious. The traditional teaching is that Judaism ceased to exist with the coming of Jesus. Thus it condemns us to meeting an anachronistic people, a sure way not to relate to them. On the contrary, says the French Bishops' Committee, "Christians, even if only for themselves, ought to acquire a true and living knowledge of Jewish tradition." Why? Because "the permanence of this people through the ages, its survival across civilizations, its presence as a rigorous and exacting partner vis-a-vis Christianity are facts of the first importance which we can treat neither with ignorance nor with contempt." Courageously, the bishops affirm that "the first covenant was not nullified by the new." They speak of the "particular vocation of this people by the Sanctification of the Name . . . which makes the life and prayer of the Jewish people a benediction for all nations of the earth."[12]

Indignant traditional theologians have reacted violently, clamoring that the bishops' statement "breaks with church tradition";[13] that "the Jewish people was the chosen people for two thousand years . . . but this election was temporary";[14] that it is "false to continue to speak today of a special election of the Jewish people . . . that it is equally wholly mistaken to write that the 'first covenant was not nullified by the new";[15] that the French bishops' position "is politically odious and theologically destructive."[16] Then comes the anguish-filled cry, "Is faith in Christ no longer sufficient?"[17] and the defensive-aggressive statement, "We have no right to change the faith."[18]

Thus, though the bishops state at the outset of the document that the enduring, living presence of the Jewish people constitutes "more and more for Christians a given situation which may facilitate for them a better comprehension of their own faith and enlighten their life,"[19] yet a quasi-visceral fear blocks the way for many to an authentic relationship with our fellow Jews.

Fear

This fear is demonstrated in the "tightening up of the basic explanations of the Gospel message," as observed by John Pawlikowski. It is, of course, partly a backlash from Vatican II, and was to be expected. But did we foresee that it would become so powerful? Apparently we underestimated the depth of the need for security in many Christians. To them, faith is a safety valve, not a challenge; it is static, not mobile. To them God is not, as He is for Teilhard de Chardin, "the eternal Discovery and the eternal Growth."[20] To them, belief means the assent of the mind to a dogmatic proposition.

This has never been the meaning of the verb *lehamin* in Hebrew, which, after all, was the language of the first Christians. The word does not denote an intellectual process; "to trust" renders the original meaning more accurately. Trust is a living experience. It is not given once and for all but grows with the person's own growth; its aspect changes with the passing of time; its roots thrust deeper and deeper through daily encounters, which are welcomed as blessings by a resilient faith. Most people, however, are used to and prefer a faith hammered into their heads like a dead, rigid beam; it frees them of any responsibility save that of holding on to the beam. Therefore, anything which tends to unsettle the beam is greatly feared. For this reason, the French bishops' declaration has drawn a sharply divided response: excoriation from those who value inert security above all else, and acclaim from those who welcome the disturbing breath of the Spirit, those who "believe," those who "trust." For the latter, the document is a joy and a light to their own Christian faith.

Liturgy

Regarding the liturgy the problem, as John Pawlikowski points out, is both difficult and particularly important, because of the "kind of 'halo' quality which intensifies the value of the texts." I have some insight into the pitfalls through Robert F. Markham's scholarly study of the problem of "the Jews" in the Fourth Gospel, which he presented to our Steering Committee of the Project on the Jewish-Christian Dimension in the New Testament Translation, a research endeavor within the National Conference of Christians and Jews.[21]

In connection with the fateful phrase "His blood be upon us and upon our children," I was privileged to discuss the question with Dr. Michael Wyschogrod, who contributed a most valuable new insight to the interpretations already attempted by those who have been anguished at the extensive use of this cry by anti-Semitic fellow Christians. We have long recognized that: (1) The fateful cry is found in Matthew only. (2) If uttered at all, it was voiced by a mere handful of Jews, since the square in front of Pilate's palace could not possibly have accommodated large numbers. (3) The gathering may have been a paid rabble. (4) It is dishonest to infer that the crowd was the same as that of Palm Sunday, especially since the latter scene, according to scholarly research, may suffer from a chronological displacement of the Feast of Tabernacles,[22] (5) In any event, the crowd did not represent the whole of Jerusalem, much less Judea and Galilee, and least of all the Jews of the Diaspora, whose population was three or four times that of the Jews in Palestine. (6) As Jules Isaac pointed out, the cry reported by Matthew and commented on by a vicious Christian anti-Semitic tradition lacks total plausibility because it came from a people at that time under the heel of a conqueror. Dr. Wyschogrod added importantly to these considerations by his disclosure to me that the purported cry seems to refer to a legal formula then in use by Jewish courts in Palestine, "His blood be on *him* and on *his* children" (emphasis added), and that this formula may have been wholly misrendered by the Greek translator, confused by the fact that Jesus had no children.

These interpretations command attention. But despite their persuasiveness, as long as the question has not been fully clarified, we can at least abstain from using Matthew's sentence in the liturgy and our catechisms. Wise selection, as advocated by John Pawlikowski, is indeed our best policy today.

I also agree that there is an urgent need for revising the Holy Week liturgy. Foremost on the agenda should be the elimination of the Reproaches. Beginning with a line from Micah 6:3, "O my people, what have I done to thee, or in what have I grieved thee?" then continue with a heart-rending lamentation put in Jesus' mouth: "I led you out of the land of Egypt and you prepared a cross for me. I opened the Red Sea before you and you opened my side with a lance," etc. Gregory Baum argued with me a few years ago that "O my people" refers to us Christians and not to Jews. This, to my mind, is wishful thinking. Does not everyone read the biblical facts into this prayer rather than struggle to find a hidden innuendo reproachful of Christians? The Bible says that the *Jews* were led out of Egypt and that the sea was opened before *them*. Let us not fool ourselves. It is high time that this emotion-charged text against the Jews, still used this very year even in New York City, be shelved for good. So should be this passage from the Oriental liturgy:

> Awake, singer David . . .
> The people who do not know mercy,
> pitilessly pierced the hands of the Son
> Like dogs, they have surrounded him who keeps silence . . .
> Awake, noble Malachi,
> make the wicked people ashamed who crucified Christ . . .
> Awake, prophet Daniel,
> look at Emmanuel whom Gabriel reveals to you,
> tortured by the children of Israel.
> Woe to the prevaricating people . . . [23]

There is much to be done in selecting new texts for the liturgy.

Let me turn now to the recent inclusion in the liturgy or readings from the First Testament (I wish to eschew the invalid connotation that has come to surround "Old Testament"), and the lack of response to them from parish congregations, as noted by John Pawlikowski. Indeed, the obstacle here is ignorance. It seems to me that the best solution would be to teach children the beautiful biblical stories. The children would tell them to their parents and transmit them to their own offspring in later life, so that gradually successive generations would become familiarized with the First Testament. What we need to convey is that "we do not support the root, but the root supports us,"[24] that "salvation is from the Jews,"[25] that we are grateful for the original recounting of the Word of God, that we respect Judaism and accept it as a legitimate, living religion.

There is one point on which I disagree with John Pawlikowski. It does not seem advisable to me to introduce other readings than those from the Bible at Mass. Who is to make such selections? What kind of social or political bent will govern the choice? I would rather the priest concentrate on First and Second Testament texts, than be at the mercy of his or others' personal likes or dislikes.

From personal experience I have no illusion that to reverse a current nineteen centuries old is an easy task. But let us not forget that, contrary to what is presently believed, inculcating Christian anti-Semitism in the people following the church's identification with political power was no easy task either; it took seven centuries. Given today's mass media, the church can undo what it has done in a much shorter time—if it desires this.

It is most important that Christians be reeducated so that they can unmask and combat the disguised anti-Semitism of today, which calls itself by such names as anti-Zionism and anti-capitalism. In this connection I should like to ask John Pawlikowski what kind of liturgy and catechisms are used in Poland currently. Poland has few Jews today, but its Christians, for their own good, should be receiving guidance regarding the Jews that implements the statement of Vatican II. Are they? In Communist countries, the governments object to religion but tolerate the church to a certain extent, whereas the Jews are forbidden any kind of religious practice. Do Christians, in those countries, offer the use of churches to their Jewish brothers and sisters? Do Christians make a point of learning Hebrew? In short, are they conscious of their solidarity with the persecuted Jews?

Anywhere in the world of our time, given the present trend, the initiative to further authentic relations with Jews will not come from those in power; it must arise from the grassroots in each country, as it does in France and the United States, where many religious and lay people and a few priests have taken it upon themselves to reeducate other Christians. Fierce opposition, born of fear, as I noted earlier, already confronts us. We can expect more of it; while remaining open to valid criticisms of our specific actions, we must stand firm in our cause. The mutiheaded monster of anti-Semitism will leave us no peace. Jules Isaac used to quip wryly, "It's not easy to be a Jew." To a lesser extent, it's not easy to be a friend of the Jews either, as some of us have already realized.

The Jewish Question: Touchstone of Spirituality

And yet, here lies the decisive factor for the direction the world will take. Not only did traditional Christianity die at Auschwitz; Western civilization died too. Had the Christian church cried out forty years ago, denouncing in no uncertain terms the extermination of the Jews at Auschwitz and other death factories, the world would not be what it is today. Had the Christian church taken an unequivocal stand against the Nazis, upholding the moral and spiritual values Hitler flaunted, it might have suffered severe persecution, but it would have saved the respect due those values; and thus it might have remained a beacon on earth, especially in the West. In capitulating to unspeakable evil through its indifference to the fate of the Jews, the church as an institution not only signed its own moral death warrant, but also unleashed in the world unrestrained reliance upon violence as a solution for all personal, interpersonal, national, and international conflict. In the most critical hour of its history, the church betrayed its mission. Today, the whole world suffers the consequences.

However, because we are the younger brothers and sisters of those who, as a people, brought to humanity the hope of ultimate liberation, we refuse to give up the staggering task of reeducating Christians regarding Jews. We know that, to human eyes, what we accomplish is negligible in the face of nineteen centuries of Christian "indoctrination." We know also, as sociologists tell us, that today the overt religious impetus behind anti-Semitic manifestations has been replaced by social and political stimuli, or both. Nevertheless, as previously observed, we cannot believe that nineteen hundred years of pounding contempt and hatred into people has ceased to color and influence their reactions to Jews, even when such people are anti-religious, let alone when they are Christians.

The very protean character of anti-Semitism makes the fight against it a model for the worldwide fight against any minority hatred and oppression. Moreover, the attitude toward the Jewish question remains the barometer which reveals the state of spiritual health of any human being, group, church, or civilization.

Auschwitz. Humanity's shame. The church's betrayal. The beginning of a new era? A murky dawn where a handful of us, Christians and Jews, are groping for each other's hands, struggling toward what many believe to be an impossible reconciliation. But it is not for us to know how and when that reconciliation will be fulfilled. Sufficient for us be it to live daily, bearing witness to the coming of the Messianic age in our thoughts and actions, as we are faced over and over again with the monster of Auschwitz masquerading under myriad masks. Already our commitment has proved not so easy, and it will probably become increasingly heavy to sustain. May our Jewish sisters and brothers not find us wanting.

Response to John Pawlikowski

THOMAS HOPKO

I can hardly offer a word of disagreement with John Pawlikowski concerning the mindless anti-Judaism which has existed and still exists among those who claim to be Christians. Certainly in those lands where the Orthodox church was established there have existed erroneous doctrines and pernicious mythologies about the Jews which have resulted in violent attacks on the Jewish people. Fortunately today, even with large Arab membership in the Orthodox church and the fiercely anti-Jewish sentiments of those who blame the Bolshevik revolution in Russia, and everything else considered to be wrong in the world, primarily, if not exclusively, on "the Jews," the theological and spiritual appreciation and understanding of Judaism has greatly improved among the Orthodox, at least in the Western world.

Generally speaking, it cannot be held today that Orthodox Christian religious education materials in the free world—the only place where such materials exist, and that quite minimally—place any collective blame on the Jews for the crucifixion of Jesus, or foster the idea that the Jewish people are cursed and rejected by God. I believe that the materials, especially those published in recent years, are extremely sensitive to the issue of Jewish-Christian relations. The texts generally, however, do teach a *fulfillment* theology—a point I will deal with below—and present the people of Israel primarily as "prototypical" of all people, especially Christians, in their relations with each other, their leaders, their neighbors, the secular powers, the devil, and with God Himself. Jesus and the first Christians are consciously presented in the manuals as Jews, with very strong emphasis on the fact that Christian faith and worship are totally incomprehensible outside the biblical categories, an emphasis which deeply irritates and scandalizes anti-Jewish people in the church and serves to demonstrate their blind and sinful prejudice.

Although the present position of the Orthodox is far from that called for by John Pawlikowski, I believe the situation is both positive and hopeful, especially for a church body which very recently could produce in America voices of protest over the publication of photographs in educational manuals "by courtesy of the Israel Information Service."

As to the liturgy of the Orthodox church, there do exist liturgical ex-
clamations of a provocative character in the Byzantine order of worship, particularly during the week before Easter, which are open to
pernicious interpretation and evil influence when torn from the total
context and contents of liturgical worship and biblical faith. I personally believe, however, that the violent anti-Jewish sentiments among
many members of the Orthodox church, as well as the violent physical
attacks and murders of the infamous Easter pogroms in Russia, had
and still have little to do with theological teaching and liturgical understanding. The texts of the liturgy, with the readings from the Bible,
were—and largely still are—virtually incomprehensible to the masses
of the Orthodox people; and, as mentioned above, the anti-Semites are
scandalized by the Jewish elements in our faith, rather than inspired
by its anti-Jewish teachings. The herd violence against the Jews in Orthodox countries, as well as the sophisticated idiocies of paranoid
pseudo-intellectuals, have been the sick and stupidly sinful result of ri-
diculous mythologies, pathological anxieties and insecurities, unen-
lightened religious zeal, and social, economic, and political fears and
frustrations rather than of clear catechetical instruction, deep liturgical
inspiration, and sound spiritual experience. Indeed, these latter realities were, and to a large extent still are, conspiciously absent among the
Orthodox populace in most places, among the supposedly "educated"
as well as the great masses of the people. Therefore I believe that it has
been the absence of educational instruction and liturgical participation, and not its presence, which has caused the horrors and tragedies
of the past in Orthodox lands.

Concerning the liturgy today in the free world, ambiguous and provocative liturgical and biblical texts are more often reasonably questioned than blindly accepted by the general church membership. In
America I find people very sensitive to the pluralism of religious belief; they demand explanations of those elements of their faith which
are offensive to them and to others, and this applies also to the treatment of the Jews in the Bible and the liturgy. This is the case generally
in Western Europe, a condition acutely accented by the Second Vatican Council, and by events in the Middle East and in the Soviet Union.
As more and more people are beginning to understand and think about
what is actually being said and done in the church—a situation occurring perhaps for the first time in history—it is inevitable that questions
will be asked which will challenge old beliefs and impressions. This
can only be for the good of the Jewish-Christian dialogue. Although
there is obviously still much to be considered and done on this issue in

the Orthodox world, there is reason for hope today where in the past, humanly speaking, there was virtually none.

My main disagreement with John Pawlikowski concerns the question of *fulfillment*. I do not see that the "fulfillment" understanding of Christianity can be abandoned without the destruction of the Christian faith. Nor do I believe that it necessarily follows that if one believes that Christ is the fulfillment—not only of Israel, but of all humanity and the whole of creation—one must have contempt for all non-Christians and support violent persecutions, inquisitions, and holocausts.

John Pawlikowski calls for the abandonment of the teaching that Jesus is the Christ who has inaugurated the Messianic age. He states that although Christians may "still call Jesus the Messiah," they will have to "radically reshape" their "definition of this term." He admits that he does not know how this reshaping will be done, and that the attempts which have so far been made are "provisional." Nevertheless, he clearly understands these attempts as the first steps which will "profoundly alter Christianity's self-definition and make possible a more realistic relationship to Judaism and to all other non-Christian religions." I personally do not see how there can be a Christian faith in which Jesus is understood to be anything other than the fullness of God in human form, the second person of the Holy Trinity, who as the perfect Adam embodies in his human flesh all of the fullness of deity bodily, and as such realizes and recapitulates in his own person the entire cosmic history and destiny of man, making him divine by grace. This, I believe, is the Christian faith. It is certainly the faith of the Orthodox church and of the apostles, martyrs, and saints of Christendom. I believe that John Pawlikowski is right when, in rejecting this faith, he calls for the reinterpretation, alteration, and virtual rejection of the apostolic scriptures and the classical Christian liturgies.

I do not think, and certainly do not hope, that Pawlikowski's plan will be realized. Nor do I think and hope that the realization of this plan is the only way in which Christian contempt of the Jews can be undone. I believe and hope, rather, that the classical Christian faith can be fully accepted without resulting in the contempt, hatred, and violent persecution of those who do not accept it. Those who have truly held the Christian faith in the past, including those in the early church, have not been led to such conclusions and actions.

The central and most essential article of faith for those who truly believe in Jesus as the embodiment of all the fullness of God in human form is that they themselves fall under the judgment of his life and teaching. The apostolic scriptures are very clear in their presentation of

Jesus: that he taught contempt for no man, that he condemned no one, and that he gave his life in love for all as the realization of the love of God for the world. It is equally clear that Jesus taught his disciples to do what he did. Where the teaching of Jesus has been broken and his way not followed, the transgressors, even though they carry his name, stand condemned. This has always been the teaching of the Christian prophets and saints. Thus in no way can it be said that contempt and condemnation of others have been of the essence of Christian faith and practice. Where these horrors have occurred in Christian history, they must be absolutely condemned in Jesus' own name, and always have been by the genuine followers of Christ. It must be noted as well that virtually all of those who are now called Christian teachers and saints have themselves suffered at the hands of their co-religionists for their insistence on following the way of their master. This is certainly true in the recent history of anti-Judaism among Christians. The scandal has been that there have existed so few true Christians. Throughout the ages the Christian prophets and saints have denounced the sin of identifying the "fullness of God" with human institutions, and have soundly rejected the heresy of reducing the church of Christ to one human organization among many, exercising power and authority over man, rather than perceiving the church as the mystical reality which judges all powers and authorities, primarily those of Christians themselves, both ecclesiastical and secular.

I believe also that the Christian scriptures and saints have witnessed that faith in Jesus as the incarnate Son of God is meant to liberate believers from all human pretensions, pride, and prejudice, and allow them to acknowledge, love, and serve "whatever is true, whatever is honorable, whatever is just, whatever is pure, whatever is lovely, whatever is gracious, if there is any excellence, if there is anything worthy of praise" (Phil. 4:8), wherever and in whomever these realities are to be found—in Judaism and in any and every philosophy and religion of man. And, conversely, faith in Christ should provide the believer with the possibility and the power, the freedom, humility, and courage to discern and reject whatever is untrue, dishonorable, unjust, impure, unlovely, ungracious, without any excellence, and unworthy of any praise, wherever and in whomever such realities are to be found—first of all in and among Christians themselves. That believers in Jesus have failed to think and act in this way, and have reduced the Christian faith to a doctrine of salvation by association in an earthly organization, with contempt for nonmembers, is a disgrace and sin before God and man for which they, according to their own master, will one day have to answer.

John Pawlikowski, as I understand him, rejects such a vision and considers it to be both theologically unsound and practically harmful. He holds theologically that Christianity ought not to be understood in this way, and claims that if it is so understood it will inevitably lead to contempt of and violence toward those of contrary opinions. If we are dealing here with the question of *theology*, then dialogue as I understand it can continue. The debate can continue about the nature of the Christian faith, how it is to be understood and lived, how it orders its believers to relate to those of other faiths, how it appreciates these other opinions, etc. But if it is a question of *practicality*, and if it is held that classical Christian belief in Jesus as the "fullness of grace and truth," and in his church as "his body, the fullness of him who fills all in all," and the contempt of non-Christians are essentially and necessarily connected, then, I believe, we have a different and much more serious problem. It is a problem wider than that of Jewish-Christian dialogue. It is a problem of whether or not there can be *any* religious or philosophical view of man and the world which claims a universal significance for all mankind, in the light of which its adherents judge themselves and others, and which does not, by the very fact of its universalist pretensions, essentially foster contempt and lead to violence against those of differing views.

If it is contended that when some claim to have a vision of reality applicable to all, they become dangerous by that very fact—which seems to be John Pawlikowski's point—then, in my opinion, we are placed in a very dangerous spiritual situation and are confronted with a dilemma. We are in a dangerous situation, first, because man's basic freedom to form universally applicable opinions, if he so desires, and to claim that God has effected a universally applicable self-revelation, if he so believes, is denied. We are in a dangerous situation also because, practically speaking, such a contention portends the end of all meaningful religious and spiritual dialogue among men before such a dialogue even begins. This is the case, as I see it, because unless it is admitted that universally applicable beliefs are possible and permissible, there really cannot be "two words" about any essential and ultimate religious question in the life of man, but only a great number of private and personal opinions and ideas incapable of reaching out and touching one another in any deep and challenging way. The result of such a situation can only be a sterile relativism, a monistic spiritual syncretism devoid of creative, truly pluralistic conflict and fruitful, truly creative tension. There can be no debate here about the meaning of life and how, if at all, one comes to find it. The dilemma inherent in this view is that such a thoroughgoing relativism becomes itself a universally applicable view, and the door is open once again for its proponents themselves to be contemptuous of those who dissent.

In the area of the physical sciences, a relativist attitude would be the end of all progress and development in human understanding and action. The scientist, by vocation, must claim that what he sees and believes, within the framework of his perspective, is true for all, and that those who believe otherwise are, with all due respect, wrong. If this were not the case, there would be no scientific progress. I believe that exactly the same principle holds true in the areas of philosophy and religion.

People of religious and spiritual vision must declare that what they see and believe is true for all. They must stand by their convictions and live by them. They must confront and challenge others with their views, exposing them to criticism and judgment. Where people discover that with the eyes of faith and reason they see the same things, they must affirm their unanimity without pride or prejudice or fear. When they discover that their visions conflict with and contradict each other, they must continue to search together, engaging in free and charitable dialogue without fear of intimidation, coercion, contempt, or violence in any form, physical or psychological. Each must be free to explain, demonstrate, and defend his position, calling others to see what he sees by means of voluntary persuasion, using only intellectual argument, moral example, and the call to empirical spiritual experience as his weapons. There must be a free and open marketplace of ideas and beliefs coexisting in charitable and respectful conflict with the purpose of achieving one mind and one heart among men, in the unity of one vision, action, and life realized and expressed in a multitude of varying and mutually enriching forms. Contradiction must be the only enemy, disharmony the only adversary to be conquered and destroyed. Any other way, in my mind, is to have no dialogue at all, but is the way to the end of man's spiritual growth and unification.

I subscribe to the view that a "new era" has come to mankind in our time. I believe that the Holocaust—and the myriad other holocausts in human history, particularly the recent histories of unholy and unhappy memory in Russia and elsewhere—have brought about a new consciousness in many people which cries out "never again" to religious and ideological persecution and violence. I believe that the day has come when we will insist more and more on the freedom of all to confront one another in ideological and spiritual debate; without fear of recrimination and persecution in any form. I believe that more and more people will soon come to support the right of all to say openly what they think, even about the deepest and ultimate destinies of man, with mental and moral persuasion as their only means of dispelling disharmony. I believe also that if we refuse the gift of entering into meaningful debate, perhaps for the first time in human history, about the ultimate meaning of man in the universe—a gift given to us not only by the scientific achievements of our day, but more significantly by the blood of millions of men, women, and children who have been killed in the era of violence and contempt which hopefully has passed—then, to borrow John Pawlikowski's allusion, "our last state" shall indeed be "worse than our first." We have at hand the most genuine possibility to cultivate and develop the spirit of the world. I personally hope that the debate can continue with nothing less than the broadest visions of the truth and the deepest spiritual unity of mankind as its goal. May the God of our fathers lead us on in our common task.

PART V

Theological Reflections on the State of Israel in the Light of the Yom Kippur War

Introduction

Three years after the end of the Holocaust the world saw the restoration of a Jewish homeland. For many Jews it seemed like a resurrection from the dead, a new sign of hope, a symbol of the people's survival. Since then the existence of Israel as a political entity as well as symbol, and the continuing precariousness of its existence, is raising new questions for Jews and Christians alike, though they differ in nature. Some of these questions, along with Israel's relationship to the Holocaust, are explored in the three papers which follow.

However one defines the relationship between the Holocaust and the State of Israel, the existence of a relationship is undeniable. In the major paper of this section, *Emil Fackenheim* finds several common denominators between the two events.

Both events are unique. Fackenheim has asserted again and again in his writings (*God's Presence in History, Quest for Past and Future*) that the Holocaust is not simply one more catastrophe in an endless chain of catastrophes in human history. It is unique, because never before had genocide been made into its own end, serving no other purpose than itself. The Holocaust is the "celebration" of evil for its own sake, and the face of the world has been changed once and for all as a result.

The uniqueness of the State of Israel appears to Fackenheim in several ways. A prayer by the Israeli Chief Rabbinate with which he opens his paper makes a link between the modern state and the beginning of the Messianic era. This represents a new development in Jewish tradition. For while the rabbis of old never ceased speculating about the end-time, they always avoided linking the Messianic future with a tenuous, contingent historical event. The future is absolute; the present, by its very nature, precarious. And yet, must not a link between the two be attempted, lest the future become evanescent and forever elusive? The boldness of the prayer referred to dares to make this attempt. The inherent tension is not dissolved here, but affirmed.

Israel is unique for Fackenheim also in the sense that the state cannot be defined in purely secular terms. While Zionism, as a modern political movement, may resemble other nationalisms, it does so on the surface only. Nothing but "a will in touch with an absolute dimension" could have overcome obstacles which no other nation has had to face: bringing a people home from eighteen centuries of Diaspora in every culture and climate; reviving an ancient language; creating a self-government and self-defense, etc. What began as, and has often seemed, an attempt at Jewish normalization, has deeper wellsprings, which simply cannot be accounted for in purely secular terms. The traditional distinction between "religious" and "secular" breaks down in the case of Israel—a view expressed also in Irving Greenberg's paper.

Fackenheim rejects any possibility of explaining either the Holocaust or the State of Israel at the historical or theological level. If, historically, the state can be seen "as a near-necessity," it is equally possible to see it as "a near-impossibility." Would it not have been far easier to give up once and for all, rather than resurrect a people and state out of the ashes of the Holocaust? As to those who seek theological explanations for the Holocaust, Fackenheim's answer follows Jewish tradition. The problem is not to *explain* God, but how to *live* with him.

If explanation is impossible, however, a response is demanded. It is here that the link between the Holocaust and Israel is most clearly visible. Jews responded to the Holocaust in a variety of ways. Some, like Rabbi Daniel, exhorted their people in the moment before the slaughter to praise the Name of the God of Israel and perform the Kiddush Hashem. Others, like the butcher in Yosef Gottfarstein's chronicle, or the Warsaw Ghetto fighters, fought unredeemable evil with bare teeth or guns. What both types of response have in common is the determination to resist, even when there is no hope of personal survival. Faith in the future of the people endures, or is reborn, through despair. Commitment to and belief in Jewish survival has transformed the patient waiting of centuries into the heroic action of the present. This, and this alone, has the power to break what Fackenheim calls the "millennial, unholy alliance of hatred of Jews with Jewish powerlessness." It may not be broken yet. But commitment to the autonomy of Israel is part of the battle which began in the Warsaw Ghetto.

The two responses to Fackenheim also deal with Messianism, but from different perspectives. *Seymour Siegel* sees Messianism, Zionism, and the Holocaust as closely related. The modern Zionist movement, for him, is built on Messianism, chosenness, and the land. It has brought about a radical change in the traditional Jewish concept of Messianism by abandoning the view that the coming of the kingdom must be left to God alone, and stressing instead the need for human effort. This makes it a purely secular movement for him. The Zionist conviction that human effort is required if Jews are to be safe has been confirmed by the Holocaust, which showed all too tragically that Jews could rely on no one but themselves for their survival, since the rest of the world was silent.

Siegel does not, however, identify secular Messianism with the whole of Jewish Messianism, and warns against equating a secure state with the Messianic kingdom. Jews must seek to avoid the temptation, on the one hand, of doing nothing (pessimism and quietism), and, on the other, of relying on human effort alone (utopianism). Precisely, however, because Israel is not yet the Messianic kingdom, it is forced to use secular tools, like other nations, to protect itself. The resulting challenge to Christians, for Siegel, is to assist in this effort, and help insure Israel's existence. Despite what has been achieved, Israel's existence is still precarious at best.

Eva Fleischner also takes up the issue of Messianism, but from the viewpoint of a Christian theologian. Seymour Siegel in his response stresses the differences in Jewish and Christian Messianic expectations. For Judaism, redemption will be acknowledged only when it is visible, public, taking place on the stage of history. For Christianity, on the other hand, it is a spiritual, inner, unseen event. Without denying these differences, Fleischner suggests that certain elements in Christian theology are narrowing the gulf which has for so long existed between the two traditions. As Christian theologians today wrestle with the Christ question ("Who do you say that I am?"), there comes to the fore in Christianity a tension of unfulfillment, of the "already" and "not yet," which in some ways is analogous to Fackenheim's perception of Israel as both sign and anticipation. A Christian theology which is more tentative, less absolutist than in the past, is closer to the tension in Judaism which dares to link Israel, in all its historical ambiguity, with the Messianic future. Thus the common ground for discussion and understanding between Jews and Christians is broadened, and new avenues of exploration can be opened up.

Christian support and affirmation of Israel's existence is not an open question for Fleischner, but a sine qua non. The nature of this support, however, is less clear-cut. No Christian understanding of Israel is valid that does not take Jewish understanding into account. But this Jewish understanding is manifold and varied. Hence Christians must learn to listen, to hear the many Jewish voices, and all the different tones in which they speak. If along with such listening Christians seek to build a climate of trust, so that Jews will no longer feel isolated and abandoned, then they may be able to speak words of both honesty and love which may help to bring healing to the torn world of the Middle East. Thus for Jew and Christian alike, Israel represents a new challenge in a post-Holocaust world, the repercussions of which will be momentous for Jewish-Christian relations, though they cannot yet be gauged.

The Holocaust and the State of Israel: Their Relation

EMIL L. FACKENHEIM

I

"Our Father in Heaven, Rock of Israel and her Redeemer, bless the State of Israel, the beginning of the dawn of our redemption. . . ."

This prayer by the Israeli Chief Rabbinate does not hesitate to describe the State of Israel as "the beginning of the dawn of the redemption" of the Jewish people. That the official rabbinate of Israel should formulate such a prayer is in itself surprising; what is positively astonishing, however, is its wide acceptance by Jews everywhere. Religious Jews inside and outside Israel recite it in the synagogue, and secularist Israelis who neither frequent synagogues nor recite prayers recite *this* prayer, as it were, not with their lips but with their lives.

Messianic expectations by religious Jews are not new or unusual; neither is the association of these with the ingathering of the exiles in a restored Jewish commonwealth. More than merely unusual, however, if not altogether without precedent, is the linking of these, even by fervent believers, with a historical event *already clearly and unequivocally present.* No matter how cautiously interpreted, the Messianic future cannot be shorn of an element of absoluteness, whereas the historical present is inexorably ambiguous in essence and precarious in its very existence. The State of Israel is not exempt from the condition of historicity. Hence a prayer which links this present state with the Messianic future reflects a boldness which the ancient sages of the Gentiles might well have considered tantamount to hybris, or tempting the gods.

The rabbis of ancient Israel would have doubts of their own. Unlike the gods, their God is Lord of History. Moreover, He has given promises, the reliance on which is not hybris but rather fidelity. But *when*

The writer wishes to thank the Canada Council for a research grant enabling him to spend two summers in Jerusalem on a project, among the first results of which is the present article, prepared for the *Encyclopaedia Judaica Yearbook.* It was presented at the Symposium, and is published here with permission of the *Yearbook.*

will the time be ripe for "the End"? And *how*—if at all—can one detect the signs? These questions receive only reluctant and conflicting answers from the rabbis. To be sure, they *must* link history with its Messianic fulfillment, but prudently shrink from extending this linking to *particular* events *already present*. Thus the rabbis too, understand, no less well than the sages of the Gentiles, that—this side of its Messianic transfiguration—all history is precarious.

For this reason rabbinic imagery picturing the Messianic days as gradually unfolding is inevitably at odds with its opposite, which views "the End" as ushered in by catastrophe. At one extreme, it is imagined that all foreign domination over Israel will cease *before* the coming of the Son of David, and that the "mountains will grow branches and bear fruit" for its returning inhabitants (B.T : Sanh. 98a). At the other, the End is pictured as preceded by impoverishment in the land, and indeed by a terror in Jerusalem so extreme that her gates will all be equal—not one will furnish escape (ibid.). The one projection can be furnished with a proof-text (Ezek. 36:8) which makes it the "clearest sign" of the End. But so can the other (Zech. 8:10, also Ps. 119:165). These and similar conflicting projections cannot but produce in all (or most) rabbis the insight that they are mere speculations—that all attempts to link the precarious present with the absolute future are themselves precarious and cannot be otherwise.

This condition cannot be transcended even when a sober appraisal of actual history brings about a near-consensus among the rabbis. Under the influence of idealism, some modern Jewish thinkers were to conceive of Messianism as a mere ideal which, on the one hand, could only be approached and not reached and, on the other, was *being* approached in a linear or dialectical progression *already present*. Such notions are foreign to rabbinic realism, to which the Messianic days are more than a mere ideal, and which, at the same time, can see no clear Messianic direction in past or present. Recognizing catastrophe as a persisting possibility, this realism creates the imagery of a pre-Messianic travail—the "birth-pangs of the Messiah"—as an all but normative check on all gradualist or sentimental utopianism. Yet even so normative an image can bring about no firm link between the absolute future and historical events already present. Thus in the midst of catastrophe the pessimistic Rabbi Hillel can despair of Messianism altogether, holding that King Hezekiah has already been the promised Messiah, and that no other is to be expected (B.T. Sanh. 99a). For his part, Rabbi Yochanan cannot go beyond the admonition that "when you see an age in which suffering pours like a stream, then hope for him" (B.T. Sanh. 98a). But hope is not a certainty, and suffering, however harrowing, is not a proof. Thus the link between the forever precarious historical present and the Messianic future is itself forever precarious, a fact poignantly expressed in Midrashim in which the Israelites plead with God to make an end of the painful historical alternation between exile and redemption, and bring the final redemption.

Yet unless the Messianic future is to become ever-elusive and thus irrelevant, its linking with a *possible* present, however precarious, is indispensable, and, with its risks paradigmatically shown by Rabbi Akiba's support of the Bar Kochba rebellion, this too becomes normative for the Jewish religious consciousness—and remains so, through the ages. Thus at one extreme, the mystical Nachmanides (1194–1270) does not hesitate to rob empirical history of its intrinsic precariousness by means of the suspect ancient device of "calculating the End," maintaining that the rabbinic strictures against the practice no longer apply when the End is so near.[1] (This view was to be reiterated by more than one rabbi during the Nazi Holocaust; with increasing conviction by those surviving to see the birth of the State of Israel.)[2] Yet he *stays with* empirical history and when he sees Messianic (albeit negative) *evidence* in the fact that, while many Gentile nations have succeeded in destroying the land, not one has succeeded in rebuilding it (Comm. on Lev. 26:32). At the other extreme, the sober Maimonides (1135–1204) assimilates the Messianic future to the historical present, sufficiently so as to reaffirm a rabbinic view that "the sole difference between the present and the Messianic days is delivery from servitude to foreign powers" (B.T. Sanh. 91b). At the same time, he must ascribe an *absolute* perfection to future men (Jews and Gentiles alike) to be able to assert that the kingdom of the Son of David, unlike David's own, will be destroyed neither by sin within nor by aggression from without. He does not resolve but only expresses this tension by echoing the rabbinic saying that those be "blasted who reckon out the End" (B.T. Sanh. 97b).[3]

In view of this inherent and inevitable tension between contingent historical present and absolute Messianic future in the Jewish religious consciousness, it is not surprising that the modern world should have produced a deep and widespread desire or need to get rid of that tension. This is done covertly when the absolute future is projected into an irrelevant infinity, and overtly when it is abandoned altogether. The result is a "normalization" which occurs when Jewish existence is classified without remainder in available categories, such as "religious denomination" or "ethnic subculture," and, above all, of course, when there is total assimilation.

The modern Zionist movement originally appears on the scene as another normalization effort, and, indeed, at one extreme one as radical as total assimilation is at the other. No Jewish self-classification as "religious denomination" or "ethnic subculture" can ever be quite successful, not the one because one is born a Jew, not the other because one is somehow obliged to remain one, and various identity crises reflect these difficulties. In contrast, Zionism characteristically seems to come on the scene with the aim of making Jews "a nation like any other nation," just as, at the opposite extreme, assimilationism aims at dissolving Jews *into* other nations. Thus Jewish "normalization" seems complete only at the extremes.

However, as Zionism unfolds in thought and action, it gradually emerges that the Messianic future, ignored or even repudiated, lives on within it, changed or unchanged, as the hidden inspiration without which the movement cannot survive. To be sure, Herzl's "If you will it, it is no dream" is a strikingly secularist appeal, exalting as it does the will above all else; it may even be understood as an antireligious protest. Yet the goal aimed at by this will is so radically at odds with all the "natural" trends of modern history as to require a mainspring far deeper and more original than the imitation of the varieties of nineteenth-century European nationalism, and one more positive and radical than escape into "normalcy" from what was then known as anti-Semitism. To this day this deeper inspiration has found little articulation in Zionist *thought*. Yet had it not existed throughout Zionist *life*—from the days of the early settlers through the Yom Kippur War—Herzl's dream would either not have become real at all or else not have stayed real for long. No other twentieth-century "liberation movement" has had to contend with all (or any) of these problems: the reuniting of a people rent apart by vast culture gaps of centuries; the reviving of an ancient language; the re-creation, virtually overnight, of self-government and self-defense in a people robbed of these arts for two millennia; to say nothing of defending a young state for a whole generation against overwhelming odds, and on a territory virtually indefensible. Only a will in touch with an absolute dimension could have come anywhere near solving these problems; and even those acting on this will may well be astonished by its accomplishments. Hence it has come to pass that the categories "religious" and "secularist" (whatever their undiminished validity in other contexts) have been radically shaken by the Zionist reality, a fact which has produced strange bedfellows. On one side, ultrareligious Jews waiting for God's Messiah and secularist Jews wanting neither God nor Messiah are united in hostility to the will that animates the Zionist reality, obtuse to its meaning. On the other side, religious Zionists do not count on miracles, while secularist Zionists have been known to be astonished. These two are united as well, if not when things appear normal, at any rate in those extreme moments when all appearances fall away and only truth remains.

II

The Holocaust is unique in history, and therefore in Jewish history. Previously genocide had been a means to such human (if evil) ends as power, greed, an extreme of nationalist or imperialist self-assertion, and at times this means may even have become, demonically, an end *beside* these others. In the Holocaust Kingdom genocide showed itself gradually to be *the sole ultimate end* to which all else—power, greed, and even "Aryan" self-assertion—were sacrificed, for "Aryan" had no other clear meaning than "not non-Aryan." And since the Nazis were not anti-Semites because they were "racists" but rather racists because they were anti-Semites, the "non-Aryan" was, paradigmatically, the Jew. Thus the event belongs to Jewish and world history alike.

Nor is "genocide" adequate to describe the Holocaust Kingdom. Torquemada burned Jewish bodies to save Jewish souls. Eichmann created a system which, by torturing with terror and hope, by assailing all human dignity and self-respect, was designed to destory the souls of all available Jewish men, women, and children before consigning their bodies to the gas chambers. The Holocaust Kingdom was a cele- bration of degradation as much as of death, and of death as much as of degradation. The celebrants willingly or even enthusiastically de- scended into hell themselves, even as they created hell for their vic- tims. As for the world—it tolerated the criminals and abandoned the innocents. Thus the Holocaust is not only a unique event. It is epoch- making. The world, just like the Jewish world, can never again be the same.

The event therefore resists explanation—the historical kind which seeks causes, and the theological kind which seeks meaning and pur- pose. More precisely, the better the mind succeeds with the necessary task of explaining what can be explained, the more it is shattered by its ultimate failure. What holds true of the Holocaust holds true also of its connection with the State of Israel. Here too, the explaining mind suf- fers ultimate failure. *Yet it is necessary not only to perceive a bond be- tween the two events, but also so to act as to make it unbreakable.*

Historians see a causal connection between the Holocaust and the foundation of the State of Israel. The reasoning is as follows. Had it not been for the European Jewish catastrophe, all the centuries of religious longing for Zion, all the decades of secularist Zionist activity, together with all such external encouragement as was given by the Balfour Declaration, would have produced no more than a Palestinian ghetto. This might have been a community with impressive internal achievements, but rather than a "national home" for homeless Jews, it would have been itself at the mercy of some alien government of dubious benevolence. Only the Holocaust produced a desperate determination in the survivors and those identified with them, outside and especially within the Yishuv; ended vacillation in the Zionist leadership as to the wisdom of seeking political self-determination; and produced a moment of respite from political cynicism in the international community, long enough to give legal sanction to a Jewish State. Even so, "the UN Resolution of 1947 came at the last possible moment."[4]

This reasoning is plausible; no more so, however, than its exact opposite. Why were the survivors not desperate to stay away from Palestine rather than reach it—the one place on earth which would tie them inescapably to a Jewish destiny? (After what that destiny had been to them, the desire to hide or flee from their Jewishness would have been "natural.") Why did the Zionist leadership rise from vacillation to resoluteness rather than simply disintegrate? (Confronted by absolute enemies, it was at the mercy of its friends.) As for the world's respite from political cynicism, this was neither of long duration nor unambiguous while it lasted. Ernest Bevin and his Colonial Office were rendered more—not less—intransigent to Zionist pressures by the catastrophic loss of lives and power which the Jewish people had just suffered. And the five Arab armies that "surged in upon the nascent Israeli nation to exterminate it and make themselves its immediate heirs" were "encouraged by the way Hitler had practiced genocide without encountering resistance."[5] Thus while, as previously argued, the State of Israel after the Holocaust may be viewed as a near-necessity, yet we now see that it may be viewed, with equal justice, as a near-impossibility. Historical explanation falls short in this manner because all human responses to the Holocaust are ultimately incalculable.

If historical explanations (seeking merely causes) remain precarious, theological explanations (seeking nothing less than meaning and purpose) collapse altogether, not because they are theological but because they are explanations. They fail whether they *find* a purpose, such as punishment for sin, or merely *assert* a purpose without finding it, such as a divine will, purposive yet inscrutable. This theological failure is by no means overcome if the Holocaust is considered as a means, in-scrutable but necessary, to no less an end than the "dawn of redemp-tion," of which in turn the State of Israel is viewed as the necessary "beginning." No meaning or purpose will ever be found in the event, and one does not glorify God by associating His will with it. Indeed, the very attempt is a sacrilege. (I have elsewhere argued that Jewish thought at its deepest level, especially vis-a-vis catastrophe, does not express itself in explanatory systems but rather in conflicting Midra-shim, the goal of which is not how to explain God but how to live with Him. Radicalizing the midrashic approach, I have also argued that to find a meaning in the Holocaust is impossible, but to seek a response is inescapable.)[6]

What, then, must be said of such as Rabbi Israel Shapiro of the city of Grodzisk, who told his Jews at Treblinka that *these* were at last the *real* birth-pangs of the Messiah, that they all were blessed to have mer-ited the honor of being the sacrifices, and that their ashes would serve to purify all Israel?[7]

First, this response must be revered *as a response;* however—in equal reverence for all the innocent millions, the children included, who had neither the ability, nor the opportunity, nor the desire, to be willing martyrs—it must be *rid totally of every appearance of being an explanation.* Did God *want* Auschwitz? Even the ancient rabbis some-times seem to view the Messianic birth-pangs not as a means used by a purposive (if inscrutable) divine will, but rather as, so to speak, a cos-mic catastrophe which must occur before divine power and mercy can find their redemptive manifestation.

Second, Rabbi Shapiro's extreme of pious hope must be juxtaposed by opposites no less pious, and no less to be revered. The pious men of a *shtibl* in the Lodz Ghetto spent a whole day fasting, praying, saying psalms, and then, having opened the holy ark, convoked a solemn *Din Torah,* and forbade God to punish His people any further. (Elsewhere God was put on trial—and found guilty.)[8] And in the Warsaw Ghetto a handful of Jews, ragged, alone, poorly armed, carried out the first uprising against the Holocaust Kingdom in all of Europe. The rabbis showed religious piety when, rather than excuse God or curse Him, they cited His own promises against Him. The fighters showed secular piety when, rather than surrender to the Satanic Kingdom, they took up arms against it. The common element in these two responses was not hope but rather despair. To the rabbis who found Him guilty, the God who had broken His promises in the Holocaust could no longer be trusted to keep *any* promise, the Messianic included. And precisely when hope had come to an end the fighters took to arms—in a rebellion which had no hope of succeeding.

With this conclusion, every explanatory connection between the Holocaust and the State of Israel has broken down, the causal historical kind in part, the teleological religious kind entirely, and even the hope connecting the one event with the other competes with despair. Yet, as we have said, it is necessary not only to perceive a bond between the two events but also so to connect them as to make the bond unbreakable. Such a bond is *possible* because to seek a *cause* or a *meaning* is one thing, to give a *response* is another. And it is necessary because the heart of every *authentic* response to the Holocaust—religious and secularist, Jewish and non-Jewish—is a commitment to the autonomy and security of the State of Israel.

The Chronicler Yosef Gottfarstein reports:

> The Jews of Kelme, Lithuania were already standing beside the pits which they had been forced to dig for themselves—standing ready to be slain for the Sanctification of the Name. Their spiritual leader, Rabbi Daniel, asked the German officer in command of the operation to allow him to say some parting words to his flock, and the latter agreed but ordered Rabbi Daniel to be brief. Speaking serenely, slowly, as though he were delivering one of his regular Sabbath sermons in the synagogue, Rabbi Daniel used his last minutes on earth to encourage his flock to perform Kiddush Hashem in the proper manner. Suddenly the Geraman officer cut in and shouted at the rabbi to finish so that he could get on with the shooting. Still speaking calmly, the rabbi concluded as follows: "My dear Jews! The moment has come for us to perform the precept of Kiddush Hashem of which we have spoken, to perform it in fact! I beg one thing of you: don't get excited and confused; accept this judgment calmly and in a worthy manner!"
>
> Then he turned to the German officer and said: "I have finished. You may begin."

Gottfarstein continues:

> At Kedainiai the Jews were already inside the pit, waiting to be murdered by the Germans, when suddenly a butcher leaped out of the pit, pounced on the German officer in command, and sank his teeth into the officer's throat, holding on till the latter died.
>
> When Rabbi Shapiro, the last Rabbi of Kovno, was asked which of these two acts he thought was more praiseworthy, he said: There is no doubt that Rabbi Daniel's final message to his flock concerning the importance of the precept of Kiddush Hashem was most fitting. But that Jew who sank

his teeth into the German's throat also performed the precept in letter and in spirit, because the precept includes the aspect of action. "I am sure that if the opportunity had presented itself, Rabbi Daniel would also have been capable of doing what the butcher did," Rabbi Shapiro added.[9]

"I have finished. You may begin." We search all history for a more radical contrast between pure, holy goodness and a radical evil utterly and eternally beyond all redemption. The German officer saw what he saw. He heard what he heard. So did his men. How then could even one go on with the shooting? Yet they all did.

This unredeemable evil must have been in Rabbi Shapiro's mind when he did not hesitate to rank a simple, presumably ignorant, and perhaps not very pious butcher with a saintly rabbi learned in the ways of the Torah and earnestly obeying its commandments. For us who come after, the resistance as faith and dignity of Rabbi Daniel and his flock, the Kiddush Hashem of the butcher, and the judgment concerning these two forms of testimony made by Rabbi Shapiro of Kovno, itself a form of testimony, are nothing less than a dual revelation: a holy dignity-in-degradation, a heroic war against Satanic death—each a resistance to the climax of a millennial, unholy combination of hatred of Jews with Jewish powerlessness which we are bidden to end forever.

To listen to this revelation is inevitably to be turned from the rabbi, who had only his faith, and the butcher, who had only his teeth, to the Warsaw Ghetto fighters in their ragged dignity and with their wretched arms. Of the second day of the uprising, one of the leaders, Yitzhak Zuckerman, reports:

> By following guerrilla warfare theory, we saved lives, added to our supply of arms and, most important, proved to ourselves that the German was but flesh and blood, as any man.
>
> And prior to this we had not been aware of this amazing truth! If one lone German appeared in the Ghetto the Jews would flee *en masse,* as would Poles on the Aryan side. . . .
>
> The Germans were not psychologically prepared for the change that had come over the Jewish community and the Jewish fighters. They were seized with panic.[10]

Amazingly, the Holocaust Kingdom was breached. At least in principle, the millennial unholy combination was broken.

This fact re-created in Zuckerman hope in the midst of despair: "We knew that Israel would continue to live, and that for the sake of all Jews everywhere and for Jewish existence and dignity—even for future generations—only one thing would do: Revolt!"[11]

Another leader of the uprising, Mordecai Anielewicz, was to perish in the flames of the ghetto. Yet in his last letter he wrote: "My life's aspiration is fulfilled. The Jewish self-defense has arisen. Blissful and chosen is my fate to be among the first Jewish fighters in the ghetto." "Blissful" and "chosen" are almost exactly the words used by Rabbi Israel Shaprio of the city of Grodzisk as he led his flock to the crematoria of Treblinka, sure that their ashes would hasten the coming of the Messiah.

But *was* Jewish destiny so much as touched by the handfuls of desperate men and women in the ghettos and camps? And is it *true in any sense whatever* that the millennial, unholy combination of hatred of Jews and Jewish powerlessness has been so much as breached? Rabbi Shapiro was unable to sustain his faith in God without also clinging to the "aspect of action" in Kiddush Hashem, as performed by the butcher. The fighters were unable to persist in their fight without staking their faith on future Jewish generations. Was not, in both cases, the faith groundless and hollow, overwhelmed by despair?

Mordecai Anielewicz died in May 1943. Named after him, Kibbutz Yad Mordecai was founded in the same year. Five years after Mordecai's death, almost to the day, a small band of members of the kibbutz bearing his name held off a well-equiped Egyptian army for five long days—days in which the defense of Tel Aviv could be prepared, days crucial for the survival of the Jewish state. The Warsaw Ghetto fighters had not, after all, been mistaken.

Their hope, however, had not been a rational one, much less a calculated prediction. It had been a blessed, self-fulfilling prophecy, for the heroism and self-sacrifice of the prophets had been the indispensable element without which the prophecy could not have been fulfilled. The battle for Yad Mordecai began in the streets of Warsaw. To this day the justly larger-than-life statue of Mordecai Anielewicz dominates the kibbutz named after him, reminding the forgetful and teaching the thoughtless that what links Rabbi Daniel, the butcher, the two Rabbis Shapiro, and the ghetto fighters with Yad Mordecai is neither a causal necessity nor a divine miracle, if these are thought of as divorced from human believing and acting. It is a fervent believing, turned by despair from patient waiting into heroic acting. It is an acting which through despair has recovered faith.

Behind the statue stands the shattered water tower of the kibbutz, a mute reminder that even after its climax the combination of hatred of Jews and Jewish powerlessness has not come to an end. However, the shattered tower is dwarfed by the statue, and is at its back. The statue faces what Mordecai longed for and never despaired of—green fields, crops, trees, birds, flowers, Israel.

"Our Father in Heaven, Rock of Israel and her Redeemer, bless Thou the State of Israel, the beginning of the dawn of our redemption. Shield her with the wings of Thy love, and spread over her the tabernacle of Thy peace . . ."

Response to Emil Fackenheim

SEYMOUR SIEGEL

Emil Fackenheim's paper brought to memory a chronicle I had read in a collection called *Kiddush Hashem* ("The Sanctification of the Name"):[1]

> Thousands of people, living, healthy, life-loving, marching with shuffling feet, apathetic, indifferent. The shadow of death already hovers over all of us . . . near me there stands out the figure of a tall, old Jew with a patriarchal gray beard. . . . He carries his *talis* and *tephillin* under his arm. Nothing more. . . . He jumps up with a strong and confident voice. "Jews, do not be troubled. Do not be melancholy! Why do you sit thus? Not in sadness, God forbid! If I would have something to drink I would propose a *lechayim*. Do you not see how we are going to greet the Messiah?"

What did this Jew mean when he said that "we are going to greet the Messiah"? Did he believe that the suffering of his fellow Jews was redemptive and thus would bring the coming of the Redeemer? Did he mean that if the awful suffering continued God would have to release the Messiah and allow him to come to earth? Perhaps . . .

Perhaps he was thinking of the well-known passage in the Mishnah:[2]

> In the footsteps of the Messiah [i.e, in the period of his arrival] presumption will increase and respect disappear. The empire will turn to heresy and there will be no moral reproof. . . the wisdom of the sages will become odious, and those who shun sin will be despised. . . truth will be nowhere found. On whom shall we then rely? On our Father in heaven.

I do not know what the Jew in our chronicle thought. But it is certain that the Messianic idea, or rather the Messianic vision, has accompanied the Jew throughout the exile, especially in times of great suffering.

The Messianic idea is inexorably tied up with the movement of Zionism as well as with the Holocaust, and therefore Emil Fackenheim is right in focusing on Messianism as the central notion around

217

which we marshal our thoughts to try to cope with the awesome events of the past decades of Jewish and univeral history. When I was in Israel a few months ago, I found that there is a spate of new books in which mystics and visionaries are now looking for the signs that the time of the Messianic arrival is near.

The Messianic idea as Gershom Scholem points out,[3]

> is totally different in Judaism and in Christianity; Judaism in all of its forms and manifestations, has always maintained a concept of redemption as an event which takes place publicly, on the stage of history, and within the community. It is an occurrence which takes place in the visible world and which cannot be conceived apart from such visible appearance. In contrast Christianity conceives of redemption as an event in the spiritural and unseen realm; an event which is reflected in the soul, in the private world of each individual, and which effects an inner transformation which need not correspond to anything outside.

The Messianic redemption would be visible on three levels.[4] It would mark the reconciliation of Israel and its land; it would mark the reconciliation of all the nations to each other; and it would mark the reconciliation of nature and its God. In the bolder and more daring speculations of the kabbalists, Messianism and redemption meant even the redemption of God Himself from His brokenness.[5]

This grand idea was not without its costs. First of all, it meant the possibility, unfortunately frequently manifested in Jewish history, of false Messiahs.[6] Secondly, the Messianic idea compelled a life lived in "deferment," in which nothing can be done definitively and in which no achievement has any lasting value because it falls short of the total redemption, and is therefore only provisional and precarious.

Zionism which antedated the Holocaust, brought about a radical change in the understanding of Messianism. It made a bold, even heretical thrust. It taught that in order to realize the first part of the Messianic dream—i.e., the return of the Jews to their homeland and the establishment of their own independence—the passive stance which Messianism had fostered would have to be abandoned.[7]

The Talmud reports that Israel made three oaths (it is generally assumed that this was a reaction to the ill-fated Bar Kochba rebellion): "One that Israel shall not go up by a wall [i.e., wage war]; the second, that whereby the Holy One, blessed be He, adjured Israel that they shall not rebel against the nations of the world; and the third is that whereby the Holy One, blessed be He, adjured the idolaters that they

shall not oppress Israel too much" (B.T., Ket. IIIa). With the advent of
the Zionist movement the oath was revoked. Israel would wage war for
its own survival.

There were, of course (and there still are), people who fully identified the Messianic redemption with Zionist achievement. The vast
number of Jews, however, saw the redemption of Zionism as the *beginning* of a process. The Almighty, in His own good time, would complete the process. Zionism, therefore, is in essence *secular,* using human efforts. The Jews are not tourists in the secular city. They have
been living there for a very long time. Zionism's most meaningful
pamphlet was *Auto-emancipation* by Leo Pinsker.[8] A dispirited and
dispersed people would be inspired to return to its ancient land in the
face of fierce opposition. Zionism was born out of the feeling that the
Jews could not depend either on the nations of the world or on God to
free them. There would have to be auto-emancipation.[9] This auto-
emancipation would liberate, not subjugate. It would bring freedom
instead of bondage.

Since we live in a period of the depreciation of words, the term
"Zionism" has been debased in our time, either out of ignorance or out
of malice. Though Zionism was a national liberation movement which
predated most of the efforts now current, the term "Zionism" is today
presented as something reprehensible, especially—though not exclusively—by adherents of the various varieties of the Left—New Left,
Old Left, Catholic Left, and Jewish Left.

When Zionism first appeared it was strongly opposed by many Jews.
There were those who, dreaming of a bogus universalism, denigrated
all nationalisms, especially Jewish nationalism. There were those who
clung to the old belief that only a miraculous redemption brought
about by God would save Israel; all efforts at auto-emancipation were
seen as heresy. There were those who believed that the universal forces
of peace and justice or the establishment of a socialist order would
solve the "Jewish problem." Everything else, Zionism included, was
seen as a diversion. There were those who believed that somehow it
was not proper for Jews, dedicated to the spirit, to dirty their hands in
politics and state-building.[10] The latter group, both Jews and Christians, was guilty of one of the most persistent of all heresies, the heresy
of overspiritualization, of the denial of the concreteness of the Hebrew
Bible, and the failure to recognize that the promises in Scripture were
involved in real, concrete things—like lands and farms. "The Hebrew
Bible," writes Abraham J. Heschel, "is not a book about heaven—it is a

book about the earth. The Hebrew word, *eretz,* meaning 'land,' occurs at least five times as often in the Bible as the word *shamayim,* meaning 'heaven.' "[11]

The great Protestant thinker Reinhold Niebuhr understood this point very well. He wrote: "I do not see how it is possible to develop this prophetic overtone of high religion in the Jewish community fully if the nation does not have a greater degree of political security."[12]

Jewish consciousness did not give up the full dimensions of the Messianic idea. It decided, however, to begin to implement at least part of the vision through secular means. Perhaps this would shame God into bringing the total redemption.

Zionism was not only concerned about the *physical* survival of Jews. It was also concerned about Judaism or Jewishness. Jewishness was threatened by assimilation—a more painless form of death, but death nevertheless. Everywhere Jewishness represented a minority culture. There is a certain grandeur in being a perpetual minority. But the demands of the covenant, the central concept of Jewish self-understanding, must be fulfilled also under conditions of autonomy. Martin Buber, in a letter to Mahatma Gandhi, expressed this eloquently:

> We went into exile with our task unperformed; but the command remained with us. We need our own soil in order to fulfill it; we need the freedom to order our own life—no attempt can be made on foreign soil and under foreign statute. We are not covetous, Mahatma. . . . Our only desire is that at last we may be able to obey.[13]

This demand for cultural autonomy could be understood in secular, cultural terms. It could also be understood in theological terms, as covenant autonomy. The Jewish spirit needs to be released from bondage in order to flourish anew. Here the ancient idea of chosenness finds new meaning in Zionism.

To the two elements of Messianism and chosenness, a third element was to be added: the concept of the land. The land is the Land of Promises. It is also the Land of the Beginnings. It is where Judaism began, and where the great culmination will occur. The land is the thread which runs throughout all of Jewish history. The God of Israel is a universal God. But Jewish history reflects a dialogue with the land, even when the people reside outside of it. "The love of this land was due to an imperative, not to an instinct, not to a sentiment. There is a covenant, an engagement of the people to the land. We live by Covenants. We could not betray our pledge or discard the promise."[14]

Thus three interrelated themes—prominent in Jewish theology—intertwined to form Zionist ideology: Messianism, chosenness, and the land. They were transmuted, transformed, and translated into secular terms. But their power was reflected in the movement of return and renascence.

The events of the Holocuast did not *create* Zionism. They *confirmed* the insights of Zionism.

The nations of the world showed their ferocious enmity. The withdrawal of the Jewish people from history had resulted in destruction, degradation, and Holocaust. We are only now beginning to understand the awesome dimensions of the enmity of the nations toward Jacob. The Hitlerian butchers were the prime criminals. But there were others who stood by while six million died. There were those who were silent in the Vatican even when the dimensions of the slaughter became known. There were the rulers of the "workers' paradise," who made a pact with Hitler, and who even now refuse to acknowledge the fact of Jewish suffering. Nor can we forget the complicity of the Arabs, some of whom openly sided with Hitler, among them the grand mufti of Jerusalem, who was given a place of honor in the courts of the butchers of the Jews. The need for active participation, for the transformation of the passive Jew into one who would fight for his physical existence with force and with blood; one who would seek political power in order to defend himself against the demons which seem to possess the nations of the world when they deal with the House of Jacob—this need became vividly clear.

The events of the Holocaust have confirmed that while ultimately our trust is with the God of Jacob, He will, apparently, not protect us unless we protect ourselves.

The events of the Yom Kippur War and their aftermath have further confirmed the insights of the Zionist leaders and the truths which emerged from the Holocaust.

The treachery of the nations was now expressed not only by those who professed the God of Jesus. The most ferocious now were those who worshipped Allah and those who bowed at the altar of Marx. We listened with bitterness and unbelief to the "debates" of the United Nations during and after the war. The USSR, which has created millions of refugees without making one gesture to compensate them, which ruthlessly crushed the Hungarian uprising and throws dissidents into Siberian labor camps, spoke sanctimoniously in the name of honor and morality. The Third World, filled with brutal dictatorships, spoke in the name of self-determination. Terrorist murderers of children spoke in the name of justice. The treachery of the nations was coupled with a naïveté about the would-be murderers of innocent women and children. In the June 5, 1974 issue of the *Christian Century,* the editor of that prominent journal spoke of Nayef Hawatmeh, a Palestinian resistance leader, as representing a "ray of hope" in the Mideast darkness becuse he "virtually acknowledged that Israel has a right to exist as a state." It was this same "ray of hope" who ordered the massacre at Ma'alot!

Hanoch Bartov, an Israeli novelist, wrote in a recent issue of *Commentary* that "the experience [of the Yom Kippur War] was a kind of national trauma, the Yom Kippur war may well become a turning point in the formation of Israel's identity; or, to put it more precisely, in the formation of Israel's Jewish identity. The trip to normalcy is over, for the time being at least. We are back to *abnormal.*" [15]

Auto-emancipation, chosenness, and the land stand stronger than ever before as the foundation pillars of Zionism and the State of Israel.

It should be noted that a secular Messianism is not the sum total of Jewish Messianism. The fulfillment of Zionism is not the Messianic kingdom. The dream of Jewish Messianism cannot be severed from the dream of universal peace from the regeneration of human nature and the incursion of the Transcendent to heal the lesions of nature and the cosmos. We must stand on guard against *premature* Messianism. The Messianic idea is subject to two distortions: pessimism and quietism in which we wait for God to redeem us, and utopianism where we think we can achieve the complete redemption. The one expects too little of us, the other too much. The Jews, even those in Israel, live in an unredeemed world. They share the human predicament of estrangement and sin. They know too well the lack of universal brotherhood. The State of Israel is salvation, but not redemption. Because Israel is not the Messianic kingdom, it must use secular means to deal with the concrete problems of security and boundaries. Israel as a secular political structure cannot endanger its national life even for universal aims. Borders have to be set by diplomacy in light of considerations of security and of realistic hopes for peace. Israel came into being as a result of the Messianic vision. However, because the Messiah has not come, Israel must use secular means to protect itself and, if possible, find a modus vivendi with its neighbors, using the ordinary procedures of sovereign states.

What does all this mean for Christians? If we are indeed younger and elder brothers, then you share with us the divine patrimony. We are members of one family. Christians, therefore, have a responsibility to protect the Jewish people from its enemies—to help insure that the Jewish body and the Jewish soul will have a secure resting place. The establishment of the state is one step on the long road toward the redemption of the world. The Messianic dream, the challenges of the covenant, have resulted in the return of the Jewish people as active participants in the historical process.

These achievements, precarious as they now seem to be, are not a call to be at ease. How could one be at ease, especially in Zion?—for God is beckoning us to be restless until His fulfillment comes.

When Ernie, the hero of the novel *The Last of the Just,* together with a group of children and his own wife, is led to the gas chamber, he prays wearily and believingly: "O God, O Lord, we went forward like this thousands of years ago. We walked across arid deserts and blood red seas, through floods of salt-bitter tears. We are very old. We are still walking. O let us arrive finally."

We still walk through deserts. Although Jacob has found a resting place, he still dreams of arriving!

Response to Emil Fackenheim

EVA FLEISCHNER

My response to Professor Fackenheim is not in the form of taking issue
with him, but rather to suggest a Christian perspective of some of the
points he raised. As I share the platform today with him and Seymour
Siegel I do so with a strong sense of responsibility. For I believe it is
incumbent on the Christian of the post-Auschwitz era to speak out on
the subject of Israel, however difficult and complex it may at times be
for us to do so. If Emil Fackenheim has indeed provided Judaism with
an eleventh commandment, that "Jews must not grant post-humous
victories to Hitler,"[1] a new commandment is perhaps also laid upon
Christians: We may not be silent. It is not enough for us to feel whole-
heartedly committed to Israel; we must give expression to this commitment. Otherwise we shall incur a new burden of guilt, at a time when
we have as yet barely come to terms with our guilt for the Holocaust.

A New Theological Climate among Christians

Let me take as my starting point that of Emil Fackenheim, the prayer
by the Israeli Chief Rabbinate. If he finds its most extraordinary aspect
in the fact of its wide acceptance by Jews everywhere, non-Jews are
still more baffled by this. It only compounds our problem of trying to
answer the question, Who is a Jew? What are we to make of people who
call themselves secular Jews, agnostics, even atheists, yet who can
identify with this prayer? Tough soldiers who have been raised with
the Bible as simply the history book of their people, yet who wept as
they reached the Western Wall in June 1967? The question, Who is a
Jew? is a constant source of puzzlement to non-Jews, especially to
Christians. For it has been fairly simple to define the Christian, at least
until recently: one for whom Jesus Christ is the full and definitive
revelation of the Father and (in the case of Roman Catholicism), one
who accepts the authority of the church and the bishop of Rome in
doctrinal matters.

In recent years, however, the definition has become more difficult
also for us. Many people today sincerely consider themselves Christians who, not so long ago, by older standards and according to tradi-

tional church discipline, would have found themselves outside the church, whether they liked it or not. We have increasingly moved into an era of theological ferment in which even some of Christianity's most sacred tenets are no longer considered beyond the pale of examination. This ferment opens up new avenues of exploration between Jew and Christian. For the purposes of this panel, let me take the topic of Messianic expectation, which forms a substantial part of Emil Fackenheim's paper.

Messianism

It is not Messianism as such that divides Christianity and Judaism, for both are Messianic faiths. They conceive of Messianism, however, in radically different terms. Christians believe that in Jesus Christ the Kingdom has appeared and redemption has occurred. For them Christ's coming marks the center of human history, a new starting point in time.

Jews, on the other hand, know of no caesura or midpoint in history. The deep wounds in our world are unmistakable signs for them that redemption is not yet. Even if partial realizations or beginnings of the Kingdom may seem to appear from time to time, Emil Fackenheim has pointed out that their very transitoriness reminds Jews of the precariousness of history.

This constitutes a very real difference between us. Yet it is too simple to say that Judaism is wholly geared toward the future, while Christianity looks only to the past Christ-event. Christians also pray for the coming of the Kingdom. They still await its full manifestation in the Parousia, or Second Coming. The Kingdom has come, and it has not come; it is present and operative, yet hidden except to the eyes of faith. Meanwhile Christian existence is lived in the tension of what already St. Augustine called the "between-time," the "already" and the "not yet." We share with Jews a common expectation, though with major differences (also regarding the nature of this final manifestation). Some of these may be lessened in the years ahead, as Christology breaks fresh ground. Let me briefly sketch here some of the new avenues of thought.

Jesus appeared on the world scene at one of the many moments in Jewish history when Messianic expectation was at a high point. His followers saw themselves standing on the threshold of the long-awaited new age. "Lord, will you at this time restore the Kingdom to Israel?" the apostles asked. For Paul, Jesus was "the first fruits from the dead," who would soon be followed by those who had faith in him (1 Cor. 15). The early Christians did not look forward to a new historical era, but to the imminent transformation of history into the Kingdom of God in the return of Jesus, who in his historical coming had been the Christ only in hidden form.[2] The expectation of the Parousia was one of the driving forces of primitive Christianity, sending Paul on his almost feverish mission of spreading the Gospel throughout the then-known world.

We know what happened when this return was delayed, indefinitely it seemed. Instead of giving up their faith and hope, as Jews before them had done and were to do again and again—without, however, ever losing their hope—the early Christians maintained their belief in Christ and interpreted the delay of his return. Rosemary Ruether speaks of a twofold process that now took place: a spiritualizing of the eschatological expectation, making it into an already present, inner, invisible reality (not unlike what happened among the followers of Sabbetai Zvi in seventeenth-century Poland),[3] and a historicizing of it. The coming of Christ was postponed into an indefinite future. In the meantime the historical events of Christ's coming, life on earth, dying, and rising, originally seen as signs of the approaching kingdom, were interpreted as historical events already identical with the kingdom. Is it possible, Ruether asks, to return the theological symbols of Christianity to their original prophetic context? This would mean that we not appropriate them as "historical events which lie behind us as institutional foundations. Rather, they must remain eschatological, must loom ahead of us as realities toward which we are still moving."[4]

Such efforts to reinterpret the Christ event are in continuity with the process that engaged the early church. The New Testament gives us no dogmatic formulations of Christology; these are the outgrowth of prolonged theological speculation, frequently aimed at combating heresy. Instead, it seeks to understand, through different modes of thought, the miracle that God was in Christ. Thus in Acts 3:19–21 Peter speaks of the coming of the Messiah as being still in the future, and that this Messiah will be Jesus. We have here an expression of the first Christians' faith in the Parousia, as well as of their struggle to understand who this man Jesus was.

Certain contemporary Christian theologians continue this struggle of the early church (Pannenberg, Moltmann, Stendahl, Ruether, etc.). Can we see Jesus, they ask, as having begun something "which gradually is changing things and will, in due time, lead to the kingdom, so that, when the ultimate future of man is fulfilled, we can say of the 'King' of that age that, in him, Jesus has returned 'as the Christ'?"[5] This robs Christianity neither of its rooting in the historical Jesus nor of its eschatological expectation, but requires a tension between the two.

I suggest that if there is a deep Jewish awareness of all of history as being precarious, so that projections about "the End" are and always were recognized by the rabbis as just that, and nothing more, Christian theologians today are moving closer to such a view of history: far more tentative, less dogmatic and absolutist. Closer, perhaps, to that "boldness" of the prayer which links the present state, in all its historical ambiguity, with the Messianic future. Insofar as Christians ask themselves, In what way was Jesus Messiah? and become more aware of the "already" and the "not yet" of the kingdom, while Jews link the Messianic future with a possible, however precarious, present, the common ground for discussion and understanding between us is broadened. That is the best we can hope for. It is neither likely nor desirable that all differences between us be eliminated; but the opening up of new avenues of exploration is to be greeted as a welcome phenomenon.

Let me next touch briefly on some points made by Emil Fackenheim regarding the Holocaust.

Uniqueness and Universality

The Holocaust is, at one and the same time, unique in Jewish history and goes beyond it, to be inscribed once and for all in the history of the West; that is to say, Christian history. I consider it imperative that in our teaching we begin by stressing the uniqueness. Particularly with young people, who in their lives have already lived through so many horrors, and who often ask, What is so special about the Holocaust? This is a delicate subject. There is something odious about playing the numbers game. Every single human life is precious, as the rabbis of old remind us. But we can attain universality only through particularity, there are no shortcuts. The more we come to know about the Holocaust, how it came about, how it was carried out, etc., the greater the possibility that we will become sensitized to inhumanity and suffering wherever they occur. If we take shortcuts we are in danger of losing all distinctions, of what Yosef Yerushalmi calls the "debasement of our vocabulary." We may soon, then, have simply one more word which for a short time was a new and powerful symbol, but which quickly became emptied of all meaning. The Holocaust happened at a specific time in history, it was perpetrated by a specific human group against another human group, the Jews. The only other people that shared the Jews' fate were the Gypsies, whose tragedy is occasionally mentioned, but rarely if ever told, let alone retold. The Holocaust is not on a par with the brush fires in California in the fall of 1971, to which the press referred as a holocaust; nor with the tragic recent shootout in Los Angeles, when six members of the Symbionese Liberation Army perished in the flames.

To stress the Jewish dimension of the Holocaust is not to be indifferent to the millions of others who were murdered by the Nazis, at Auschwitz, in other camps, in Russia. We must not lose sight of the fact, however, that all these other victims had a choice, were in some way considered enemies of the regime, whether for political or religious reasons. Only in the case of the Jews and Gypsies did the Nazis have nothing whatever to gain from their deaths; only here can we truly speak of "genocide." It is my conviction that if six million Christians had been done to death in the way six million Jews were killed, the world would not have remained silent, least of all the pope. To this the eighteen-hundred-year-old Teaching of Contempt has heavily contributed. We Christians must come to grips with this, must work it through and accept it. Not so as to beat our breasts forever after (I share Yosef Yerushalmi's unease about "a giant mea culpa"), but so that we will do everything humanly possible to see to it that it will not happen again. Or, in the event that it does happen again, we will perhaps freely accompany our Jewish brothers and sisters into the gas chambers the next time, as a few Christian martyrs indeed did during the Nazi period. The slogan "Never again" must become ours too.

The Holocaust: Revelatory Event

The Holocaust does indeed defy explanation; yet it can be considered a revelatory event by Christian as well as Jew. Let me briefly suggest a Christian perspective as counterpart to Emil Fackenheim's remarks.

It has opened our eyes—or the eyes of some at least—to the heretofore unimaginable results of distorted Christian teaching about Judaism. Enough has been said on this subject by others at this Conference (Ruether, Pawlikowski, Claire Huchet-Bishop, etc.) for me not to elaborate on this statement.

If the Holocaust reveals much about Christians, it reveals much about Jews also, to Christians. That any Jews, let alone thousands, perhaps millions, went into the gas chambers with the Shema Yisrael on their lips is something I shall never be able to understand fully, even though I know we have our own galaxy of Christian martyrs. For me as a Christian the Jew has become, through my encounter with the Holocaust, the witness to the Living God in the world.

Secondly, the Holocaust revealed again, but in more extreme circumstances than ever before, perhaps, the deep, indestructible drive for life in the Jewish people. The life instinct runs deep in all of us, of course, yet I find something uniquely Jewish revealed in the Holocaust. It is more than life instinct, instinct for survival. It is survival for a reason, so that the people may live. I first became aware of this in reading *Treblinka* some years ago.

The word "life," which recurs throughout the book, gives expression to the deepest meaning of what these men and women strove to achieve in their world of death. Whether it is the young girl Lydia, who worked with the SS in order to learn their plans; or the old woman whom Berliner undresses as she arrives at Treblinka, and who says to this man whom she is seeing for the first and last time, "Swear to me that you will stay alive"; or Chocken, who, having escaped, returns mortally wounded in order to call the camp to revolt: all these act as they do in order that the people may live. "Of what use is Israel if there are no more Jews?" This life of the people, this faith in the people, sustains and animates their actions.

In reading this book the familiar words "people" and "life" took on a new meaning for me. I was reminded of the text from Deuteronomy, "You shall be My people," and "Choose life, then, that you may live." What a costly witness it took to show the world that the words of Scripture had not been spoken in vain—these words which, thirty centuries later, restored to the members of this people the power to come back to life from the pit of hell.

Fackenheim spoke of the "unholy alliance" between hatred of the Jew and Jewish powerlessness, which has lasted for centuries, and has now been broken thanks to the existence of the State of Israel. Surely Israel's determination to live is evidence that he is correct. Jews will never again let themselves be led as sheep to the slaughter. But what of the attitude of Christians toward the state? We touch here the great complexity and ambiguity raised for Christians by Israel's existence. Let me address myself to this in the last part of my response. In so doing I know that I shall not be able to hew rigorously to that objectivity which, in the minds of many, should mark all scholarly, including all theological, discourse.

The State of Israel and the Christian

I recall last October—none of us here present are likely to forget it. I was attending the Yom Kippur service with a Jewish friend, one of my former students. It was there, in Temple Shalom, Cedar Grove, New Jersey that we first received the news of the outbreak of the war. As I look back over the past year it has been marked for me, as few other years I recall, by a constant back and forth between hope and—if not despair, something very akin to it at times. Certainly fear, great fear; and pain, great pain. Fear—for the future of Israel, its growing isolation in the community of nations, the almost solid loss of sympathy for Israel in the Third World, the growing rift with one-time liberal Christian supporters of Israel here at home, the possibility that even we, the United States, might sell Israel down the drain in return for Arab oil. Pain—over the so senseless bloodshed and loss of lives. Pain, mixed with ambiguity. It is this ambiguity, which has only grown over the months, that I have found most difficult to live with.

I know that some Jews share my sense of ambiguity. I have read Elie Wiesel's letter "To a Concerned Friend,"[6] in which Wiesel assures his young correspondent, who is worried that Israel will develop a conqueror's mentality, will become a power defined by its conquests, that his fear is groundless; that "victory, in the Jewish tradition, does not depend on defeat inflicted on the adversary. Every victory is first victory over oneself." I remember being deeply moved when I first read this essay in the spring of 1970 in Paris, and asking myself: Is it really possible that the Jewish people will overcome the temptations of power to which every other people has succumbed, as it has for so long overcome the ravages of powerlessness and so much inhuman suffering? Everything in me wanted to say yes; wanted to believe in the normally unattainable, in the dream. And I did, in a kind of blind act of faith.

This act of faith has become more difficult this year, though I still affirm it (what else is faith, if not affirmation in the face of difficulty?). The ambiguity and tension have become increasingly difficult to bear. Two weeks ago, the day after the tragedy of Ma'alot, I remember my shock at reading in the *New York Times* the outcries of some of the mourners as the bodies of the terrorists, and of the dead and wounded children, were brought out of the schoolhouse: "Let's give them another Auschwitz!" I understood the rage, I could imagine myself acting similarly in a moment of hatred and revenge. But I shuddered because the outcry came from the lips of Jews. Was I falling, I asked myself, into that same double standard vis-à-vis Israel of which I frequently accuse my fellow Christians?

I will not, I cannot, I may not judge or condemn. The sins of my own faith community are too numerous and far greater. Jesus said to those who wanted to stone the woman caught in adultery, "Let him who is without sin cast the first stone" (John 8). But if I may not judge or condemn, is there something I may do, must do, as a Christian, as one who cares deeply about Israel's future, lest I incur that guilt referred to earlier? This is a key question for me; I believe the answer is yes.

We should recognize that we, the non-Jewish world, are to a large extent responsible for Israeli intransigence, for what we often deplore as Jewish phobia, or the Masada complex. We have not, by and large, given tangible evidence to Israel that, when the chips are down, it will have any choice but to go it alone. We have almost invariably judged Israel by a double standard, beginning with the Beirut airport raid in December 1968. With the exception of one German newspaper, there was a universal outcry against the Israeli destruction of the Lebanese civil air fleet in the international press; almost no mention was made of the extraodinary fact that the Israelis had gone to great lengths, risked the very success of their operation, to insure that not a single human life would be lost.

Compare that to the terrorist attacks—during the Olympic Games, at Kiryat-Shemona, at Ma'alot. How many times have the world, the United Nations the Security Council, condemned Israeli reprisals, yet passed over in silence the actions which led to these reprisals? Can we blame the Israelis for feeling that they are "damned if they do, damned if they don't"? How is it possible that Ma'alot and the Israeli reprisals are mentioned in the same breath? I do not suggest that we should be callous to the reprisals, that they should not also tear us apart. But I do say that we may not mention them in the same breath. Let us first look at the one in all its horror, and then at the vicious circle by which violence begets violence—a vicious circle which the non-Jewish world started; not in the recent war, not in 1967, or 1956, or 1948, but long ago.

I believe that one reason for the double standard is an undeniable ambiguity, religious in nature (hence all the more dangerous) on the part of Christians vis-à-vis the State of Israel. It is rooted in many centuries of the Teaching of Contempt (cf. the papers by Ruether, Pawlikowski, Huchet-Bishop). The image of the Jew rejected by God, cursed, wandering homeless over the face of the earth, has been deeply engraved in Christian tradition (though never, fortunately, in official church doctrine). Homelessness, landlessness, until the end of time, God-willed, God-imposed—these were for nineteen centuries considered part and parcel of Jewish existence by the Christian world, to the point where to this day one can hear Christians voice indignation and surprise that Jews should claim the right to have a land of their own. This ambiguity quite possibly plays a role in the Vatican's refusal to grant official recognition to the State of Israel. There are signs that beneath the officially maintained stance things are changing in Rome, yet the facts remain.

At the same time, there are signs of hope. In what I consider the finest and most radical theological document to have been issued about the church's relation to Israel, the French bishops, in their Pastoral Guidelines of April 1973, affirm the Jewish people's right to return to Eretz Israel, and urge Christians to take into account Jewish interpretations of the return to the land. (cf. Claire Huchet-Bishop's paper.) Christian support for Israel during the Yom Kippur War was greater than it had been in 1967. Let me give one example of a change at the theological level, of a major change that took place in the space of twenty years in the thought of Karl Barth.

In an interview with the World Council of Churches in 1948 in Amsterdam, Barth said that the way in which the names of Jerusalem and other holy places were being bandied about sounded to him like a parody of their biblical meaning.[7] Yet two years later, in 1950, events in Israel appeared to him, in their similarity to Old Testament events, as a sign of God's election and love of Israel.[8] Nor was the evolution of his view of the state at an end. In 1962, when asked about the meaning of the state, Barth answered as follows:

> A possible explanation is that it is another and new sign of the electing and providentially ruling grace and faithfulness of God to the seed of Abraham, a very visible sign, visible for every reader of the papers, the whole world—a sign which is not to be overlooked. . . . The reappearance of Israel, now as a nation in the political realm, even as a state, may well be called a miracle for all that have eyes to see.[9]

Still later, in 1967, in a discussion with students of the Mennonite School in Basel, Barth called the State of Israel "an eschatological sign," and spoke of the events since 1948 as a repetition of the biblical account of Israel's entrance into the promised land.[10] Perhaps there is

no radical difference between the thinking of Barth here and that remarkable prayer by the Israeli Chief Rabbinate.

There are signs of hope. Yet we should not too quickly sit back and
reassure ourselves that the mind-set of centuries is now a thing of the
past. Rather, let us confess our guilt. But to confess it, while essential,
is not enough—indeed, if we go no further it may be dangerous (cf. the
remarks by Yerushalmi). If guilt remains guilt it will paralyze us,
weigh us down so much that it will take but a flip of the coin to vent
itself anew on those who occasion it. Guilt unassumed, undigested, is
dangerous. We must work through and transform it into a deep sense of
responsibility, which will free us for constructive action, will permit
us, perhaps, to speak the right word at the right moment.

"The right moment"—how do we recognize it if and when it comes?
Not long ago I assisted at a panel, in New York, of four editors of Jewish magazines and journals. One of the editors shared with his audience a painful dilemma in which he found himself, and invited their
help in solving it. He had tried to find someone to write an article for
his magazine that would be constructively critical of Israeli policy. It
had been no easy job, but finally an author was found, the article written. It reached his desk just after the Yom Kippur War broke out; he felt
he could not publish it, that it was not "the right moment." He still has
not published it. Some discussion ensued in the audience: What is the
right moment? On the surface of it, surely not the time when Israel is
fighting for survival. But is another view possible? Is it perhaps precisely at moments of crisis that a prophetic word must be spoken?

It was Jews, that night in New York, who asked these questions, and
who have been asking them in Israel. Christians must try to listen, hear
what Jews have to say about the present situation. Some of us have begun to do this with regard to the Holocaust, thanks in large part to the
eloquence of an Elie Wiesel, the impact of whose message is no less
powerful for Christians than it is for Jews. But we still have difficulty
listening with regard to Israel. Or we hear only one side, which is indeed more vocal and easily heard. If we listen carefully, however, if we
succeed in winning the trust of some Jewish friends, so that they will
dare speak frankly with us, we shall hear that there are many, often
sharply dissenting voices (some of which can be heard at this Symposium), within Israel, within Diaspora Jewry. The ancient prophetic conscience is not dead among Jews today. But Christians must remember
that the prophets, and the ancient rabbis, and Jesus, who stood in the
same tradition, addressed their reprimands and often fierce accusations
to their own people, as members of that people. Jews have not forgot-

ten how quickly and easily these same texts were turned against them by those who had become outsiders to the community of Israel, whether their names are Justin Martyr, or Barnabas, or, to come to the present, Daniel Berrigan. It is not enough for Christians today to assert kinship with Israel, for us to call ourselves "true Jews" and thereby arrogate to ourselves the right to take Israel to task. We can earn that right only through consistent commitment and effort; only if we have acquired a certain kind of sensibility, a deep empathy which enables us to speak to and about Israel from within the covenant relationship. Whether or not we have attained this the sons and daughters of Abraham in the flesh are better qualified to judge than we ourselves. My plea to my fellow Christians, then, is to let go of our still too often arrogant and absolutist stance, which presumes the right to tells others who and what they should be or are. Let us, instead, free Jews to speak the liberating word to their fellow Jews, and gradually also to non-Jews, and let us listen to them. Then, perhaps, we will at the crucial moment be able to speak ourselves—the kind of word that may be spoken, that can be heard, because it is spoken in love. Let me close with a few lines from the letter by Elie Wiesel referred to earlier—it is still part of my act of faith:

> You know and esteem the Jewish people enough to realize that the secret of its survival—and the antagonism this survival arouses—is linked to its unrelenting will not to assume a destiny other than its own. The setting and circumstances are immaterial. For the duration of its torment, the Jewish soul has remained Jewish—that is, vibrant to everything human—and Jewish it will remain now that we can see a glimmer of light.[11]

PART VI

Radical Theology, the New Left, and Israel

Introduction

The speakers concern themselves with the New Left more than with radical theology; in their evaluation of the former, they are at odds on the relative importance of the Jewish problem as well as the very existence of a New Left at the present point in time.

Shlomo Avineri develops the history of political liberalism's stance toward Jews and Judaism. It is complex and not as clear-cut as some liberals would like. He begins his account with the nineteenth century, and explains the basis of Marx's *On the Jewish Question* as a refutation of Bruno Bauer's demand that Jews cease being Jewish before they are accepted as equals in a secularized state. No such demand was made of Christians.

The emergence of racial theories enabled socialists and other secularists of the nineteenth century to absorb elements of anti-Semitism without being accused of following the old ecclesiastical anti-Judaism. The later linkage of Marxism with Darwinism, inaugurated by Engels, was so powerful a combination that Kautsky, as chief theoretician of the Second International, felt compelled to rebut racist anti-Semitism for the socialist movement. In a second edition of his *Rasse und Judentum* in 1921, however, Zionism had become a political issue. Kautsky does not admit that Jews are a nation or have a claim on Palestine. According to him, the fate of the Jews is bound up with revolution in their own Eastern European countries. Kautsky considers Zionism a reactionary movement. Like Lenin, he disregards the strong socialist elements among the Jewish settlers and concentrates on the views of Herzl and the capitalist philanthropists.

With the advent of Nazism the Zionists found strong support among the non-Communist Left, but early critical attitudes carried over into recent New Left literature. Avineri quotes two such sources, the American Black scholar Stephen Halbrook and the French Marxist writer Maxime Rodinson. Avineri believes that disagreement with certain aspects of Israeli policy is not only permissible but probably justified. Yet such an attitude does not warrant a negation of the very legitimacy of the state, as maintained by these two authors.

The Arab-Israeli conflict is, in the Hegelian sense, a situation in which two conflicting conceptions of justice collide with another. The solution, explains Avineri, short of annihilation of one of the partners, is a compromise of sorts. Such a compromise must eschew all Manichaean temptations. It calls for patience, not triumphalist solutions.

Paul Jacobs criticizes Avineri's equating Zionism with Jewish existence. He also points out that Avineri, in his historical expostiton, makes a leap from Kautsky in the twenties to the New Left in the early sixties. For Jacobs, moreover, socialist opposition to Zionism does not necessarily derive from anti-Semitism.

The relationship between internationalist-socialist ideals and national self-determination has long been a vexing question. Zionism sought a refuge for Jews and never considered the class struggle a primary problem. Even among agnostic labor groups, Zionism always relied on a secularized Messianic element. Ben-Gurion's "social-cultural" Messianic vision was only recently supplanted by the ideology of a national liberation movement. Jacobs traces the relationship between Zionism as defined by Nachman Syrkin—that is, a movement for Jews of middle-class, intellectual background—and socialists of the Menshevik party. In the early years of Zionism, many Marxists opposed it because of their commitment to fight for Jewish rights within their own countries. Later, American socialists were opposed or indifferent to Zionism, until the Eichmann trial and the 1967 war made them change their position. Reform Jews, until a few years ago, opposed Zionism often more zealously than some gentiles and Jewish socialists. As late as 1950, the overwhelmingly Jewish ILG-WU called on Israel to free itself from narrow nationalism and ameliorate the fate of Arab refugees; they even asked for an internationalization of Jerusalem.

The New Left, until the mid-sixties, did not greatly concern itself with the State of Israel. The civil rights movement, the cold war, and many other problems were of greater importance. Only with the rise of Black power did Jews of the New Left become increasingly aware of their Jewish identity and power. The 1967 war, finally, led to a polarization: Jews, including Jewish radicals, overwhelmingly supported Israel, while Blacks identified with the Palestinians. Tensions between militant Blacks and the established Jewish community increased as Blacks seemed to threaten American society, and thereby Jewish security and status.

Jacobs no longer considers the New Left a force in American political life. Yet its ghost has, as it were, been endowed with demonic qualities, "associated with Black anti-Semitism, Jewish self-hate, and gentile indifference to the Arab threat to exterminate the Jews."

Milton Himmelfarb complements Avineri's historical account by pointing out pre-Christian anti-Semitism and the influence of pagan writers on the deists and atheists of the nineteenth century. He reminds us that traditional Christianity at least tolerated the survival of Jews and Judaism, while Voltaire and others advocated that they "disappear from the world." He quotes George L. Mosse, who aptly summarizes the problem by saying that "revolutionary socialism desired to put an end to Jews and Judaism."

Himmelfarb declares that the New Left and radical theology are simply heirs of older leftist and/or theological attitudes. Opposition to Israel is merely another aspect of the earlier rejection of Jews and Judaism.

Radical Theology, the New Left, and Israel

SHLOMO AVINERI

One should really start with Bruno Bauer. Here, at the threshold of modern radical theology, oscillating between the prophetic vocation of the church and the new role of the secularized theologian as a social and political critic, one finds the traditional Christian images of Judaism translated into a political program with clear anti-Jewish overtones. The religious prejudices become secularized, and as Karl Marx observed in his critique of Bauer's essays on the Jewish question, Bauer was unable to transcend the theological limitations of his frame of mind.[1]

Bauer's position has deep roots within the Western philosophical tradition, which, even while emancipating itself from Christian theology, nevertheless preserved much of what can be called, with all due caution, a "Gentile" way of looking at Judaism. "Universal" philosophy and history, which were basically "gentile" philosophy and history, were elevated to the status of a norm, while Jewish thought and Jewish history were relegated to the realm of the particular and separate, which somehow had to be gauged by what became known as "universal" criteria.[2] Seen from such a perspective, Feuerbach's image of Judaism is of crucial importance in such a context.[3] Yet for all his importance both for nineteenth-century theology as well as for the contemporary emergence and revival of radical Christianity, Feuerbach's argument about Jews and Judaism still limits itself to a purely *theoretical* understanding of the historical phenomenon of Judaism; and though the possibilities of secularizing the orthodox Christian arguments against Judaism are already inherent in Feuerbach's position, it appears that he himself has not yet made the transition from the pulpit to the forum.

It is with Bruno Bauer that the argument becomes political, and therefore significant to the way in which a certain combination of radical theology and political radicalism may result in an attitude which denies the legitimacy of Jewish existence on a multiplicity of levels. It is, therefore, also worth noting that Bauer's views were expressed not in his theological writings but in polemical pamphlets, explicitly addressed to the question of the political emancipation of the Jews.[4] This was done in two treatises, *Die Judenfrage* (Brunswick, 1843), and "Die Fähigkeit der heutigen Juden und Christen frei zu sein," published in Georg Herwegh's *Einundzwanzig Bogen aus der Schweiz* (Zurich and Winterthur, 1843), pp. 56–71.[5] Within the general movements toward liberalization which engulfed Prussia in the early 1840s at the accession of Friedrich Wilhelm IV, the issue of Jewish civic and political rights was raised once again. Although in the wake of the French Revolution and the Napoleonic Wars Jews in Prussia, and in Germany generally, were freed from many of the traditional restrictions imposed on their lifestyle by medieval Christian legislation, they still did not enjoy equal civil rights and could not participate in public life on an equal footing with members of the Christian majority. Jews were excluded from any participation, active or passive, in whatever limited elections did take place in the various provinces, could not hold public office or enter the civil service and the army, nor could they teach in public schools or universities or perform any other function that had a public aspect, like that of a lawyer or notary (it was this fact, it will be recalled, that led Marx's father to convert, so as to be able to practice as a lawyer in Trier).

Like his fellow Young Hegelians, Bauer could be called a radical within the political context of the 1840s. He certainly stood for the introduction of reforms that would lead German public life toward responsible parliamentary government, if not outright republicanism, abolishing the legitimist-bureaucratic structures of the Prussian state. But when it came to the question of Jewish emancipation, his two pamphlets oppose granting equal political rights to the Jewish minority. The paradox is compounded if one recalls that Hegel, who certainly could not be called a liberal in the accepted sense, came out more than twenty years earlier in favor of *full* civil and political rights for the Jews, maintaining that a state that did not grant full equal rights to the Jews "would have misunderstood its own principle."[6] Bauer, on the other hand, as a radical, leftist Young Hegelian, emerges as an opponent of Jewish emancipation, going back, so to speak, to a pre-Hegelian position, as if the Hegelian postulate about the universality of the state had never been voiced.

This is a truly fascinating paradox. In his writings Hegel painted, after all, a highly uncomplimentary picture of Judaism; yet when pronouncing on the political status of contemporary Jews, he made it a point to divorce his historico-philosophical views on Judaism from the criteria according to which the issue of civil rights for the Jews should be judged. In Bauer, on the other hand, there is a regression: while accepting Hegel's view of historical Judaism, theological considerations are introduced into the political realm under a secularized disguise. This is obviously a Feuerbachian influence. Although Bauer calls for a separation of church and state, his views on Jewish emancipation amount to a call for a secular conversion of the Jews as a condition for their emancipation.

Bauer's argument is quite complex, but its general contours can be summed up as follows. The demand for Jewish emancipation is based upon a secular conception of the state. In a Christian state, naturally, Jews have no place as equals; only if the state ceases to consider itself Christian can there be any validity to the claim that the Jews should become members of the body politic. But if the Jews wish to become free citizens in this secularized state, they cannot make this demand while still remaining Jews. Has not the Christian majority stripped its own Christian state of its Christian trappings by the very fact of allowing non-Christians to participate in its public life? If so, the Jews should follow suit and strip themselves of their Judaism before being accepted into the secular state. They don't have to be converted to Christianity, but they should cease to be Jews, since the state has ceased to be Christian.

The basic fallacy and intellectual dishonesty perpetrated by Bauer's argument has been criticized most forcefully by none other than Karl Marx in his *On the Jewish Question*. Because this essay is by itself famous for some of the nastiest remarks about Judaism made by a modern progressive thinker, it has usually been overlooked by almost everyone referring to it that this is basically an *anti-Bauer* essay. While Bauer appears to accuse the Jews of wishing to eat their cake and have it (demanding a de-Christianization of the state while preserving their religion intact), it is he who is, in fact, applying a double standard to the problem. The secularization of the Christian *state* does not imply by itself that any Christian *person* has to give up his self-identity as a Christian, while this is precisely what Bauer is asking the Jews to do as a prerequisite for being admitted into the commonwealth. Separation of church and state, while certainly diminishing the power of the church's dominion, cannot be equated with asking Jews to relinquish their religion.

Secondly, and this is tied up with the imbalance in the argument just mentioned, Bauer's thoughts imply a basic normative inequivalence between Christianity and Judaism. For him it is not simply the case that Christianity happens to be the religion of the majority, while Judaism is that of a minority. As religions, they appear to him not of the same order. Even while advocating the overcoming of religion, Bauer argues at the same time from a position which acknowledges the Christian theological claim of supremacy vis-à-vis Judaism; the emancipated theologian might have emancipated himself from his God, but not from the hybris his religion has bequeathed to him in the realm of prejudices. "The Christian," Bauer argues, "has only to raise himself one degree, to rise above his religion, in order to abolish religion in general. . . . The Jew, on the contrary, has to break not only with his Jewish nature, but also with the process toward the consummation of his religion, a process which has remained alien to him."[7] *Extra ecclesiam, nulla salus:* a Christian may reach atheism directly; a Jew, on the other hand, needs the mediation of "Christianity in dissolution" to reach atheism. As Marx rightly points out, to Bauer "it is still a matter, therefore, of the Jews professing some kind of faith."[8] The conversion of the Jews is still on the agenda: Christianity may be passé, but Judaism has already been abolished by the advent of Christianity itself. Hence Jews are not viewed as coeval with their Christian brethren, precisely because the theologian-turned-atheist still believes Christianity to contain a higher element of truth than Judaism and denies Judaism, even in its dissolution, an equal rank with Christianity in *its* dissolution. The most adequate commentary would probably be 1 Kings 21:10

Bauer's views should not be dismissed as a mere idiosyncrasy on the part of a perhaps eccentric, if not muddled, theologian transformed into a political radical. His views raise the crucial issue which was to bedevil the status of Jews in the emancipated West, namely, is there legitimacy to Jewish existence in a secularized, post-Christian world?

It is for this reason that the relationship between political liberalism and the Jewish question has been much more complex than claimed by conventional wisdom, as expressed, for example, by Seymour Martin Lipset in a somewhat surprised tone when confronted with some anti-Israel attitudes which he found among several New Left groups. Lipset maintains that "for a century and a half, the left supported Jewish political and social rights against existing establishments which tried to deny them."[9] Lipset himself is well aware in his essay that the kind of anti-Semitism called by August Bebel "the socialism of fools" was not an isolated phenomenon. We now have Edmund Silberner's detailed cataloguing of anti-Jewish statements by socialists of various schools in his *Sozialisten zur Judenfrage* (Berlin, 1962), as well as

George Lichtheim's brilliant essay, "Socialism and the Jews" (*Dissent*, July–August 1968).[10] These studies amply document that various tendencies within the socialist movement reacted to the immense success and mobility of significant sectors in the Jewish population in the nineteenth century in a very complex way. As Herzl put it, when the walls of the ghetto came tumbling down, Jews found themselves in the midst of bourgeois society. But while they became economically and socially quite prominent, especially in Western Europe, due to their ability to get ahead in a modern, literate, and industrial environment, they did not manage to get an equivalent share in political power, hence were unable to control the political environment upon which their continued prosperity depended. For all their phenomenal success in business as well as in the professions, the Jews remained excluded from the commanding heights of their societies; hence their vulnerability and marginality did not diminish. On the whole, the Jews are one example that belies the mechanistic thesis that economic prominence automatically means political power. This imbalance has to be viewed as a cardinal factor in driving so many of the Jewish intellectuals to the revolutionary movement; for its part, this disproportionate share of Jews in revolutionary circles helped to sustain the traditional distrust of them on the part of those very powers-that-be which the upwardly mobile Jews were trying to join.[11]

This crossfire in which Jews thus found themselves is perhaps best illustrated by an almost incredible piece by Bakunin. Referring to his quarrel with Marx, Bakunin writes in 1871:

> A Jew himself, Marx is surrounded—in London and France, but especially in Germany—by a crowd of little Jews, more or less intelligent, stirring up intrigue, troublemakers, as is the case with Jews everywhere. Traders or bankers, literateurs, politicians, correspondents of journals of every shade and opinion, courtiers of literature as well as of finance, with one foot in banking, the other in the socialist movement, and their behind sitting on the daily press of Germany—they have taken over all the newspapers, and you can imagine what a nauseating literature this gives us.
>
> And so this whole Jewish world, which constitutes an exploitative sect, a bloodthirsty people, tightly and closely organized not only across state borders but across different political views—this Jewish world is today, to a great extent, at the disposal of Marx on the one hand, and the Rothschilds on the other. I am sure that the Rothschilds appreciate the merits of Marx, and that Marx, for his part, feels an instinctive attraction and deep respect for the Rothschilds.
>
> This may appear strange. What can there be in common between com-

munism and the world of high finance? Ah! It is that Marx's communism seeks the powerful centralization of the state; and where there is centralization of the state there must needs today be a central bank of the state; and where such a bank exists, the parasitical nation of the Jews, speculating on the labor of the people, will always find a means of making a living.[12]

Revolutionary zeal is apparently quite able to preserve a whole set of traditional images: Bakunin's outburst in not limited to what may be called "social anti-Semitism," i.e., a critique of the role of Jews, or some Jews, in bourgeois society, but is based on characterological concepts obviously based on a blanket denunciation of Jews as such.

The prevalence of such images received a further boost from the emergence of racial theories toward the end of the nineteenth century. This development broadened the base of the variety of themes to be found in anti-Jewish sentiments generally, and enabled even extremely secular movements, like socialism, to absorb elements of anti-Semitism without opening themselves to the accusation of following in the lead of the old ecclesiastical anti-Jewish ideas. Anti-Semitism could thus be linked with scientific, i.e., progressive, thinking.

With the linkage between Marxism and Darwinism inaugurated by Engels, this could lead to an extremely powerful combination. Such was the force of these developments that Karl Kautsky, the chief theoreticain of the Second International after Engels's death, came up with an attempt to define the socialist position on the Jewish question with special reference to the racial aspect. His *Rasse und Judentum,* first published in 1914, became the classical socialist rebuttal of racist anti-Semitism. The very necessity to issue such a rebuttal ex cathedra became, however, itself an indicator of the gravity of the problem.

Yet even this eloquent attack on anti-Semitism raises a highly complex question: the second edition of the tract, published in 1921, has a postscript dealing with what at that time appeared as a wholly new phenomenon—Zionism. Here the question is no longer that of the civil and political rights of the Jews as individuals, nor is it a campaign against a collective vilification of all people of Jewish descent. Here the question is that of the self-determination of the Jews on the basis of their national self-consciousness, and from this point of view there seems to be no corollary between a defense of Jewish social and political rights and a defense of the claims for Jewish self-determination: an ardent defender of full Jewish emancipation will not necessarily feel obliged to defend the claim for Jewish self-determination. The Bund, which had, at times, the largest working-class membership of any socialist organization in the Czarist empire around the turn of the century, found itself faced with similar problems in its relationship with the Russian Social Democratic party, and particularly with its Leninist wing. When the claim for Jewish ethnicity referred not to cultural autonomy (which could, at least, be easily defended within the socialist movement on the basis of the Austro-Marxist concept of cultural pluralism), but to a political renaissance involving Palestine, some socialist reactions present a number of problems which deserve a closer study.[13]

In his pamphlet Kautsky refers to the idea of national self-determination in the Middle East, and finds it inextricably bound up with the democratic and socialist traditions. The Arabs, who had just recently come under Western imperialist rule, are naturally entitled to exercise this right. The Jews, however, are not to be numbered among the nations:

> It is already two thousand years since the Jews have utterly ceased to be a nation. They lost not only their common territory, but also their language. What can, perhaps, be called a living Jewish tongue, Yiddish, is nothing else than corrupted German. This language receives its Jewish national appearance only when it is written, not when it is spoken. It is German written in Hebrew.[14]

As for the future of Jewish life in Palestine, Kautsky has nothing but a gloomy forecast:

> Jewish colonization in Palestine must collapse as soon as British-French hegemony in the Middle East will collapse. This is only a question of time, and probably of very short time.
> There is no doubt about the ultimate victory of Arabism. . . . Whatever will be the form of this process of change, the poor and weak Jewish settlers in Palestine will be the principal sufferers, both during the Arab fight for independence as well as after their victory. Of all the European elements in the Middle East, these Jews are the most defenseless, they will have the greatest difficulty in fleeing, and are, at the same time, viewed by the Arabs as their worst enemies, since through their efforts at settlement they have proven that they would like to stay in the country. . . .
> One can however view it as an exceptional stroke of luck for suffering Jewry that the Zionist settlement policy will proceed very, very slowly. Hence one may hope that the number of victims caused by Zionism will not be very great. . . .
> Not in Palestine, but in Eastern Europe will the fate of suffering and op-

pressed Jews be fought for—and this will happen now. No emigration can save them: their fate is bound with that of the revolution in their home countries.[15]

Zionism, Kautsky concludes, is therefore not progressive but reactionary. Like Lenin, Kautsky was completely oblivious of the strong socialist element in the structures of Zionism as realized in Palestine. In his account of the origins of Zionism, Herzl figures, naturally, most prominently, as does the philanthropic work of the Rothschilds. But nowhere does Kautsky mention that the first call for a return to a modern, secular Zion came from none other than the socialist Moses Hess, who started from extremely universalistic premises, yet in his *Rome and Jerusalem* (1862) reached the conclusion that the Jewish question as a national and social problem, not a religious one, is actually the *last* nationalities problem, and has to be solved on the basis of Mazzinian national self-determination in a Jewish socialist commonwealth in the historical land of Israel: there, only there, can the Jewish proletarian masses from Eastern Europe and the Middle East solve their national problem within the context of a social transformation.

What is even more astounding in Kautsky is the fact that within the Second International he was aware of the emergence of various Zionist socialist parties, whose contribution to the Jewish immigration to Palestine was crucial. Nothing of this awareness is reflected in his assessment of Zionism in his study. For a thinker who was one of the first socialists to broaden the principle of national self-determination to include non-European peoples, this is an ominous blind spot.

With the advent of Nazism, however, this initial suspicion of Zionism gradually disappeared within the socialist movement, and in its crucial years of struggle the Zionist movement, by that time already led by Labor Zionists, found in the left-wing non-Communist movement one of its strongest supporters. But much of this early socialist critique of Zionism, denying self-determination to the Jewish people, has reappeared in the recent New Left literature on the Middle East conflict and Israel.

One should be careful about generalizations. There are numerous groups belonging to the New Left which have supported Israel consistently, whatever criticism they might have voiced about various aspects of Israeli policy (in Brussels, in the late 1960s, there even appeared a Marxist-Leninist Zionist group). But insofar as there is a critique of Israel's very existence on the part of left-wing groups, we find a number of basic themes in this critique. Under the aegis of misplaced scholarship, a collection of half-truths and heaps of documented ignorance have been used in the intellectual arguments surrounding the tangled issues of the Arab-Israeli conflict.

One example can be seen in an article by an American Black scholar, Stephen Halbrook, entitled "The Class Origins of Zionist Ideology."[16] Here Herzl appears not as a rather unsuccessful supplicant who tried to woo the Rothschilds to the idea of Zionism; he is characterized as the ideological spokesman and agent of the Rothschilds. All Zionist ideology is bourgeois. Moses Hess is indeed mentioned; not however, as a protagonist of what later became Zionist socialism, but as a spokesman for French imperial interests. The reason for this accolade is Hess's attempt to enlist the French revolutionary tradition of support for national movements of liberation in the service of both Jewish *and* Arab renaissance. That Hess thus called upon the French to support national independence for Syria and Egypt as well is conveniently forgotten by Halbrook; nor would it obviously appear to him legitimate to criticize Italian nationalism because of the support it received from Napoleon III. Halbrook also sees Hess's calling for Jewish settlement in Palestine as a way to "palliate" class struggle among the Jews. The truth of the matter, of course, is that Hess saw the Jewish proletariat as capable of waging a class struggle *only* in Palestine. In the Diaspora, Hess argued, Jewish class struggle is deflected because of the national issue and anti-Semitism; only within a Jewish socialist commonwealth in its historic homeland could the Jewish proletariat come into its own.

Halbrook's semi-scholarship reaches its peak of ignorance when he tries to confront the role of socialist Zionism in the actual emergence of a Jewish society in Palestine. He has this to say on what became the mainstream of Zionism, the major social and political force in the Jewish community in Palestine and later in the State of Israel:

> So-called Labour Zionism, founded by Syrkin, Aharon David Gordon, and especially Ber Borochov, never posed a real third choice in the place of revolution or (bourgeois) Zionism. It accepted all the racial elements of Zionism proper, and can only be considered as a special ideology within the Zionist context to meet the particular interest of the members of the middle and petty bourgeoisies and the labour aristocracy who personally carry out the work of colonization. . . .
>
> In other words, just as the Jewish upper bourgeoisie needed a foreign market (e.g. for the export of capital), the Jewish middle bourgeoisie need-

ed a domestic market. They would have their own national territory, cheap raw materials, vast resources of labour (the Eastern Jews), and profitable investment. [p. 103]

Anyone reading this would not, of course, guess that the reference to Labor Zionism is to the force that has been heading Israel's political life since its inception.

The suppression of the socialist aspect of the dominant element in Zionism and Israeli politics is a recurring theme in many of the left-wing critical writings on Israel. Overlooking this aspect makes it possible to obviate the embarrassing problem of having to confront a situation that cannot be viewed through the dichotomic and Manichaean simplicities of black and white which sometimes are the hallmark of so much of the uncritical naivete characterizing the discussion of the Middle East conflict.

The simple truth of the matter is that the Arab-Israeli conflict is not a clash between European imperialism and Third World anti-colonialism, but a conflict between two national movements: both movements are extremely complex in their historical associations, both are intertwined with religious backgrounds, both have had to contend with sometimes unprecedented problems of social structure. But just as Greek nationalism was linked to the Christian tradition of the Greeks in their fight against the Muslim Turks, yet was nevertheless a national, not a religious, movement, aiming at the creation of a nation-state, so both Zionism and Arab nationalism are basically secular, nationalist movements.[17] Jewish dispersion, as well as the fact that both national movements claim a bond to the same piece of territory, the Land of Israel/Palestine, have tended to complicate and sometimes obfuscate the issue involved. Any confrontation with either of the two national movements must be premised on an adequate realization of their nature.

Similarly, both Zionism and Arab nationalism have, in their checkered histories, relied on British imperialism: in 1917 the British supported the Arab revolt against the Turks at the same time that they issued the Balfour Declaration. The association with British imperial interests, which characterized *both* movements, cannot be taken out of its historical context and used as an argument solely against *one* of these movements.[18]

Furthermore, an utter disregard for the social and political realities and historical roots of Zionism appears in several of the standard left-wing writings on the subject. This is astonishing when it comes from critics with a Marxist background of sorts, who should have been more careful in their historical analysis of the forces involved. Thus historical falsification creeps in under the disguise of progressive scholarship. A scholar of the stature of Maxime Rodinson manages to write a whole book (*Israel and the Arabs*) on the history of Zionism and Israel *without even once mentioning the Holocaust and the extermination of most of European Jewry.* In another book, the same author comes up with the conclusion:

> I believe the preceding pages have shown that the creation of the State of Israel on Palestinian soil is the culmination of a process that fits perfectly into the great European-American movement of expansion in the 19th and 20th centuries whose aim was to settle new inhabitants among the other peoples or to dominate them economically and politically.[19]

Such an analysis obviously creates a problem for Rodinson when he comes to the discussion of Jewish resistance against the British in Mandatory Palestine in the 1940s. If the Zionists were nothing else than an outpost of the British imperial interests, how does one expalin that the only force in the Middle East around 1945 actively fighting for self-determination against the British were the Jews in Palestine? Rodinson's answer is a masterpiece of double-think: "Militant minorities among them [the Jews in Palestine], soon decided to begin terrorist activities against Britain, which they regarded as a colonial repressor."[20]

Two points should be mentioned. Never in his book does Rodinson call Arab activities "terrorist"—even if they were aimed at civilian Jewish targets; neither the mufti-led activities in the 1930s nor the more recent Fatah activities are called terrorist. The only time in the book when an activity of some group is labeled with the adjective "terrorist" is when it describes Jewish activities against the British *army* in Palestine. Secondly, those Jews who fought against the British (and they certainly were not a minority, but a majority of the Jewish population) are not granted by Rodinson the honor of fighting against imperialism: they were fighting only against Britain, "which they *regarded* as a colonial repressor." When Arabs fight against the British, this is anti-colonialism; when Jews fight against the British, this is terrorism and cannot be regarded as anti-colonialism. Seldom has a more racist double standard been applied from the Left with such blatant intellectual dishonesty to problems of nationalism. George Orwell would have been proud.

I do not intend here either to list the particulars of the New Left indictment of Israel nor to defend Israel against such accusations.[21] It is even further from my intention to maintain that all these criticisms are by themselves false. As a citizen of Israel, I find myself quite often criticizing this or that policy of my government, and thus I am sometimes in agreement with some of the issues raised by these critics of Israel.

But this is not the point. No country can be beyond criticism, nor can a society consciously modeled on a social ideal, as Israel has been modeled, ever fully live up to the ideals which inspired its birth. One may disagree about this or that aspect of Israel's policy or Israeli society, one may even oppose some of the very tenets directing this policy: yet all this cannot amount to a negation of the very legitimacy of the body politic involved.

The conflict in the Middle East lies, as I have already reiterated several times in this paper, between two national movements. One may, if one so wishes, be opposed to nationalisms all and sundry; but one cannot deny the right to self-determination to one nation while condoning and encouraging it in another.

The conflict is one about legitimacy, and its immediate victims are the Palestinians—but not because Israel denied them the right to self-determination or uprooted them from their homeland. Ironically it was Israel which recognized the right of the Palestinians to self-determination in 1947, when the Zionist movement accepted the United Nations proposal for the partition of Mandatory Palestine into two sovereign states, a Jewish one and an Arab one. This compromise plan, accepted by the Jews and rejected by the Arabs, would have made possible the peaceful coexistence of two nation-states in the historic area of the Land of Israel/Palestine; if carried into practice, it might have led to an economic union or even to some sort of federation or confederation. Unfortunately it was rejected both by the Arabs of Palestine as well as by the Arab States in the surrounding area, and the first Arab-Israeli war (1947–48) started with an Arab attempt to prevent the establishment of a Jewish state, according to the United Nations proposal, in that part of Palestine in which Jews were a majority. The tragedy of the Palestinians is an outcome of their denial of the Jewish right to self-determination in *part* of what both national movements consider their common, and hence disrupted, homeland.

The Israeli-Arab conflict is thus a truly tragic conflict in the Hegelian sense of the term, as Hegel saw it epitomized in *Antigone*. It is a situation in which two rights, two conflicting conceptions of justice, collide with each other. Unless one thinks in terms of the annihilation of one of the partners, the only solution is a compromise.

Such a tragic view of history is much more difficult to sustain than the Manichaean view, deeply embedded in the heritage of Christian theology turned secular in the New Left, which sees the world in terms of the battle between the Sons of Light and the Sons of Darkness. It calls for the patience needed to work out compromises, not triumphant one-sided solutions. It must realize that the two ancient peoples concerned, burdened by their own histories and traumas, do not fit into slick generalizations about progress and/or reaction. It has to realize that both Jews and Arabs have a historical link to the same piece of land—a link which the New Left cannot grasp because of its ahistoricity, and which it is difficult for some radical theology to stomach when it comes to Jews and their land.

All these elements are present in Father Daniel Berrigan's remarks about Israel in the wake of the Yom Kippur war.[22] To this one can add the specific personalitistic-existential bent of his thought, which makes it extremely difficult for him to face historical contexts or historical links not under the aegis of his *historia sacra.* Instant feeling makes historical knowledge superfluous, and self-righteousness chases facts out of the Temple.

I shall not dwell here upon the long list of Berrigan's distortions, inaccuracies, and falsifications; this has already been done in some detail elsewhere by others.[23] I would like to limit myself to pointing out what appears to me the ultimate scandal of Berrigan's position. It is contained in the oft-quoted passage in which Father Berrigan describes himself as "a western Christian in resistance against my Government and my Church, a Catholic priest in resistance against Rome, an American in resistance against Nixon, and a Jew in resistance against Israel."

This is the crux of the whole argument, and here Berrigan carries further one of the church's most obnoxious traditional attitudes toward Judaism. By saying that he, Father Daniel J. Berrigan, S.J., is speaking as "a Jew," he is saying nothing else than what the traditional church has always implied when it referred to itself as "the true Israel." If he, Berrigan, is a Jew, possibly the only true Jew, if he is *verus Israel,* then the real, living Jews, the real, besieged Israelis, are nothing but idolaters, can be dispensed with, and have no legitimacy as Jews. It is also convenient to refer to them as "Zionists" whenever possible.

This delegitimization of the Jewish people had already occurred once in the early days of the church. The present attempt at a Christian-Jewish dialogue is trying to heal some of the wounds caused by this delegitimization. By reverting to what has often been called the church's original sin against the Jewish people, Daniel Berrigan is not only reopening one of the darker pages of ecclesiastical history. By presuming that he has the power to issue such prophetic condemnations of the Jewish people, he is also assuming, within his own theological frame of reference, the very identity of Christ. What, if not such a belief in one's own identity as Christ, can be the source of such ultimate hybris? Berrigan's idolatry is the worst and ultimate of all idolatries: he created his idol in his own image.

One of the paradoxes of modernity is that despite the disappearance of the orthodox Christian theological justification for the reprobation of the Jews, both emancipation and liberalized theology did not automatically suspend the tensions inherent in Jewish existence within a non-Jewish majority culture. Emancipation raised—and did not adequately answer—the question of a secular self-identity of the Jewish people, now perceiving itself not as a religious community but as an ethnic entity. And many who were ready, indeed eager, to grant full social and political rights to the Jews as *individuals,* did not come up with a similarly enthusiastic response to a Jewish quest for a modern, secular, national, *collective* identity. Similarly, a radicalized theology does not necessarily mean heightened awareness of the Jewish claim for legitimacy on a par with Christianity. Sometimes even a reverse development is possible, when the prophetic mode is added to a reformed zeal to suggest a postulate which boils down to the maxim that charity should start with the Jews. In some cases this means a neo-Christian delegitimization of Jewish existence in a world which is imperfect, and in which Jewish existence is also necessarily imperfect. What some left-wing attitudes as well as radical theological positions imply is that someone else will decree to a people, to a community—in this case, to the Jews—what are the legitimate modes of its existence. Morally and theoretically, such a position is untenable. In a world which stands for self-consciousness and a quest for identity, this has to include Jewish self-determination as well. It is in the light of this universal principle that the Jewish quest for a particular self-identity has to be seen and accepted.

Response to Shlomo Avineri

PAUL JACOBS

Thirteen years ago, during the Eichmann trial, I telephoned Martin Buber to ask if I could talk with him. And although I was an unknown to him, characteristically he agreed. We met in the study of his Jerusalem home, he sitting behind his desk, his head not much higher than its top, I in a chair facing him, almost too awed to speak. But I did inquire why he had not written about his objections to the nature of the Eichmann trial, objections which he had voiced, openly, a number of times.

Slowly, he answered. "I would like to write about the trial but in order to do this properly, I would first have to write about the history of anti-Semitism in Europe. Now I am just finishing a book on the Bible and when that is done, I must start on another. Perhaps, when I finish the second book, I can then begin to write about Eichmann."

Today, I know better what Buber meant. To discuss Professor Avineri's thesis properly, it would be necessary to write one paper analyzing whether Zionism is a movement of national *liberation*, as that concept is generally understood; another dealing with the relationship of sovereignty to power; a third explaining why and how the majority of Jews in the world shifted from anti-Zionist to pro-Zionist views; a fourth to explore the significance of anti-Semitism in socialist movements; a fifth to trace the real as distinguished from the mythical history of socialist and radical attitudes toward Zionism and Israel; a sixth to deal with the phenomenon of assuming that serious criticism of Israel must be rooted in anti-Semitism; plus two or three other papers on related subjects.

But my responsibility today is to produce only a short commentary on Avineri's paper, a task which has turned out to be even more difficult than writing a book would be. The difficulty stems in part from the limitations on time, but in addition, the subject of the paper does not lend itself to either easy or purposive analysis, from my special viewpoint.

Shlomo Avineri describes and analyzes at length the relationship between the anti-Semitism found in radical theology and socialist theory during the nineteenth and early twentieth centuries. I accept the thesis

255

that some important socialist thinkers may also have been conscious or unaware anti-Semites and that this anti-Semitism has its roots in radical theology; I am prepared to advance the further argument that some modern socialist societies may display anti-Semitic tendencies. Others do not, of course, and the question of the variations among them depends, to a great extent, on the character of the society in its presocialist period.

But having established the fact that anti-Semitic tendencies existed in the European socialist movement, which no intelligent socialist would deny, Avineri then suggests, at least, that a fundamental socialist critique of Zionism, as distinguished from a criticism of specific Israeli policies or actions, also derives from anti-Semitic roots.

I do not accept the notion that socialism and anti-Semitism are inextricably linked, although I assume it is conceivable that under specific historical circumstances "a certain combination of radical theology and political radicalism," to use Avineri's phrase, "may result in an attitude which denies the legitimacy of Jewish existence on a multiplicity of levels."

Obviously, for Avineri the question of Zionism is subsumed under the rubric of "Jewish existence," and therefore if a socialist ideology denies the legitimacy of Zionism, it follows that it must also deny the legitimacy of Jewish existence.

Thus, in an astonishing one-sentence leap in time and space, Avineri links Karl Kautsky's opposition to Zionism to the New Left. The many years between Kautsky and the "New Left" period are disposed of with the single statement, which I believe to be an oversimplified inaccuracy, that "with the advent of Nazism, however, this initial suspicion of Zionism gradually disappeared within the socialist movement, and in its critical years of struggle, the Zionist movement, by that time already led by Labor Zionists, found in the left-wing non-Communist movement one of its strongest supporters." (It is not clear which period Avineri means when he refers to "crucial years of struggle," and I hope he will elaborate on this question during the discussion today.)

In fact, the nineteenth-twentieth-century socialist rejection of Zionism as a legitimate movement of self-determination worthy of support grew from a different perception of the meaning of "self-determination" than that espoused by the Zionists. And, indeed, it is not true that socialists have singled out the Jews as the only people not entitled to "self-determination" as that concept has been defined differently at various times by Zionists. Socialists also have rejected other movements described by their adherents as "self-determination." In the United

States, for example during the 1930s, the entire non-Communist left fought vigorously against the Communist party's thesis of establishing a "black belt" which would have given American Blacks sovereignty over a group of southern states.

For the purposes of this discussion, I do not wish to debate the correctness of the socialist position vis-a-vis the "black belt." Nor do I want to discuss whether the socialist movement was correct in its rejection of Zionism. But I do want to argue that the socialist movement's historical opposition to Zionism did not derive, necessarily, from anti-Semitism. And, indeed, it is striking that this concept is comparatively modern: in the heated debates between Zionists and socialists that took place before the Holocaust and World War II and even afterwards, the issue of anti-Semitism hardly arose. (I am omitting, deliberately, any discussion or analysis of the Communist position on Zionism, since Avineri does not discuss it, and it would require still another paper to deal with the subject adequately.)

The problem of the relationship between internationalist socialist ideals and national self-determination has always been one of the most vexing questions confronting the socialist movement and Marxist theoreticians.

In the case of Zionism, the problem has been even more perplexing, because at least a few of the many rationales advanced to justify Zionism contradict socialist theory. Thus, since Zionism's primary objective has always been the salvation of Jews, Zionism has never attributed to the class struggle the primacy of position it has always had for the socialist movement. Further, the socialist analysis of society and the Zionist perceptions of the world are based on two totally different and opposing views. Zionism, even that special form of Zionism espoused by the admittedly agnostic Labor Zionists, has always contained secularized Messianic justifications, while socialism rejects *Mashiach*. For Labor Zionists like Ben-Gurion, the Messianic vision of Zionism was, in his phrase, "not a metaphysical but a social-cultural one." He went on then to illuminate his notion with, "I believe in our moral and intellectual superiority, in our capacity to serve as a model for the redemption of the human race . . . The glory of the Divine Presence is within us, in our hearts and not outside us." (It is interesting that this Messianic justification for Zionism has been supplanted, lately, among some Zionists, by the justification of Zionism as a "national liberation movement.")

Obviously, the concept of Jewish "moral and intellectual superiority" is contrary to both orthodox Marxism and to non-Marxist socialists whose vision of the world does not include the notion of one group's superiority over all others.

But the socialist movement *never* perceived Zionism as a movement of national liberation, as that concept was generally understood during the nineteenth and twentieth centuries, since in the formative years of the Zionist movement its adherents did not seek to justify it as such a movement. Rather, Zionism sought to establish some kind of sovereignty for Jews because of the Zionist belief that Jews needed a place of refuge from the anti-Semitism which pervaded European Christian society. And the idea of refuge was of more importance in early Zionism than was Palestine as being the only possible "Eretz Israel." Indeed, in Theodor Herzl's original formulation of creating a "sovereign Jewish state" to avoid the consequences of anti-Semitism, he did not mention Palestine as Zion, nor Hebrew as the language of the Zionists. And in later years, even after Palestine had become fixed as the physical center in the aspirations of some Zionists, the pressing need many others felt for a place of refuge led more than 60 percent of the delegates to the Zionist Congress of 1903 to vote in favor of sending a commission to explore the possibilities of accepting the British government's offer of Uganda (now Kenya) as at least a temporary homeland for the Jews.

Is it any wonder, then, that the socialist movement did not perceive Zionism as a movement of national liberation? Would Jewish colonization of an already colonized African society identify it as a movement of national liberation?

The people who formulated the theories of Zionist socialism understood very well the contradiction between their ideas and those of the socialist movement.

"Socialism will solve the Jewish problem only in the remote future," wrote Nachman Syrkin, the Russian Jew who was a founder of the Zionist Socialist party. "First of all, the Jews suffer from a hatred which is unique; secondly, the class struggle cannot help the Jewish middle class or intelligentsia. The only practicable alternative for the Jew is emigration, especially from Eastern Europe. Zionism can be accepted by all Jewry, in spite of class differences. The form of the Jewish state is the only debatable issue involved in Zionism, and we must struggle to see that it is a socialist state."

Obviously, Syrkin's thesis was unacceptable to the socialist movement. Lev Martov, the theoretician and leader of the Menshevik party, scorned the Zionist Socialists in his memoirs by observing that "their socialism bears the imprint of abstract utopianism and that the idea of the class struggle was absolutely alien to them. While we looked upon them as men who had to move the whole working class, as a tool in the hands of the revolutionary organization, they considered themselves as individuals who have outgrown the masses and created a new cultural milieu."

Martov and the Mensheviks were not alone in criticizing the socialist Zionists. The Bolsheviks, of course, rejected Zionism as a substitute for the class struggle and revolutionary activity. And the Bund, the militant Jewish, as distinguished from Zionist, organization, which organized thousands of Polish and Russian Jews, heaped even more opprobrium on the Zionist Socialists than any other group: The Bund insisted that social, cultural, and political freedom for the Jews could only come about if the Jews fought for socialism in their own countries.

"Farewell and don't look back," Medem, a Bund leader, said bitterly to the Jewish youth who had started emigrating to Palestine in the first days of the twentieth century. "Turn your back on our life, on our struggle, on our joys and sorrows. You have deserted the Galut."

Was anti-Semitism the basis for the arguments of the European socialists and East European Jews against Zionism? Perhaps Martov was an anti-Semite in his heart, a self-hating Jew, although I have never seen any reports attributing anti-Semitism to him. Perhaps, too, the Bund leaders' insistence on preserving Yiddish culture was another form of anti-Semitism, but I doubt it.

I suggest, instead, that in the early years of the Zionist movement, many Marxists, of all kinds, opposed Zionism while still remaining committed to the fight for Jewish rights within their own countries. And I propose, further, that opposition to Zionism or indifference to it was characteristic of the American socialist movement until, first, the Eichmann trial and then, much more importantly, the 1967 war.

Thus, in the years from the latter part of the nineteenth century through World War II, the Jewish socialist movement in America maintained the same kind of strong opposition to Zionism as had been true for the Bund, and the non-Jewish socialists also opposed Zionism.

During this period, anti-Zionism was even stronger among American Jews than Gentiles. The middle-and upper-class Jewish community's opposition to Zionism grew from the emergence of Reform Judaism, which believed in the assimilation of American Jews into the American society rather than the maintenance of a separate Jewish political identity. The Jewish socialist view of Zionism as "bourgeois chauvinism" dominated the Jewish working class, which had emigrated from Eastern Europe.

So Zionism had little support either in the cafes of the Lower East Side, where Yiddish intellectual culture reigned, or from Jewish workers in the sweatshops, where almost totally Jewish unions were being organized.

The 1922 convention of the International Ladies Garment Workers Union reflected the characteristic attitude of the Jewish labor movement toward Zionism. One speaker, Abraham Shiplakoff, appeared before the convention, to greet it, as he said, "in the name of a movement that is temporary and if I am to tell the truth, somewhat unpopular . . . " He went on, apologetically, with, "I have come to greet you in the name of the United Hebrew Trades Campaign for the Jewish workers in Palestine. I don't want to be misunderstood. I have not become a Zionist." Mr. Shiplakoff concluded his speech by stressing the importance of Palestine as a place of refuge and omitting completely any discussion of a "return to the homeland." "The Jewish delegates at this convention as well as the Italian will sympathize," said Mr. Shiplakoff, "with the hundreds of thousands of Jewish wandering people who are badly in need of emigrating without any place to which they can emigrate and will do all they can to help them."

Again and again, the appeals for help from Palestine directed to the Jewish socialist and labor movements stressed the notion of refuge rather than homeland or national liberation. In October 1936, the predominantly Jewish Cap and Millinery Department of the United Hatters, Cap and Millinery Workers Union was asked to support the Histadrut because it "has created a haven of refuge for a vast number of Jews who are compelled to migrate to Palestine, being driven from their countries by severe persecution and the spread of race hatred."

Even after World War II had started, the Jewish trade-union leaders in the United States retained some of their earlier critical stance toward Zionism. In December 1945 in *Commentary* magazine, Zachariah Shuster, of the American Jewish Committee, arguing the standard AJC line of that time against the thesis that the Jews must leave Europe, defended his position by quoting from Jacob Pat, then chairman of the Jewish Labor Committee. Acceptance of the exodus notion, wrote Pat, would mean "that the Jewish people, all over, agree that it is a non-Jewish world, an Aryan world where there is no place for Israel. Europe without Jews means a victory of Nazism . . . . It means also a strengthening of anti-Semitism in other countries where there are Jews. It would be a suggestion, a lesson: Expel the Jews."

Two years after the creation of Israel, the 1950 convention of the the ILGWU asked Israel "to make new and extraordinary efforts, free from

narrow nationalism, to eliminate the bitterness and ameliorate the difficulties caused by the Arab refugee problem growing out of the war
which led to its birth."

The same convention even called for the internationalization of Jerusalem! Considering the fervid opposition of the Israeli government
and the Zionist movement to that kind of status for Jerusalem today, is
it conceivable that such a position would be adopted by the ILGWU
today? Or by any other union, in fact? Would a resolution suggesting
Israeli responsibility for Arab refugee be passed by the ILGWU today?

Just as the Jewish socialist and labor movements first opposed Zionism and then supported its efforts in Palestine only as creating a place
of refuge, so did the American socialist movement in general. During
the 1930s, for example, the theoretical organs of the Socialist party
published no more than a few articles on the Palestine question. And
the articles that were published reflected a basic antipathy to Zionism.
In 1936, for example, the *American Socialist Quarterly*, an official
party publication, printed a statement accepted for discussion by the
Central Bureau of Jewish Socialist Branches and submitted to the
party at large, which attacked "the continuation of the chauvinist policies of the Zionists of all kinds in Palestine.

"Zionism, in accordance with its illusion of building a homeland for
Jews in Palestine is continually pursuing the policy of taking over the
economic position of the native population."

And in language close to that used by some New Left groups, the Socialist party statement warns that the Palestinian Arabs fear that "the
small Jewish minority, supported by hated English imperialism is
about to conquer their lands."

Even as late as the 1950s, the American socialist movement held ambiguous views about Israel and Zionism. Norman Thomas, the out-
standing American socialist leader, for example, is described by his bi-
ographer, Harry Fleischman, as being sympathetic to Zionism, but as
"seeing clearly that in their zeal for the new Palestine, Zionists themselves created problems." And Fleischman also writes in his book of
the consequences to Thomas from his "opposition to certain nationalistic features of Zionism": some pro-Zionists characterized him as
"anti-Semitic."[1] (More than likely, today, he would incur a similar
charge from a large part of the organized Jewish community.)

Dissent magazine, created in 1954 to be the voice of the left-wing
non-Communist movement, provides an even more striking example of
that movement's indifference to Middle Eastern problems or opposition to Zionism. From the time of its first issue until after the 1967 war,

only two or three articles on the Middle East were published in the magazine. And the tone of those that were printed is reflected in the article written by Stanley Diamond, a *Dissent* editor, following the 1956 Suez War: "We should, therefore, condemn the combined attack on Egypt as a special example of immoral, impractical, antiquated and ultimately ineffectual political behavior."[2]

The *Dissent* editor went on to denounce the "cultural chauvinism of many Israelis, their lack of insight into or sympathy with Arab culture," and stated, flatly, that the border incidents used by Israel to justify its role "did not constitute a threat to Israel's immediate survival."[3]

If I may use a personal example for a moment, I should like to point out that as late as 1961, I was criticized, severely, for an article on the Eichmann trial in which I raised the question of whether some Jewish radicals might have become involved in the radical movement as a way of rationalizing their own desire to be non-Jews. A few years later, Lewis Coser, associated for many years with *Dissent* favorably reviewed my book *Is Curly Jewish?*,[4] which discusses at some length the problem of the relationship between radicalism and "Jewish identity," but said that I ought to stop worrying so much about the question of my Jewish identity since it wasn't that important anyway.

I cannot quarrel with the right of *Dissent* editors and union officials to change their views; but Avineri's paper makes it essential to have an accurate record of the positions that were held. Only then is it possible to seek an explanation for the changes that have taken place.

A whole series of events brought about a shifting of socialist position concerning Zionism and Israel. Initially, of course, the Holocaust shattered the complacency of those Jews, including socialists, who believed that it was possible and desirable for Jews to be absorbed into society, retaining some vestiges of their Jewishness. During the rise of Nazism, Palestine appeared as the only place to which Jews could escape; after the defeat of the Nazis, Palestine again appeared as the only possible home for the refugees. (I cannot discuss, in this paper, the failure of organized Jewry in the Western world to challenge, in any serious way, the refusal of their own governments to admit Jewish refugees on a large scale, although the subject is certainly worthy of a serious examination.)

Fortuitously, Palestine existed then as a refuge for the European Jews, in the absence of other countries willing to admit them; and as a living proof, to the Zionists, that they were correct in their dour prognoses about the nature of the Gentile world.

After Israel was created, the 1948 war erupted between Israel and the

Arab states. By then, the cold war had developed into a full-scale international political conflict, and much of the anti-Communist Left aligned itself alongside the U. S. governemnt in the worldwide struggle against the Soviet Union and Communism.

Israel, too, picked its side and became a trusted ally of the United States. Slowly, the non-Communist and anti-Communist Left groups began to shift in their attitude toward Israel, deterred slightly by the 1956 Suez war. But still, Israel's problems were not high on the agenda for these groups, and most of their members were appallingly ignorant about the Middle East, and especially about the Arab presence there.

Meanwhile, what became known as the New Left was born, nourished by the attitudes of the "beat generation" and the active resistance to segregation laws carried on by young black college students and joined by young whites, many of them Jewish.

One other basic tenet of the New Left, from its genesis, was a total rejection of the cold war, and especially of its intellectual sponsors with past histories of radicalism.

Israel and the Middle East, however, were not discussed in the first New Left documents. Instead, the foci of the New Left's attention was on Cuba, the escalating war in Asia, the civil rights movements, the Black uprisings in the cities, the rise of Malcolm X, the cold war, the fight against bureaucracy, the battle for control of the Democratic party, drug laws, the invasion of the Dominican Republic, and the need for new modes of change in American society.

Understandably, then, Irving Howe's lengthy, detailed attack on the New Left, "New Styles in Leftism," made in April 1965, contains not a single criticism of any New Left views on Israel, Zionism, Arabs, or the Middle Eastern problems: no New Left views on these questions were visible to be attacked.

But by 1966 a decisive shift had taken place within the civil rights movement as the Black militants moved away, sharply, from the concept of integrated action to that of "Black Power," leaving the white supporters of the movement, especially the Jews, bewildered and distressed.

"Jewish identity" and "Jewish power" began to evolve within New Left groups as young Jews, faced by Black Power, became aware of their Jewishness and sought, self-consciously, for meaning in that Jewishness long before the Old Left was aware that the problem existed.

The eruption of the 1967 war sent shock waves throughout the world. Diaspora Jewry virtually panicked, seeing the war as an extension of Nazi genocide, as another pogrom. Frantically, Jews outside Israel rallied in support of Israel, and not even the tremendous sense of relief felt at Israel's smashing victory allayed the deep fears which had surfaced when the war began. Suddenly, millions of Jews became aware of their Jewish identity, just as the Jewish radicals in the New Left had become self-conscious Jews earlier.

Within the New Left, too, the 1967 war had important repercussions. The Blacks identified with the Palestinians, who had become visible in the sharpest possible way. And since Israel was linked so closely to American policy, it was easy for them to extrapolate opposition to the war in Vietnam into opposition to the U.S. support for Israel. Many young Jewish New Left adherents, already alienated from the Blacks, supported Israel.

Simultaneously, the Israeli-Arab issue became even more complicated by the increasing tension between the militant Blacks and the established Jewish community, including Jewish intellectuals. The Blacks were seen as threatening those institutions of American society, like the school systems and the university, which were the very places in America where Jews had achieved some measure of security and status.

In Israel, flushed with victory, little or no attention was given to the New Left or to the anti-Israel positions adopted by one wing of it. And when the New Left finally did penetrate into the Israeli consciousness, it was scorned rather than taken seriously. But in America, even though no unanimous or even majority New Left view of Israel prevailed, larger and larger numbers of Jews were alienated from it, seeing not the reality but a frightening specter of a movement united in violent opposition to Israel's existence.

Thus, even after the New Left began disappearing as a force in American political life, its ghost remained alive. The fact that the "enemy" no longer existed did not end the ceaseless attacks upon it. Even now, when an autopsy would be the only appropriate form of inquiry about the New Left, it is still treated as if it were a strong, powerful movement with a huge constituency.

Perhaps the explanation for this phenomenon is that the phrase "New Left" has a significant symbolic value. After the 1967 war, the New Left was endowed with demonic qualities, associated with Black anti-Semitism, with Jewish self-hate, and with Gentile indifference to the Arab threat to exterminate the Jews. And the fact that the New Left no longer exists is not important because the symbol itself is still real: the words "New Left" conjure up all the enemies of Jews and of Israel.

Response to Paul Jacobs

By SHLOMO AVINERI

Shlomo Avineri made a brief response to Paul Jacobs' paper, which appears here. Some of the remarks to which he refers, especially under no. 4, were made spontaneously by Paul Jacobs, and do not appear in his paper as printed above.

There are only a very few remarks I would like to make, as I basically agree with the historical account given by Paul Jacobs, although obviously the conclusions I draw from it are different.

1. It is, of course, true that the Soviet Union supplied Israel with arms in the War of Independence of 1948, while the United States initiated an arms embargo on the Middle East, which hurt Israel much more than the Arab states, which were then lavishly supplied by the British and the French. But these Czechoslovak arms were *sold* to Israel, not given for free, and Israel paid for them in U.S. dollars raised by voluntary Jewish contributions in America. So the picture is a little more complex than suggested by Jacobs.

2. I don't think I ever suggested in my paper that whatever anti-Zionist sentiments existed in the socialist movement were motivated by anti-Semitism. I only wanted to point out that the traditional socialist attitude, which usually supported Jewish claims against anti-Semitism, did not necessarily mean support for Jewish national rights as against Jewish civil rights.

3. I fail to see why socialism and Zionism are by nature incompatible. Socialism is, of course, transnational and internationalist; but it does not negate the very existence of nations, it only hopes to transcend them. But you can transcend only what you already have. It was for this reason that Marx supported Polish, and German, and Italian nationalism, and the same argument can be made—and was made—for Zionism. I am perfectly ready to see the State of Israel wither away into a socialist internationalism—when all the other states will wither away, but not one moment earlier. To find fault with the very existence of Israel while not advocating the disappearance, simultaneously, of all other states is not internationalism, but a very bad case of double standards.

4. Lastly, terrorism. I was deeply disturbed by Jacobs' peroration, which while condemning specific acts of inhuman murder like Ma'alot, still gives them indirect support by suggesting that so long as the Palestinians remain dispossessed, such acts will continue. I think I do not have to repeat what I said earlier about my views and hopes for an Israeli-Palestinian reconciliation, based on mutual recognition and acceptance. But to postulate a deterministic view of the inevitability of terrorism because a community feels dispossessed is truly scandalous: other communities also did in the past, and do in the present, feel dispossessed, and not all of them had recourse to brutal and indiscriminate murder. The Jews felt dispossessed for two thousand years, yet they never resorted to the murder of children; as a universalist, I would like to apply this as a yardstick for all human behavior. What I would find repugnant in my own people, I think I have to criticize in others as well, and failure to do so is a moral failure.

Response to Shlomo Avineri

MILTON HIMMELFARB

There is little I would wish to add to Professor Avineri's "Radical Theology, the New Left, and Israel"; I would suggest only a slightly different emphasis.

Shlomo Avineri is aware, of course, of the non-Christian—indeed pre-Christian and classical pagan—literary background to the contempt for Jews and Judaism on the Left and in the works of such major figures of the Enlightenment as Voltaire: witness his reference to Arthur Hertzberg's *French Enlightenment and the Jews*. Still, I would suggest that we need to pay more attention to the disdain for Judaism and the Jews that has come down to us from pagan antiquity. Sometime ago I had occasion to write about an article that appeared not long after the 1967 war in *Soldier of Freedom*, published for the troops by the Polish Ministry of Defense.[1] The author was Kazimierz Sidor, a high-ranking member of the Communist party—which is to say, a Marxist; which is also to say, an atheist, hostile to religion generally and to Christianity specifically. Among other things, this Marxist expert on Israel, the Jews, and Judaism told the Polish soldiers of freedom that the Bible lies in asserting that Moses led the children of Israel forth from the Egyptian house of bondage at God's command. The real truth, he said, was that the Egyptians had expelled the Israelites, because the Israelites were lepers.

At the time I noted that this anti-Jewish account of the Exodus had originated with one Manetho, a hellenized Egyptian priest who wrote three centuries before the rise of Christianity. Since then the line of transmission between Alexandria 2,250 years ago and Warsaw today has become clearer to me. That line of transmission has been traced by several colleagues of Shlomo Avineri, notably by Samuel Ettinger in an article in *Zion*.[2] Ettinger makes a number of points: (1) John Toland is the only English deist who can be said to have been friendly to the Jews. (2) It was the deists who revived certain pagan anti-Jewish doctrines and gave them a new respectability. (3) The French Enlightenment received the neopagan teachings about Judaism and the Jews from the English deists. When deism was abandoned for atheism, first of the simple, late-Enlightenment kind, and then of the Left, Hegelian kind, the revived pagan teachings remained intact. Ettinger shows how not only the deist Voltaire, but also the atheist d'Holbach, repeated what English deists had said long before them. (He cites the classical pagan accusation of leprosy, as well as lice and stinks, against the Jews in the deist writings.) While d'Holbach may not have needed the deists to rediscover Tacitus on the Jews, d'Holbach did call the Hebrews "enemies of the human race"—Tacitus' phrase. Ettinger's article concludes by quoting H. S. Reimarus and J. S. Semler, theologians who were to have a great influence on advanced German Protestant thought in the nineteenth century.

Avineri is informative and judicious about Bruno Bauer. Zvi Rosen, also in an ariticle appearing in *Zion*,[3] traces Bauer's views on Jews and Judaism directly to his readings in Voltaire and d'Holbach—who, as we have seen, had read the English deists, who had read the ancient pagans.

The deists, and all the more so the atheists, were not Christian. They were ex-Christian. It probably is true, as Avineri suggests, that the prejudice against Jews and Judaism of their later years was an emotion that persisted from the Christian formation of their childhood and youth. That is important and must not be overlooked. It is also important and not to be overlooked that the intellectual justification the deists gave for their prejudice was largely, and in some cases almost exclusively, pre-Christian. Nor is it to be overlooked that intellectual ly, and in most cases politically, deists and atheists were men of the Left.

(A notable exception was the skeptic Hume, a Tory, who for that reason was considered by Jefferson to be not so much a skeptic as a cynic—for, thought Jefferson, who hated and despised Hume, how otherwise could he bring himself to be a Tory? Another exception was Lord Melbourne, the eighteenth-century infidel and Whig, who said of himself that he was a buttress rather than a pillar of the church. He supported it from the outside.)

In this respect, from a Jewish point of view traditional Christianity, hostile and oppressive as it was to the Jews and Judaism, is superior to post-Christian Enlightenment and revolution. At least traditional Christianity tolerated, both in theory and practice, the continued survival of the Jews and Judaism. If Christendom had wished to destroy the Jews and Judaism, it could have done so easily (cf. Yerushalmi's paper). After all, the Jews were a tiny, powerless minority. What Christendom could do when it really wanted to destroy religious dissenters we can learn from the fate of the Albigensians. Expulsions of Jews were frequent—from England, France, Spain, parts of Germany. Destructions, and especially sanctioned destructions, were rare. It is in Rome—Rome!—that Jews have their oldest uninterrupted settlement in Europe, from before the days of Julius Caesar. By contrast, this is how Jacob Katz concludes his recent study of Voltaire's view of Judaism and the Jews:[4]

> Of the traditional outlook [on Judaism and the Jews] there was left [to Voltaire] only a residue of revulsion and jeering contempt. In the absence of an ideology of justification [of Jewish existence] from another [divine] source, Judaism is exposed to shattering criticism and is condemned to total obliteration—like an errant survival from an earlier age, with no recognized place in the new scheme of things. The conclusion is inevitable: that Judaism must and should disappear from the world.

The continuity is striking. George L. Mosse's "German Socialists and the Jewish Question in the Weimar Republic"[5] is a thorough and meticulous examination of all the sources, from Marx's polemic with Bauer to the rise of Hitler. Mosse is able to summarize the whole problem in one sentence: "Revolutionary socialism desired to put an end to Jews and Judaism."

Avineri rightly pays his respects to Karl Kautsky. One of the first books—perhaps the first—brought out by the American Communist publishing firm, International Publishers, in the 1920s, was an English translation of the second edition of Kautsky's *Rasse und Judentum*, under the title *Are the Jews a Race?* For Communists, Kautsky the Social Democrat was the notorious "renegade," yet on the Jewish question he was, even for them, an impeccably Marxist authority. This is how Kautsky concludes his book:

> We cannot say we have completely emerged from the Middle Ages as long as Judaism still exists among us. The sooner it disappears, the better it will be, not only for society, but also for the Jews themselves.
> The disappearance of the Jews will not involve a tragic process like the disappearance of the American Indians or the Tasmanians. . . . It will not mean a mere shifting of domicile from one medieval ruin to another, not a transition from orthodox Judaism to ecclesiastical Christianity, but the creation of a new and higher type of man.[6]

Note the singularity: the disappearance of any other group but the Jews is a tragedy. Only the disappearance of the Jews will not be a tragedy, only the disappearance of the Jews will instead be a blessing. Actually, we may infer that the Jews' refusal to disappear—but only theirs—is not merely itself tragic but also wicked, since anything that deliberately obstructs the creation of a new and higher type of man may rightly be condemned as wicked. Here, as Mosse reminds us, Lenin and Stalin were faithful disciples of Kautsky: "Lenin and Stalin were ready to grant . . . autonomy to other suppressed nationalities but not to the Jews. . . . they applied Kautsky's theories to the Jewish question . . ." (p. 126). "[The Social Democrats] had largely succeeded in liquidating the heritage of Marx's Jewish questions, and Kautsky's became an increasingly lonely voice within his party. The Communist party continued the older tradition, and was here indeed the inheritor of orthodox Marxism" (p. 134).

One of the last Communist pronouncements on Judaism and the Jews before Hitler's rise to power was Otto Heller's *Untergang des Judentums* (Berlin, 1931), which Jacob Katz mentions as a twentieth—century descendant of Voltaire. Part of Mosse's summary paraphrase of this elegant treatise is as follows: "not only is trade their [sc., the Jews'] way of life, but they have also acquired other undesirable characteristics; they are a nervous people who gesticulate." This is a grave Marxist criticism: "The Jew gesticulates."

For Marx the purpose of Jewish emancipation—i.e., civic equality—was the emancipation of the Jews from their Judaism, and indeed the emancipation of society from *its* Judaism, namely, the worship of money; for what else is Judaism but that? The idea that Jewish emancipation really meant or necessarily implied the Jews' abandonment of Judaism was widespread. At the beginning of the nineteenth century, Reimarus included a propensity to swindle in a gloating enumeration of Jewish inferiorities and vices. Toward the end of the century, the philosopher Eduard von Hartmann, politically of the Left, published a book in which he accused the German Jews of having swindled Germany. The swindle consisted in their failure to honor a clause in the contract they had implicitly signed with the German majority, when that majority graciously bestowed emancipaion upon them. The implicit clause in the implicit contract was that thenceforth the Jews would feel and behave like real Germans. But feeling and behaving like a real German was impossible for a Jew who retained a sense of Jewish solidarity. The philosopher proposed a test. How many Jews could conscientiously say that when having to choose between helping a German who was not a Jew and helping a Jew who was not a German, they would have no hesitation about helping the German who was not a

Jew? Jewish inability to make that choice without hesitation proved the Jewish swindle.

Since there can be no Jews and Judaism without a sense of Jewish solidarity, Jews and Judaism are wrong. It is wrong, it is unethical, for Jews and Judaism to continue to exist.

More than a hundred years earlier, Frederick the Great's cultural adviser, the Marquis d'Argens, a member in good standing of the French Enlightenment, recommended to his master that Moses Mendelssohn should be allowed to live in Berlin because, as he put it, Mendelssohn was "a bad Jew." A bad Jew is a Jew on the point of ceasing to be a Jew. Clearly, no case could be made allowing a good Jew to live in Berlin. ("Living in Berlin" symbolized admission into society.) D'Argens called himself a bad Catholic and Frederick a bad Protestant, but it would not have occurred to either of them that good Christians should not be allowed to live in Berlin.

The French Revolution granted citizenship to the Jews of France. The principle of that grant of citizenship was expressed concisely in the famous declaration by Clermont-Tonnerre: "To the Jews as individuals everything, to the Jews as a people [*nation*] nothing." (His *nation* meant, in accordance with the usage of time, something like "collectivity.") Hardly anyone is familiar with the words that immediately followed. The distinguished historian Salo Baron reminds us that Clermont-Tonnerre added: If the Jews refuse to accept these terms, "let them be banished."

During the seventy years or so of the Third Republic, there was an oddity of the French school system that has been little commented on. We are accustomed to a five-day school week, Monday to Friday. The Third Republic had a school week of four full and two half days: Monday, Tuesday, Wednesday, half (or no) Thursdays, Friday, and half (or all of) Saturday. May we say that the French government went out of its way to insure that every Jewish child in a state school would have to violate his Sabbath? I am sure that was not the intention. It was, however, the consequence: in practice, "to the Jews as a people nothing" could mean "taking away from the Jews as a people everything." Yet the French Jewish community, and even the French rabbinate, seem not to have protested. It is as if they feared that by protesting against an arrangement of the school week which not only was absurd but also singled them out for injury, they would be accused of seeking something for theselves as a people—an unthinkable crime.

This brings me to what for a Jew may be the most painful thing of all. The Otto Heller of the *Untergang des Judentums*, who had such a horror of gesticulation, was or had been a Jew. In *Midstream* of January 1974, Martin Jay's "Antisemitism and the Weimar Left" first reminds us that

> Marxists, beginning with the founder himself and his controversial reply to Bruno Bauer on the Jewish Question in 1843, have tended to deny the uniqueness of antisemitic oppression. That is, they have tended to subsume it under the more general rubric of the exploitation of the working class and as a result have relegated it to a secondary role. Or worse, at times they have even condoned Judeophobia, implicitly or explicitly, as an expression of anti-capitalistic resentments. [p. 42]

He adds that some of "the socialists in question were from Jewish backgrounds, however assimilated."

At first I though Jay was referring to what happened in Russia in the early 1880s, when many Populists (Narodniki) greeted a wave of pogroms against the Jews as a sign that the formerly inert masses were beginning to stir against their exploiters; but Jay had something more particular to Weimar in mind. He mentions "an ugly speech by Ruth Fischer on July 25, 1923, in which the masses were exhorted to 'trample the Jewish capitalists down, hang them from the lampposts'" (p. 47). (Ruth Fischer was one of those "socialists . . . from Jewish backgrounds." Jay continues: "In 1930 . . . comparable appeals to antisemitism ywere also sounded by the KPD [the German Communist party]. Although these incidents ought not to be overemphasized, they certainly suggest that the KPD was far from vigorous in its response to antisemitism"(ibid.).

One need hardly speak, therefore, of the New Left—or of radical theology, if that is to be taken as new—and Israel. The New Left and radical theology are faithful heirs of the Old Left and the theology extending from pagan antiquity, by way of the English deists and the French Enlightenment, to the Left Hegelians. Then there was no State of Israel to reject, only Jews and Judaism. The new rejection of Israel is an aspect of the old rejection of Jews and Judaism.

PART VII

The New Romanticism and Biblical Faith

Introduction

In considering the planning and executing of the concentration-camp structure, much attention has been paid to the role of technology and to the scientific world-view. The mentality of science has been seen as subordinating the
value of life to the value of efficiency, thus blunting sensitivity to suffering and
facilitating the destruction of millions of people. If this criticism is justified, are
we not, then, compelled to turn to the critics of scientific rationalism, who find
in the expansion of consciousness as such, in the prizing of experience for its
own sake, an alternative to the depersonalization of technology? In short, is
the New Romanticism a cure for the ills of scientism, or is it only another aspect of the disease?

Michael Ryan's view of the New Romanticism points both to its dangers and
to its salvific possibilities. Recognizing the difficulty of defining "romanticism," Ryan is still able to discern certain salient characteristics which, taken
together, constitute a definite pattern. These common features include a sense
that consciousness itself is of crucial importance, and that personal consciousness can be identified with the new direction history is taking. This view risks
the danger of taking the part for the whole, the individual for the direction of
world history. Turning to the Old Romanticism of the nineteenth century, Ryan
argues that its digressions from religious orthodoxy served the interests of recovering a more genuine religiosity, and that it was, at its best, capable of condemning anti-Semitic dogma. While these tendencies are not always found in
the New Romanticism, they provide evidence for romanticism's positive possibilities. Like its predecessor, the New Romanticism places a special value
upon nature, less out of aesthetic considerations, which characterized this interest in the Old Romanticism, than from a desire to save the planet's rapidly
dwindling resources. Moreover, the New Romanticism is not in this respect at
variance with the biblical attitude, Ryan argues, since for biblical man the
world is the gift of a loving God. A major difficulty in the New Romanticism lies
in its attempt to incorporate widely divergent, even contradictory, psychological strands and cultural symbols. Individual consciousness becomes protean,
slipping easily from one role to another with little affective dislocation.

While Ryan points to the dangers of the New Romanticism as well as to its
strengths, *Arthur Waskow* argues that counter-culture critics, as exponents of
neo-romanticism, correctly attack the apocalyptic character of our age while at
the same time praising its promise, and thus call attention to the dimension of
Messianic change in our epoch. Thus, if we are indeed at the end of days, we
can expect the restoration of what was taken away at the beginning: the full
humanity of women, the harmony of man and nature, work which is fulfilling
rather than arduous, and the absence of violence or, to put it otherwise, universal peace. The torments of the present age represent the travail, the birth-
pangs, of the Messiah in accordance with the traditional warnings, but the in-

ner dialectic of Messianism entails the reversal of the negative conditions of our age. Furthermore, Waskow argues, we must not allow the signs to go unheeded. Instead, a new and radically conceived Messiancic "path" must be constructed which could lead humankind back to its original wholeness.

Where Waskow perceives the harmony of biblical and romantic consciousness, *Edith Wyschogrod* sees a sharp dichotomy between biblical claims and romanticism's aspirations. She distinguishes the two worldviews as two metaphysical types, the metaphysics of experience (the romantic) and the metaphysics of event (the biblical).

She is largely in accord with Ryan's description of the New Romanticism, but adds that its most striking feature is its emphasis upon personal freedom and expressiveness. Unlike Ryan and Waskow she locates the phenomenon of Auschwitz along the same gradient as romanticism itself, suggesting that technology provides the tools for the implementation of a fantasy whose content is at least partially the product of romantic consciousness. In contrast, the biblical world does not speak of consciousness, inner life, or experience valued for its own sake. The lives of the patriarchs are narrated in terms of the most quotidian events, punctuated only by the intervention of divine claims. Most significant is the fact that transhistorical judgment determines the significance of these events.

Despite the dangers of romantic criticism, all three contributors agree that at its best romanticism provides a compelling critique of narrow rationalisms and contains elements which can become signposts of hope in a world after Auschwitz.

The New Romanticism
and Biblical Faith

MICHAEL D. RYAN

The banks of the Thames are clouded! the ancient porches of Albion
   are
Darken'd! they are drawn thro' unbounded space, scatter'd upon
The Void in incoherent despair! Cambridge & Oxford & London,
Are driven among the starry Wheels, rent away and dissipated,
In Chasms & Abysses of sorrow, enlarg'd without dimension, terrible.
Albion's mountains run with blood, the cries of war & of tumult
Resound into the unbounded night, every Human perfection
Of mountain & river & city, are small & wither'd & darken'd
Cam is a little stream! Ely is almost swallowed up!
....
Jerusalem is scattered abroad like a cloud of smoke thro' non-entity:
Moab & Ammon & Amalek & Canaan & Egypt & Aram
Receive her little ones for sacrifices and the delights of cruelty.
           —From *Jerusalem,* by William Blake[1]

A clue to at least part of what is meant by "The New Romanticism" is
furnished by the theme of this Symposium, "Auschwitz: Beginning of
a New Era?" It was not suggested as part of the historical game of periodization in order to become the occasion for yet another outburst of
revisionist histories, playing around with the data. There is a periodization that historians superimpose on the data, such as that delimiting
the age of the Renaissance. But there is a periodization demanded by
the events themselves. Such is the new era suggested by the horrendous complex of events symbolized in the single word—Auschwitz.

New eras are created by historical catastrophes like the fall of Rome,
which had the effect of leaving its citizens with a consciousness as
shattered as the empire itself. All of the normal expectations of life associated with the political, economic, and cultural institutions of Rome
were radically transformed. Everywhere people became strangers in
their own land, extruded, as it were, pushed out against their will from
one age, from one way of life, into another not yet fully formed. Uncertainty, an acute sense of the transitoriness of life, an urgent need for a
whole new departure of personal and social existence—all this, inter-

mixed with bitterness, or cynicism, or resignation, characterized the consciousness of those who felt that the events of history had closed the gates of one epoch behind them and left them to find their way in a strange and threatening world. As such an extruded citizen, St. Augustine wrote *The City of God* to help his fellow citizens find their way in the new age after the fall of Rome.

What I shall attempt to discuss here under "The New Romanticism" is the manifestation in varying expressions in our society of such a consciousness of having been extruded from the past by the horrendous events of our century, and the different postures assumed either toward, or in terms of, biblical faith. But because "New Romanticism" suggests definite analogies to what is presumably "Old Romanticism," I wish first to characterize that movement.

The "Old" Romantic Consciousness

By the "Old Romanticism" I refer to the consciousness of those Europeans who in one way or another understood themselves as living in a new epoch in the years after the French Revolution and during the Napoleonic Wars. This new epochal consciousness found expression in concrete manifestations as diverse and as varied as the interpretive reactions to the events themselves. William Blake's vision of a militarized Britain on the way to becoming an empire was crystallized in the apocalyptic stanzas of his long poem *Jerusalem: The Emanation of the Giant Albion,* as can be seen from the lines cited above. Lord Byron, commenting on the battle of Waterloo and the defeated Napoleon, whom he saw wearing "the shattered links of the World's broken chain," wrote:

> Fit retribution! Gaul may champ the bit
> And foam in fetters;—but is Earth more free?
> Did nations combat to make One submit?
> Or league to teach all Kings true Sovereignty?
> What! shall reviving Thraldom again be
> The patched-up Idol of enlightened days?
> Shall we, who struck the Lion down, shall we
> Pay the Wolf homage? proffering lowly gaze
> And servile knees to Thrones? No! prove before ye praise![2]

Byron's Childe Harold is the extruded citizen of old Europe sojourning through familiar landscapes in a strange new time. Napoleon may have been defeated and the old order reasserted, but the aura of moral-religious authority is gone. There are no more kings by divine right in Childe Harold's world, only by the assertion of naked power, or perhaps by historical sentiment.

Georg W. F. Hegel also found himself in a new world after Napoleon. The last section of his *Philosophy of History,* the lectures of 1830–31, is devoted to the world-historical significance of the French Revolution. He understood the "French oppression," as he called it, as a providential improvement of the political condition of Germany. It exposed "the deficiencies of the old system," dispelled "the fiction of an Empire," and left standing the more genuine political reality of several sovereign states. In Prussia it meant that feudal obligations were abolished and the role of the monarch diminished by the emergence of a new bureaucracy of the state manned by persons with "talent" and the capacity for "adaptation"—all of which suggested to Hegel that the Spirit of God, of Absolute Reason, was at work in the events.[3] On this more solid foundation the political history of Prussia, and of all Europe, could proceed. If Blake and Byron were romantic pessimists, Hegel was the epitome of romantic optimism.

Arthur O. Lovejoy was so right when he argued in his essay "On the Discrimination of Romanticisms"[4] that many entirely different, even contradictory complexes of thought have been labeled "romantic," resulting in a debasement of the term.[5] This state of affairs has been so generally acknowledged that the word "romantic" has become synonymous with mild muddle-headedness, if not outright confusion. Horace L. Friess, in the introductory essay to his translation of Friedrich Schleiermacher's *Soliloquies,* furnished a rationale for the radical heterogeneity of romantic thought and expression. Referring to German romanticism, he wrote, "it is . . . the attempt to embrace magic and science, poetry and politics, Hellenism and Protestantism, romance and toil in the compass of a single life that is strikingly romantic and peculiar to the ambitions of modern society become more conscious of its diverse riches."[6]

Yet for all the heterogeneity, there remain some salient common characteristics that apply as much to the poets Blake and Byron as to the philosopher Hegel and the pious Friedrich Schleiermacher:

1. Consciousness of a new epoch. Each in some respect identified himself with the new era, saw in his own life the first fruits of the new epoch, and accordingly indulged in iconoclastic criticism of what he considered to be outworn beliefs or atavistic tendencies on the part of his contemporaries.
2. Preoccupation with consciousness as such. In the reflex of his own

preoccupation with history, each came to see history reflected in his own consciousness; that is, consciousness was historicized so that each came to reflect on consciousness itself as the clue to the essential reality of history, and by way of history, as the essential reality of nature as well.

3. Identification of personal consciousness with world history. In the case of both Hegel and Schleiermacher, their own personal consciousness was understood as furnishing the clue for the total direction of world history. Therefore, they sought in the nature of consciousness itself the unity that was implicit in the manifold of reality that presented itself as radical diversity. Consciousness was for them at once *self*-consciousness, *historical* consciousness, *world* consciousness, and finally *God*-consciousness. Thus, in the "Old Romanticism" consciousness was the key to reality, and so its proponents came to understand their own intentional acts as *participation* in world history.

Lord Byron expressed all this poetically:

> Tis to create, and in creating live
> A being more intense that we endow
> With form our fancy, gaining as we give
> The life we image, even as I do now—
> What am I? Nothing: but not so art thou,
> Soul of my thought! with whom I traverse earth,
> Invisible but gazing, as I glow
> Mixed with thy spirit, blended with thy birth,
> And feeling still with thee in my crushed feeling's dearth.[7]

The Old Romanticism and Biblical Faith

The primary exponent of the Old Romanticism and biblical faith is Friedrich Schleiermacher, professor of theology at the University of Berlin from the time of its founding in 1810 until his death in 1834. His *Speeches On Religion*, published in 1799, when he was a young pastor in Berlin, were an iconoclastic attack on the apotheosis of human rationality by the thinkers of the Enlightenment. In addition to Goethe, the followers of Immanuel Kant were especially scandalized, among them Georg W. F. Hegel. Here was a blow, not from the stronghold of Christian orthodoxy, claiming that religion, too, could be reasonable, like secular philosophy, but from someone—obviously a student of rationalism—claiming that reason, by itself, is insufficient to constitute the essence of human nature, that reason alone could not really define human nature through a reflection on itself, but rather through reflection on an essence that lies deeper in the human being than the capacity to know and to do. This was a radical relativizing of that power of reasoning which apparently had succeeded in relativizing all positive historical religions. Had not reason successfully analyzed them and extracted from finite particulars a universal rational essence called natural religion?

The romantic strategy of Schleiermacher was to counter the analyzing-dividing thrust of rationalism with a synthesizing description of consciousness that had the effect of absorbing reason by showing its role in a larger field of awareness—one that includes feeling and aesthetic experiences as well as analytical processes. Thus reason by and for itself could not furnish the description of the human essence. Only through interaction with states and stages of consciousness could reason play a role in arriving at the essential human being—namely, as that finite being who has a capacity for an awareness of the Infinite in and through the consciousness of the finite.[8] Scandal of scandals! Schleiermacher was arguing with reason against reason as that which finally constitutes the human essence. *Homo religiosus* lay deeper in human nature than *homo sapiens.* For the rationalists that was indeed a foolish reactionary babbling that seemed to prefer the dark night of the Middle Ages to the daylight of the eighteenth century. For Schleiermacher, whose romantic consciousness, like a great boa constrictor, had swallowed the Kantian system whole, it was a sober assessment of the limits of human reason and a discovery of the manifold richness that lies at the heart of being human. For, according to him, to be rational without being religious is a truncation of human beings, a failure to develop the human consciousness to its fullest capacity. It is to misperceive one's relation to culture and to the world within which civilization and culture appear. As he put it to the cultured despisers of religion, "I know how well you have succeeded in making your earthly life so rich and varied, that you no longer stand in need of an eternity. Having made a universe for yourselves, you are above the need of thinking of the Universe that made you."[9]

Convinced as he was that being religious was the essence of humanity, it followed for Schleiermacher as a Christian theologian that Jesus Christ, the revelation of very God and very man, was a perfect religious person. His volume on dogmatics, *The Christian Faith,* first published in 1822, is written on the premise that in Jesus of Nazareth a perfect religious consciousness, a perfect God-consciousness, had appeared in the world. Since religious consciousness is an awareness of sheer dependence, or of being dependent purely and simply upon God (*schlechthinige Abhängigkeit*),[10] Jesus shared this with all human beings; but he differed from all others in the quality and constancy of that awareness of sheer dependence, which for Schleiermacher meant his sinlessness.[11]

Jesus' awareness of himself as the Messiah of God and his idea of the kingdom of God occurred to him spontaneously at the same moment when he perceived the uniqueness of his own consciousness of God compared with that of those whom he encountered.[12] According to this portrait of the historical Jesus, his consciousness of "the power indwelling him," and simultaneously his awareness of the dire need of others outside of him, became for Jesus "a single impulse of constant Self-communication."[13] Schleiermacher believed that the Christian church had a solid historical basis for this judgment about Jesus as one who constantly communicated his own consciousness of God to others. He was convinced that the Gospel of John was written by an eyewitness to the ministry and passion of Jesus. He even argued that the Fourth Gospel might possibly contain the *verba ipsissima* of Jesus, since Jesus might have been self-taught in Greek as well as in Hebrew.[14] The famous "I am" statements of the Gospel of John—"I am the bread of life" (John 6:35); "I am the light of the world" (8:12b); "I am the way, and the truth, and the life" (14:6), etc.—are words that reflect his perfect self-communicating God-consciousness. The synoptic Gospels, Matthew, Mark, and Luke, with their contrasting language and styles, were the compositions of redactors who received from the tradition a transmuted impression that Jesus made upon those outside his immediate circle. Hence they were not as accurate in their representation of the words of Jesus as was the author of the Fourth Gospel.

The Christian church emerges in Schleiermacher's historical conception as a community of people whose consciousness of sin and grace was their response to the impact of Jesus' God-consciousness upon their own. The result of this impact was that their own God-consciousness was conflated with his, so that they could no longer think of God apart from him. Redemption meant assumption into living fellowship with Christ by sharing his God-consciousness.[15] Thus the Christian church is a God-consciousness with a history that contains its historical origin within itself. The revelation of God was thus radically historicized, which Schleiermacher came to express in a doctrine of the

Trinity that he claimed to find in Sabellius, who came to Rome circa 215 C.E. The Trinity is God revealed, and the revelation is threefold: in creation and preservation of the world—God the Father; in redemption as justification and regeneration of sinners through Jesus' impartation of his perfect God-consciousness—God the Son; and in sanctification as the maintenance of living fellowship with Christ—God the Holy Spirit.[16] But God in and for God is One, the true *Monás*, the Most High, the Unity that admits of no distinction within the divine life, and as such is beyond all of the distinctions and the anthropomorphisms that are appropriate for understanding the Christian revelation.[17]

The Jewish character of his description of the Godhead as pure unity did not escape even Schleiermacher himself. He believed that Judaism, on the one hand, and Greek paganism, on the other, both left abiding imprints on the Christian religion.[18] But both constituted extremes to be avoided. He saw Judaism as animated by an understanding of revelation that was too external, too bound to words and laws that come from without.[19] Greek polytheism indeed fostered the idea of indwelling divinity, but it degenerated into a multiplicity of deities and so was demoniacal and transitory, lacking the power to perpetuate itself.[20] Schleiermacher's Christian arrogance was betrayed in his assessment of Judaism as a child-like religion that had long since died because it was too capricious for adult minds to take seriously.[21] From his own perspective as part of the established church of Prussia, Judaism appeared in his society as a dead fragment, with its own sons and daughters, many of whom—like Henriette Herz, whom he knew personally—had abandoned the faith of their forebears for rationalism or some version of Christianity. His descriptions of Judaism never got beyond a caricature. That is to say, he never succeeded in doing with Judaism what he invited the cultured despisers to do with religion— namely, to penetrate the teachings and rituals of a community of faith in order to grasp the animating vision of the world and the self-understanding of a community before God. There is no indication that Schleiermacher ever understood the fundamental role of covenant, either in the Hebrew Scriptures or in the New Testament. The Scriptures were worn like a wax nose to fit the contours of his romantic conception of religion and life. The peculiar roots, air, and light of the Scriptures themselves were ignored or suppressed.

It must be noted, however, that Schleiermacher's attitude toward the Jewish religion was not carried over into the political struggle of the Jews of Prussia for full citizenship. Throughout the eighteenth century the Jews of Prussia, including wealthy merchants, bankers, and court Jews, were still considered a separate "nation" within Prussia by Jews themselves as well as by Christians, and the old medieval laws were still in force that obliged Jews to pay special taxes for protection and for travel. Jews were still denied access to most trades, professions, and offices in the government. The unyielding attitude of the government toward Jewish demands for full citizenship, in spite of the record of patriotism and loyalty exhibited by such notables as Moses Mendelssohn (1729–86), was a source of frustration for the Jews of Prussia toward the end of the eighteenth century. It led David Friedlander (1750–1834), a silk manufacturer and prominent disciple of Moses Mendelssohn, to suggest a desperate solution.

In an open letter representing the heads of some Jewish households in Berlin, Friedlander, the author of the anonymously published epistle, advocated that Jews be granted full citizenship through conversion to Christianity, but that the conversion should not entail subscribing to any dogma, or assuming any liturgical obligations that would violate the canons of rationality current among enlightened Christians and Jews.[22] In short, it was to be a conversion to a deistic expression of Christianity. The suggestion set off a great furor and debate, not a little of it apparently anti-Semitic in character, although the word "anti-Semitic" had not yet been coined. Friedrich Schleiermacher, then in the process of publishing his *Speeches on Religion,* also wrote a letter (April 17, 1799), which was published anonymously as part of a larger correspondence evoked by Friedlander's letter.[23]

Schleiermacher's reaction was to reject the proposal on the grounds that citizenship should not be impaired on the basis of a person's positive religious affiliation; therefore, citizenship should be extended to all Jews, and not simply to Jews who effect a "quasi-conversion" to Christianity.[24] Since it was apparently an open secret that David Friedlander was the author of the open letter, Schleiermacher appealed to him as one who had fought for full citizenship of Jews without the requirement that they abandon the ceremonial laws.

> How deeply hurt especially the admirable Friedlander must be! I am eager to see whether he won't come forward and raise his voice against this betrayal of the better cause; he who with such high hopes—so it seemed at least—once departed the battlefield, who—more genuine disciple of Mendelssohn than this one here—did not even want to consider an abolition of the ceremonial law, but rather asserted decidedly that Jewish orthodoxy constitutes no obstacle for his people. . . . Reason demands that all should be citizens, but it does not require that all must be Christians. It

should therefore be possible in a number of ways to be a citizen and yet not be a Christian . . .[25]

Schleiermacher then went on to attack the real basis for governmental resistance to full citizenship for Jews. He saw it not in the government's supposed wish to maintain the protection tax, but rather in a "lazy reason" of the statesmen, which considers the remnants of "the old barbarism as ineradicable and believes that the conflicts which could arise therefrom, and which are considerable indeed, as insurmountable."[26] But this "lazy reason" was hiding behind a facade, namely, "the dogma of an inward corruption of the Jews, and behind the maxim that it is therefore dangerous to accept them into civil society."[27] In the last part of his letter, Schleiermacher cited some of the blatant prejudices extant in Prussian society with regard to Jews that would be used against their receiving full citizenship even as converted Christians. It would be charged "that the Israelites who convert to Christianity would not leave behind their inborn corruption"; and that "neither the water of holy baptism, nor other moral means of Christians in which they could participate, would furnish power for that."[28] The task of right reason, as Schleiermacher saw it, was to make it impossible for a state which identified Judaism with an anti-civil attitude to employ such a dogma and maxim for its repressive policy. Schleiermacher saw no need to keep Christianity pure from such an "inborn corruption of Jews," because he did not believe that it existed. He wanted to protect the church from having to fight a false struggle with this sort of perverted thinking, which he believed would find an occasion for self-expression if a policy of "quasi-conversion" of Jews to Christianity for the sake of citizenship were to become official.[29]

The pertinent conclusions from this survey of the thought and issues of the "Old Romanticism" for our discussion of the "New Romanticism" are that the Old Romanticism self-consciously moved out of religious orthodoxy in the interest of recovering a more purely conceived vital essence of historical religion; that it tended to read its own meanings back into the texts of biblical religion; but that it was capable of recognizing and condemning anti-Semitic dogma and maxims as contrary both to reason and to its own apprehension of the human essence.

The New Romanticism

The New Romanticism is the self-alienated spirit of Western culture, which, like a great and sad genie uncorked from its modern bottle, has descended on the consciousness of Western liberals. The mass destruction of human life, and the despoliation of whole sectors of the biosphere by corporations and governments that offer political and economic rationales for their destructive use of technical reason, has simply shocked the liberal self-consciousness of the West.

This self-contradictory use of technical reason has evoked a new radical negation of reason as that capacity which by itself defines and preserves genuine human being. Especially where Eastern philosophy and religion are advocated by Westerners as the purer, truer, more humane way of being in, and to, a world, or of arriving at the awareness of an ultimate nonworld, there Western analytical reason is employed in a self-negating exercise for the sake of that purer vision. The transition in the West from Western to Eastern thinking can only take place by way of a pathetic self-negation of Western thinking. The results of the transition are usually published in books that employ Western discursive reasoning to illuminate the Eastern mysteries, and Western mass media to communicate the Eastern "meaning." Even more painful to behold than this self-sacrifice of Western intellect is the contempt and scorn for the New Romantics by the managerial elite of business and government, who would rather continue their destructive enterprises than make a public admission of their collective wrongs.

Because the New Romanticism is a Western pheonomenon even where it embraces Eastern thinking, the discussion here will be limited to its more patently Western expressions.

Like the Old Romantics, the New understand themselves as having been extruded from the past by the massively destructive events of the last thirty-five years. They are not able to identify positively with the institutions and values that perpetrated such horror for the sake of the so-called greater good of mankind. Auschwitz represents the definitive end, the *telos*, of European civilization. It was a veritable revelation of the dark underside of European imperialism for the whole preceding millennium. Vietnam likewise revealed the animating spirit of the American empire, and as such now signifies proleptically the end of that empire for the New Romantic consciousness. The present technocratic civilization, manipulated by American-based multinational corporations, appears to be only the corpse of an empire whose grand moral idealism simply died in Vietnam, as a tiny nation was pulverized, and moral objections to the American bombing were dismissed for allegedly more realistic reasons of state. In the meantime fuel and natural resources that could have served peaceful purposes for years to come were burned up in one decade. For the New Romantics this is the definitive self-contradiction of the militaristic capitalism of the mori-bund American empire. Even apart from the draining effect of Watergate, American political institutions after Vietnam have lacked the moral majesty that is claimed for them by the words "with liberty and justice for all" in the pledge of allegiance.

While the Napoleonic Wars were as shocking for the Old Romantics as Vietnam has been for the New, the former saw themselves as extruded from the small five-thousand-and-some-years-old world of Christian and Jewish orthodoxy. They understood themselves as living in a world whose temporal-spatio dimensions exploded that small, apparently utterly knowable world. It was as if the back-end had been kicked out of history, as the old dates of creation were called into question and pushed farther and farther backwards in time.[30] In the new epochal consciousness of early-nineteenth-century romanticism, the past seemed to extend backward to infinity, and the future forward to infinity. The world suddenly became mysterious and vast. Human history appeared to be made up of relatively constant elements—government, religion, culture, and economics; but, like pieces of glass in a kaleidoscope, they would rearrange themselves in ever new patterns in succeeding ages of history. There was no reason to think that the world might soon come to an end, but only that the elements of culture and history would strike a new pattern after Napoleon.[31]

The new epochal consciousness of the late twentieth century seems to be a return to a world of the proportions of the pre-Napoleonic era. The extinction of the human species has suddenly become conceivable in more ways than one. The Old Romantics looked forward to many millennia of human civilizations. The New Romantics think in terms of only a few centuries of survival for civilization as we know it. The Old Romantics turned from a preoccupation with nature to history as the story of human mastery over the natural environment. The New Romantics are turning to a new preoccupation with nature, which is rapidly proving to be beyond human control, as death and disaster threaten the activities of humans who have ignored the fundmental conditions for the survival of organic life. For the New Romantics, the biosphere and the way it delimits the possibilities for the survival of an expanding human population within it are the great new facts of history. The world itself is now perceived as finite, and the question of the future is not, How shall human beings dominate nature? but rather, How shall they learn to live with nature in a finite, not an infinite, world?

The turn toward an understanding of human life within history as entailing only finite possibilities has led to a new introspection and a new exploration of consciousness itself. The experience of radical limitation of physical growth in outer space has led to the exploration of inner space and a quest for a new life-style in which the external patterns and social arrangements would not only be appropriate for a finite world, but would also imply a whole new set of values based on a richer, more abundant inner life. This means that, in addition to the traditional emphasis on reason and intellect, other powers of consciousness will be cultivated, such as extrasensory perception, levitation, etc. In a world based on an abundance of possibilities for perceiving, evaluating, and appreciating it from within consciousness, human beings carry their own capacity for enjoyment, and hence their own possibilities for satisfaction within themselves. They might very well be rendered immune to the life-style that conceives of satisfaction in terms of the accumulation of material things that have social-status value. This is not to suggest that there is no possibility at all for social-status values in the New Romantic consciousness. Now, however, the richness of one's capacity to see and appreciate beauty and to evoke in others that capacity determines social status and not the material things of life.

At this juncture the New Romanticism completely corresponds with the Old. The turn to preoccupation with consciousness itself has carried with it, in many cases, the conviction that through a change in consciousness, one can change history itself. It is believed that the external historical conditions for human existence in time and space can be altered by a radical change in human consciousness understood as the key to all external patterning and organization of human life. Pushed to the extreme, it results in the rather naive assumption that one's own consciousness can be viewed as a reliable indicator of the direction that history itself is taking. Hence the autobiographical sketch of one's own developing consciousness takes on the value of universal history, as it apparently did for William Irwin Thompson, whose book, *At The Edge of History,* will be discussed below.[32]

What lends credibility to this assumption, in spite of the rather bizarre interpretation of history it may produce, is the mounting pressure for a change in human values, and hence for a change of human consciousness, created by the increasing evidence of the limits to the physical and economic growth of our industrial civilization, as witnessed in the rapid depletion of the world's finite natural resources. If all the signs in the external public world are pointing to the inevitability of resource depletion and to the necessity for developing a new, steady political life-style and economic system, then it is not difficult to project a

massive rethinking of the human condition itself amounting to a transvaluation of the *present* value system, which is represented by the hope
for an ever increasing gross national product. When the conclusion is
drawn that human survival, at any significant level of health and spiritual vitality, will depend upon such a transvaluation of present values,
then one may assume that such a change in consciousness will take
place, that indeed it may already be taking place. The new epochal
consciousness thus becomes a clue for the direction of history. As long
as one remembers that it is the pressure of external events that renders
the transvaluation possible and necessary on a broad social scale, and
not a change of consciousness that has created pressure on existing institutions and social structures, one can keep a healthy perspective of
the power and efficacy of one's own changing consciousness. Unfortunately, not all of the New Romantics have a proper appreciation for the
finitude of their own consciousness.

The Variety of New Romanticisms

The New Romanticism is every bit as mercurial and heterogeneous
as the Old. The new effort to embrace arbitrary and self-contradictory
values and enterprises in the compass of a single life has been
identified by Robert Jay Lifton as "protean man."[33] This ongoing identity crisis, incapable of abiding loyalty or commitment in terms of any
particular symbol of the self because it entails heterogeneous symbols
of the self, is representative of much, but not all, of the broad stream of
the New Romanticism. Lifton understands protean man as a creature
of two historical tendencies characterizing modern life:

> The first is the world-wide sense of what I have called *historical* (or *psy-
> chohistorical*) *dislocation,* the break in the sense of connection which men
> have long felt with the vital nourishing symbols of their cultural tradi-
> tion—symbols revolving around family, idea systems, religion and the life
> cycle in general. . . . The second . . . is the *flooding* of *imagery* pro-
> duced by the extraordinary flow of post-modern cultural influences over
> mass communications networks.[34]

Just as many perspectives on culture, on institutions, and on several
epochs of history were entertained in the consciousness of Jean-
Jacques Rousseau and of Friedrich Schlegel in a way that resulted in
several conversions for each in his own lifetime, so a similar process is
occurring, but more intensively, through the glut of contemporary im-

agery, in the consciousness of protean man—this creature who is constantly being converted, ever falling in love, always embracing new symbols for the thematization of his experience. It has the same effect as if he were never converted at all. For protean man, genuine conversion would mean conversion from a constantly converting consciousness to a symbolization of the self that one may maintain through the several remaining stages of one's life. Protean man is not concerned with the question of the orthodoxy or heterodoxy of one's appropriation of the primary symbols of culture; rather, he does not want to be defined by any one symbol of the many being beamed at his consciousness.

The representative spokesman for protean man, according to Lifton, is Jean-Paul Sartre, with his understanding of human consciousness, or the for-itself, as "a sheer activity transcending toward objects."[35] Having no father, which for Lifton means no classical Freudian superego, Sartre's man is father to himself, and the continuity of his consciousness consists in the exercise of freedom as the constant negation of any objective criterion, which is to say—of any *being,* for the definition of self. Sartre's self *is* itself by constantly mocking itself. The tone of mockery is characteristic of protean man, according to Lifton, who finds it expressed in pop art, in camp, and in literature, especially Gunter Grass's *The Tin Drum.*[36] This new pessimistic romanticism, with its vaunting of the self through self-mockery, or self-negation, or through pure self-assertion in the face of nothingness (death), seems to be the animating spirit of a significant stream of twentieth-century philosophy and literature from Sartre to Camus and Martin Heidegger. In drama it appeared as the theater of the absurd, and in art it has found poignant expression in the mixed media paintings of Elizabeth Korn.

Charles Reich

In stark contrast to this largely European pessmistic romanticism, Charles Reich's *The Greening of America* appeared as apple-pie American optimism.[37] The pain of the stabbing opening sentence of the book, "America is dealing death, not only to people in other lands, but to its own people," is immediately dispelled in the next paragraph by the promise of a nonviolent revolution, already aborning, which will bring about "a new and enduring wholeness and beauty—a renewed relation of man to himself, to other men, to society, to nature, and to the land."[38] For Reich, the new revolution will result in a " 'new head'—a new way of living—a new man."[39] All this will occur, "with amazing rapidity" as part of a necessary and inevitable process working itself out in American society.

Reich's book is a romanticized description of the American consciousness, which he sees as three distinctive phases of the historical American consciousness maintining themselves side by side and in conflict with each other in the present time. What he called "Consciousness I" was really the American expression of the Old Romanticism. It was the rugged individualism of the founding fathers of America, the belief that individuals, granted the freedom to work, to pursue their own happiness, would indirectly create the good society. It animated the nation's westward thrust and the development of the first great industrial enterprises. The pioneers, the settlers, and the famous industrial barons all shared in its optimism and innocence, and unfortunately also its shallowness. At the present time Consciousness I lives on as a nostalgia for a romanticized past, out of touch with the social consequences of myopic individualism.[40]

Consciousness II represents the technocratic managerial revolution, which has superimposed a substitute man-made reality upon the natural environment in a manner which destroys local community and its traditions. Disneyland is its emblem.[41] The organizational world, with its division of labor and specializations ranked in order of importance and motivated by technical achievement (meritocracy), despoils individuals, drains them of creativity, and harnesses their efforts for the production of a great variety of artificial substitutes for the natural reality that can be immediately appropriated by the human body.[42] The overall result is the consumer society, a structure profoundly hostile to life-sustaining values. As Reich put it, "Football on Sunday TV is not the same as physical play, but it serves as a placebo to lessen our awareness of loss."[43]

Consciousness III is the revolutionary rejection of the consumer society of Consciousness II and the affirmation of the values of growth in community awareness, of personal receptivity to the physical world, and of creativity. According to Charles Reich,[44] it is an ever expanding consciousness, in constant flux—this center of the new redemptive agent of society and mankind at large. But one must hasten to add that this, too, is but another expression of America's perennial proclivity—only here it appears as the romanticized future of America. *The Greening of America* is but the latest version of American "Manifest Destiny." But it is the value system of American youth that is to shape the future of the world, instead of that of the American industrial estab-

lishment. Reich's book is at once profoundly true and hopelessly mistaken. It lays bare the essential character of the American spirit, which
can neither affirm nor negate itself, its past, its present and future, except by way of a romantic exaggeration of itself as now the *best,* now
the *worst,* and finally as the *most redemptive* of all collective spirits in
the world. In self-affirmation and in self-negation the essence of America is revealed as sheer romanticism, beneath that brittle, Yankee-trader
exterior.

   The Greening of America was a straightforward attempt to speak to
the masses of America. It was romanticism for the masses, and Reich
never gave his reader any indication that it was anything else. That is
the redeeming feature of the book. He told his readers that his three
types of consciousness are "highly impressionistic and arbitrary; they
make no pretense to be scientific."[45] The fact that the Yale professor
dedicates a book written for the masses to his students does not mean
that he did not make a distinction between his book and genuine social
science (although he may not have distinguished between his students
and the masses). All this has, after all, the ring of authenticity.

Midcult Romanticism

   In Theodore Roszak and William Irwin Thomspon we encounter a
romanticism of another sort. The "counter-culture" consciousness of
Theodore Roszak and the "edge-of-history" consciousness of William
Irwin Thompson are expressions of what Dwight Macdonald called
"Midcult" in his book *Against the American Grain.*[46] According to
Macdonald, Midcult is a bastard cultural pheonomenon between
"High Culture," the literature and learning of discipline both in con-
tent and form of communication, and "Masscult" as the parody of
High Culture, or the play to popular tastes in a form which is indiffer-
ent to all standards of discipline. "Midcult," he says,

> has the essential qualities of Masscult—the formula, the built-in reaction,
> the lack of any standard except popularity—but it decently covers them
> with a cultural figleaf. In Masscult the trick is plain—to please the crowd
> by any means. But Midcult has it both ways: it pretends to respect the
> standards of High Culture while in fact it waters them down and vulga-
> rizes them.[47]

Roszak and Thompson, each in his own way, have attempted to express
a counter-culture ethos and pilosophy which is at once sophisticated
and earthy. Common-sense insights are parleyed with language that

combines allusions to classical antiquity with modern technical, mostly psychoanalytical jargon to remind the reader of the high-culture origin of this counter-culture talk. The result is Midcult romanticism, purveyed primarily for the readers of *Time* and *Newsweek*.

Roszak gave himself away when, in his *Making of a Counter Culture*, he defended Alan Watts's westernized and popularized version of Zen and Taoism. Referring to Watts's style he writes:

> It is a style easily mistaken for flippancy, and it has exposed him to a deal of rather arrogant criticism: on the one hand from elitist Zen devotees who have found him too discursive for their mystic tastes (I recall one such telling me smugly, "Watts has never experienced satori"), and on the other hand from professional philosophers who have been inclined to ridicule him for his popularizing bent as being, in the words of one academic, "The Norman Vincent Peal of Zen." It is the typical and inevitable sort of resistance anyone encounters when he makes bold to find a greater audience for an idea than the academy or any restricted cult can provide—and it overlooks the fact that Watts's books and essays include such very solid intellectual achievements as *Psychotherapy East and West*.[48]

By condemning, as he goes on to do, aristocratic strictures handed down from a small circle of experts, Roszak declares his loyalty to Midcult—to the task of westernizing Zen on a Midcult wavelength. What is interesting about this stance is the implicit attack on Zen by providing a rationale for it in Western terms. When Zen devotees protest, they are accused of being elitist, that is to say, "High Cultic," a very bad thing indeed! Roszak is hardly counter-culture at this juncture, but hopelessly Midcultic, insisting that Watts's westernized brokerage of Zen can be justified on the grounds of its broader impact on the culture than that of Zen masters.

The devotee of Midcult clearly sees himself in the role of linguistic broker to the larger culture for esoteric and explicitly high-cultic ideas and concepts. Roszak claimed this role for himself as the interpreter of the "counter-culture" to the larger reading public. What is interesting is that his primary source materials were not the writings and expressions of young people, but rather the prose of such older proteans as Herbert Marcuse, Norman O. Brown, Allen Ginsberg, Alan Watts, and Paul Goodman. The radical student newspapers receive a passing reference. The *Berkeley Barb* is cited a few times, and Daniel and Gabriel Cohn-Bendit are lauded in a bibliographical note;[49] beyond that, Roszak produced his book on the premise that if one understood the books that young people are reading, one would understand them.

This overlooks the very important matter of how young people respond to what they have read; but Roszak does not permit his reader access to this. He claims to show how they have understood Marcuse, Ginsberg, Brown, et al. Unfortunately he furnishes merely his own interpretation of these more profound thinkers as the authentic counter-culture stance.

Roszak's book *Where the Wasteland Ends* starts where *The Making of a Counter Culture* leaves off—namely, with a Western romantic consciousness that absorbs Eastern philosophy and religion in terms of Roszak's own interpretation of William Blake. Under the rubric of "the shamanistic world-view," the radical conflation of East and West in Roszak's consciousness is affirmed as the liberation from technocracy. Traditional Western religion is dismissed as at once the historical source and midwife of the evil technocratic society. Eastern religion is present only as a pinch of salt here and there in Roszak's dish of interpretation. The redemptive role is reserved for radical Western romanticism, which relativizes all symbols—of the West and of the East—in its own arbitrary game. Eastern principles employed to dismiss Western symbols are not thereby affirmed as primary. The game is to negate any and all symbols as primary in order to affirm the sheer power of symbolization of the human consciousness. The result is to commit oneself to the process of constantly destroying old symbols in the effort to create new ones. The place to stand against the culture is nowhere, but rather one must constantly move with a permanently revolutionary consciousness. The religious implication is to negate every concrete religion, whether of East or West, by the affirmation of human religious sensibility.[50] It is a psychedelic version of former President Eisenhower's "having faith in faith," a self-apotheosizing consciousness.

Roszak is indeed a modern cultured despiser of Judaism and Christianity, but one must hasten to add "midcultured" despiser of these communities of faith. He repeats what Schleiermacher perceived as the great error of the eighteenth-century cultured despisers. Roszak is not a rationalist as they were, but he nevertheless identifies Judaism and Christianity as communities which destroy religious vision for the sake of religion reduced to propositional statements interpreted literally. Roszak maintains a deliberate external stance, never once attempting to appreciate their own peculiar religious vision—the thematization of lived experience in terms of Jewish or Christian symbols.

Judaism is for Roszak the historical source of an iconoclastic spirit which purges the world of its sacramental capacities so that "it dies the death of the spirit."[51] The prophetic utterances of Judaism inevitably cool down and leave its adherents "prey to small-minded literalism." "It becomes a word which is not the spirit, and which kills the spirit. It congeals into law, and at last it lends its lifeless carcass to the creed makers and theologians."[52] Roman Catholic sacramental theology amounts to an ineffective attempt "to straddle sacramental consciousness and the Judaic tradition of iconoclasm."[53] Protestantism represents the final triumph of Judaic dead literalism. It eradicated sacramental perception from culture, so that finally "all knowledge becomes a single-visioned knowledge of mere objects, an *objective* knowledge from which, we feel certain, mastery, security, affluence flow."[54]

Roszak is here a faithful follower of William Blake. In his consciousness Judaism and Christianity are metamorphized into something entirely contrary to their essence. In the radical conflation of epochs and institutions in Blake's consciousness, Judaism becomes deism, the religion of this world that worships the god of this world—Satan. In Blake's words:

> Man must & will have Some Religion! if he has not the Religion of Jesus, he will have the Religion of Satan, & will erect the Synagogue of Satan. . . . Deism, is the Worship of the God of this World by the means of what you call Natural Religion and Natural Philosophy, and of Natural Morality or Self-Righteousness, the Selfish Virtues of the Natural Heart. This was the Religion of the Pharisees who murderd Jesus. Deism is the same & ends in the same.[55]

Roszak similarly confuses Judaism and Protestant Christianity with a philosophical positivism that allegedly generated technology, and led to the spread of death in the form of the artificial environment.[56] The evidence for all this is nothing more than the magical power of Roszak's consciousness, which makes it so by his mere imprecation. Because he has identified technological exploitation with Judaism and Christianity, it is so. Why should a consciousness so endowed with the power of such vision into the inner mystery of these historical religions be bothered by such trivia as historical evidence and a disciplined use of reason to support these identifications? If Roszak's interpretation of Judaism and Christianity were true, then one would have to say that the visions of Isaiah and Ezekiel were aberrations, and that the author of the Apocalypse of St. John was no Christian. As Hitlerian apocalyptic vision identified a so-called culture-destroying Judaism with capitalism, democracy, and communism—all at one time, so Roszak does with technology as the new elaborated essence of these "isms."

In William Irwin Thompson's *At The Edge of History,* a whole new outburst of Blake's fourfold vision of the human being, culture, and history is distributed in the charts, symbols, and prose of the book, waiting to set fire to the reader's consciousness. Convinced that the human imagination of history has a profound effect upon society,[57] Thompson takes his reader with him on a journey through his own particular development of historical consciousness as an expatriated citizen of Los Angeles. The reader is brought to a place where Thompson claims he stood outside of history and from that vantage point saw the great panoramic development of history from the primitive tribal communities through all of the succeeding phases—from agricultural society and industrial civilization to the new scientific planetary civilization now forming.

The whole new morphology of history is laid out in chapter 4, "Values and Conflict through History," as a fourfold elaboration of the simple fourfold tribal society in a succession of three circles extending from each quarter of the primary circle. The result is a huge X of circles, like the crystals of a magnified snowflake. From the top left clockwise around the primary tribal circle there is the shaman, the headman, the hunter, and the clown.

From the shaman religion developed in agricultural society, and from that circle education in industrial civilization emerged, and from education, science emerged in the new planetary civilization.[58] From the headman in the top right quarter there developed the state in agricultural civilization, government in the industrial, and managers in the new scientific planetary civilization. From the hunter at the lower right quarter there developed the military in the agricultural phase, then industry, and finally technicians in the last civilization. From the clown there emerged art in the agricultural phase, media in the the industrial, and critics in the planetary civilization. Each circle of each phase has a fourfold division of opposites striking a homeostatic balance, just as the shaman was a counterbalance and opposite to the hunter and the clown to the headman in the primal tribal culture.

Each phase of history, each civilization , is at once a repristination and elaboration of the former. The opposites of each circle are locked in fierce conflict with one another, producing the tension within which new multiplicities are created. They in turn adhere to one another, entropically producing a new level of dynamic complexity, until in the fourth planetary phase each circle fully replicates all of the others. At this level something like cultural entropy is reached. More a Greek than Roszak, Thompson is convinced of the tragic character of history. Every excellence (*areté*) contains its own tragic flaw (*harmartiá*),[59] and "every institution must subvert the value for which it was founded."[60]

Thompson conceives of two possible stances toward this panoramic whole of cultural history, each of which must be assumed in terms of self-conscious relativism:

> This field condition of values thus presents us with a relativism in the context of a universal absolute. If we stand furiously in our personalities in the theater of conflict of history, our actions can only be tragic or comic, appropriate or inappropriate. If we stand in our daimonic consciousness outside of history, we become full of truth because we can hold on to no thing. But man lives at the place where time and eternity meet, that is a place of crucifixion where the opposites cross. In the human world of conflict, every action creates its equal and opposite reaction, and so static values can only be mocked by the very dynamic process of history itself.[61]

The two possible stances are thus detachment or attachment to one's own role as understood from what Thompson calls the "mythical perspective of the whole field."[62] In detachment one seeks to escape one's own destiny and avoid all conflict, since even one's enemy is right. Or one may attach oneself (the way of the monkey?) to one's destiny. Thompson says:

> When a man accepts the tragedy and goes forth to action, as Faulkner says, "knowing better," he begins to be more of a mythical creature than a historical being. Whether it is a Gandhi sustained by God or a Mao sustained by the dialectics of history, the mythical creature is a hero whose proportions are frighteningly larger for the rest of us who cower in the chorus[63]

There, "at the edge of history" in the vision of the person who accepts his or her destiny, Thompson recognizes the radical possibility for transcending the relentless flux of protean consciousness through a resolute decision and action in the world. One chooses from outside history, outside value-laden time, to live the given moment. One dares to act in time; one permits oneself to be defined by a symbol; one decides in terms of it what is important and so, by means of the relative, one relativizes all of the other symbols of consciousness. The proteans look in horror at the committed person, not because he has acted, but because he has permitted a relative symbol to define him.

In the radical last chapter of the book, entitled "The Re-Visioning of History," Thompson seriously entertains the cataclysmic theory of history, especially the stories about Atlantis, the lost civilization. If one radically transvaluates all values and revisions history from the standpoint of myth, if one's history has become myth, then, Thompson asserts, one should take seriously the idea that myth is history. Here Thompson takes a flip from symbolic to literal meaning of the myths, and proceeds to explore the literal reality of the Atlantis myths based on hard archaeological evidence and the prognostications of Edgar Cayce. In view of his own morphology of the succeeding civilizations of history, however, a much more radical possibility heaves into view.

If the old Hebraic mythic consciousness, which conceived of all reality in terms of the six days of creation, is radically inverted—that is, if one does not consider it any longer as a crude cosmogony, as the mistaken reflection of all reality, but rather takes it seriously as history—then the 5,734 years of the Hebrew calendar can be viewed as the history of the development of civilizations from phase one to phase four. We may thus understand ourselves mythically as living in the sixth millennium before the Sabbath rest, before the end of human history. Biblical eschatology would appear as a radical possibility, especially as that insight converges with the vision of ecological disaster and the possible destruction of the biosphere through fate-laden corporate human action. In this radical inversion, ecological consciousness becomes eschatological consciousness, and the day of the Lord may be expected imminently.

Here it becomes possible to entertain a convergence of biblical faith with the New Romanticism, one in which biblical faith ultimately furnishes the symbols for the definition of consciousness. In this inversion biblical faith appears as the judge and the negator of protean consciousness. What is clear is that with regard to protean consciousness or biblical faith, one must choose to define one by the other. Both cannot dwell side by side, for each understands itself as the other's redeemer.

Thompson's vision of history is indeed suggestive and fascinating, but finally it is just that—Thompson's vision of history. While the sheer power of his imagination will undoubtedly influence many, it will remain for the serious historian a piece of playful retrospection. It will not stand up to a close comparison with a work like Derek de Solla Price's *Science Since Babylon*, which penetrates the inside of ancient Babylonian culture through its mathematics, and by means of a close scrutiny of primary sources tells the story of the transition from agricultural to industrial stages of scientific development.[64]

But Thompson's vision is not worthless. It is very important for setting out in bold relief the fundamental polarity between biblical faith, or any concrete adherence to a community of faith—be it Eastern or Western—and protean consciousness. Concrete religious faith and protean consciousness are, in Thompson's sense of the word, "opposites" in conflict with one another. The question to be explored now is whether biblical faith can be a viable alternative to protean consciousness in the world after Auschwitz and Vietnam.

The New Romanticism or Biblical Faith

If Theodore Roszak were alone in his conviction that Judaism and Christianity were *the* formative influences that finally produced life-destroying industrial civilization, and that they are currently serving as moral support for the attitudes and values of that civilization, one might simply ignore this view as his own peculiar way of dumping all of his sour grapes into one basket. Unfortunately many, if not most, of the leaders of the ecological revolution share that conviction. Ian McHarg, professor of landscape architecture and regional planning at the University of Pennsylvania, has flung the gauntlet at biblical tradition in an address entitled "Man: Planetary Disease:"

> If any of you has the slightest theological bent, what you say in passing is that the basic attitude of man and nature is explicit in Genesis, central to Judaism, absorbed and changed into Christianity. It says in the first chapter of Genesis that man is exclusively divine—which means that everything else is rubbish—man is made in the image of God. Man has preempted the image of God. The second line says man is given dominion over life and nonlife. Dominion is not a negotiating term. You cannot love anything as St. Francis did and have dominion over it. Dominion means that the other thing lies down before you. If there is any doubt about the relation of man and nature, the third line clinches it when it says, "Man is licensed to subjugate the earth."
> If you want to understand the Western view of man and nature, in the Judaic-Christian-humanist tradition, all you have to know is these three lines: Man is exclusively divine and everything else is rubbish; Man is given dominion over life and nonlife, and Man is enjoined to subdue the earth. Understanding that text, look retrospectively back to the despoliation of all the land which has been accomplished by man, particularly Western man, and you will recognize that the men who believe this to be so can only accomplish destruction.[65]

I have repeated a good portion of this pathological outburst to show how, in the minds of many intelligent people, anti-technocracy and anti-industrialism have now become emotionally linked with anti-Judaism and anti-Christianity. What is noteworthy is that Christianity is here seen as sharing the guilt for spreading an anti-human doctrine of death. In spite of his disclaimer that his view is not meant to be anti-Jewish or anti-Christian, the charge is made in terms that leave the reader with no other conclusion—namely, that such doctrine is "central to Judaism and absorbed and changed into Christianity." Furthermore, having identified as "planetary pathogens" all those who act on the basis of such a doctrine, McHarg suggests that they ought to be placed in rocket capsules and shot into outer space, apparently not minding the fact that this new form of genocide would be even more polluting than Hitler's. In a world headed for ecological disaster and pathological human reactions to it, this identification of industrial exploitation with the basic faith of Judaism and Christianity is indeed ominous. It suggests the possibility of a new wave of scapegoating pogroms, a new set of victims earmarked for persecution and death because of the alleged role that their historic community played in bringing about the situation in which wars over dwindling resources and famine and plague begin to happen.

This identification is all the more unfortunate because, if the ecologists were to take the trouble to find out what the Bible is *really* saying in the creation story, and what is really central to Judaism that was absorbed and changed into Christianity, then biblical faith would be rightly recognized as an ally in the struggle to bring about a transvaluation of American values for the sake of a steady political society and a sense of planetary citizenship. What Ian McHarg is attacking is not authentic biblical faith, but rather a romantic interpretation of it.

Viewed from the outside, what could be more protean than a religious community with a four-thousand-year history? The story of Israel is a grand spectacle of the cultural-historical transformations of a people whose nomadic forebears, the Hebrews, formed a tribal confederacy—Israel—conquered a land, became a settled people, fell apart in civil strife, were themselves subjected to piecemeal conquests and carried off into captivity, restored to their own land as vassals, yet lived in Diaspora for the most part, enjoyed a brief period of liberty and home rule, were again conquered, sent once more into dispersion, and after almost two millennia returned to the land of their forebears (now considered sacred by two other religions), and yet still live for the most part in Diaspora.

The story is one of constant cultural adaptation and assimilation, first to Egyptian, then to nomadic tribal, then to Canaanite society. Then the same process occurs wih a series of imperial societies from Babylonian to Persian, Greek, and Roman, to European Christian, and finally to the American empire. But if the story were only one of cultural adaptation and assimilation, it certainly would not have lasted longer than the first episode in Egypt. It is the religious inside of this story that accounts for its longevity. There always remained a corporate identity, an unassimilated center of consciousness that constantly reasserted itself in every epoch, creating new occasions for the cultural adaptations throughout its long history. That religious center is the covenant faith of the people of Israel. It is that non-negotiable corporate identity which refused to allow itself to be absorbed by any one of the host cultures from ancient Babylon to modern America.

The essence of Israel is not an arid rationalistic transcendental mentality that desacralizes all of life and culture, as Roszak would have us believe. It is a passionate, transhistorical, transcultural and even transrational conviction that its own corporate consciousness, and the whole world in which that consciousness is always imbedded, and in which it is somehow strangely preserved, is sacred, the gift of the God who in lovingkindness has made life itself a sacred celebration of his presence in the world. The idea of a history of salvation, of a *Heilsgeschichte*, is misleading, as if nature, the land, the rivers and oceans— the totality of the productive world (the *tevel*)—were not also sacred for Israel.

The liturgy for the presentation of the first-fruits in Deuteronomy 26:1–15 is indicative of the way that Israel's consciousness of the sacred encompassed nature *and* history. Reflecting the period after David and Solomon, when Israel lived a settled existence in the land, the liturgy had a twofold significance. One indicated the sacred character of the land as God's gift, and the other, the historical existence of Israel— the corporate consciousness of the people as God's gift. Land and history were both sacred as the gift of the Lord.

The bearer of the basket of first-fruits hails the priest of the sanctuary with the words: "I declare this day to the Lord your God that I have come into the land which the Lord swore to our fathers to give us" (Deut.26:4).

After the priest receives the basket and places it before the sanctuary, the holy history is recited which begins, "A wandering Aramean was my father, and he went down into Egypt" (v. 5). It tells the story of bondage and deliverance from Egypt, of the gift of the land, and ends with "and behold, now I bring the first fruit of the ground which thou, O Lord, hast given me" (v. 10).

The law of the fruits of the land also required a third-year tithe to "the Levite, the sojourner, the fatherless and the widow, that they may

eat within your towns and be filled" (v. 11). Far from teaching waste
and despoliation, the Deuteronomic priests taught care of the land and
concern for all who were found within its borders—including sojourn-
ers.

The Torah is a reflection of the covenantal consciousness of Israel
from its nomadic preliterate days before 1500 B.C. to the period immediately after the Babylonian captivity. The Torah is like a Bach
fugue, repeating the covenant theme throughout the scrolls with variations in color and tone. The Torah has remained with Israel throughout
the rest of her history as the precious fuel ever reigniting the fire of her
sacred consciousness.

The liturgy of the first-fruits, as already indicated above, reflects the
celebration of life during the period of settlement. Then the land itself
was the sign of the covenant. Everything one could see, could touch,
even the air one breathed, was part of the covenantal sign. What happened when that sign was taken away, when the land was assailed and
conquered and its people carried off into captivity in Babylon?

In Babylon the Israelites began to gather for worship in houses. The
tradition of the synagogue has its roots in that experience, and along
with it—scholars generally agree—the practice of circumcision as the
sign of the covenant. When the land as the sign of the covenant was
taken away, the covenant for Israel was not abrogated, which is to say,
the sacred corporate consciousness of Israel was not extinguished. The
sign of the covenant was transferred from the land of Israel to the flesh
of Israel. Thus the sign of the covenant went with Israel into captivity,
and from thence also into the Diaspora.

From that time to this, Israel as a people became the living ark of the
covenant bearing in its hands the sacred scrolls, and in its flesh the sign
of the covenant. This is the sacred center that can never be simply assimilated, but rather finally only carried by the host cultures and civilizations on Israel's sojourn through world history. For Israel the world
in which she sojourns is not a desacralized negative pole to her own sacred consciousness, and therefore "rubbish." This world is also the
world given by God to live in and to celebrate his presence. Therefore
it is never to be destroyed, but cared for as the sacred gift of life itself.

The story of creation in the Torah belongs to the poetic praise of the
Lord of the covenant and the recitation of his mighty deeds. That story
has its meaning as part of the prelude to the central theme of deliverance from Egypt as the community-forming act of God. Dominion over
the earth in some arbitrary sense is not central to Judaism. But more
important to the story of creation, as we find it in the final redaction,
which combined a newer with an older version as part of a new whole,

is the symbolization of the human predicament that we find in the third chapter of Genesis. (Let us get beyond the pulverizing criticism of Protestantism and give the ancient priests credit for knowing what they were about when they combined them!) The human predicament in history, where the knowledge of good and evil reigns, is that humans are subject to the temptation to vaunt themselves, to think that they are "like God" (Gen. 3:5). Here is the appropriate part of the story for the subject of the human despoliation of the earth. It is the consciousness of fallen mankind playing God, the consciousness that refuses to recognize any limits to the human enterprise upon earth; that suggests that there is a human solution for all of the problems we face; the consciousness that says "the energy crisis is not real because technology is rapidly developing new sufficient forms of energy." This is the consciousness that is in the process of destroying the earth, the sacred gift. In fact, in its refusal to accept its own finitude it is a form of protean consciousness, and it is this "unlimited-growth protean consciousness" that constitutes the essence of the new bondage that is American GNP civilization.

The covenant consciousness is what, to employ McHarg's words, "was central to Judaism [and] absorbed and changed into Christianity." All of the New Testament images of the church—the "people of God" (1 Pet. 2:9–10), the people "called to freedom" (Gal. 5:13), the "body of Christ" (1 Cor. 12:27), the scattered seed waiting to be harvested (Matt. 13:1–15)—are expressions of Christian covenant consciousness. The church understands itself as a people called to be servants to the world, even as it understood Jesus of Nazareth as the Son of Man who "came not to be served but to serve, and to give his life as a ransom for many" (Matt. 20:28). The authentic church is therefore the "Covenant of Service to the World" as the response to the Word of God heard in the proclamation of the life, death, and resurrection of Jesus of Nazareth as the Messiah of God. The authentic church of Jesus the Messiah understands itself as sharing the covenant consciousness of Israel as wild olive shoots grafted into a tree of which the covenant of God with Israel constitutes the natural root, as St. Paul taught in Romans 11:17–21. As such, the authentic church takes seriously the admonition of Paul when he wrote "Do not boast over the natural branches!" Wherever, therefore, in the history of the world Christians vaunted themselves as the true sons and daughters of the covenant over Israel and engaged in wicked defamation and persecution of Jews, there the church became apostate; and where it still vaunts itself, there it remains apostate and not church of Jesus the Messiah.

Unfortunately the history of the Christian church is the history of its repeated apostasy from the covenant of service. But as such it has also been a history of grace, a history of God's faithfulness in ever calling the church through word and sacrament back to the covenant of service. Properly understood the Mass is covenant renewal, the announcement and bestowal of the grace of God for the forgiveness of sins and the reception of that mercy with gratitude expressed as a renewed avowal to live a life of service in the world. This has been the true center of the church from its earliest history in the diaspora, in which the documents of the New Testament were produced for purposes of communication between those scattered communities. It was the church's true center through the long period beginning with Constantine, when it became a legal estate of European civilization, an estate beside others which developed its own bureaucracy, levied taxes, held court, maintained a diplomatic office and an army. It is still the true center of the church now that it has entered into decline as a legal estate of civilization, and in most, if not all, nations of the world has entered a new diaspora. The story of apostasy and covenant renewal goes on.

The process of returning to diaspora has been painful for the Christian community, because it involves a total repentance from the triumphal majority consciousness that has characterized European and American Christianity for most of their history. There is much disorientation and confusion involved in the turn toward diaspora, as Christians wonder what it really means to be the church in a society which, for all practical purposes, has *established* the church because it asks it to serve the corporate self-interest of the American nation rather than God and the world as understood from tradition and Scripture. As has been true for the people of the covenant throughout history, Christians are beginning to discover that obedience to the covenant is something contrary to the service demanded for the values of the host culture. In America today the church is asked to serve the gross national product of the United States. This is the new idolatry, the new god, who is acclaimed as the giver of every good to the people who serve it.

Now that it is possible to recognize clearly that service of that end means not only a widening gap between the rich and the poor of the world and starvation for millions of the latter, but also the possible destruction of the biosphere as the matrix for all organic life, the church in the United States must choose whom it will serve—the gross national product, or God.

The church must make this choice knowing very well that service according to the Gospel will mean a lower standard of living for the United States, possibly even grim depression, if Christians take the Gospel seriously and actually buy fewer products, make things last longer, eat less, consume less energy. With eyes and minds wide open to the possible consequences for their own standard of living and life-style, the Christians of the new diaspora are discovering their true service for our time. It is to help Americans lose themselves in genuine concern for human well-being; hence to help American corporate structures lose themselves in a process of dedevelopment, in order that they and millions of people about to be born into this finite world might find the means to survive in a stable, well-cared-for *tevel,* or productive world.

In the new era after Auschwitz, Christianity and Judaism appear as sister communities sharing a common biblical heritage, albeit appropriated and applied differently in separate traditions of interpretation. The triumphal consciousness of Christianity before Auschwitz explicitly attacked and denied the validity of Jewish covenant consciousness. After Auschwitz Christianity's claim to have superseded Judaism has become simply incredible for any Christian or non-Christian who knows the history of Christian anti-Judaism. This claim ultimately served the cause of genocide and not the love of God and neighbor. Now Christianity must reconceive the meaning of its covenant of service as it recognizes the validity—not only of its roots in ancient Israel, but also of its counterpart in contemporary Judaism.

The appropriate expression for this volte-face in relating to Judaism must be the abandonment of any intention to convert Jews to Christianity, and support in deed and word for the State of Israel. Because Christianity in the past employed the Roman ban of Jews from Jerusalem as evidence of God's displeasure with Judaism and gloried in Judaism's misery, Christianity now is obliged to share the social, political, and economic responsibilities that come with the recognition that the State of Israel is a moral necessity in a world where anti-Semitism is a pervasive presence.

Unfortunately many Christians are ignoring the significance of Auschwitz, and have yet to find their way to a ministry of service that does not entail the purpose of undermining the personal and corporate identity of Jews. For those who have found their way to understanding, the world after Auschwitz is a common field of service for Jews and Christians, as each community of faith draws on its own moral and spiritual resources for the horrendous challenges that lie ahead.

The Choice:
Romanticism or True Messianism?

ARTHUR I. WASKOW

It is not new for Jews to contemplate a Holocaust, not only to seek in agony to incorporate Holocaust within the tradition, but also to seek in anger to make the tradition transform itself in the dark light of Holocaust.

Midrash Rabbah on *Eicha,* the commentary on the Book of Lamentations, tells the story that when the Temple was destroyed and the Jews began their death march to Babylon, Abraham, and then Isaac and then Jacob, came before the Holy One to mourn and to challenge.[1] One by one God refuted and rejected them: "Israel has whored after strange gods and I am a jealous God. I will not stand for it: they must be punished." The ministering angels themselves accused God of breaking the covenant, but God scornfully told them to stop stringing together dirges. The Torah herself, and the letters of the *alephbeit,* came to be defense witnesses for Israel. All were turned away, the petitions of all were denied. Even Moses pleaded, and even Moses was denied. God's fury continued to burn, unabated.

Then Rachel arose to speak: "You say you are a jealous God. Well, I was a jealous woman. I knew that my father planned to trick Jacob and give him my sister for a wife, not me. I was so jealous that I arranged with Jacob signals to let him know if my father tried to trick him. But at the last moment I could not do it.—I loved my sister, I loved her so much that I gave her my signals, I hid beneath the bed and answered for my sister so Jacob would not realize.

"Yes, I was a jealous woman—jealous of real flesh and blood. Yet I, a mortal woman, found mercy and love in my heart. And you, you are a jealous God—jealous of what? Of empty things—of sticks and stones, of idols? For this you will destroy your people? And you an eternal God of Mercy? How dare you!"

And God turned back his anger to end the exile and redeem the people.

This *'drash* is the radical post-Holocaust theology of the tradition. It

307

does not ignore God; it does not deny God; it does not celebrate God by finding higher purposes in the Holocaust. It challenges God at the deepest level. It points to that which is most God-like, most *tzelem elokim,* in humanity, and demands that God act at least as human, as mentschlich, as Godly. It demands redemption—and it wins redemption.

And perhaps it was no accident that the rabbis saw that Abraham, Isaac, Jacob, Jeremiah, Moses would fail: that only a woman could succeed in calling forth redemption.

What does this midrash have to teach us?

We are not, because of the Holocaust, to ignore or deny God, to become secularists and to seek a secular redemption only.

We are not, because of the Holocaust, to despair of the *tzelem elokim,* the Godly image in humanity. We are not to curse humanity and die. We are not to turn away from human need and human caring, to abase ourselves before the awesome God of Terror.

There is only one answer to the Holocaust: to challenge God, Who has already shown a fury as pitiless as the worst of human hatred, now to show a lovingkindness as warm as the best of human caring. To challenge God, to demand the redemption. And in order to do so, to open up the tradition beyond the patriarchs and "brotherhood"—to enrich the tradition with mothering and sisterhood, in men as well as women.

How do we, today in the dark light of our own Holocaust, do what Rachel did? How do we demand the redemption?

There is no doubt that the present global social and political upheaval is encouraging the emergence of religious movements and energies that challenge most of the existing Jewish and Christian understandings of biblical faith. Are these challenges to be feared, as simply presaging attacks on Jewish (and perhaps Christian) communities? Or are they to be understood *within* the context of biblical faith, as early—no doubt flawed—efforts to respond to events prophesied by the Bible and in ways demanded by the Bible? Put starkly, are these movements (which Michael Ryan has denounced) *merely* romantic—or are some of them the precursors of, pointers toward, a serious Messianic—not pseudo-Messianic—impulse?

I would summarize my own answer to this question by saying: first, the world now lives in the situation prophesied by the Hebrew Bible and Jewish tradition as the birth-pangs of Messiah; second, in that situation *one* response has been and will be intensely dangerous appeals to orgies of blood and floods of sex; but, third, there will also be more and more effective hearing of the Messianically productive calls of the Bible to make peace, liberate women and men, transform alienated toil into creative work, bring about harmony between human beings and nature, and achieve the self-determination of all peoples on their own lands—all this in the context of a new spiritual life in which people-hoods become holy, their life practices become unified into a holy path and their calendars into hallowed time, and in which flowingness and spontaneity become more characteristic of the relation between humanity and a God who is *chaver,* comrade, not king.

In the struggle between the dangers of Gog and the hope of Messiah, I count William Blake and his spiritual descendants on Messiah's side. I think they are calling us not to reject the Bible, but to hear the repressed and buried side of biblical faith.

The Messianic tradition has been buried and repressed in Jewish history out of the sense of a small people that Messiah is dangerous— out of the memory of the different kinds of disastrous results that were visited on Jewry by Christianity, Bar Kochba, and Sabbetai Zvi. In Christian tradition also, the Messianic tradition has been buried, repressed, but out of a sense of bigness, rather than smallness: having celebrated the Messiah fulfilled and swiftly married itself to the princes of the world, Christianity pushed out to the margin every cry that the Messiah still needed to be brought and the princes overthrown. What conventional Judaism and Christianity shared was this: since the Messianic transformation had not arrived in real social and spiritual fact, it is dangerous to reach toward it—dangerous to established practice.

Is this the same as seeing it as a danger to biblical faith? No. What is dangerous to biblical faith is to deny the biblical prophecy that in fact the Messiah will come in the real world, in real time; or to abandon the effort to act toward that vision. Does reaching it shatter the practices that we know as Jewish and Christian, and therefore shatter those communities? Let us recall the story of the rabbi who counseled that in a year of rampant plague, the whole Jewish community eat on Yom Kippur. "Rabbi, you are lenient concerning the mitzvah to fast," says one of his congregants. "No," answers the rabbi: "I am strict concerning the mitzvah to save life." We do not propose being lenient with the mitzvot to live in ordinary history; we propose to be strict concerning the mitzvot for living in the birth-pangs of Messiah. *And we do this because of an empirical judgment, just as the rabbi had to make an empirical judgment: his was of great and widespread danger to life, and so is ours.* We need only look at the title of our Symposium and then remind ourselves that the invention of Auschwitz and the invention of Hiroshima were simultaneous, to understand how widespread and how great the danger is. Of course it is possible to be mistaken in projecting from any social cataclysm to the birth-pangs of Messiah, but the mistake can be in either direction. As Franz Rosenzweig wrote,

> The expectation of the coming of the Messiah, by which and because of which Judaism lives, would be a meaningless theologumenon, a mere "idea" in the philosophical sense, empty babble, if the appearance again and again of a "false Messiah" did not render it reality and unreality, illusion and disillusion. The false Messiah is as old as the hope for the true Messiah. He is the changing form of this changeless hope. He separates every Jewish generation into those whose faith is strong enough to give themselves up to an illusion, and those whose hope is so strong that they do not allow themselves to be deluded. The former are the better, the latter the stronger. The former bleed as victims on the altar of the eternity of the people, the latter are the priests who perform the service at this altar. And this goes on until the day when all will be reversed, when the belief of the believers will become truth, and the hope of the hoping a lie. Then—and no one knows whether this "then" will not be this very day—the task of the hoping will come to an end and, when the morning of that day breaks, everyone who still belongs among those who hope and not among those who believe will run the risk of being rejected. This danger hovers over the apparently less endangered life of the hopeful.[2]

The first step of our process must be to examine our world history in the light of the Messianic prophecies, so that our empirical judgment may be as careful and clear as possible.

In 1945 Martin Buber wrote:

> For the last three decades we have felt that we were living in the initial phases of the greatest crisis humanity has ever known. It grows increasingly clear to us that the tremendous happenings of the past years, too, can be understood only as symptoms of this crisis. It is not merely the crisis of one economic and social system being superseded by another, more or less ready to take its place; rather all systems, old and new, are equally involved in the crisis. What is in question, therefore, is nothing less than man's whole existence in the world.[3]

Almost three decades later, the crisis continues to convulse the human race. Buber wrote before we had full knowledge of the Holocaust or Hiroshima; before we invented the H-Bomb and the ICBM; before the Chinese Revolution transformed the lives of one-fourth of the human race; before the manipulation of human genetics became a reality; before the earth's population had grown by two billion in a single generation and promised to do so again; before we knew that we were poisoning the very air and oceans.

Humanity's "whole existence in the world": how do we deal with such a question?

To go further: How do we deal with the eruption of new longings in our very selves, the changes in our own hopes and fears, the transformation of our own characters and personalities, that occur at the same time that the world changes around us? Millions who thought we were firm in our feelings about violence, work, sex, and families, about how we travel and what we eat, about our place in the world, about God— have discovered ourselves changing from within as well as shaken from without. We have experienced moments of joy, of fear, of hope, of anger that we never expected to experience. Some of us have indeed experienced transcendent moments of love—for ourselves, our sisters and brothers, our natural world, our God—that we had never imagined possible.

What language, what categories of thought, can we use in such an outer/inner crisis?

We propose to try to use an old and well-shared language: the language of *the unfulfilled Messiah,* which imagines "in the latter days" the deepest convulsion of human history and—with God's help—the passage of human life to a new level of experience. That language is most available to me in Jewish usage, because there the Messiah is most clearly understood to be still on the way, not yet arrived. But some strands of Christian and post-Christian thought also focus on the unfulfilled Messiah, and perhaps other religious traditions—Muslim, Buddhist, Native American—also contain strands of the unfulfilled Messiah that we need to understand. At this stage, however, we are not yet ready to learn from those traditions.

Two cautions. We are *not* talking about a secularized Messianism which sees purely human institutions—state, party, movement, even church—as Messiah; and we are *not* talking about a carrot-for-the-donkey Messianism, which sees Messiah only as a receding vision, never actually to come.

The Messianic language has, of course, been heard in many different ways across the generations. It may, indeed, carry a different truth for different generations. We can only read it in our own way, and can only offer that reading to others of our generation who may have shared experiences sufficiently like ours to make that language useful to them too. We propose a reading that may help us without plunging us into the dangers that have afflicted some who in the past have taken serious- ly the Messianic vision—dangers that we may be better able to avoid through knowing their mistakes. Not that we can avoid all dangers. But surely we need *some* language to deal with "the greatest crisis humani- ty has ever known," and we believe that the other languages usually tried—Marxism, Eastern mysticism, "muddling through"—are, on bal- ance, less effective or more dangerous than this one, although they probably express truths that a revivified Messianism ought to hear.

Let us begin where tradition suggests the Messianic strand begins: not in the days of the end but in the days of the beginning, in Eden. The story in Genesis suggests—at least to ears sensitized by the partic- ular earthquakes of the past two generations—that four major process- events were involved in the departure from Eden into normal human history:

1. The rigidification of sex roles, the subjugation of women, changes in the nature of sexuality and birth (painful childbirth), etc.
2. The beginning of enmity between humanity and nature
3. The beginning of the necessity of hard labor to eat
4. The advent of violence: Cain kills Abel

The Messianic strand of the tradition suggests that the Days of Mes- siah can be seen as a re-creation of Eden on a higher level—a level in- fused this time by full human consciousness, and created in part by human struggle to create it, rather than solely by divine gift, as Eden was. But this image might direct our eyes to the four process-events sketched above, and might suggest that the advent of Messianic times would involve the reversal of these four:

1. Equality of women and men, the transformation of sex roles, sexual- ity, reproduction and birth
2. The reharmonization of humanity and nature
3. The achievement of prosperity without toil
4. The abolition of war

An examination of the prophets suggests that at least three of these four are indeed seen explicitly as criteria for the Days of Messiah. Al- though most of the prophets ignore the transformation of sexuality, Jeremiah (31:22) hints at the end of male dominance and the rigidity of sex roles: "And the Lord shall make a new thing on the earth: a female shall encompass a warrior." The kabbalists also saw the inner history of sexuality as a form of exile and redemption. They saw the alienation of the Supernal Male and Female, the Holy-One-Blessed-Be-He and the Shechinah, or Presence, as a cause/index of the "exile" of the universe; and their reunion as Messianic event to be celebrated/enacted on earth through marital sex.

The prophets added a fifth major "event" as an index to the Days of Messiah: turmoil in the life of the Jewish people and its return to the Land of Israel. This fifth event is quite different from the others in its particularity, in its addressing *one* people rather than all humanity; we shall come back to this and examine it more closely.

The prophets assert that the time immediately preceding the Days of Messiah will be dreadful, the worst days of human history. Gog and Magog will do battle. It would seem reasonable to assume that this upheaval-in-general would result from, or be shown forth by, upheavals in each of the five particular areas.

If we examine current world history in this light we see that—

1. The very basis of human sexuality and sex roles is being questioned, not only at the levels of equality between men and women, and of assertions of ultimate differences or nondifferences between them, but even at the level of the possible manipulation of human genetics, reproduction, and birth. These are not only unprecedented, but there is *no more* fundamental issue that could be raised in regard to sexuality. In short, some kind of crucial threshold has been reached in human history.
2. The very basis of life-exchange between humanity and nature is threatened, since human activity now threatens the biological potential of the earth itself; but simultaneously the whole life-exchange process can now be described and explained for the first time. Again, this is both unprecedented and unrepeatable: a crucial threshold has been reached.
3. We have developed a technology that could support life for all humans without toil. True, the technology itself and the fruits of its use have been so maldistributed that some humans dispose of enormous wealth, while others live in desperate misery. Indeed, precisely because of the new technology, the disparities of wealth are greater than ever before. But what could be achieved now if the proper social decision were made was not even possible before: any one human can, through a matrix of production, and using known tech-

niques, help make more than enough food-clothes-shelter than is necessary to support him/her self and his/her children or disabled dependents—without physical or mental exhaustion. Yet the very same technology and social process have been put to uses and managed in ways that divorce human beings from directly providing for their needs by their own work or their own property. Thus at the same moment the liberation of all from toil and the subjugation of all to alienated work and to utter proletarianization are made possible. This is a third unprecedented/unrepeatable threshold.

4. The technology has been achieved by which war can kill the entire human race, and at the same time allow any human being on the face of the globe—or even beyond—to speak with any other: a fourth unprecedented/unrepeatable threshold.

5. The Jewish people has suffered the most horrendous destruction since the defeat of Bar Kochba, and for the first time since that defeat a sizable proportion has assembled in the Land of Israel.

We see, then, that all five of these arenas-of-action suggested by Eden and the prophets as proto-Messianic are in an unprecedented upheaval. They seem, moreover, to be intrinsically connected: a massive development of human technology, which in some ways seems a leap from previous history but clearly grows out of it, has made them possible. They are not coincidental; they seem to emerge from a deep process of human history.

In all five areas there seem to be the seeds of either overwhelming disaster or overwhelming promise. On the one hand, as Buber points out in analyzing the world crisis, there is the devouring of almost all I-Thou relationships by the I-It mode of life, the swallowing up of communal processes by stateliness. The new technology was born from that necessary part of human life which was reserved to the I-It mode. But it has broken the controls that the I-Thou relationship tried to put upon objectification and causality, and has threatened to objectify the I-Thouness of the God-human, human-human, God-nature, and nature-human relationships. In so doing it has become truly lethal.

Yet at the same time the new technology could serve life at an unprecedented level, if it were newly suffused with and made to serve the I-Thou relation. For the first time technology gives us *means* to abolish toil and poverty, war, sexual exploitation and role rigidity, and the war of humanity against nature. For the first time the knowledge exists to understand how to be apart-from-nature in that we understand and "name" it, but part-of -nature in that we flow in-and-through it as we live. For the first time the peoples of the whole world are in touch with each other, know each other, can make peace with each other. For the first time we are able to know the roots of sexuality.

In short, the new technology for the first time makes it both *possible* and *necessary* to encompass all the social classes, all peoples, all sexes, and all of the earth in an I-Thou relationship. Perviously there was no way to reach out to all; previously there was no need to reach out to all. Now, if we do not reach out we die; now, if we do reach out we can address the other and hear the answer.

The unprecedentedness of this situation can itself teach us a great deal about the Messianic tradition, about how to read its language anew so that it speaks to us, and how to understand the problems of other languages. For we may be able to understand the previous failures and mistakes of Messianic movements in a new way. I suggest two hypotheses:

1. The long warfare of the classes, sexes, and nations against each other and of humanity against nature—the warfare inherent in I-It, the warfare that creates technology—are a necessary but not sufficient precondition to the achievement of the Messianic age.
2. "Turning" our faces to face a Thou so that we can achieve an I-Thou among all humanity and from humanity to nature and God is necessary to complete the achievement.

When we look at the explicitly Messianic movements from early Christianity on, we find they have tried to make the leap of turning toward a universal I-Thou before the time was ripened through the I-It struggle. When we look at the more recent secularized Messianisms—especially Marxism—we find they tried to complete the struggle without transcending it, without turning in love to humanity, nature, and God.

Let us look more closely at these obverse failures.

Traditional Messianism seems to teach that the "great turning" and therefore the Messianic age might have come, might come, at any moment of human history; it depends only on turning below and on redemption above. Some of the tradition focuses on the need for God's action, some on the need for human action. But even if human action is necessary to bring Messiah, the tradition seems to say it is human action *now;* any now, at least any now that God wills the hearts to be ready. The tradition does not suggest, or at least does not work out in any detailed way, that the great turning may depend on the previously woven fabric of human history and society—that God might have willed a discoverable historical process to be the necessary preparation for *tshuvah*.

Since many communities have turned as fully as they knew or could image, they have been the more bitterly disappointed to discover that even the strongest turning has been unable to achieve *Mashiach*. They have learned chiefly exhaustion, malaise, and hopelessness from these historic disappointments.

Marxism, on the contrary, has taught that the Messianic leap into freedom can come only after the long class struggle has brought both a high technology and a conscious proletariat into being. Marx himself, and a long line of followers down to Rosa Luxembourg and Herbert Marcuse, thus argued that socialism must be achieved first in the most highly industrialized nations.

But neither in the developed nations—where the revolution never came—nor in the nonindustrial world—where it came but was unable to achieve such goals as the withering away of the state, "to each according to his needs," etc.—could Marxism achieve the kind of society that a secularized Messianism sought. Why?

Classical Marxism, of course, rejects the notion that anything *besides* human history, the class struggle, is necessary. It rejects as empty mystification the notion of the Divine Comrade with Whom humanity talks and wrestles. And with it, rejects the possibilty of infusing even the struggle with love. Here Messianism has something crucial to say: that our Comrade is essential; that the absence of a commitment to the non-human Other makes it too easy for human narcissism to become idolatry; that without the love of God it is too hard to turn from a history of struggle to the love of humanity and nature; that the hope of an atheist humanist socialism is, if not doomed to failure, at least inclined toward failure; that even "good cases," like the kibbutz, show the danger of relapse from humanism into idolatry.

Perhaps in our generation we can put names to these vague fears. Unless we of the developed world enter the dialogue Buber talked of, encounter a Partner in that dialogue, are we more likely to build Nazism or Stalinism than socialism? Were indeed Nazism and Stalinism a radical embracing of the "inverse Messianic" possiblilities of industrialism without God, as the H-bomb is a radical embracing of the "inverse Messianic" possibilities of postindustrial, ultrascientific technology without God? Perhaps Gog and Magog can in our time be newly understood as the monstrous engine of the one-dimensional society?

If this description of the complementary failures of traditional Messianism and classical Marxism is correct, one of the major intellectual and spiritual tasks that we face is to bring the two traditions into an encounter:

Can Marxism open up to the possibility that the spiritual values which some Marxists (such as Marcuse) are finding more and more central to human need and revolutionary transformation have their grounding *not only* in human evolution and history but *also* in the basis of the universe?

On the other hand, can God-centered Messianism become open to the fact that neither obedience to a religious code of behavior nor religious ideals have been sufficient to strengthern human beings to transform the world, nor even to reform the world, nor even to preserve the religious paths? Why has it been so easy for believers to cramp and reduce the Living God into a deadening idol? Why have the religiously committed so seldom been among those who moved human beings to change as much as humanists? Can the religious who found it possible to see modern natural science as a clarification of God's will expressed through nature—despite the professed atheism of many modern scientists—treat an evolving Marxism as a clarification of God's will expressed through human history—despite the professed atheism of most Marxists?

In short, can we now affirm the great *interplay* between God and humanity in bringing Messiah?

But how are we to enter this great interplay? How are we to go about reaching out to all the social classes, all the peoples, all the sexes, all the earth—and to God? The Messianic tradition or message, as we have sketched it so far, might be described as a message about "content" or "result"; how human beings should act in the Messianic age. If the message were complete it would also talk about "process," how to achieve the transformation. And in so doing it would have to speak about ourselves: about the inner transformations we have already felt, and those other transformations we would need to feel in order to share in the Messianic transformation.

We suggest that the Messianic tradition does include such a message about process, and that it flows from the same five arenas that we have already discussed as the crucial ones of the transition from Eden to ordinary history and from ordinary history to the Days of Messiah.

Before we try to show the linkage between the five "result" arenas and the five "process" arenas, let us say first that our perceptions of these new arenas of process have flowed from new feelings of our own selves, new feelings from within that have drawn us to new ways of seeking change outside.

We have felt drawn to some new form of relationship to God: neither rejection nor obeisance, but some form of puzzled and independent love.

We have felt drawn to make our lives "whole," to unite the separate roles played by work, politics, the family, leisure, religion, into a seamless life-process.

We have felt drawn to thinking and acting more and more as part of a community, rather than either boss or follower.

We have felt drawn to actually growing, in the present, seeds of the future that we imagine—rather than simply opposing the present or pleading for change.

We have felt drawn to the dimension of time rather than space as most important to liberate and hallow our own lives.

We have felt drawn to a looser, more spontaneous flow of life and thought for ourselves.

These changes seem to be validated across the generations and across time by prophecy—since we find in the Messianic tradition not only what the Days of Messiah should be like, but how they should be achieved. What is more, just as the external upheavals have been keyed to the five crucial arenas of Messianic "content" or "result," so the internal upheavals have been keyed to five analogous crucial arenas of Messianic "process." We see this if in each of the five arenas we ask the question: If we project this view of relations among people into the relations between people and God, what would the Messianic relationship be? For instance, if among humans there is to be peace and an end to violence, what is to be analogously changed in the relationship between God and humanity? If among humans there is to be freedom for women and the "womanly" within men, what is to be analogously changed in the relationship between God and humanity? It is as if the five arenas exist in both a "lower" and "higher" sphere. The "lower" is concerned chiefly with Messianic relationships among human beings—transformations in the way in which violence, sexuality, ecology, etc., are carried on—and describes the "result" that we are to achieve in the Days of Messiah. The "higher" sphere is concerned chiefly with Messianic relationships between humans and God, and describes the "process" by which the Days of Messiah are to be achieved. For the deepest questions of process in human life are wrestled out more inwardly and upwardly than outwardly, with more subtle vibrations of the spirit and fewer exertions of the flesh.

None of these five arenas in the sphere of process is utterly new, for in each case there have been during ordinary history what might be called "Messianic flashes"—contacts with God that presage the Messianic situation. But it would be new to focus on these processes as the dominant forms of change.

Let us, then, examine the five arenas in the sphere of process.

First: What is analogous to the arena of human violence (ordinary history) versus human love (Eden and Days of Messiah)? Elevated to the sphere of process and more direct relationship with God, it becomes the arena of fear-and-anger-toward-God (ordinary history) versus comradeship-with-God (Eden and Days of Messiah). The first kind of relationship is characterized by the alternation between rebellion and cowering before God's wrath, by most human beings in most of human history. The second kind of relationship is characterized—in a "Messianic flash"—by Moses' "friendly" challenging of God, as well as by Jacob's unfearful and unfurious wrestling. First, then, and most basic to the process of creating the Days of Messaih, is the wrestle/dialogue/interplay between God and humanity, between human turning and divine redemption.

In this interplay human choices, human decisions, will not always be correct, even if they are based on the most thoughtful and "hearing" assessment of past revelation and God's Voice within us, within history, and within nature. We must seek always to hear the Voice anew, and correct our own choices by what we hear. But neither refusal to hear the Voice nor refusal to act on our own best hearing can ever be the correct choice. If we choose hearingly, we will receive further revelation.

Second: What is analogous to the arena of self-alienated toil and exploitation in making a living (ordinary history) versus self-unified, unalienated work and sharing in making a living (Eden and the Days of Messiah)? Elevated to the sphere of process and more direct relationship with God, it becomes the arena of the kind of divided, categorized work-with-God that produces not a life but a conglomeration of divided, partial lives in separate boxes (ordinary history) versus the kind of wholly-directed work-with-God that creates a seamless, unified life-path (Eden and the Days of Messiah).

What, concretely, would this mean? How does the prophetic outlook on the Days of Messiah offer guides to such a messianically oriented life-path? For example: In the Days of Messiah, there are to be no wars. Could this be developed into a path in which communities would act according to Messianic rather than normal-time prescriptions, and not participate in war—hoping thereby to bring closer the full onset of Messiah?

In other areas: In accordance with the prophetic call for peace between animals and humans, perhaps a path oriented to Messiah may prohibit all slaughter? In accordance with the prophetic call that the woman encompass the warrior, perhaps a path oriented to Messiah must prohibit all subjugation of women and the "womanly"?

If we seriously attempt to develop the rather general and vague prophetic prescriptions about the Messianic age into a specific path, we will need to ask ourselves a number of specific questions. Perhaps, in order to see the dimensions of the task, it would be useful to lay out a few of these questions, divided into the five areas that we have already suggested as crucial to Messianic transformation. Before we undertake this effort, which should help us understand more deeply the "result" or "content" level of the Messianic transformation, let us continue with our examination of the remaining three "process" arenas.

Third: What is analogous to the arena of war-with-nature (ordinary history) versus harmony-with-nature (Eden and Days of Messiah)? The equivalent of nature, for God, is *olam:* space-time. Elevated to the sphere of process and more direct relationship with God, the arena of relations with nature therefore becomes the arena of asserting control over God's space or territory (ordinary history) versus achieving the liberation of God's time (Eden and Days of Messiah). Most theories of social transformation—including the secularized Messianism of Marxism—have focused on the liberation of space, territory. But their own history has shown that this is insufficient—and perhaps also that in the modern world it is increasingly difficult, nearly impossible. Where today, in a modern state, can a movement find a geographically isolated "Yenan Province" in which to make a model of the revolution? Perhaps a fully Messianic movement should learn how to move into the Messianic age by liberating chunks of time, rather than space, in our lives: turning the weekend into the Sabbath, turning summer "vacation" (emptiness) into a month of study and spiritual development, pressing forward in a reserved piece of time, one that is comparatively well protected from the dis-integral society, to develop the Messianic life-code for that kind of time, and then, when that time-span is relatively well liberated, hallowed, moving forward to a new, somewhat more precarious piece of time.

Fourth: What is analogous to the arena of Jewish captivity (ordinary history) versus Jewish autonomy in the Land of Israel (Days of Messiah)? Elevated to the sphere of process and more direct relationship with God, it becomes the arena of a dispersed, dis-integral collection of individuals spiritually captive in Egypt or Babylon (ordinary history) versus holy-peoplehood (Days of Messiah). The notion of the holy people teaches a "universal particularity"—it is not through a dispersed, lonely crowd in which all humans are *only* human, and therefore have no smaller community than the whole race, that humans can build the Days of Messiah—but only if peoples can be fully themselves, each walk its own path as a community, be fully plural in making up humanity. Moreover, holy-peoplehood calls the *whole* people, not merely a saving remnant of priests or prophets—to be holy. It calls for a community that is not frozen into hierarchy.

The inner meaning of the holy people has a great deal to do with social change. It is in harmony with a basic principle of Godly social action, stated over and over by the Messianic tradition: the most important *means* of social action is to try to create in the present a miniature, a model, a foretaste, of the future toward which the world is striving. Thus Moses acts out in his own person, in miniature, the history of the people: first he plunges into Egypt, then he rebels, then he flees, then he receives revelation. Thus the Sabbath is explained as a foretaste of the Messianic age. Thus Jeremiah "acts out" the captivity by wearing a yoke around his shoulders for years.

Fifth: What is analogous to the arena of sexual role-rigidity and the subjugation of women (ordinary history) versus sexual role-flowingness and the equality of women and men (Eden and Days of Messiah)? Elevated to the sphere of process and more direct relationship with God, it becomes the arena of rigidity, clock time, and precise prescription (ordinary history) versus flowingness, spontaneity, and open-endedness (Eden and Days of Messiah). As might be expected, this arena—what might be called "transforming the sexuality of process"—is as hard to pin down in the tradition as is its analogous arena of transformed sexuality in the sphere of Messianic "content." Yet there is some precedent, some hint, of Messianic change.

Perhaps the strongest hint comes from the Song of Songs. Images of spontaneity and evanescence—goats streaming down Mount Gilead, dreams, fruit and flowers, the playful response to the appearance/disappearance of the lover, are summed up over and over in the line, "Do not stir up love until it please!" This outlook—held by woman who seems to set the viewpoint of the Song of Songs—is counterposed to that of the brothers, who warn her to guard her vineyard and want to guard her with artificial adornments; to that of Solomon's retinue, which guards his palanquin; to that of the night-guards, who beat her up for wandering after her beloved: all images of male rigidity, guardedness, and prescriptiveness. It is as if the whole traditional "male process"—strict calendars, the strict codes—were being put in question by this one book of the Bible. We might thus lean from it to surround and infuse a Messianic life-process with much more possibility of spontaneity and choice, much less rigidity of prescription, than has been characteristic of traditional life-codes.

Let us, then, bring together the elements of process that we have discerned:

> creating a forestaste or miniature of the Messianic future in the form of a Messianic path, a miniature which will grow organically toward that future.
>
> involving the whole community in the process of deciding the content of the Messianic path.
>
> liberating/hallowing time in the lives of the participants, so the expansion of time spent living a Messianic path is a major form of the organic growth toward the birth of the Days of Messiah.
>
> infusing and encompassing both the discussion of the path and its content with spontaneity, fluidity, and openness.

All this would be done in the hope and expectation that each step in the process is an act of turning, to be done with ears open to God's Voice and to the possibility of an act of redemption in response: a spontaneous response which could be unexpected, wholly unpredictable, because it is the gift of an infinite God.

These elements of process in bringing Messiah to birth would help prevent the dangers and failings that have beset Messianic movements in the past, quite aside from the difficulty that the preconditions for the Days of Messiah had not yet been met when most of those movements flourished.

The danger of idolizing a particular Messianic hope, institution, or form would be avoided by openness to the infinite and living God and to the always unpredictable and unimaginable interplay with that God.

The danger of using disastrous means in reaching for an infinitely desirable end should be avoided by creating the end through prefiguration, by creating a foretaste of the end itself; for in this way the means and the end tend to be collapsed into each other, so that only means that will grow into the end can be used.

The danger of antinomianism, of destroying all community through individualism and the abandonment of any path, and the state-centered bureaucratic legalism this breeds, should be avoided by the creation of a new communal path.

The danger of a rigidified and idolatrized path should be avoided by emphasizing openness, fluidity, and spontaneity in particulars.

The dangers of elitism or of hysterical response to a single leader should be avoided in insisting that the *whole* community take part in shaping the new path.

The danger of a cycle of ecstasy-and-despair should be avoided by the focus on organic growth, leading toward birth when the new creation is mature enough for birth—rather than toward bursting out of the redemption on schedule.

Can we fuse these elements of process into the first stages of growth? Already there exist in North America the very first bearers of the process: the religious communities that are already striving to shape a seamless life-pattern, already beginning to share thoughts with an eye to the re-creation of a path.

These groups may be exemplars of the early stages of the Messianic growth-process, but many of them have not consciously defined their imagined path as a Messianic one. Perhaps the process does not need to be fully conscious in order to grow in a Messianic direction, but it would seem that a different context might evolve for a path that is a conscious response to the Messianic vision than from inward promptings alone.

In the belief that the present world-situation partakes of the immediately pre-Messianic, and that therefore ten areas are crucial—one on the "content" level and one on the "process" level of each the five arenas of Messianic change—we propose to begin by asking questions in each of the areas. We are, however, open to the process of interplay with God in reassessing these questions and the ten basic areas.

I. In the sphere of "content" of human behavior in the Messianic Age:

1. VIOLENCE, WAR, AND THE MODERN NATION-STATE. In Eden there was no violence, only loving solidarity, between humans; in the Days of Messiah, as Isaiah, Micah, Hosea, and other prophets say, there will be no war.

A. What wars are clearly forbidden? What ought to be the path of the Messianically committed in regard to—
    (1) direct participation in war as soldiers?

(2) indirect participation in war as planners, munition-makers, strategists, weapons researchers, etc.?

(3) indirect participation in war as taxpayers?

B. What war *preparations* are prohibited—e.g., nuclear overkill-stocks? stocking of anti-personnel weapons? strategic planning for massive nuclear war? strategic planning to control, conquer, or destroy small nations? What ought to be the path of the Messianically committed who are citizens of states carrying on prohibited preparations?

C. Would a Messianic path require that "wars" of self-defense and of liberation now be fought only through civilian nonviolent resistance?

D. Would a Messianic path urge upon us efforts to live wholly without a centralized state (a "king," as in the call of the prophet Samuel)?

E. How are the new religious communities and movements dealing with these issues?

F. What are prohibited behaviors of a state and of its citizens in regard to questions of wealth, poverty, slavery, etc.? Are there modern forms of slavery (e.g., the pass-system in South Africa, any workplace not controlled by the workers?)

2. HUMANITY-AND-NATURE, FOOD, AND OTHER SUBSTANCES INCORPORATED FROM NATURE INTO THE HUMAN BODY. In Eden Adam "named" but did not damage or exploit nature. Adam was to eat of the herbs and fruits, but evidently not of animal life. In the Days of Messiah, says Hosea, God will make a "covenant on behalf of Israel with the wild beasts, the birds of the air, and the things that creep on the earth."

A. Ought ecology, the science in which humans "name" and describe nature but do not alienate themselves from it, the science of the web of life, be seen as the Messianic science?

B. In a Messianic path, ought the eating of all meat be prohibited?

C. Since ingestible substances are one chief nexus between humanity and the natural world under the aegis of God, should a Messianic path require the holiness of nature, protection of nature, nondisturbance of God's universe, etc., to be used as criteria of judgment for a new kashrut in regard to such substances, along with criteria based directly on the physical health of human beings? How would one judge diethyl stilbestrol, tobacco, marijuana, hard alcohol, chemical preservatives, addition of various substances to the general air and water environment, etc., under these categories?

D. Should some equivalent of the talmudic principle of *oshek* (nonconsumability of food grown by exploited labor) apply in a Messianic path?

3. WORK AND THE WORKPLACE. In Eden, Adam was to work the garden (but not in toil or pain), and could freely eat of its trees; and in the Days of Messiah, says Isaiah, "They shall build houses and dwell in them, they shall plant vineyards and enjoy their fruit. They shall not build for others to dwell in, or plant for others to enjoy."

A. Ought a Messianic path end all practices by which some toil for the enjoyment of others? Should it search out the kinds of economic relationships that would make work directly related to the human needs of the workers, rather than alienated from them? For example, are all the people who have mixed their labor with a commodity to be the owners in common of the resulting property, and would depriving them of it be theft? Are the new communities and movements raising these questions?
B. Are there any working conditions and relationships among workers and owners that are "Messianic"? For example, is the kibbutz to be considered a preferred form? Are there equivalent forms applicable to large concerns, urban enterprises, etc., such as, workers' councils?
C. Are new technologies, sources of energy, etc., to be pursued so that small groups of workers can more directly meet their own human needs—"build houses and dwell in them"—instead of depending entirely on a remote chain of economic life?

4. SEXUALITY, THE FAMILY, SEX ROLES, CHILDBIRTH, CHILDREARING. This is the area in which the Messianic tradition is least explicit. The Eden story, however, is very thorough in describing the sexual implications of the expulsion from the garden. What is more, despite millennia of male-chauvinist interpretations of the Eden story, the text itself opens up some of the earliest images of liberation from rigidified sexual roles. In Eden, the man and woman are not confined to the "normal" biological role of women and the "normal" social role of men. To begin with, Adam—the human who is created from *Adamah,* the humus—is both male and female. The story could, then, have said simply that the two were separated, or that the female aspect of Adam gave birth to the male. Instead, surprisingly, it is the male aspect of Adam that gives birth to the female, Eve, and it is, surprisingly, Eve who then takes the assertive and initiative role in the story of the Tree of Knowl-

edge. It is as if the men who wrote down the story of Eden were trying wistfully to say that in the harmonious world, men would be able to give birth and women be able to take the lead in decision and action—just as in the reduced and alienated world of normal history, men ruled over women and childbirth was painful.

To these images the prophets added little about the Days of Messiah, except that Jeremiah imagined the female—open, receptive—encompassing the aggressive warrior male. Perhaps that imagery accords with the wistful sense of humanness beyond the sex roles that flows from the Eden story. Here are some questions that arise from these images:

A. Should a Messianic path include obligations in the areas of housework, childrearing, economic production, etc., all deliberately extended fully and equally to both men and women? Do the new movements and communities move in these directions?

B. Should men and women become fully equal in all obligations and capacities regarding marriage and divorce?

C. Is the very nature of marriage and the family being reexamined, e.g., are group marriages permissible? desirable? Are homosexual marriages permissible? desirable? Are sexual liaisons without marriage permissible? desirable? with communal knowledge and sanction? secretly? Is permanent nonmarriage to be elevated as a live option? Is group childrearing permissible? preferable? What should be encouraged as optimum relationships between sex and love or deep friendship, and what should be accepted as permissible relationships between them?

D. Are all obligations regarding prayer, religious study, and observance being applied fully and equally to men and women?

E. What kinds of celebration/prayer, etc., are being created to mark the sexuality of women and men (e.g., menstruation, intercourse, the onset of puberty, childbirth, etc.)?

F. What are desirable practices and limits in the manipulation of human genetics?

5. PEOPLEHOOD/LAND/GOD. The outlook of the prophets is that in the Days of Messiah the Jewish people shall again shape its own destiny in the Land of Israel, but shall do this in accordance with God's will rather than idolatrously. For Jews this poses a number of specific problems, but for all peoples it poses questions about the relationship between a people, a land, and God:

There is a traditional linkage between "religion" and "ethnic group" that is not a one-to-one equation, yet cannot be dismissed. To the degree an *ethnos* is a way of relating to a wider society—through language, legal or moral codes, food, clothing, etc.—it is likely to express itself in a "religion" (or in several competing ones that all draw in overlapping ways on the history and symbols of that people): a religion, that is, a way of understanding and relating to the world in the deepest sense—where the people came from, why that particular people is in the world, what is its role in or out of history, how it relates to birth and death. On the other hand, sometimes a new outburst of religious feeling may melt down old ethnicities and create new ones among groups that share work and time out of a religious concern.

A. Would a Messianic path require the re-creation of a strong relation between ethnic identity and religious faithfulness?

B. Would a Messianic path require the treatment of a land as God's-but-on-lease-to-a-people?

C. Would a Messianic path require peoples to reexamine the treatment of "strangers within the gates"?

D. Would a Messianic path require a restoration and extension of the traditional prohibitions on interest, on the permanent ownership of private property, on the subjugation of workers, etc.?

E. Would a Messianic path require an ecological planning process for the land, equivalent to the Sabbatical year but broader, in accordance with a modern technology and economy?

F. What is the relation of ethnos to religion in recent American life in the Jewish, Irish, Italian, Black, Appalachian, Greek, Polish, Chicano, Québecois, and Woodstock Nation communities?

G. Just as American society during most of the last half-century has operated so as to freeze religious feeling and prevent ecstatic communitarian religious paths from emerging, did it also freeze ethnic feeling and attempt to merge all serious independent ethnic patterns into a culture defined by, led by, and profitable to those who ruled the nation?

H. If so, has this double freeze begun to thaw, so that both ethnic identity and religious orientation have begun to attract more and more Americans who identified their lack of religion or ethnos as an oppression or denial?

I. What is the role of the family in linking ethnos to religion?

J. What are the dangers of ethnocentrism, ethnochauvinism, and ethnic-interest politics, and the relation of these to the possibilities of "holy war" between various religious movements?

II. In the sphere of "process" of religious communities engaged in Messianic search:

6. INTERPLAY BETWEEN HUMANS AND GOD, TURNING AND REDEMPTION.

A. What is the nature of mystical experience in the new communities and the relationship of mysticism to social action?

B. What are the problems and possibilities involved in fusing the "religious" and the "political": the use of religious language to cope with new earthquake social possibilities, such as the death of humanity, universal leisure, biotransformation, etc.; political "liturgies" and ritual or ceremony as the physical enactment of ideology; the link between the social and nature universes; the rooting of ethics/politics in ultimate, not changeable, concerns; the relation of production and work to religious concerns; relation between "religious" visions of future reality and present political possibilities, etc.?

C. What are the social and political results of the more body-centered, God-exploring communities that arise from other than Jewish and Christian traditions: the "Eastern," "encounter," and "rock-drug" communities?

7. THE PATH-OF-LIFE.

A. What efforts have been made in the various religious movements and communities to create a concrete path of life, a code of conduct?

B. Have these been chiefly personal, or social-political, or both?

C. How have such codes been enforced? If they are regarded as universally applicable, do they pose dangers of religious struggle and war?

8. HALLOWING OF TIME.

A. How have new communities and movements been dealing with time in the life-cycle—birth, puberty, adulthood, old age, death?

B. How have they been dealing with time between the life-cycles of the generations, and with the "binding of time" that may be involved in the passing-on of tradition?

C. How have they been dealing with time in the natural cycles—day, month, year?

9. HOLY-PEOPLEHOOD.

A. Have the new religious communities seen themselves as models, the future-enacted-in-the-present?
B. Have they transformed the religious process by involvement of the whole community in guidance, decisions, spiritual breakthrough, celebration, etc., as a "nation of priests," or are they reestablishing hierarchies—charismatic or bureaucratic?

10. FLOW/SPONTANEITY.

A. Are new forms of religious experience and new ways of understanding God, more "open," flowing, and spontaneous, more responsive to the moment and less to the clock, the calendar, and rigidification, emerging in the new religious movements and communities?
B. Are the attributes of God traditionally associated with maleness being reexamined, reinterpreted, and is the God-concept itself being infused with attributes more traditionally female?
C. What effects are such changes, or questions, having on the daily lives of religious groups?

The basic formulation of a world-outlook that has been presented here, and the questions that flow from it, are only a beginning. I expect them to change. But I propose to begin by posing these questions to a number of people who are involved in or studying the new religious currents, and to draw on their responses for the next stage of learning. In this way I intend to examine the emerging religious communities and movements, fresh currents in the established religious institutions, and the general religious sensibility of North America by the expectations, standards, and categories of Messianic change. In the ten areas outlined, is change indeed taking place in the directions we have pointed out? Where are such changes most encouraged, where are they rejected and dismissed? Does change in one area tend to reinforce or retard change in another? What choices are being made?

I believe that these choices are of world-historical importance. I recall a great image of choice, set out by the prophet Elijah, that faced the Jewish people three thousand years ago: A bird, hopping on a branching twig, comes finally to the point where the two branches separate so much that it can no longer walk on both at once. It must choose. So Elijah spoke to Israel; and Israel chose God.

I believe that the human race now faces in a new way the choice between life and death. It has always faced that choice, as the branches have always diverged, and it has always walked on both at once: choosing a little life and a little death. But now, I believe, the branches diverge beyond the point at which it is possible to fudge the choice: now it is either the great death or a renewed and transformed Messianic life that confronts the human race.

Can we choose the branching path that leads to the Days of Messiah?

Romantic Consciousness
and Biblical Faith

EDITH WYSCHOGROD

Michael Ryan has given us an illuminating account of the Old Romanticism and the New, indeed a phenomenology of romantic perspectives. I should like, however, to distinguish the New Romanticism and its implications from the biblical view more sharply than Ryan has done, and to interpret this split in the light of somewhat different categories. I should like to develop both perspectives, the romantic and the biblical, as two types of metaphysics, the metaphysics of experience as opposed to the metaphysics of event. By the term "metaphysics" I shall understand the theoretical foundations of a given world view, the premises upon which it is based.

Ryan has already pointed to the vastly expanded role of individual consciousness in the Old Romanticism, to the identification of personal consciousness with world-historical consciousness and with Providence. God, self, and history, at least for Hegel, can be taken as identical items in a tautologous proposition: self, God, and the historical process are one. I shall assume as a minimal point of agreement between Ryan and myself that the term "romanticism" entails the view that individual consciousness, the reflective awareness of self as experiencing subject, values its own experiences as both the formal and material basis for the understanding of culture. Thus individual consciousness becomes a shard, as it were, which, to the archaeologist of consciousness, provides a clue for comprehending the thought structures of a civilization.

I shall, however, assume in addition, and as a necessary corollary of this view (and also as particularly important for understanding contemporary romanticism) the premise that freedom (in a sense to be explained) is the *telos* of expanded consciousness. We can trace the emphasis upon freedom to Kant's distinction between pure and pure practical reason in which a dichotomy between freedom and nature is established. Hegel sustains this distinction to the extent that (despite spirit's central role in his thought) spirit and matter remain radically split. Thus Hegel claims: "The nature of Spirit may be understood by

331

a glance at its direct opposite—Matter. The essence of Matter is gravity, the essence of Spirit—its substance—is Freedom."[1] What is essential for Hegel (in addition to his insistence that genuine freedom can only be exercised in a state) and crucial for neoromanticism is the understanding of freedom as the unhampered exercise of spirit, consciousness playing with itself, with its history, consciousness as the "bacchanalian revel where not a member is sober."[2] Spirit is centered in itself: "Matter has its substance outside of itself; Spirit is Being-within-itself (self-contained existence)."[3] Freedom for Hegel is thus independence from the strictures of "matter" so that identity is derived from *oneself*, an infinitely wider self than is entailed by mere personal history, a self which has now interiorized the totality of spirit's own trajectory. It is a self free to play with the totality of cultures, which cannot be jostled by the impediments of spatio-temporal limitation. Thus Hegel writes: "For when I am dependent, I refer myself to something which I am not; I cannot exist independently of something external. I am free when I am within myself. This self-contained existence of Spirit is self-consciousness, consciousness of self."[4] Consciousness, free to manipulate the detritus of history, is the progenitor of modern romantic consciousness, a consciousness in which every experience is valorized so long as it is the product of spontaneous, unhampered (i.e., "free") imagination from which repressive prohibitions and limitations have been removed.

Before turning to what I call the "metaphysics of experience" in contemporary romanticism, I should like to develop my last remark concerning the imagination from which prohibitions have been lifted. For I take it to be a hallmark of the New Romanticism that the unhampered flow of consciousness involves the remanding of restrictions imposed by an older metaphysics rendering possible the shift from valuing experience as the servant of ends extrinsic to itself to valuing experience for its own sake. This alteration in perspective is well illustrated in Nietzsche's attack upon "the lie of unity, the lie of thinghood, of substance and of permanence."[5] Once these assumptions are undermined, the independence of a realm of values apart from experience is destroyed, along with the metaphysics upon which it is based. No longer can one seek values, for they are nowhere to be found; instead they are to be fashioned, a new *techne* of values replacing the older image of discovery. One could even claim that the only value which remains is the value of creating values. The highest human type becomes the shaper, the artisan of values, avant-garde consciousness being defined by the recognition that there are no longer instantiations of value lodged in the world anterior to the act of their discovery. Since no value is privileged, i.e., preexists its discovery, freeing oneself of antiquated restrictions becomes the goal of consciousness; the content of this new freedom cannot be stipulated since there is no standard of reference to be used as its measure. Freedom is to itself its own measure, the measuring rod being "the resistance which must be overcome . . . the exertion required to remain on top."[6] Furthermore, for Nietzsche only the free spirit is worthy of love: "I love him who has a free spirit and a free heart, thus his head is only the entrails of his heart."[7] Because there is no truth for Nietzsche, to become truthful is to accept the new freedom, to glory in it and to risk oneself on its behalf.

Nietzsche's destructuring of metaphysics depends largely on a reading of metaphysics as a thought structure reflecting the corruption of a once "pure" language.[8] Thus language enforces the "perspectival falsifications" which everyday existence imposes, and which have a certain pragmatic value but nevertheless reflect the illusion of immutable truths.[9] Nietzsche writes:

> What then is truth? A mobile army of metaphors, metonyms, and anthropomorphisms—in short, a sum of human relations, which have been enhanced, transposed, and embellished poetically and rhetorically, and which after long use seem firm, canonical and obligatory to a people: truths are illusions about which one has forgotten that this is what they are; metaphors which are worn out and without sensuous power; coins which have lost their pictures and now matter only as metal, no longer as coins.[10]

Following the course of Nietzsche and other romantics, Heidegger takes language to be a fundamental condition for the disclosedness of human existence. It is characteristic for Being-in-the-world to see something *as* something, e.g., that which is environmentally available is interpreted as this table, book, etc. All Being-in-the-world presupposes language, but language is now interpreted as having authentic and inauthentic functions. "Idle talk" represents the erosion of language, its attrition in the public domain, its use to convey information rather than to express the ownmost being of *Dasein*. Thus an authentic task of human existence is to recover the original possibilities for the disclosure of Being lodged in language. Only the poet (the true philosopher) can recover this primordially unconcealing language. In the neoromantic reconstruction of Nietzschean sensibility, Norman O. Brown reaffirms the centrality of language as the key to opening up a new mythological dimension of experience. Thus Brown writes: "The key to *The New Science* [the title of a work by Vico which is the subject of Brown's *Closing Time*] is mythology but the key to mythology is etymology."[11] Or yet again: "The New Science is etymology:/ In the beginning was the Word, and the Word was/ Man./ Man is grammar:/ Tenses and Persons of the Verb/a city is syntax . . . Annihilisation of language so that it can be abnihilated again; created out of nothing."[12] The coinage "abnihilated" is deliberate: it conveys simultaneously the annihilation of language and the consequence of such a destructuring, i.e., philosophical nihilism, the absence of privileged nodes of value to be found lodged in the world.

What has been undermined in the romantic critique of language is not language as such, but the presumed concomitance of language and reason, the notion that the limits of discourse and the limits of intellect are identical. Thus the critique launched against language is actually an attempt to expand the possibilities which are taken to be restricted by criteria of coherence (the logical compatibility of ideas) and correspondence (the notion that language is limited by its function of referring to objects, facts, etc.). Norman O. Brown writes: "As rational metaphysics teaches that man becomes all things by understanding them (HOMO INTELLIGENDO FIT OMNIA), this imaginative metaphysics shows that man becomes all things by not understanding them (HOMO NON INTELLIGENDO FIT OMNIA)."[13] What is wanted is an expanded notion of cognitivity which is to include affective and appetitive elements: the sensuous free play of consciousness now becomes part of the cognitive process. Cognitivity is now coextensive with "life," cosmic, historical, and personal. There is a reversal of the order of the repressed: heretofore affect and becoming were subject to repression; the new age heralds the suppression of permanence and restrictive reason. This reversal is seen to release unprecedented power: in *The Birth of Tragedy* this power is expressed as Dionysian consciousness, the loss of individuation via mass participation in the powers of nature, in *Zarathustra* through the birth of the overman to whom man is merely a bridge to the *typos* of the future. No longer is the ideal formal, conceptualizable, viz., expressible in language. The old view is supplanted by an apotheosis of the undetermined. Thus Nietzsche remonstrates: "One must still have chaos in oneself to give birth to a dancing star."[14] Similarly Hegel's world-historical individual is possessed by the "vast congeries of volitions, interests and activities of the World-Spirit."[15] The negative repressed elements of Spirit are now released within the sphere of cognitivity itself: "We may affirm without qualification that *nothing great* in the world has been accomplished without passion."[16]

A consequence of this widened conception of reason has been the valorization of death, of the negative element which clears away the historical "rubbish" of the old age and makes way for the new. Thus one finds in both Hegel and Nietzsche not only an invariable concomitance between passion and death but a valuing of death which expresses itself in the will to risk in order to make way for the millennium. Armageddon is now more than cosmic: it is both personal and world-historical; individuals and civilizations must die in order to make way for the new age. In the cult literature of the New Romanticism Hitler's orgies of destruction are interpreted as a regrettable but necessary antidote to Western rationalism, as demonic possession, the price man must pay to inaugurate the new age of giants. Thus, for example, in a work by Pauwels and Bergier, *Morning of the Magician*, Nazism is interpreted as demonic possession and therefore inevitable: "With the coming of Nazism it was the 'other world' which ruled over us for a number of years. That world has been defeated, but is not dead, either on the Rhine or elsewhere. And there is nothing alarming about it; only our ignorance is alarming."[17] For the New Romantic the millennium is never too costly. This is sometimes expressed in the admonition to see the new age in the perspective of very great periods of time so that, if prorated over cosmic aeons, the cost can, so to speak, be taken as negligible. This is the standpoint of Teilhard de Chardin. Another strategy is to return to a Neoplatonic or Vedantic devaluation of the body by acquiring spiritual powers which bypass the body and depend upon transcendent principles. The acquisition of a "supermind" through such progressive spiritualization of body is the course taken by Sri Aurobindo. "There is no slayer and there is no slain" according to the *Katha Upanisad*, a key text of Aurobindo's spiritual heritage. The true self and the body are radically dichotomized, the demise of body in no way experienced as jeopardizing the life of spirit. Thus, for Aurobindo, perfected mankind frees itself from the chains of matter by tapping the hidden spiritual resources of the universe.

The difference between the Old Romanticism and the New (the "New" including both the counter-culture and the more serious bridge-builders between nineteenth-century romanticism and this very counter-culture—figures such as Sartre, Heidegger, Buber, Marcel) lies less in the difference between their theoretical suppositions than in the power available to the twentieth century to implement what had heretofore been merely fantasied. For what the contemporary metaphysics of experience presupposes is not merely the valorization of consciousness—although this is one of its premises—but techniques for the im-

plementation of its content. Nineteenth-century romantic philosophers
and poets valued self-reflective awareness, expanded consciousness,
experience for its own sake, but twentieth-century affluence and technology are able to make available in actuality what had merely been
fantasied by their predecessors. Michael Ryan alludes to Robert Lifton's chronicle of the succession of roles made possible to man grown
protean not merely in fantasy but in fact. No one *is* anyone any longer
so that a young patient of Lifton's is able to ask: "Is it futile for the ac-
tor to try to find his own face?"[18] Abetted by psychoanalysis, which
lifts impediments to choice in ways never anticipated by Freud, men
and women are now able to actualize their wildest dreams. Philip Rieff
writes:

> When psychoanalysis frees a patient from the tyranny of his inner com-
> pulsions it gives him a power to choose that is not otherwise his. Thus the
> aim of psychoanalysis is the aim of science—power; in this case a transfor-
> mative technology of the inner life. Where science is there technology will
> be. This ultimate technology aims at increasing the range of choice. Yet,
> without a parallel range of god-terms from which choices may be derived
> and ordered, choice itself may become a matter of indifference or man will
> become a glutton choosing everything. There is no feeling more desperate
> than that of being free to choose, and yet without specific compulsion of
> being chosen. . . .This is one way of stating the difference between Gods
> and men. Gods choose, men are chosen.[19]

What is perhaps most significant in many of the new strategies for
liberation is the absence of elitist criteria. Nietzsche's overman, Hegel's world-historical individual, Kierkegaard's knight of faith, Dos-
toievsky's Grand Inquisitor assume the separation of mass and class.
The avant-garde in each of these cases constitutes an "aristocracy"
whose credentials consist of the strength required to attain uniqueness.
This attitude is maintained in Heidegger, Teilhard, and Aurobindo.
But what had in these thinkers been maintained as the provenance of
an elite becomes, in the romanticism of the counter-culture, democra-
tized; expanded consciousness is the goal of a new wider proletariat, is
disseminated to a new constituency in much the same way as Judaism
was spread among the Gentiles in the first century and in the course of
that spread altered both doctrinally and institutionally, or as Therava-
da Buddhism was altered preceptively through its democratization
into Mahayana Buddhism. The change in quantity (in numbers of adherents) becomes a change in quality, in the tone, aesthetic character,
and promise of romantic consciousness become common property.

The democratization of experience leads to a striking paradox. On the one hand, the grounds for legitimating expanded consciousness rest on a rationale which assumes a *consensus gentium*: X's experience is like Y's, Y's like Z's. One does "what people do," so that both the content of and the right to hedonic quality are established by the fact that the new consciousness is Everyman's. Thus Norman O. Brown writes: "The Vico Rd. is a public way, it is the Joycean principle of HCE Here Comes Everybody."[20] On the other hand, each claims the singularity of his or her experience, legitimates the veracity of experience by referring to its individuality. Uniqueness rather than homogeneity becomes the determining factor in validating experience now seen as personal, irrefragable, and nonduplicable, and enabling one to say *my* experience is as interesting as anyone else's. The products of subjectivity fascinate, command attention, simply by virtue of having issued from personal consciousness. Thus, for example, dreams take on the status of literature, accidental assemblages, the status of art. Nothing which issues from subjectivity remains a spontaneous concatenation: *everything* is now interesting. This paradox of romantic consciousness, the legitimation of experience by proclaiming its homogeneity and extensiveness while simultaneously arguing for its individuality, thus holding in tension a set of conflicting values, itself represents a level of neoromantic sensibility. Paradox is taken as a sign of life and valorized.

The experiences now valued for themselves are those which most deeply challenge social stability: sex and violence. The erotization of the public sphere is attested by the ubiquitous appearance of erotic symbols saturating every aspect of the life of the culture. This tendency already appears in nineteenth-century romantic sensibility through the sexualization of the commonplace. George Steiner writes: "Many elements are in play: the 'sexualization' of the very landscape, making of weather, season, and the particular hour a symbolic restatement of the erotic mood: a compulsion to experience more intimately, to experience sex to the last pitch of nervous singularity, and at the same time to make this experience public."[21]

The eros of romanticism is largely narcissistic: the other is loved as part of the panorama of self. The correctives to self-love are often themselves romantic working to create heightened feeling through recognition of the other in his or her own being. Thus, for example, while Buber's philosophy of dialogue attacks personal narcissism by sacralizing the space *between* persons and preventing the one from incorporating the other, this spatiality is conceived as a locus for the interaction between two psyches attuned to one another for the enhancement of psychic life, for the enlarging of an already impoverished psychic landscape. What transpires here takes on the character of a visual model: what was heretofore background (the sphere of interpersonal relations) becomes foreground (the objects of the world organized for utilitarian ends), while the foreground becomes backdrop for the reciprocity of dialogue through which the experience of each is seen to be enriched.

Neo-romanticism can also be seen as lifting all restrictions against violence. The products of fantasy, the mythic motifs of earlier consciousness, can now be actualized through a facilitating technology. George Steiner notes:

> The concentration and death camps of the twentieth century, wherever they exist, under whatever regime, are *Hell made immanent*. They are the transference of Hell from below the earth to its surface. They are the deliberate enactment of a long precise imagining. . . .
>
> We know of the neutral emptiness of the skies and of the terrors it has brought. But it may be that the loss of Hell is the more severe dislocation. . . . The absence of the familiar damned opened a vortex which the modern totalitarian state filled. To have neither Heaven nor Hell is to be intolerably deprived and alone in a world gone flat. Of the two Hell proved the easier to recreate.[22]

Not only have scenes from Dante's *Inferno* been brought to life, but in recent years sadistic appetites have been created by bringing within the range of a vastly expanded public the bizarre, the outre, the grotesque, through extending to violence the privileges granted to sport. Thus not only are hockey and football spectator sports, but as part of the same conspectus the incineration of thousands in warfare as well as shootouts between police and fugitives, as in the recent match between the Los Angeles police and the Symbionese Liberation Army, are included. Moreover, interest in the spectacle lasts the length of time it takes to run the film, for as Andy Warhol noted, in the future everyone will be famous for fifteen minutes. *Tout est permis* becomes not merely a slogan of the imagination but an apothegm for life, a goal to be implemented.

The new metaphysics of experience is made possible by a radical alteration in the relationship between space and time. Their inseparability as organizing structures of experience is already grounded in Kant's transcendental aesthetic, in which they are taken to be equiprimordial. The objects of experience for Kant can be intuited as representations only in terms of a formal structure involving their extension and sequentiality. The lived quality of space and time has, however, been radically altered by current technology. The subject no longer lives within a surrounding space, that is, inside a framework of what is contiguous to him. This framework is extended not merely by one's ability to travel distances but by a far more radical dislocation. The alteration in our concept of spatiality is the consequence of our ability to be in more than one place at the same time. One *is* in Paris when one phones Paris although one *is* in a phone booth in Chicago in a quite different sense; one *is* in Moscow when one is tuned to the television set in New York. Thus one feels oneself to be in several places at the same time, a sense of multipresence. But one cannot say in which of these one is really located, for the body's insertion into a particular locale does not definitively determine "where one is at."[23] In effect, what happens to one's life world when one can be in several places simultaneously is that spatiality is experienced as temporalized: simultaneity and sequentiality supplant extension and depth as forms of the imagination. One consequence of this alteration in the sense of time and space has been to make the occult conceivable. Ryan has already pointed out that Eastern religions have become an element in romantic sensibility. I would suggest further that the occult features of many of these religions have, as a consequence of this new mode of temporalization of consciousness, become plausible to the contemporary imagination. For example, clairvoyance, the experience of being elsewhere (of "seeing" beyond one's actual locale), becomes natural for an imagination which technology has schooled to multipresence. Similarly, where extension is eroded as a basic category of the imagination in favor of sequentiality, the "tangible" is less vivid than the "intangible," matter less interesting than spirit. This sensibility has led to a renewed valuing of gnosticism. Thus Theodore Roszak writes:

> In the gnostic myth, the *apocatastasis* is the illumination in the abyss by which the lost soul, after much tribulation, learns to tell the divine light from its nether reflection. So a new reality replaces (or rather *embraces*) the old and draws the fallen spirit up, wiser than if it had never fallen. For us it means an awakening from "single vision and Newton's sleep," where we have dreamt that only matter and history are real.[24]

This new valuing of the old gnosis ignores its antisexual bias, but even where the antisexual is explicit, as in Aurobindo, it is not incompatible with the new sexuality. For both the gnostic *critique* of body and the quite different *valorization* of sexuality, with its emphasis on the lived body as the field of experience, spring from a common root. This root is the new sense of space which erodes the experience of spatiality, since one is in several "spaces" at once. Now the body must *concentrate*, as it were, our remaining sensations of spatiality: it is only here, through body, that extension is still fully lived and tangibility is primary. Thus body becomes both subject and object of its own sense of the extended: one listens to it, feels it, takes its pulse with intense interest, since it is all that is left of unidimensional spatiality. This concentration of the sense of space in body is heightened by the homogenization of the environment, where spatial markers, such as buildings or natural features, trees, rocks, coastline, are demolished and replaced with interchangeable constructions. The body in this context is the last instance of spatial uniqueness. Thus not only the lifting of taboos against sexual expression by the Old Romanticism, but the dependence upon the body as the last field of spatiality, make possible the emphasis upon the sexual. This stress gives to the New Romanticism still another pair of contradictory features: asceticism of the new cults (through the temporalization of consciousness), and the endless quest for sexual experience (the attempt to reconstitute spatiality at its last frontier, the body).

It is widely assumed that at least the attitude of the New Romanticism toward technology is unequivocal, that technology is seen to restrict imagination and is thus at the root of affective dislocations. This attitude is found in sensibilities as different as those of Roszak and Buber, Marcel and Heidegger. Heidegger's attack presents some features worth noting: not *all* mechanical devices are denigrated; those which lend themselves to use, are guided by the hand, show marks of human concern, are regarded as "authentic" tools. Thus for Heidegger an older technology of simple agricultural implements and the tools of handicraft are valorized. The same type of technology is valued by some elements of the counter-culture for quite different reasons: such technology is thought to avoid the radical depletion of natural resources. But not all romanticism discredits technology. Modernism in the visual arts (Dada, Surrealism, etc.) regards the machine itself as capable of widening experience. Thus artists have not merely subjected technology to negative criticism, as in the paintings of Leger, the assemblages of Rauschenberg, the films of Rene Clair, Chaplin, or Kubrick. Instead, other artists have themselves become makers of machines designed to create hedonic quality.[25] For example, a machine which throws balls back and forth to the spectator by running them first through its labyrinthine interior provides at once a critique of the senselessly mechanical and a pleasurable experience for the viewer-participant. Some artists have used complex gadgetry to create mood-stimulating environments: electric light bulbs are made to seem as though extending infinitely in all directions through a complex arrangement of mirrors. But what constitutes this technology as romantic is its nonutilitarian character, its only end being the creation and satisfaction of hedonic needs.

The metaphysics of event, the other pole of my analysis, is based upon a quite different set of suppositions.[26] In the biblical world, as distinguished from the neo-romantic, a life acquires significance through the episodes of divine intervention which interrupt its expected course. The patriarchal narratives are "stories," the recounting of events which transpire within the compass of life: divinely commanded wandering, the quest for a wife, the birth of sons, the transmission of religious and cultural patrimony, death. What one learns of the inner life, the introspective content of consciousness, of the biblical protagonist remains meager. Inner life as such is simply not a category for biblical imagination. When the contents of consciousness appear, they are confined within the context of response to divine commands: God's word is accepted or rejected.

Events themselves happen within a framework of a naturalized cosmos, one from which nodes of noumenality that remain constant are missing. Thus the sacred groves of Greek or Canaanite religion are absent or rendered innocuous. The watering places established by the patriarchs, for example, are not cited as places sanctioned for divine worship, but are interpreted as milestones punctuating the lives of the patriarchs. Furthermore, the human and the divine are seen as discontinuous. In the Homeric epic the narrative line proceeds in terms of continuity between the Olympian and the heroic (but nonetheless human) realms: the gods are little more than men, the heroes little less than gods. The biblical imagination could not tolerate such a mixed scenario, one in which gods and men inhabit a common psychological and physical cosmos. God must enter history through a special act. The fact that for biblical imagination there *is* a natural order makes it necessary to account for a break with that order. Thus Greek experience acknowledges the extraordinary but not the miraculous, for miracles depend upon the concept of a natural order in which the appearance of the divine is interpreted as a disruption. So "natural" is this order of the world that even the holy land, Canaan, is *merely* a land flowing with milk and honey: it is sacralized only through the presence of its Israelite inhabitants. In a sense, of course, as Ryan has shown, the whole earth is sacred because created by God, but no specific locale is numinous because of the gods who inhabit it.

It is at this point that we may consider possible relationships between the metaphysics of event and the metaphysics of experience. Does not the relative desacralization of space, together with a heightened awareness of event, suggest that biblical consciousness recognizes the primacy of time over space? The answer to this question is, I believe, a qualified yes. Sequentiality is the form of organization of *both* types of consciousness. But biblical consciousness does not value personal consciousness, heightened affectivity, passion, for their own sakes. It values obedience. If other affective consequences flow, they are seen as incidental rather than central to religious consciousness. The consciousness of each is the consciousness of all: the individual psyche is the repository of tribal events, of freedom from bondage, of the realization of divine promises, and, in the exilic period, of Messianic expectation. The life events of the individual are absorbed into a pattern of temporalization imposed by the Lord of History. The fact that transhistorical judgment is possible transforms the mere sequentiality of indifferent events into historical events, that is, renders some events meaningful, others insignificant, by assuming God's sanction or disapproval as hanging over all events. Consciousness thus temporalized is sequential, but the pattern is imposed by a quite different set of concerns than those which are based upon the valorization of experience for its own sake. Self-importance is not humanly created for biblical imagination, but conferred by divine choice.

I have tried to point to differences between what I take to be opposing worldviews and to certain negative possibilities entailed by a commitment to several versions of the metaphysics of experience. I should also like to suggest, however, that insofar as we are all contemporary men and women we cannot shed our skins. We are in a world where the antidotes to brute positivism are romantic in the ways I have suggested. Thus those who are sensitive to values not determined by a narrow positivism, a narrow pragmatism, or a narrow rationalism are, by virtue of their situations, thrown into some version of the metaphysics of experience. Nor is it possible to find in a fundamentalist biblicism the corrective to romantic narcissism, and the potential for violence which the valorization of experience breeds. Rather it is important, if one chooses to tread the path of romanticism, to do so with fear and trembling, with a sense not only of its opportunities for personal gratification, but for its darker, bleaker, more demonic side.

PART VIII

Auschwitz and the Pathology of Jew-Hatred

Introduction

A confrontation with Auschwitz must neither "redeem evil through explanation" nor seek justification through theodicy, urges *Lionel Rubinoff*. What is required is an existential encounter in the form of an "imaginative reliving" and renewed affirmation of and commitment to Jewish survival, as propounded by Emil Fackenheim.

A lesson to be learned from the Holocaust is that a highly developed culture and indifference to evil do not exclude one another. Rubinoff quotes George Steiner, "Men are always accomplices to whatever leaves them indifferent," a maxim obviously not heeded by the world at the time of Hitler. In Steiner's sense, Germans must inquire into their history, Christians into Christian anti-Semitism through the ages, and everyone in the Western world must, in accepting their complicity through indifference, undergo profound personal change, which should lead to a commensurate change in future actions.

Psychodynamically speaking, Jew-hatred appears as normal, rational behavior. The "final solution" is an extreme example of "functional rationality," as defined by Max Weber and Karl Mannheim. Race-hatred, under that guise, can be rationalized by confusing the means with the rationale by which the "realization of those means can be justified." Behavior associated with functional rationality may provide an outlet for the expression of aggression which under normal circumstances must be repressed. Treating human beings as means instead of ends appears justified under functional rationality.

Rubinoff discusses some images from myth and literature to explain more clearly why evil may be perpetrated without feelings of guilt. Satan, for instance, can be experienced as an external force to be used by the individual, to project an interior reality onto an exterior source. Bureaucracy may appear as a modern disguise of the satanic, a means for uncritical acceptance of authority which relieves the person of responsibility.

The promethean and faustian approaches to learning help to understand further the psychodynamics of anti-Semitism. The former applies knowledge in a "thoughtful" way and for the good of others. The latter exploits knowledge for selfish purposes in order to gain power over other people. Promethean rationality places ends over means. Evil, in our time, is committed for political, economic, and technological purposes which are experienced in the logical context of functional rationality. For that reason, we have not been able to articulate the concept of evil.

Rubinoff quotes Milgram's study, which seems to prove that an authority recognized as legitimate may seduce an individual into performing acts that are in conflict with one's moral standards.

The Third Reich represents yet another archetype, identified as "ultra-mythic," i.e., a preoccupation with the events in one's personal life as part of a grand cosmic drama. Quoting Sartre, Rubinoff identifies hate as an escape from personal responsibility. Translated into anti-Semitism, this means security through anonymity, abdicating one's responsibility for dealing with Jews. The Jew is treated as an object, just as the self is conceived as mere object.

While a moral individual distinguishes between good and evil "in fear and trembling," bad faith makes the world a place of certainty. Thus, anti-Semitism provides a definitive answer by proclaiming the Jew an evil, whose elimination becomes an act toward the good.

Auschwitz and the
Pathology of Jew-Hatred

LIONEL RUBINOFF

I

There, is perhaps, no greater challenge to contemporary scholarship than the obligation to engage in a full-fledged confrontation with Auschwitz. But in attempting to comprehend the absurdity of Auschwitz and the horror embodied within it, we must be careful not to pretend that once interpreted and explained the event has somehow been redeemed. The temptation to confound explanation with redemption, as conveyed by the classic motto *tout comprendre, c'est tout pardonner,* has been endemic to the social sciences since their inception.

Yet notwithstanding the risks inherent in the effort to bring absurdity before the court of understanding, there is a sense in which such a confrontation is a sine qua non of continued authentic Jewish existence, if not of all human existence. To adapt a comment from Goethe's *Faust,* "what from our fathers we inherit as tradition, we must earn in order to possess it."[1] For Jews and Christians alike, tradition is earned through a confrontation with Auschwitz. Such confrontation involves an imaginative reliving of the event in ways analogous to the reliving of sacred events. Just as Judaism traditionally urges Jews of all generations to live again the miraculous and sacred events of biblical times, in order to reaffirm the covenant, so Jews must live again the horrors and nightmares of the past. Catastrophe no less than fortune forms the context in which Jews are called upon to affirm their commitments. I do not apologize for the Nietzschean tone of this statement. It is a case, rather, of acknowledging the Hebraic dimensions of Nietzsche's doctrine that we must learn to say "Yea!" within the cycle of eternal return, the return of evil as well as good. Viewed from within this context, Irving Greenberg's notion of "moment faith," as explained in his contribution to this Symposium, takes on special significance.

It is, then, for the purpose of reaffirming the Jewish commitment to survival, in order to fulfill the Messianic covenant (however that might be interpreted) that the reliving of Auschwitz should be undertaken.

Only under these conditions can such an investigation be expected to occasion a theological advance in the history of Jewish-Christian dialogue.

This should not be confused, incidentally, with the tendency to redeem Jewish existence by assimilating it to a grand cosmic drama. The Messianic covenant is essentially the promise to exist between revelation and redemption and to work toward redemption through witness and "through the sweat of one's brow," which means, through the "labor of the notion" as well as one's body. In this process the Jewish people bear a profound responsibility for bringing about the conditions under which the meaning of their past can be made to bear fruit. There is all the difference between the posture of witness, of waiting for the Messiah, and the posture of conceiving oneself and one's people as a mere medium through which the inexorable laws of history and/or providence work themselves out. Thus, just as the confrontation with Auschwitz must avoid the temptation of seeking to redeem evil through explanation, so must it avoid the scandal of seeking justification through theodicy—as was the case, for example, during the Crusades, the Inquisition, and the era of Christian Social Darwinism. Scholars confronting Auschwitz cannot ask with Hegel, "To what principle, to what final purpose, have these monstrous sacrifices been offered?" For Hegel that principle is freedom, which is God's purpose with history and the world. And it is for the sake of freedom, according to Hegel, that "all the sacrifices have been offered on the vast altar of the earth throughout the long lapse of the ages."[2] After Auschwitz, not to speak of Munich, Lod, Kiryat-Shemona, and Ma'alot, such a view seems not only blasphemous but perverse and obscene.

Thus, while I am convinced that Auschwitz defies explanation and justification as these terms are normally understood—indeed, the radical uniqueness of Auschwitz lies as much in its refusal to be comprehended in terms of the normal categories of scientific inquiry as in its effects on the lives of its victims—I am equally convinced of the necessity to confront it through an existential encounter that takes the form of an imaginative reliving. Perhaps all that can be expected is for each one to suffer the event for oneself. Rather than pretend to announce the truth in the sense in which scientists give us explanations and theories, the historian of Auschwitz can only express, through the telling of the tale, the truth of his own unique encounter: a uniqueness which gives rise to universality only when it is responded to through affirmation and renewed commitment to Jewish survival. What is the character of this affirmation?

For the authentic Jew, tradition can sometimes be affirmed by stepping outside that tradition and its accompanying commitments, thus calling it into question. According to the dialectic implicit in this notion of criticism, the believer exposes his faith to criticism. This brings him into the midst of doubt and despair with respect to his formerly held beliefs. He then steps back once again and becomes critical of his criticism, with the result that, although he transcends his original commitments, he is yet able to return to them, albeit transformed. In this transformed state the believer continues to participate in his tradition and to celebrate his fundamental commitment to uphold the Messianic covenant. But this celebration of tradition no longer occurs in a religious immediacy which has never been challenged, and which has never exposed itself to the risk of total despair. Auschwitz constitutes such a challenge to Jewish faith.

Notwithstanding the risk inherent in such encounters, I wish to stress that they are enacted in the hope that they will lead to a renewed affirmation of Jewish commitment. To respond in turn to such affirmations requires a similar affirmation, which then becomes the basis of a shared understanding.

But how does one share the meaning of an encounter with radical uniqueness? The radical uniqueness of Auschwitz lies in its radical absurdity, in the fact that it is pure demonic evil. Jews were punished for having maintained fidelity to a covenant which promised survival to the Jewish people, and which identified that survival as a condition for the renewal of the world. Yet the more faithful Jews have been, the more has their survival been threatened. To face such absurdity and respond to it is, therefore, the greatest test the Jew has ever had to endure.

II

Faced with the absurdity of Auschwitz, can we expect our response to it to be any less absurd? Some have responded by arguing that Jews should give up their Jewishness. Some years ago Norman Podhoretz confronted this alternative and responded with the question:

> Will this madness in which we are all caught never find a resting place? Is there never to be an end to it? In thinking about the Jews I have often wondered whether their survival as a distinct group was worth one single hair on the head of a single infant. Did the Jews have to survive so that six million innocent people should one day be burned in the ovens of Auschwitz?[3]

It is not, of course, unreasonable for a group of people who have suffered as have the Jews to emerge from an experience such as Auschwitz with the temptation to question the very basis of their historical existence. Boris Pasternak confronts the issue in his novel *Dr. Zhivago*.[4] Here the Jewish problem is presented as a question. What is the sense of being a Jew in a non-Jewish world? Why should there be Jews at all? Typical of the astonishment which perennially plagues the non-Jew is the exclamation by Zhivago's mistress, Lara:

> It is strange that these people, who once liberated mankind from the yoke of idolatry, and so many of whom devote themselves to its liberation from injustice, should be incapable of liberating themselves from their loyalty to an obsolete identity that has lost all meaning; that they should not rise above themselves and dissolve among the rest whose religion they have founded and who would be so close to them if they knew them better.

When this attitude is internalized by the Jew himself the result is the surrender to self-hate as represented by Pasternak's Mischa Gordon. How is it, Mischa Gordon wonders, "that a human being with arms and legs, like everyone else, and with a language and way of life common to all the rest, could be so different—a being liked by so few and loved by no one. " He could not understand how it was that if you were worse than other people you could not improve yourself by trying. "What did it mean to be a Jew? What was the purpose of it? What was the reward or the justification of this unarmed challenge which brought nothing but grief?"[5]

To the question, Why be a Jew?, Gordon could find no answer. For him assimilation would seem the only rational response. Gordon has decided that to remain a Jew is as irrational as the cruelties perpetrated upon him, as irrational even as the traits attributed to him in order to condone the malice and sadism from which he suffers. Gordon thus represents the generation of exhausted Jewry no longer able to grapple with the historic mission of the Jew. Whereas the Jew has never been unaware of the absurdity of Jewish existence, he has, for the most part, resisted the temptation to escape absurdity by renouncing his tradition. Of course we have yet to see what it means to affirm tradition in the face of Auschwitz.

The fact remains that until Auschwitz, the Jewish record of transcendence had been exemplary. Nevertheless, the temptation to surrender is perennial. "Oh let me hear no more of Jews and Judaism and of myself as a Jew! Let me put an end to this inexhaustible torment," says the hero of Albert Memni's autobiographical novel, *The Pillar of Salt*.

It is only because he refuses to give up his separateness that the Jew
suffers in this world. For as long as they cling to their traditions Jews
must pay for it with voluntary martyrdom. But why be that invalid and
called a Jew when you can be a man? Why forsake so many splendid
adventures to remain vanquished among the vanquished? As Mischa
Gordon declares in his deepest moment of self-hate:

> Their national idea has forced them century after century to be a people
> and nothing but a people. . . . But in whose interests is this voluntary
> martyrdom? Who stands to gain by keeping it going? So that all these in-
> nocent old men and women and children, all these clever, kind, humane
> people should go on being mocked and beaten up throughout the centu-
> ries? . . . Why don't the intellectual leaders of the Jewish people ever get
> beyond facile Weltschmerz and irony? Why don't they . . . dismiss this
> army which is forever . . . being massacred nobody knows for what?
> Why don't they say to them: "That's enough, stop now. Don't hold on to
> your identity, don't all get together in a crowd. Disperse. Be with all the
> rest."[6]

Others respond by telling us that the best we can do is continue to remember and tell the tale. But consider how poor and inadequate is human language when confronted by the terror of Auschwitz! We remember, yet we cannot speak. Perhaps, then, the only authentic language of
that memory is silence.

Yet even silence is Being. Confronted by the poverty of language,
language can no longer become a substitute for action. Instead of seeking evidence of the divine presence in explanations and theodicies,
consciousness now experiences the silent power of the divine presence
through action. The Jewish response to the Holocaust thus takes the
form of action, both the universal action of love, charity, piety, and
creativity, and the uniquely Jewish action of stubborn commitment to
remaining Jewish. But we must act *as Jews*, as Jews who remember
Auschwitz, and not simply as members of the universal class of human
being. There is all the difference in the world between the love of man
qua man and the love of a Jew whose Jewishness has been nourished
by the memory of Auschwitz. For when I reach out my hand to my fellow man, in love and in trust, it is the hand of a man who still bears the
charred memory of Auschwitz in his bones.

If I respond to Auschwitz through affirmation of my Jewishness,
then my response can, in turn, be responded to and shared, either directly by other Jews who respond in kind with personal affirmation, or
else by non-Jews who respond by affirming the Jew's right to survive as

a Jew so that the Messianic promise can be fulfilled. Each, in its own way, is absurd. For a Jew it means to respond in the shadow of a God who, although absent, yet commands. The essence of such response is trust. For the Christian and non-Jew it is absurd because he must affirm an uniqueness in which he cannot directly share. The essence of this response is also trust.

But while we might agree that the uniqueness of Auschwitz lies beyond rational comprehension in mere language, and that nothing less will do than to respond to what Emil Fackenheim has called a commanding voice that speaks from Auschwitz,[7] we might also agree that there is a universal essence to Auschwitz, the importance of which can be neither altogether ignored nor minimized. There is universality in several senses. There is universality in the sense that it demonstrates that culture and cold-blooded murder do not necessarily exclude each other.[8] It demonstrates also that culture and indifference to the spectacle of evil do not exclude each other. For Auschwitz carried out what the world, by and large, was prepared to see carried out. The Jew was the victim not only of demonic evil, but of the indifference of humanity to what was happening. God's failure was matched by man's. And, as George Steiner charges, "Men are always accomplices to whatever leaves them indifferent."[9]

There is universality, then, in the responses that all must make. For Germans Auschwitz requires a ruthless examination of their whole history. For Christians it provokes the need for a pitiless reckoning with the history of Christian anti-Semitism, and for confronting the kind of reasoning that led a leading theologian to declare during the rise of Nazi terror: "The Church of Christ has never lost sight of the thought that 'the chosen people,' who nailed the redeemer of the world to the cross, must bear the curse for its action through a long history of suffering."[10] And finally, for the whole world Auschwitz demands an inquiry into the grounds for its indifference for twelve long years.[11]

Such inquiries should not be confused with theories of suffering-in-general or persecution-in-general, which only permit the real issues to be evaded. For as Emil Fackenheim explains, Auschwitz is the rock on which, throughout eternity, all rational explanations will eventually be shipwrecked and break apart.[12] Such investigations, if they are to be meaningful at all, must take the form of self-interrogation leading to affirmation. In the case of such interrogations, there are no distinctions between fact and value, or between the "is" and the "ought." To establish the facts is equivalent to knowing what ought to be. If the Jews at Auschwitz were the victims of indifference, then to accept that diagnosis is equivalent to both condemning continued indifference to evil and to affirming the values of the victims of Auschwitz, which means assuming the obligation to bear witness to that event ever after. To recognize and accept the extent of one's own complicity in the drama of evil that was Auschwitz is to undergo substantial, not merely accidental, personal change, and to act in a manner commensurate with that change. The inquiry into Auschwitz, which it is humanity's universal obligation to undertake, cannot be like a signpost, which, although it may correctly point in the right direction, is itself under no obligation actually to follow the direction in which it points.

Resisting rational explanations, Auschwitz will forever resist religious explanations as well.[13] In particular, the attempt to find a purpose in Auschwitz is foredoomed to a total failure. Some have sought refuge in the ancient "for our sins we are punished." But it does not require much sophistication to rule this out as totally unacceptable. Secular Jews might even connect the Holocaust with the rise of the State of Israel. But while there is undoubtedly a causal connection here, to translate this into a purpose is intolerable, and would constitute a vicious example of the fallacy *post hoc ergo propter hoc.* Equally intolerable would be any attempt to justify Israel on the grounds that it is the answer to the Holocaust. So to link these events together is to diminish them both. If Israel is a free and independent State it is not because of the Holocaust, although it may be out of respect for the Holocaust that Israel assumes its determination to maintain its Messianic pledge. Thus we must agree with Fackenheim when he insists that "a total and uncompromising sweep must be made of these and other explanations, all designed to give purpose to Auschwitz. No purpose, religious or otherwise, will ever be found in Auschwitz. The very attempt to find one is blasphemous."[14]

Emil Fackenheim distinguishes—and I have followed him in this regard—between an attempt to seek an explanation and a response. But, he points out, there is no precedent for such a response either in Jewish or non-Jewish history. Jewish faith finds no refuge in midrashim of divine powerlessness, none in otherworldliness, none in the redeeming power of martyrdom, and most of all, none in the view that Auschwitz is punishment for the sins of Israel. This is what makes Jewish existence today unique, without support from analogues anywhere in the past. This is the scandal of Auschwitz, which once confronted by Jewish faith threatens total despair.[15]

Yet, however we come to characterize the failure of a theology of Auschwitz, one thing is certain with respect to the theology of response. Does it follow, after Auschwitz, that any Jewish willingness to suffer martyrdom will constitute an encouragement to potential criminals? After Auschwitz, is not even the saintliest Jew driven to the inexorable conclusion that—ironical as it may seem—he owes a moral obligation to the anti-Semites of the world not to encourage them by his own powerlessness? After Auschwitz Jews no longer seek to sanctify God by submitting themselves to death. There is no revelation in Auschwitz in the sense of purpose, but there is nonetheless a commanding voice. The Jew is commanded to survive as Jew. And whereas survival might once have been regarded as devoid of meaning, in the age of Auschwitz a Jewish commitment to survival is, in itself, a monumental act of faithfulness, as well as a monumental, albeit fragmentary, act of faith. Thus Fackenheim writes:

> Even to do no more than remain a Jew after Auschwitz is to confront the demons of Auschwitz in all their guises, and to bear witness against them. It is to believe that these demons cannot, will not, and must not prevail, and to stake on that belief one's own life and the lives of one's children, and of one's children's children. To be a Jew after Auschwitz is to have wrested hope for the Jew and for the world—from the abyss of total despair. In the words of a speaker at a recent gathering of Bergen-Belsen survivors, the Jew after Auschwitz has a second Shema Yisrael: no second Auschwitz, no second Bergen-Belsen, no second Buchenwald—anywhere in the world, for anyone in the world.[16]

The commanding voice at Auschwitz thus decrees that a Jew may not respond to Hitler's attempt totally to destroy Judaism by cooperating in that destruction. In ancient times the unthinkable Jewish sin was idolatry. Today it is to respond to Hitler by doing his work. To this idolatry the post-Auschwitz Jew responds by reaffirming the ancient tradition whereby Jews bind themselves to each other and to the past through the rituals of commemoration. Foremost among those rituals as Fackenheim reminds us, is the Yizkor, and to be a Jew is thus to be part of a community woven by memory—the memory whose knots are tied up by Yizkor, by the continuity that is summed up in the holy words: *Yizkor Elohim nishman aboh mori*—May God remember the name of . . .

III

It is in the context of these remarks, admittedly of a highly personal nature, that I wish to consider some of the structures that characterize the phenomenon of Auschwitz. Auschwitz rests on three scandals: the scandal of using others as sacrifice in order to facilitate a barbaric rite of expiation, the scandal of rationalizing evil through a myth of cosmic purpose, and the scandal of the magical achievement of identity through the notion of kinship. Perhaps the first thing we notice concerning the psychodynamics of Jew-hatred that permeated the atmosphere in which these scandals came to be is that such hatred derived from what had come to be accepted as normally rational behavior. The important thing about Jew-hatred is that it appears to those who indulge in it not as irrational and irresponsible passion, but as reason. The "final solution" was a carefully planned, bureaucratically organized application of means to ends. It was, in fact, a prime example of what Max Weber and Karl Mannheim have called "functional rationality." As against the more "substantial" rationality of "caring," which views other persons as beings of intrinsic worth, as ends rather than means, functional rationality is preoccupied primarily with the manner in which persons can be "organized" as means to the realization of ends. The organization of the means whereby the goal is achieved is more important than the ethical content of the goals themselves. The agent, having become obsessed with "means" and "techniques," is virtually anesthetized by this obsession into adopting an attitude of either passive indifference to, or else implicit acceptance of, the goals. What gives the enterprise the pretense of rationality is the fact that it is "organized," and organized in such a way that goals are achieved by means of the most efficient techniques. Thus Eichmann, for example, in his pursuit of the "final solution," regarded his actions as rational. He had organized a repertoire of technologically functional means toward the solution of a specific goal; any action which is experienced as playing a functional role in achieving the ultimate goal is, by virtue of this fact alone, experienced by him as rational. If he was an idealist, as Aarne Siirala reminds us, his was an idealism of efficiency, a Faustian idealism of fascination with the use of technique as an instrument of power—a hybris which is especially characteristic of modern secular society. It is to the logic of functional rationality that we must turn if we want to answer to the question posed by Yosef Yerushalmi in his reply to Rosemary Ruether.[17]

It is thus that one acquires a completely false sense of rationality. Just as Hume pointed out, in his well-known and widely discussed analysis of causation, that we sometimes confuse the psychological experience of "fulfilled expectancy" with the perception of "necessary connection" or "force," so it might also be pointed out that we tend often to confuse the psychological experience of the means of bringing about the end with the reason or rationality for the sake of which the end exists. The confusion of the "means," which merely produce the ends in question, with the rationale, according to which the realization of those means can be *justified,* is one of the major sources of the crisis of reason, as manifested in the extent to which Jew-hatred was rationalized during the Nazi period, and the extent to which other forms of race-hatred have become rationalized in our own time.

Such attitudes result from the learned habit of identifying, both emotionally and intellectually, the structure of rationality per se with the structure of functional rationality. At the same time we must recognize the psychological context in which such habits are acquired. Freud suggests that some habits provide outlets for the expression of unconscious urges and repressions. It is thus easy to see how the habits associated with the exercise of functional rationality may become outlets for the expression of the libido of what Freud called the instinct for aggression, which I would identify as the Faustian urge to dominate, control, and organize for the sake of gaining power over the minds and bodies of other persons.

When viewed from the standpoint of Freud, the behavior associated with functional rationality may provide an outlet for the expression of aggression, which under normal circumstances the ego must repress under pressure from the superego. For while the superego may not permit the expression of totally self-initiated acts of violence, it can permit the expression of violence through acts which are perceived as legitimate responses to the command of authority. Just as Freud's neurotic rationalizes his violence by believing himself to have been "possessed" by an external reality, so zealots believe themselves compelled to their acts by their commitment to such ideals as the "national interest," "national security," "the improvement of mankind," etc. It is under the influence of functional rationality so conceived that individuals qua individuals more easily suspend their individuality and allow their group identity to determine their actions. In other words, group identity is more likely to be a source of evil when it is experienced within the context of functional rationality than would be the case if it were experienced within the context of the rationality of "caring," which is based on the principle of respect for the person, the principle according to which we are obliged to treat others as "ends" and never as "means."

But what precisely are the psychodynamics whereby an individual can freely engage in evil without visible signs of guilt? What are some of the other social mechanisms which combine with the logic of functional rationality to facilitate and encourage this behavior? Some help in the direction of providing answers to these questions may be obtained by drawing on certain images from the fields of myth and literature which together may be taken to constitute a symbolism of evil. Of particular importance in this regard is the image of Satan.

In a provocative and insightful paper on the devil, David Bakan suggests that the image of Satan can be analyzed into two components.[18] The first may be designated as "ultra-realistic," the second as "ultra-mythic." The "ultra-realism" of Satan lies in the fact that for those who believe in him he is experienced as a foreign intruder and an embodiment of external reality. At the same time Satan is typically represented as the "Tempter," and as "calling forth the beast in man." It is he who manipulates our inner drives. The pleasures and pains which the individual experiences with respect to the committing of evil acts are experienced as having been evoked from without, from some point in external reality called "hell." In this way the individual projects the inner-felt reality associated with evil onto an external source, which must now bear full responsibility for the impulses, drives, and experiences of pleasure which constitute the content of that inner reality.

There is a close parallel between the image of Satan as an external source of temptation and compulsion, and modern man's view of his behavior as compelled by forces over which he has no control. Just as Satan represents a mythological solution to the need for finding some way of relieving us of full responsibility for our actions, so modern man has invented "bureaucracy," with its emphasis on uncritical acceptance of authority, as his solution to this need. Bureaucratic authoritarianism makes it possible for the individual to experience his behavior not as an expression of something internal to himself, but simply as a response to an external command, and as something over which he has no control. "I am simply doing my job, merely following orders." The bureaucrat is compelled by his job description in much the same way that in more ancient times certain individuals believed themselves to have been "possessed" by the devil. And just as the devil relieves individuals of the burden of responsibility for their own behavior—for doing what they secretly crave to do anyway—so bureaucracy relieves individuals of a similar sense of responsibility.

This tendency to identify with one's job description, irrespective of the moral consequences, can be further elucidated by interpreting the symbolism of the devil's fall from heaven, and man's subsequent expulsion from paradise. In the case of the devil, to have been cast out of heaven is to have been separated from being and cast into hell, the realm of nothing. The devil is thus the messenger of "nothing." He is activity without purpose. It is important, also, to remember that although the devil has fallen from being, in which case he has lost all sense of purpose, he has not lost any of his techniques, his knowledge, or his skills. He is like a lover who no longer believes in love but still retains his power of seduction. The devil, in other words, still has the "knack," as it were, but no longer the "vision." He has lost the sense of the end, and the glory to which the application of knowledge is destined. But he is a tireless worker, who dedicates himself to bringing about whatever happens to be desired without regard to whether or not it is also desirable. And whatever is done skillfully but without regard to the ends or purposes served, and to the moral consequences of pursuing such ends, whatever is done for "no reason," or for reasons which are, in reality, nothing more than disguised excuses or alibis, bears the imprimatur of the devil.

The problem to which I am drawing attention may be further illustrated by appealing to the following images from classical mythology. When the name Prometheus comes to mind, one tends to think of the compassionate hero who was so inspired by his concern for man's miseries that he risked incurring the wrath of the gods by stealing fire from heaven so that men might become their own masters and thus alleviate the conditions of adversity under which they had lived and suffered. But there is another association that derives from the etymology of the world itself. The word "Prometheus" comes from the Greek words *pro* and *mathein*, which together mean fore-thought or thoughtfulness. Putting these various meanings together, then, "promethean" may be understood to mean " the compassionate but thoughtful concern for leading mankind toward greater and greater degrees of self-mastery through understanding and knowledge." Viewed thus, the term "promethean" aptly describes the professions of science and technology in their ideal form.

A very different image derives from the mythological figure of Faust. Faust, too, has an interest in knowledge. But unlike promethean knowledge, faustian knowledge serves the appetite for personal self-interest and power. So defined, faustian rationality is clearly the opposite of the rationality upon which science and technology are ideally founded. Yet faustians have a peculiar talent for disguising their real interests under the guise of promethean rationality and creativity. For this reason we are often deceived by faustians who pretend to be promethean; by politicians, scientists, and technologists who claim to be dedicated to the classical humanistic ideals of Western culture, but for whom, in fact, the entire resources of science and technology present themselves primarily as instruments for the satisfaction of an irrational craving to exercise power.

As I have used these terms, the promethean and the faustian suggest two distinct interpretations of rationality which can easily be confused. Promethean rationality is "thoughtful." It seeks the application of means to the realization of ends that are worthy of being realized because they are understood to contribute to justice and the general happiness of mankind. For such rationality, the thinking which aims at the evaluation of ends has priority over the thinking which preoccupies itself exclusively with the determination of means. Faustian traditionality is "thoughtless." It is concerned exclusively with the organization of means irrespective of the ends. Indeed, to the extent to which it is concerned with ends at all, it is only insofar as they serve the irrational need to gain recognition through the manipulation of the means. Faustian rationality is the rationality through which the ego seeks selfhood through mastery over others. It arises in the course of the dialectic of self-consciousness, as outlined by Hegel in *Phenomenology of Mind,* which eventually leads to the relationship of lordship and bondage. Consider, for example, Hegel's claim that desire is the first form of self-consciousness and the first category for understanding the growth of both individual and collective consciousness. Desire arises as a consequence of the fact that self-consciousness, as opposed to mere consciousness, depends for the sense of self-certainty on the negation of the other, whether in the form of nature or other selves. Self-consciousness regards itself as the truth of the other, while the other is nothing until he derives his truth from being appropriated by self-consciousness. This is the ontological source of the desire to negate the other.

Self-consciousness thus arises in the context of a desire to appropriate or negate the independence or otherness of the other. What makes the other an object of desire is the mere fact that he exists as other. How does this doctrine affect our understanding of interpersonal relations and international relations? To begin with, we should become immediately suspicious of the excuses and rationalizations that we are accustomed to employ in order to justify our aggressive attitudes toward each other and toward things in general. Such rationalizations may be nothing more than masks which hide the true meaning of our behavior. For alas, in real life we are less prone to philosophical self-understanding than in Hegel's philosophical consciousness. Let us suppose that the selfhood of the nation, like the selfhood of the single individual, depends on the annihilation of the selfhood or sovereignty of the other. The nation in search of selfhood thus conceives of itself as the truth of all other nations; a view of the other as nothing cannot be openly adopted by any nation unless it can be justified by the collective superego; no nation can explicitly adopt this point of view. Instead, such a nation will manufacture excuses in order to justify its conduct. This is a phenomenon to which Freud has, perhaps, contributed more understanding than Hegel. Thus Pericles conceived Greek imperialism as a form of education. Woodrow Wilson justified the Messianic nationalism of America by appealing to "manifest destiny." Richard Nixon attempted to justify his policy of annihilation in South Vietnam and Cambodia on the grounds that he was fighting for liberty against Communist aggression, while his colleagues, the Watergate conspirators, pleaded that they acted always in the "national interest." If Watergate and its related events signify anything, it is that it was not enough merely to defeat the Democrats in an election, it was necessary to annihilate them. It was not enough merely to punish Daniel Ellsberg for breaking the law, he had to be annihilated. In the White House horrors, as John Mitchell has aptly described them, we have once again the nightmare described by Thucydides in his account of the invasion of the Island of Melos during the sixteenth year of the Peloponnesian Wars.

It is from the temptation to universalize the craving for mastery and manipulation that we find ourselves developing a kind of faustian urge to apply our technique to the implementation of goals, irrespective of their desirability, irrespective of their consequences, and irrespective of whether they will contribute to the common good. This is the attitude of technological nihilism.

As represented by the myth, the devil is clearly an agent of "technological nihilism," whose mission it is to tempt man in that direction. The satanic impulse is implicit even in such normally commendable desires as to succeed at something, to achieve for the sake of achieving, which at the very best means the promethean desire to reach transcendental standards of excellence. In itself, the desire for excellence is not productive of evil. Indeed, such a desire should be a factor in all motivation. But when it is converted into a faustian *compulsion* to achieve for the sake of achievement, and when the idea of achievement, conceived as the pursuit of the possible, is elevated or deified into an absolute goal, then such desires are positively satanic. And whenever man submits to the temptation of technological nihilism under the cover of such language as "I was only following orders," "only doing my job," he is in reality speaking *in nomine diaboli*.

But how, according to the symbolism of the myth, does the devil tempt man? Never with the prospect of evil per se, but rather with the prospect of achieving some good. The devil's chief weapon is deception. It is always through the mediation of some promethean hero that man surrenders to the faustian impulse. The promethean and the faustian derive from the same diabolical urge. This is the source of what I earlier called—following David Bakan's analysis—the "ultra-mythic." Ultra-mythicism is understood as preoccupation with an eschatology or ideology, the belief that the events of one's life are the playing out of some grand cosmic drama. According to the mythic representation, the devil is a skillful nihilist, hence the plots of these dramas can be invented at will without regard to their truth or falsity. Thus, as we were once called upon to act in the name of God, so we now find ourselves called upon to act in the name of a cause, destiny, or national purpose. As Kurt H. Wolff writes, in a paper dealing with the sociology of evil, "Evil is no longer committed in the name of God, is less than ever 'legitimated' by religious or even moral motives, and is covered over by political, economic and technological reasons, and on a larger scale than ever."[19]

Wolff suggests that the reason we are so captured by these new forces of order is that we find ourselves living in the midst of a paralyzing suspension between two impossible worlds: a world ordered by religious directives in which we can no longer believe, and a world without such directives, which we cannot bear. The result of this alienation is that we are driven to fill the vacuum by finding new gods to worship. These are made readily available to us in the form of political, economic, and technological incentives. Since the latter are experienced in the context of the logic of a "functional rationality," which, as I hope to show, tends to be confused with the very essence of reason itself, it does not occur to us that anything committed in the name of such goals could be evil. It is perhaps for this reason, as Wolff points out, that "we have not succeeded in articulating a conception of evil that would be adequate to the secularized world in which we in fact live, but which has left evil itself, in contrast to space, cancer, the Greenland Icecap, and innumerable other phenomena and problems, comparatively unexplored, ominously sacred and threatening."

The technological nihilism which characterizes the world in which individuals make use of the mechanism of projection is as much a product of functional rationality as of human psychology. In such a world the "banality of evil" becomes a matter of routine. Men acquire the capacity for engaging in evil without experiencing it as such. They learn how to perform evil acts as part of their job description. Such behavior, as Hannah Arendt and others have pointed out, is not so much the expression of innate aggressiveness or sadism as it is the result of an inability to challenge whatever discrepancies and irrationalities a person might perceive between his actions and his moral beliefs.

One of the best studies of this inability to challenge authority is a set of experiments conducted by the social psychologist Stanley Milgram during the early 1960s.[20] The aim of these experiments was to determine the amount of pain (in the form of an electric shock) a subject is willing to inflict on another, when ordered by an experimenter to do so. The punishment is represented to the experimental subject under the notion of learning, and the experiment as an attempt to study the effect of punishment on memory. Unknown to the subject, the victim, or "learner," merely pretends to be "punished." But the important point, as far as the experiment is concerned, is that the experimental subject believes the victim to be experiencing great pain, yet continues to administer higher and higher voltages of shock at the command of the experimenter. This study shows that it is possible for quite normal individuals to engage in immoral behavior at the instruction of some authority, provided that they perceive that authority as legitimate. Milgram's study shows that the recognition of conflict between one's conduct and moral standard is not always sufficient to conform the former to the latter. The agent accepts as rational the injunction by the person in authority; in spite of the apparent moral implications the order must be obeyed, the experiment must go on.

> Despite his numerous, agitated objections, which were constant accompaniments to his actions, the subject unfailingly obeyed the experimenter, proceeding to the highest shock level on the generator. He displayed a curious dissociation between word and action. Although at the verbal level he had resolved not to go on, his actions were fully in accord with the experimenter's commands. This subject did not want to shock the victim, and he found it an extremely disagreeable task, but he was unable to invent a response that would free him from E's authority. Many subjects cannot find the specific verbal formula that would enable them to reject the role assigned to them by the experimenter. Perhaps our culture does not provide adequate models for disobedience.[21]

The subject's need to respond to the symbolism of authority is greater than his need to obey the dictates of his conscience.

To these variations must be added a further one, not identified by Milgram. It is the mechanism operating in a variety of familiar cases in which people resort to what the sociologist Lewis Coser calls the "denial of common humanity" device.[22] The representation of the Jews as subhuman was an important device for facilitating the evil that was done to them. By creating a distinction between "good, decent people" and "inferior, subhuman creatures," one is able to engage in or witness evil without guilt or moral indignation.

But just as the "dehumanization" of the victim facilitates authority, so authority itself can be delegitimized by being dehumanized. It is thus not surprising that those who currently engage in acts of violent disobedience refer to the defied authorities by words such as "pig," "swine," and so on. The very language itself plays an important role in the process. It is one way of breaking down the superego's defenses, which might otherwise exercise a restraining influence on the behavior.

Milgram's general findings, as stated in his most important article, deserve to be reported in full:

> Almost a thousand adults were individually studied in the obedience research, and there were many specific conclusions regarding the variables that control obedience and disobedience to authority. Some of these have been discussed briefly in the preceding sections, and more detailed reports will be released subsequently.
>
> There are now some other generalizations I should like to make, which do not derive in any strictly logical fashion from the experiments as carried out, but which, I feel, ought to be made. They are formulations of an intuitive sort that have been forced on me by observation of many subjects responding to the pressures of authority. The assertions represent a painful alteration in my own thinking; and since they were acquired only under the repeated impact of direct observation, I have no illusion that they will be generally accepted by persons who have not had the same experience.
>
> With numbing regularity good people were seen to knuckle under the demands of authority and perform actions that were callous and severe. Men who are in everyday life responsible and decent were seduced by the trappings of authority, by the control of their perceptions, and by the uncritical acceptance of the experimenter's definition of the situation, into performing harsh acts.
>
> What is the limit of such obedience? At many points we attempted to establish a boundary. Cries from the victim were inserted; not good enough. The victim claimed heart trouble; subjects still shocked him on command. The victim pleaded that he be let free, and his answers no longer registered on the signal box; subjects continued to shock him. At the outset we had not conceived that such drastic procedures would be needed to generate disobedience, and each step was added only as the ineffectiveness of

the earlier techniques became clear. The final effort to establish a limit was the Touch-Proximity condition. But the very first subject in this condition subdued the victim on command, and proceeded to the highest shock level. A quarter of the subjects in this condition performed similarly.

The results, as seen and felt in the laboratory, are to this author disturbing. They raise the possibility that human nature, or—more specifically—the kind of character produced in American democratic society, cannot be counted on to insulate its citizens from brutality and inhumane treatment at the direction of malevolent authority. A substantial proportion of people do what they are told to do, irrespective of the content of the act and without limitations of conscience, so long as they perceive that the command comes from a legitimate authority. If in this study an anonymous experimenter could successfully command adults to subdue a fifty-year-old man, and force on him painful electric shocks against his protests, one can only wonder what government, with its vastly greater authority and prestige, can command of its subjects. There is, of course, the extremely important question of whether malevolent political institutions could or would arise in American society. The present research contributes nothing to this issue.[23]

In Milgram's experiment the mechanism of projection, as embodied in the image of Satan, is exemplified in the situation in which average individuals can be induced to inflict pain on another person, under the compulsion of a structured social situation. The devil is here represented by the social structure of authority; that structure itself is legitimized by the projection of an internal need. The correct interpretation is not that individuals were, in fact, compelled to their behavior by the prevailing authoritarian situation; it is, rather, that they *chose* to perceive and to react to such a "compelling" situation *in order* to express internal needs, in particular, the need to express violence without having to bear responsibility for it.

There is one further association of the image of Satan which could conceivably throw light on the implications of Milgram's experiment, as well as on the phenomenon of the "final solution." One of the characteristics of Satan is, as we already pointed out, that he is always represented as a master of ingenious and artful physical and chemical devices. Indeed, we cannot help but notice that one of the first products of technology was the weapon, the instrument of warfare and torture. David Bakan observes, in the paper already referred to, that historical images of hell are filled with all sorts of clever torture devices, and the "screw" has, no doubt, been used as a torture device more often than as part of machines for the production of goods. The fact that Milgram's naive subjects were taking part in a scientific experiment, using electronic and technological devices as instruments of punishment (or teaching, as it was referred to), may have had some effect on the success with which authority prevailed. Likewise the gas chambers, the ovens, and Eichmann's scientific experiments may also be understood as a manifestation of the devil's ingenuity. Indeed, it may well be that in a world such as ours, driven as it is by pragmatic considerations and functional rationality, as well as by the compulsion to "solve" everything, the application of technology to the "final solution" of the Jewish problem comes as no great surprise.

The phenomenon of the Third Reich expresses yet another of the archetypal structures of evil, which I have earlier identified as "ultra-mythic." Just as the devil is represented as playing out a cosmic role, so the Nazis presented the "final solution" as the fulfillment of a cosmic destiny. Thus Gert Kalow declares in his book *The Shadow of Hitler:*

> Would Hitler have been able to rouse the masses . . . to such delirious enthusiasm, if there had not existed in Germany the idea or expectation that something in the nature of collective redemption was possible? A "messianic expectation among the common people" . . . combined with a superstitious belief in a world history which, by evolution and impelled by a higher automatic power, was moving forward to fulfillment?[24]

Here, too, language plays an important role. Just as the language of "I was only obeying orders" facilitates the mechanisms of ultra-realism, so the language of ideology—"it is our destiny," "it is our mission," "it is our purpose"—introduces an equally external compelling force, which is made to bear full responsibility for one's acts.

In the end, then, the one overriding characteristic of the human tendency to engage in evil without compunction is that, in all such cases, one acts in accordance with what is experienced as "an external demand," whether that demand be interpreted as the demand of authority or the demand of a cosmic plan according to which reality itself is constructed. In both cases the burden of responsibility is shifted away from the self to the "other."

In a society in which functional rationality has been institutionalized, and which is based, moreover, on myths of class and racial superiority supported by an eschatology of special mission, acts of barbarism, such as choosing to violate the rights of others for the sake of realizing a cosmic goal, become possible. Yet the act of choosing is logically and ontologically prior to social structure. That man is a being for whom such a choice is a possibility has to do with his being qua man. This accounts for the grounds of his fallibility. That man then finds himself in a society dominated by functional rationality, a society which defines identity in terms of kinship, and which favors one kinship group over others, has to do with the conditions of historicity. This accounts for the possibility of a transition from fallibility to fault. To understand Jew-hatred, then, we must understand both the a priori structure of man and the historical conditions under which possibility and fallibility become converted into actuality and fault.

The historical conditions in which man finds himself are not, however, entirely a matter of accident. They are, to some extent, the product of man himself. To adapt a phrase of Kant's, "reason has insight only into that which it produces after a plan of its own."[25] The studies of anthropology and sociology thus raise questions about the intentional structure of consciousness as the source of the plan according to which society is constructed, and into which sociology and anthropology claim to have insight. The task of philosophical anthropology is, therefore, to inquire into the a priori structure of consciousness as such, in order to account for the possibility of kinship and for the ease with which it facilitates the flight from individual responsibility which characterizes Jew-hatred. Such an inquiry is indicated and developed in the philosophical writings of Jean-Paul Sartre.

In a remarkable essay on the structure and significance of human emotions, Sartre introduces the hypothesis that emotions are often employed to facilitate a magical flight from responsibility.[26] Emotion is a behavior of defeat which allows the individual to proclaim defeat even before engaging in struggle. An individual does not hate, according to Sartre, because he is outraged by the conduct of others. The individual chooses to be outraged in order to hate.

Hate now appears as an escape from the painful feeling that one is responsible toward others. The emotional crisis is thus an abandonment of responsibility by means of a magical transformation of the object into something hateful. Let us extend this analysis to cover the idea of kinship. Kinship is one expression of magic. Not only do I relieve myself of caring for others, but I endow myself and my possessions with value without having to work for it. By hating another group, I endow the kinship group to which I belong with value.

In his major philosophical work, *Being and Nothingness,* the magical manipulation of the emotions is represented as bad faith. Sartre asks, What is the structure of consciousness that man is capable of bad faith, of choosing to escape from responsibility? The answer lies in the analysis of consciousness as the effort to-be-what-it-is-not and not-to-be-what-it-is. This doctrine, as elaborated by Sartre, combines the influence on his thought of Freud and Hegel. Man *is* freedom, yet he seeks *not* to be free. Indeed, it is only to the extent that men live through this drama of ambivalence that they can be expected to reach authentic existence. The paradox of the human condition is that only for a man who recognizes in himself the temptation to escape from freedom can the exercise of freedom become a mode of authentic self-expression.

In a work published in 1946 entitled *Anti-Semite and Jew,* Sartre applies this hermeneutic to the analysis of anti-Semitism. Sartre describes anti-Semitism as a form of bad faith which seeks security through anonymity and loss of individuality. To judge the other as a Jew is simply to classify him under an abstract rule. It is an answer to the question, How shall I deal with that man? without thinking it out for oneself. I shall deal with him as a Jew—which is to say, I shall refuse to deal with him at all. Since Jews are less than human, their very presence is an outrage. What is more, in their presence I am no longer required to be an individual. I have obliterated *their* individuality in order to negate my own individuality. In treating the other as mere object, I become myself an object. For in branding him a Jew, I bring him under a code that has a collective origin. I thus become part of an anonymous crowd. My attitudes and beliefs are vindicated by the consensual validation of the many others who believe as I do—and we all believe together that we are compelled to our unanimous verdict by the brute facts of nature. We hate Jews because they *are* by nature hateful.

Through hatred, the anti-Semite seeks out the protective community of men of bad faith, who reinforce each other through a collective uniformity of behavior. Sartre's own description of the anti-Semite is worth quoting in full. The anti-Semite, he writes, is a man who has chosen to reason falsely.

> How can one choose to reason falsely? It is because of a longing for impenetrability. The rational man groans as he gropes for the truth; he knows that his reasoning is no more than tentative, that other considerations may supervene to cast doubt on it. He never sees very clearly where he is going; he is "open"; he may even appear to be hesitant. But there are people who are attracted by the durability of a stone. They wish to be massive and impenetrable; they wish not to change. Where, indeed, would change take them? We have here a basic fear of oneself and of truth. What frightens them is not the content of truth, of which they have no conception, but the form itself of truth, that thing of indefinite approximation. It is as if their own existence were in continual suspension. But they wish to

exist all at once and right away. They do not want any acquired opinions; they want them to be innate. Since they are afraid of reasoning, they wish to play only a subordinate role, wherein one seeks only what he has already found, wherein one becomes only what he already was. This is nothing but passion. Only a strong emotional bias can give a lightninglike certainty; it alone can hold reasoning in leash; it alone can remain impervious to experience and last for a whole lifetime. . . .

This man fears every kind of solitariness, that of the genius as much as that of the murderer; he is the man of the crowd. However small his stature, he takes every precaution to make it smaller, lest he stand out from the herd and find himself face to face with himself. He has made himself [prejudiced] because [in prejudice] one cannot be alone. The phrase "I hate the Jews" is one that is uttered in chorus; in pronouncing it one attaches himself to a tradition and to a community—the tradition and community of the mediocre.[27]

Sartre makes another point about the morality of anti-Semitism. Being an authentic individual, he argues, involves learning to distinguish between good and evil. But such distinctions must be made in fear and trembling, for there is no guarantee that our decisions in such matters are beyond question. In matters of morality there is no absolute certainty. But one can, through bad faith, transform the world into the kind of place in which certainty is now possible. Anti-Semitism, for example, provides a definitive answer to the question, What is evil? Jews are evil, therefore let us eliminate them. To eliminate an evil is to perform a good. There is no longer any necessity to *think* one's way toward good. Good is automatically realized through the elimination of what is recognizably and indisputably evil, like Jews. Thus Hitler writes in *Mein Kampf* in a passage already cited by Alan Davies, "today I believe that I am acting in accordance with the will of the Almighty Creator: by defending myself against the Jew I am fighting for the work of the Lord."[28] Elsewhere he writes: "Only when we have eliminated the Jews will we regain our health."[29] Again I quote directly from Sartre:

The advantages of this position are many. To begin with, it favors laziness of mind. . . . The anti-Semite understands nothing about modern society. He would be incapable of conceiving of a constructive plan; his action cannot reach the level of the methodical; it remains on the ground of passion. To a long-term enterprise he prefers an explosion of rage analogous to the running amuck of the Malays. His intellectual activity is confined to *interpretation;* he seeks in historical events the signs of the presence of an evil power. Out of this spring those childish and elaborate fabrications which give him his resemblance to the extreme paranoiacs. . . . [But] above all this naive dualism is reassuring to the anti-Semite himself. If all he has to do is to remove Evil, that means that the Good is already *given*. He has no need to seek it in anguish, to invent it, to scrutinize it patiently when he has found it, to prove it in action, to verify it by its consequences, or, finally, to shoulder the responsibilities of the moral choice he has made.

It is not by chance, then, that the great outbursts of anti-Semitism (as indeed any other form of racism) conceal a basic optimism. The anti-Semite has cast his lot for Evil so as not to have to cast it for Good. The more one is absorbed in fighting Evil, the less one is tempted to place Good in question. One does not need to talk about it, yet it is always understood in the discourse of the anti-Semite and it remains understood in his thought. When he has fulfilled his mission as a holy destroyer, the Lost Paradise will reconstitute itself. For the moment so many tasks confront the anti-Semite that he does not have time to think . . . and each of his outbursts of rage is a pretext to avoid the anguishing search for the Good.[30]

I regard this kind of thinking as an example of "magicalism"—although psychiatrists, as Sartre himself suggests, might prefer to call it paranoia. There is something magical and paranoiac about believing that one need only eliminate evil to bring about good—which completely ignores the fact that the good society is the product of labor, the labor of the mind as well as of the body, to be achieved through the "sweat of the brow."

The contribution of Sartre's analysis is that it provides a hermeneutic for understanding such scandals as the use of others as sacrifice, the rationalization of evil through the myth of cosmic purpose, and the magical achievement of identity through kinship. Each of these phenomena constitutes a mode of bad faith which has its origin in the ontological constitution of consciousness as the effort both to-be-what-it-is-not and not-to-be-what-it-is. I would not pretend that Sartre's position is without difficulties. His analysis, for example, accounts for the possibility of anti-Semitism, but not for the translation from possibility to actuality. For this we must take into account such factors as functional rationality, kinship, etc. I wish only to stress that by considering the direction in which it points, and by thus taking seriously the structure of intentionality which accompanies Jew-hatred—indeed, hatred in general—we may hope to approach a more adequate understanding of the phenomenon of Auschwitz. I would even suggest the possibility that the hermeneutic I have developed out of Sartre might provide further insights when applied to the history of Christian anti-Semitism as developed by Rosemary Ruether.

IV

For Jews Auschwitz is the symbol of a continuing Holocaust. In recent times, the descendants of Auschwitz have watched their children offered to the slaughter-bench of history; at Munich, at Lod, at Kiryat-Shemona, and now Ma'alot. As I write these words, Israeli mothers are burying their children slaughtered at Ma'alot, and Israeli youth, out of a rage which knows no limit, cry out for revenge. That the spiritual reality of a community can be consumed by hatred as well as by flames is a lesson that history teaches only too well. The great tragedy of the modern period of Jewish suffering is that where the gas ovens failed to exterminate all traces of Jewish flesh, the Arab terrorists, together with the growing conspiracy of resentment against the existence of Israel, may yet succeed in the destruction of the Jewish spirit by breeding within Jews more hatred than they can reasonably be expected to endure. Then will the most poisonous fruits of kinship ties and tribalism come to light. But while this risk continues to haunt us, I will contend that the authentic Jewish response to catastrophe takes the form of both memory and witness. As Emil Fackenheim and Elie Wiesel have often reminded us, not to remember would be blasphemy, not to be a witness would be a betrayal. Memory must be, as Elie Wiesel urges, without hatred and rage, while witness, as Irving Greenberg and Arthur Waskow remind us, takes the form of action; both the universal action of love, charity, piety, creativity, and social reconstruction, and the uniquely Jewish action of stubborn midrashic commitment to remain a Jew.

The question raised by the Jewish response is, however, whether such an affirmation is still possible in a world which remains indifferent to Jewish survival, in which Jews are still allowed to be offered as a sacrifice on the slaughter-bench of history. Whether this scandal continues into the new era hopefully anticipated by the organizers of this Symposium will depend, I submit, not simply on Jewish willingness to remember and bear witness, but on the question whether, and to what extent, Christians are also prepared to remember and to bear witness. For Christians this will involve more than the task of seeking an accommodation with Judaism, more than finding new instruments of cooperation and tolerance. It will involve an openness to Judaism as a root source of Christianity; a willingness to listen to and learn from Judaism, and thus to abandon the tradition of "theological silence" which has characterized Christian-Jewish relations in the past. As the contemporary Lutheran theologian Hagen Staack writes, in his effort to identify the roots of anti-Semitism, "The object of the theological effort of the future will have to be not only the turning to the world, but also the return to Israel. Anti-Semitism through 'theological silence,' if maintained, will render Christian theology irrelevant to the future."[31] But, to echo Yosef Yerushalmi's eloquent *crie de coeur* in his response to Rosemary Ruether's paper, the breaking of that theological silence must involve more than new theological formulations. It must involve direct and immediate resistance to the institutionalization of functional rationality, a willingness to confront directly those economic and political Leviathans that have so ruthlessly co-opted the passions of race-hatred to serve the interests of power, and which helped bring the Jews from their alleged historic role of "suffering servants" to the gas chambers of Auschwitz.

PART IX

*Blacks and Jews:
Affinity and Confrontation
On Common Theological Themes*

Introduction

All three speakers in this section share an ambiguity with regard to its title. They see the tensions and similarities between the two communities in political and sociological, rather than religious and theological, terms. Apart from this shared ambivalence, however, there are marked differences in their perceptions of the tensions and common ground between Blacks and Jews in the United States today.

In the view of *Charles Long*, Jews and Blacks share a common minority status in U.S. history, but with a difference. By the time they became a minority in the West, Jews had an ancient religious and cultural tradition behind them. Their deep sense of identity generated in them both the capacity and the determination to maintain their integrity across centuries of defamation, discrimination, and persecution in the Christian West—a determination which in turn heightened the hostility toward them of the majority population. Blacks, on the other hand, were not only uprooted from their African culture, but because of their status as slaves found themselves forced into isolation in the United States, cut off from their roots and at the mercy of their White masters.

The roles which the images of Africa and Israel have played are also somewhat different. The land of Israel has been a symbol of "at-homeness" for Jews, representing a unique phenomenon in Western culture. Africa's role in the consciousness of the slaves in the United States is less clear. Yet there is evidence that even if North American Blacks were not able to preserve and integrate aspects of their African culture in their new existence, the memory of Africa has exerted an influence at the unconscious level. For a landless people (who, unlike the Native Americans, were not living in a land which had been taken from them, but had been violently separated from their land of origin), Africa provided a "revalorization of the land" which authenticated Black resistence. This, no doubt, accounts for the fact that most Black nationalistic movements have found their inspiration in Africa.

The United States represented a bizarre reality for the slaves. They had to cope, at one and the same time, with the shock of radical cultural uprooting, and the contradiction which their condition of slavery revealed in the newly discovered American culture. They had to come to terms with the negativity of the existence imposed on them by the white majority, and simultaneously oppose this negativity in order to survive spiritually and preserve their identity. The effort to transform their existence took place primarily at the level of religious consciousness, of which Long sees the phenomenon of the blues as one striking expression. From this effort was born the power to preserve their humanity, a process not unlike that experienced by the Jews of Europe.

The fact that Blacks and Jews share a history of exploitation and oppression is a common bond, but also gives rise to difficulties between them. Long raises the question whether at this time in history, precisely because of the common experience of oppression, each may expect too much of the other. What about the charge of Black anti-Semitism? Even if it is, to some extent, justified, Black anti-Semitism differs significantly from all other anti-Semitism. For Blacks in the United States never have been in a position of power, hence are unable to give legislative expression to any negative views they may hold. Nor is there for Long any anti-Judaism inherent in Black history or consciousness. Blacks have no anti-Jewish exegesis of the Hebrew Scriptures, which, on the contrary, appear to them as the prototype of their own experience. Black confrontation of Whites and Jews, then, takes place at the level of self-definition and survival, not of racial discrimination.

Paul Ritterband sees the common issues between Blacks and Jews even less in religious or theological terms than Charles Long. He attributes the current tensions between the two communities to the widely held, but mistaken, notion that those who suffer from the same oppressor are natural allies. Precisely the opposite tends to be the case; for each is too bruised to be haunted by the other's pain. We must take the sources of tension out of the ideological framework into which we have placed them, and put them back within the political arena where they belong.

In their common powerlessness, both Jews and Blacks have tried to appeal to the conscience of the world. Such an appeal is not only doomed to fall on deaf ears, but tends to produce a sense of moral righteousness in the supplicants, which can lead them to confuse political with moral issues. There have, indeed, been times when the alliance between Black and Jew worked— because both found themselves near or at the bottom of American society. Ritterband does not believe that the alliance was ever based on moral consensus, and suggests that "an effective, partial, and fragmentary alliance was overgeneralized into an eternal love affair." That the love affair was far from eternal became all too clear in the sixties, when the self-interests of the two groups came into conflict.

It is true that both Blacks and Jews have been the objects of oppression in American society; but the sources of oppression differed, as did their forms of expression. Racial and sexual stereotypes of Blacks and Jews were conceived in opposite terms. Blacks were part of American life, though inferior; Jews remained on the outside.

Why the present sense of mutual betrayal felt by both groups? Ritterband considers it unfounded, the result of a naive misreading of each other's situation. Blacks and Jews face different problems, which can readily make them into political adversaries, as was amply demonstrated by the New York teachers strike, the growing rift between Israel and the Third World, etc.

Failure to perceive this difference leaves no room for the moral ambiguity that has traditionally characterized Black-Jewish relationships. Each group feels isolated, each seeks to become part of the American mainstream. In this effort, periods of friendship have alternated with periods of distance and hostility. Each has fallen into the trap of moral self-righteousness with regard to the other. Yet, Ritterband believes, there remains a residue of goodwill on both sides, for Blacks and Jews alike continue to perceive their position in American society as precarious. The recognition that both are objects of discrimination is a sounder basis for a common bond than high-sounding moral preaching.

The third speaker on this panel, *Charles Silberman,* is in some agreement with Long and Ritterband, but also expresses crucial differences in perception. He considers the troubled relationship between Blacks and Jews in America as stemming from their common American background. "Blacks are Christian Americans, Jews are White Americans." Unlike Long, Silberman believes that Blacks, as Christians, share the heritage of the Teaching of Contempt; Jews, on the other hand, as Whites, share American racism. In both cases the prejudice is part of their American cultural heritage. While Blacks have been more vocal and public in their anti-Semitism, Jews have tended to be muted and private in their anti-Black feelings, hence attracting less attention to a phenomenon which is no less real than the anti-Jewish prejudice of Blacks. Recent historical events have further complicated the relationship between the two groups.

How, Silberman then asks, is this situation affected by the Holocaust? Addressing himself first to Blacks, he urges them to recognize that anti-Jewish rhetoric can all too easily be misused, leading to hatred and mass murder. He takes exception to Charles Long's belief that because Blacks hold no power, Black anti-Semitism differs in mind. After Auschwitz not even powerlessness can render anti-Semitism harmless.

Silberman's primary concern, however, is the Holocaust's lesson for Jews. He recalls Greenberg's statement that the model of the Holocaust makes a repetition more likely. Greenberg challenged Christians "to quarrel with the Gospels themselves for being a source of anti-Semitism." Silberman, for his part, challenges his fellow Jews to "quarrel" with the conscious and unconscious racism within themselves. For he believes that no White—neither Jew nor Gentile—can grow up in America without absorbing prejudice. What matters is not that we are prejudiced—we inevitably are—but that we act justly and decently despite our prejudice.

If a Holocaust were to occur in the United States today—and Silberman believes it could—he sees evidence that Blacks would be its victims as much as Jews. For as Abraham Heschel has pointed out, humiliation of another human being is no less a crime than outright murder. What this moment of history after Auschwitz demands of all, and of Jews in particular, is the determination to fight against the degradation of all human beings—above all of Blacks, who have been the object of degradation in American history more consistently than any other human group. In this challenge to his own community for self-purification and righteousness, Silberman reiterates in a different perspective what Greenberg sees as the chief counter-testimony to the Holocaust: bearing witness to the preciousness and uniqueness of every human being.

Blacks and Jews:
Affinity and Confrontation

CHARLES H. LONG

I take it that this section of the Symposium has been designed to raise certain theological and religious issues from the points of view of two historical minorities in the United States. I must at the outset express a demurrer about the assignment. The term "theological" troubles me, for I think it is a very special and precise mode of religious thinking that need not characterize all religious groups or forms of thinking. It seems to me to be a Christian mode of religious thinking which is related to certain cultural power motifs in the history of Western Christianity.

On Being a Minority

To the extent that minority status, by definition, implies a majority, everyone and every group may at one time or another experience minority status. In the case of Jews and Blacks, this status has been of such long standing in Western culture and the United States that a certain tradition and cultural style have come into being.

While both Jews and Blacks constitute the dominant minority traditions in the United States, their respective traditions are very different. In the case of the Jew we are dealing with a very old tradition, older than Western culture itself, and the roots of which lie in the ancient Near East. Its history was in process of formation long before it was known in the West as a minority tradition. Although ancient Israel may be seen as unique among the nations of the Near East, it yet knew long periods when it possessed the integrity that arises from self-determination.

This tradition first experienced minority status in the Eastern world through the hegemony of the Roman Empire, and subsequently through the inheritance of this empire by Christianity. The Christian hegemony differed from the Roman, for Christians used religious and theological meaning to justify the minority status of Jews.

Already the New Testament relegates the history of Israel to a first

379

stage of God's plan for human salvation—a stage that has been superseded by the coming of Jesus of Nazareth, who is called the Christ. Moreover, the sacred text of Christians carries on a constant polemic against Judaism. The polemic and tension are not occasioned only by the argument over the proper interpretation of texts; they also represent a certain animus against the very existence of a people, and, in some cases, can be seen as an example of the imperialism of language. For from a Christian point of view, Jews come to be known as people of the Old Testament, the people who rejected Jesus and stubbornly refused the salvation he offered.

The minority status of the Jew is so deeply woven into the early traditions of the Christian Western world that any examination of this issue touches the very roots of Western culture itself. This is a negative definition of the minority status of the Jew, from the point of view of the Christian West. The desire and insistence of Jews to maintain their religious and cultural integrity as a people constitute a positive understanding of their minority status. There are, thus, two issues at stake here: the capacity of the Jewish community in the West to maintain a distinctive stance, and the resulting hostility evoked by this stance in the majority population.

The minority status of the Blacks in the United States is a modern phenomenon, since America itself is a product of modernity. It is also true, however, that the hermeneutical justification for the negativity resulting from this minority status is of modern vintage. Blacks were brought to this country as African slaves, arriving for the first time in 1619. From that time until the abolition of the slave trade in the middle of the nineteenth century, millions of slaves were imported into the country. The most obvious minority status was that of being a Black slave in a country of whites who were free.

The slaves were systematically cut off from their older cultural forms; their only recourse was to accept the language and cultural forms of their owners. Acculturation of this kind created a complexity of meaning for the new country expressed during the history of their enslavement, and notions of political and religious freedom. The constant subversion of these notions as they related to the black man constitutes a datum of the Black's experience, as well as a general structure of the American republic.

Black traditions and styles of culture have been created from the forced isolation of the Blacks from the political, economic, and cultural resources of the United States. They are the results of certain survivals from Africa.

Land and People

Israel

Jewish existence has always been related to the land of Israel—the ancient Israel as a location in time and space, as a place "to be at home." Thus the meaning of Israel has had both a locative and a utopian meaning for Jews. It was and is both an actual place and a religious datum that guided Jewish existence when Jews were a landless people, in a *u-topia,* "no place."

But not to be in Israel, that is, to be in a *u-topia,* did in fact mean to be in some place, in many places, all over the world. So there are Jewish traditions that express the sense of Jewishness in the several worlds of the Diaspora. To the extent that one can speak of eschatological movements in the Jewish tradition, they differ from Christian forms of eschatology through their insistence on the meaning of Israel as a historical-geographical, both locative and utopian, rather than a strictly otherwordly datum.

The land Israel has been for Jewish existence a mode of orientation; the persistence of this fact in Jewish experience cannot be overlooked. Even when Jews thought that they could simply be citizens of Western nation-states, the orientation toward the land of Israel remained a structure of Jewish existence. This appears as a strange phenomenon in modern Western culture; except for patriotic nationalism the religious meaning of a land has almost vanished from Western consciousness.

Hitler and Auschwitz made it clear that this Jewish orientation toward the land was, in fact, a necessity. This barbaric act of a so-called civilized Western country showed vividly that Jewish existence in the modern world is inextricably tied up with Israel, as both a locative and a utopian datum.

Africa as Historical Reality and Religious Image

It is a historical fact that the existence of the Black communities in the United States is due to the slave trade of numerous European countries from the seventeenth to the nineteenth century (slaves were being illegally smuggled into the United States as late as the 1880s). The issue of the persistence of African elements in the Black community is hotly debated. On the one hand, we have the positions of E. Franklin Frazier and W. E. B. Du Bois, emphasizing the lack of any significant elements of Africanism in America. Melville Herskovits at one time held the same position, but reversed it in *The Myth of the Negro Past*

(Boston, 1958), where he places a greater emphasis on the persistence of African elements among the descendants of slaves in North America.

One of the elements in this discussion is related to the comparative level of the studies. Invariably, the norm for comparison was the Black communities in the Atlantic islands, and in South America. In the latter the African elements are very distinctive, and, in the case of Brazil, Africans have gone back and forth between Africa and Brazil. African languages are still spoken by Blacks in Brazil. Indeed, Pierre Verger first became interested in Yoruba religion when he saw it being practiced in South America.

It is obvious that nothing of this sort has existed in the United States. The slave system of the United States systematically broke down the linguistic and cultural pattern of the slaves. Yet even a protagonist for the loss of all Africanisms, such as E. Franklin Frazier, acknowledges the persistence of "shout songs," African rhythm, and dance in American culture. Frazier and Du Bois, while acknowledging such elements, did not see them as possessing ultimate significance, for in their view these forms did not play an important role in the social cohesion of the Black community.

Without resolving this discussion, another issue must be raised here. The persistence of elements of what some anthropologists have called "soft culture" means that, even given the systematic breakdown of African cultural forms in the history of North America slavery, the slaves did not confront America with a religious tabula rasa. If the content of culture did not survive, a characteristic mode of orienting and perceiving reality has probably persisted. We know, for example, that a great majority of the slaves came from West Africa, and we also know from the studies of Daryll Forde that West Africa is a cultural as well as a geographical unit. Underlying the empirical diversity of languages, religions, and social form there is, according to Forde, a structural unity discernible. With the breakdown of the empirical forms of language and religion as determinants for the social group, this persisting structural mode and their common situation as slaves in America may explain the persistence of an African style among the descendants of the Africans.

In addition to this, in the accounts of slaves and their owners we read of "meetings" which took place secretly in the woods. It is obvious that these "meetings" were not the practice of the masters' religion. They were related to what the slaves themselves called "conjuring." The connotation reminds one of Voodoo rites in Haiti.

Added to this is the precise manner in which, by being a slave, a Black man, one was isolated from any self-determined legitimacy in the society of which one was a part, and was recognized by one's physiological characteristics. This constituted a complex of experience revolving around the relationship between one's physical being and one's origins. Even if, therefore, they had no conscious memory of Africa, the image of Africa played an enormous part in the religion of the Blacks. The image of Africa, related to historical beginnings, has been one of the primordial religious images and of great significance. It constitutes the religious revalorization of the land, a place where the natural and ordinary gestures of the Blacks were and could be authenticated. In this connection, one can trace almost every nationalistic movement among the Blacks and find Africa to be the dominating and guiding image. Even among religious groups not strongly nationalistic, the image of Africa or Ethiopia still has relevance. This is present in such diverse figures as Richard Allen, who organized the African Methodist Episcopal Church in the early nineteenth century, through Martin Delaney in the late nineteenth century, in Marcus Garvey's "back to Africa movement" of the immediate post–World War I period, and finally is taken up again among Black leaders of our own time.

The image of Africa as it appears in Black religion is unique, for the Black community in America is a landless people. Unlike the American Indians, the land was not taken from Blacks, and unlike the Black Africans in South Africa or Rhodesia, their land is not occupied by groups whom they consider aliens. Their image of the land points to the religious meaning of land even in the absence of these forms of authentication. It thus emerges as an image which is always invested with historical and religious possibilities.

The Involuntary Presence

Implied in the discussion concerning the land and the physiological characteristics of the Blacks is the significance attributed to their meaning in America. Their stance has, on the one hand, been necessitated by historical conditions, and on the other, been grasped as creative possibility. From the very beginning, their presence in the country has been involuntary; they were brought to America in chains, and this country has attempted to keep Blacks in this condition in one way or another. Their very presence as *human beings* in the United States has always constituted a threat to the majority population. From the point of view of the majority population, the Black has been simply and purely a legal person, first as a slave defined in terms of property, and then, after the abolition of chattel property, as a citizen who had to seek legal redress before he could use the common facilities of the country—water fountains, public accommodations, restaurants, schools, etc. There is no need to repeat this history, it is well known; the point I wish to make is more subtle than these special issues, important as they may be.

In addition to the image and historical reality of Africa, one must add, as another persisting datum, the involuntary presence and orientation as a religious meaning. I have stated elsewhere the importance of the involuntary structure of the religious consciousness in terms of oppugnancy. In the case of the slaves, America presented a bizarre reality, not simply because of the strangeness occasioned by a radical change of status and culture, but equally because their presence as slaves pointed to a radical contradiction within the dominant culture itself. The impact of America was a discovery, but one had little ability to move from the bizarre reality of that discovery to the level of general social rules of conduct, as happens in the case of other communities presented with an ultimate discovery. In addition to this, to normalize the condition of slavery would be to deny the slave's existence as a human being.

The slave had to come to terms with the opaqueness of his condition and at the same time oppose it. He had to experience the truth of his negativity and at the same time transform and create *an-other* reality. Given the limitations imposed upon him, he created at the level of his religious consciousness. Not only did this transformation produce new cultural forms, but its significance must be understood from the point of view of the creativity of the transforming process itself.

A musical phenomenon, the blues, is one expression of this same consciousness. What is portrayed here is a religious consciousness that has experienced the "hardness" of life, whether the form of that reality be the slave system, God, or simply life itself. It is from such a consciousness that the power to resist and yet maintain one's humanity has emerged. Although the worship and religious life of Blacks have often been referred to as forms of escapism, one must remember that there has always been an integral relationship between the "hardness" of life and the ecstasy of religious worship. It is, in my opinion, an example of what Gaston Bachelard described in Hegelian language as the lithic imagination. Bachelard referred to the imaginary structure of consciousness that arises in relationship to the natural form of the stone, and the manner in which the volitional character of human consciousness is related to this imaginary form. The Black community in America has confronted the reality of the historical situation as immutable, impenetrable, yet this experience has not produced passivity. It has, rather, found expression as forms of the involuntary and transformative nature of the religious consciousness. Let me illustrate this point by returning to the meaning of the image and historical reality of Africa.

Over and over again this image has ebbed and flowed in the Black religious consciousness. It has found expression in music, dance, and political theorizing. There has been an equally persistent war against this image in the religion of Blacks. This war against the image of Africa and Blackness can be seen in the political and social movements connected with the stratagems of segregation and integration.

The fact that Jews never gave up their traditions for the Christian Western tradition is the basis for their involuntary presence in the West. There were indeed periods of apostasy, conversion, assimilation, and accommodation, but ever since the Diaspora there have always been numerous Jewish communities in the Western world.

If Jews thought they could be simply like others, some form of persecution always reminded them of their distinctiveness vis-à-vis the Christian and secular Western traditions: the pogroms of the Middle Ages, the Dreyfus affair, and finally Nazi Germany.

The Convergence of Traditions

Because I have not discussed the traditions of Blacks as they confront Jews I have tended to imply that Blacks are not to be included when I speak of the Christian West. I have done this in a somewhat rhetorical form. For if the Christian West represents a particular historical attitude toward the Jews, an attitude buttressed by power of execution, then the Blacks are on the periphery of such a tradition. Indeed, many Christian Europeans have often taken, for very different reasons, an identical stance towards Blacks and Jews.

Several questions must now be raised: Do Blacks expect too much of Jews, given Jewish history and the Holocaust? Do Jews expect too much of Blacks, given the fact that we have consciously and systematically been exploited in this country?

If there is Black anti-Semitism, it is of a very different kind than the anti-Semitism of the majority population. For it is set within a context that Jews should understand: the context of survival. Blacks have never had the power to rule, much less exterminate, anyone except themselves.

Blacks possess no dramatic history or hallowed texts; they have no ambivalent feeling about the Hebrew Scriptures as the precursor of the final revelation in Jesus Christ. The Scriptures are more often used as an archetype of their vicissitudes, and not as a history which has been overcome. We are a people who continue to struggle within and without for the authenticity of who and what we are, and it is on this level that we confront both Whites and Jews. As modern people in the process of defining our integrity, who must exert our freedom as we see fit. We will not be silenced by cries of anti-Semitism or Black racism. Such cries are ineffectual, since to make sense, they would have to imply a power that Blacks do not have or have never possessed in modern times, neither in Africa nor in the United States.

It is time for a new conversation between Blacks and Jews in America. This conversation must be based on history, and it must be open-ended. Both groups must allow the truth to be told. Jews and Blacks should commit themselves to something beyond name-calling, something beyond American theological liberalism. For we too have suffered—not quite as long, but probably as intensely. For the novelty of America had to be borne intensely, and the demystification of America could not take place over centuries, but happened in a short time; and the legal scholars, the immigrants, the general American public, saw us only as slaves, never as people of any account.

Conscience and Politics

PAUL RITTERBAND

The issues joining together Blacks and Jews are only very marginally theological. There may be a religious component in their relationship, but it is clearly not theological. The current problematic relationship between Blacks and Jews is not a function of theological imagery or religious imagination. It is based, rather, upon a mistaken presumed relationship between the two peoples, on the notion that those who suffer by the hands of the same tormentors are natural allies and have a common perspective on the world. This presumption owes more to rationalistic liberalism than to prophetic conscience. The partial communality of fate is precisely, in part, the root of current tensions between the two groups. Neither group can afford the *beau geste*. Both have been too bruised to be obsessed with the pain of the other.

There have been times when Jews and Blacks were allies, and other times when they were antagonists. Currently, the course of events has placed significant numbers of Blacks and Jews on opposite sides of the fence. In the course of political affairs this is natural and to be expected. The current tensions become more of a problem than they need be when each group is seen as disembodied soul and conscience, when ideology, rooted in and reflecting social arrangements, is misperceived and converted into moral pronouncement. The interests of both Blacks and Jews would be better served if the issues over which they are contending could be placed back into the political arena where they belong, and taken out of the hands of moral absolutists.

Neither Jews nor Blacks as groups have shown very much talent for democratic rough-and-tumble politics. There is little in the history and tradition of either group which would have trained it to be competent in the political game as it is actually played. Both groups, with fresh memories of political powerlessness, have conducted their "external affairs" through intermediaries and intercessors. Viewing themselves and perceived also by others as supplicants, they have appealed to the conscience of America or the world. The appeal to conscience gives one a sense of virtue, but in most instances turns out to be ineffective. Paradoxically, there are times when conscience destroys that which it

would build—when trivial issues are raised to the level of moral utli-
mates precluding negotiation and compromise. At that point moral
purism becomes a luxury fit only for the powerful.

The hard fact, which has been the core of the Black-Jewish alliance
when it has functioned, is that both groups are at the bottom of the
American ethnic totem pole—Blacks at the very bottom, and Jews just
slightly above them. When exclusion has been the major issue on the
public agenda, Blacks and Jews have cooperated in developing antidis-
crimination legislation, briefing the courts, and conducting public-
relations campaigns. At times this alliance, joined by the labor movement, big-city Democratic party organizations, and other groups in
American society, has been remarkably successful in achieving its
aims. The mistake we have made, however, is to assume that cooperation in this area was based upon an ultimate moral consensus and an
absolute identity of interests. An effective, partial and fragmentary alliance was overgeneralized into an eternal love affair.

The congruence of interests on one level is counterbalanced by a dis-
similarity of interests on other levels. Within the American cultural tradition, Blacks and Jews are the objects of insult and opprobrium, but
the sources and expression of these are very different. In American racial stereotypes, Blacks are big, strong, and dumb; Jews are little,
weak, and wily. The sexual imagery which weaves through American
culture portrays Blacks as rapists and Jews as seducers. Blacks are cau-
tioned to stay in their place; Jews are told that they have no place.
Though socially excluded, Blacks are culturally integrated into American life, albeit in positions which demean their humanity. Jews, by
contrast, remain exotic, in significant part outside of the American cultural consensus.

Recent events have tended to bring to the fore the differences between the two groups, and it is only our historical naiveté and excessive moralism which have led to the sense of pain and betrayal felt by
both. Affirmative action, the relationship between Israel and the Third
World, specific events, such as the New York City teachers strike,
among other issues, have tended to underscore the fact that aside from
a common history of suffering and debasement, the issues facing the
two groups are largely different, and the solutions called for will often
make them political antagonists, though not necessarily enemies. What
we are seeing today is partially a recapitulation of past events in which
Blacks and Jews took opposing positions, each based upon the perceived interests of their own group. For purposes of illustration, let us
look at two instances of prior conflict, one dealing with international
issues, the other purely domestic.

Beginning in the 1880s Congress passed a series of bills designed to restrict immigration to those nationalities which were viewed as most desirable. The Chinese were the first group to feel the sting of a racially oriented immigration policy. During the next forty years many bills were proposed, reaching their climax in the immigration acts of the 1920s, which were in force until the immigration act of 1965. The point of similarity among all of these bills was that eligibility for immigration was to be based upon "national origins," which was a euphemism for the then current notions of race. From 1890 until America entered World War I, over 17,000,000 immigrants (mostly Europeans) entered the United States. In 1905, the year of the abortive Russian Revolution, 1,026,499 immigrants entered the United States. The flow of immigrants from the turn of the century through the World War I period came largely from southern and eastern Europe. It was this immigration which established the demographic base for the American Jewish community. After World War I, Europe was still in turmoil. Pogroms were staged in the Ukraine. The governments of the newly established nation-states increased the pressures on their ethnic minorities (including Jews). The economic and political situations became increasingly intolerable. In light of the events in Europe, the American Jewish leadership, in the main, sought to maintain the free flow of immigration.

The proponents of restrictive immigration policy included American nativists and racists and at least some of the leadership of the Black community. James Weldon Johnson, secretary of the NAACP in 1919, saw the Jewish immigrants entering the country as competitors for the moral support and concern which the Black man needed. Some other Blacks opposed Jewish immigration on the grounds that the Jews were radicals, Bolsheviks, and subversives. Interestingly enough, support for the Jews came from the Black political left, most particularly A. Philip Randolph. Jews and Blacks active in the labor movement supported one another's issues—Jews supporting anti-lynching legislation and Blacks supporting open immigration. Although the Black-Jewish-Left alliance failed in its immediate aims, it did forge bonds which remain vital to this very day. While the Black New Left (like the New Left generally) became increasingly hostile to Jews and Jewish interests, those Blacks and Jews whose political home was in the old Socialist party and the League for Industrial Democracy continued to be supportive of one another's interests.

During the 1930s another event occurred which prefigured current tensions. Harlem had been a Jewish neighborhood, one of the way stations out of the poverty of the first settlement on the Lower East Side.

By the late 1920s and early 1930s Harlem increasingly became popu-
lated by Blacks, while many of the institutions in the area remained
owned or staffed by Jews. Generally, families and individuals are more
mobile geographically than institutions and businesses. Harlem hospi-
tal was one such institution which had an increasingly Black clientele
and a Jewish medical staff. This was a period in which both Jews and
Blacks had great difficulty in securing entrance to medical schools, and
in obtaining staff appointments in hospitals. The NAACP and a Black
physicians' group pressed for the appointment of more Black physicians to the staff. Though the language used was different, the issues
raised were essentially the same as those which arose almost forty
years later in the community-control controversy and as part of government affirmative-action programs. The dispute was finally resolved by
Mayor Jimmie Walker, in a resolution which called for the dismissal of
many of the Jewish physicians and their replacement by Black physicians. However, this resolution of the immediate problem did not resolve the long-term issues of Blacks and Jews facing restricted opportunities and fated to compete with one another for those few positions
which were allotted to them.

We are distressed by these and similar events insofar as we assume
an identity of interests and/or moral perspectives which never was and
is not there now. No room is left for the moral ambivalence which, in
fact, is the leitmotif of Black-Jewish relations. Each group, feeling isolated from the American mainstream while painfully eager to enter
American society, has alternately identified with and distanced itself
from the other. We have used one another as points of comparison, as
moral test cases, complicating our relationships and making it difficult
to be honest with ourselves and one another. Jews have been pointed to
by Black spokesmen as objects of emulation and condemnation, often
for the same presumed attributes. Marcus Garvey, who was called the
Black Moses, both praised and attacked Jews for their presumed solidarity and ethnic self-consciousness. Jews have made moral capital of
the brotherhood in death of Schwerner, Goodman, and Chaney, reminding Blacks of how much we have suffered in their cause. Neither
of us is entitled to self-righteousness.

As a Jew, I am only peripherally concerned with Black anti-Semitism in and of itself. I take it as a serious threat insofar as it might disin-
hibit mainstream White America, and make possible the uttering of
that which has been unutterable in the wake of Auschwitz. I know that
Blacks did not contribute to the "Final Solution," and I have no fear
that they could do so now even if they wanted to. When political anti-

Semitism was aroused in the Black community during the sixties, my special concern was the absence of anti-anti-Semitism in the bosom of the liberal community, that community in which Jews have placed too much faith during the last century and a half. However, given the fragility of our civilization and the ease with which anti-Semitism is communicated, I will fight political anti-Semitism from whatever quarter it comes, whether from Blacks or Whites.

In the midst of recent and current conflicts, there is an important residue of goodwill for one another in both the Black and Jewish communities. Right after the New York City teachers strike, the Harris organization polled New Yorkers on their positions on the issues. As we all know, Blacks and Jews took diametrically opposed positions, and there was deep bitterness between the two groups. Interestingly enough, however, Blacks and Jews, uniquely among the various ethnic groups in New York City, saw one another as objects of discrimination by the larger American soceity. There was a common-sensical articulation by the ordinary folk of the feeling that neither Jews nor Blacks had really made it in American society. I would rather build our future relationship on that folk empiricism, eschewing special moral claims on one another. Let the White Man's Burden be carried by others.

Response to Charles Long

CHARLES E. SILBERMAN

I share Professor Long's demurrer about the way in which the topic has been formulated. It seems to me that sociological categories are more relevant than theological ones in discussing the complex and often crippled relations between Blacks and Jews in the United States.

That the relationship between these two minority groups has been troubled and problematical as often as smooth and friendly can hardly be doubted. Thirty years ago, for example, in the introduction to a volume analyzing the reactions of the Negro press to Hitler and the rise of Nazism, the late Ralph Bunche wrote, "It is common knowledge that many members of the Negro and Jewish communities of the country share mutual dislike, scorn, and mistrust."[1]

While there are a variety of reasons for this mutual dislike and mistrust, the overriding reason is the American background that both Jews and Blacks share. Blacks are Christian Americans; Jews are White Americans. Black anti-Semitism stems largely from that fact that as Christian Americans, Blacks have imbibed the anti-Semitism that is part of that heritage. The parallel phenomenon, which for want of a better term I call Jewish anti-Negroism, stems predominantly from the fact that as White Americans, Jews have imbibed the racism that is part of that tradition.

One of the clearest illustrations of the degree to which Black anti-Semitism grows out of Black Americans' Christian heritage comes from Richard Wright's autobiographical account of his childhood in the South, *Black Boy*.[2] "All of us black people who lived in the neighborhood hated Jews," the great Black novelist and essayist recalls,

> not because they exploited us, but because we had been taught at home and in Sunday school that Jews were "Christ killers." With the Jews thus singled out for us, we made them fair game for ridicule.
>
> We black children—seven, eight, and nine years of age—used to run to the Jew's store and shout: . . .
>
> Jew, Jew,
Two for five,
That's what keeps
Jew alive.

Or we would chant:

Bloody Christ killers
Never trust a Jew
Bloody Christ killers
What won't a Jew do? . . .

There were many more folk ditties, some mean, others filthy, all of them cruel. No one ever thought of questioning our right to do this; our mothers and parents generally approved, either actively or passively. *To hold an attitude of antagonism or distrust toward Jews was bred in us from childhood; it was not merely racial prejudice, it was a part of our cultural heritage.* [Emphasis added]

The "Jew's store" that Wright describes was a tiny grocery store whose proprietors were hardly more affluent than the Black customers they served. The anti-Semitism Wright describes clearly has nothing to do with powerlessness or oppression.

By the same token, and for much the same kinds of reasons, prejudice against Blacks is part of the cultural heritage of American Jews. In his history of American Jews during the colonial period, Jacob Rader Marcus concludes that "as far as can be determined . . . Jews were no different from non Jews in their treatment of Negroes."[3] Before the Civil War, as Bertram Korn has described in great detail,[4] Jews could be found on all sides of the slavery issue. Some Jews were slave owners, or slave traders, or apologists and polemicists for the cause of slavery; other Jews were active and ardent abolitionists, working and writing on behalf of the abolitionist cause. The complexity of Black-Jewish relationships since then is described sensitively and in detail by Robert G. Weisbord and Arthur Stein in their volume, *Bittersweet Encounter.*[5]

Some of the confusion that has surrounded Black-Jewish relationships over the last half century is the result of a lack of symmetry in the relationships between the two groups. Expressions of Black anti-Semitism have been public and vocal—in the Negro press, and on the part of Black writers and political spokesmen. (This is not to suggest that all, or even most, Black spokesmen have been anti-Semitic. The contrary is true, and major Black writers and leaders, e.g., Claude McKay, Adam Clayton Powell, Roy Wilkins, A. Philip Randolph, Bayard Rustin, and Whitney Young, among others, have actively opposed anti-Semitism in the Black community.) On the Jewish side, by contrast, the public posture has been consistently and uniformly friendly and favorable to Black aspirations; while pervasive anti-Negroism has been private rather than public. The result has been that Black anti-Semitism has received far more attention than Jewish anti-Negroism.

Tensions between the two groups have been exacerbated and complicated in recent years by a series of historical accidents.

1. Because Jews have tended to be more mobile geographically than other ethnic groups, areas of Black residence have tended disproportionately to be areas formerly occupied by Jews. While Jews left these neighborhoods as residents, they often remained as property-owners and storekeepers. Harlem is the prototype of this pheonomenon. As a result, Blacks and Jews have confronted one another in ways that have reinforced the negative stereotypes that each has had of the other.

2. Somewhat the same phenomenon has occurred in occupational terms. Blacks have tended to choose occupational lines—e.g., teaching, social work—that Jews had chosen as their route to upward mobility a generation earlier. The result has been tension and conflict over the criteria for appointment and promotion, and over the question of who determines those criteria. The complaints that Blacks and Puerto Ricans have voiced in recent years about the New York City Board of Examiners and its competitive examinations for teachers and administrators are remarkably similar to the complaints that Jews voiced a generation or so ago, when they were struggling to enter and acquire administrative positions in a system then dominated by Irish Catholics.

3. Tensions have been exacerbated still more in recent years as the Third World anti-Zionist rhetoric of Black nationalists has been joined to the traditional folk anti-Semitism of Blacks.

4. Tensions and misunderstandings have been compounded, moreover, by fundamental cultural differences in the role of language and rhetoric. "In white America, the printed word—the literary tradition—and its attendant values are revered," Charles Keil writes. "In the Negro community, more power resides in the spoken word and oral tradition—good talkers abound and the best gain power and prestige, but good writers are scarce. . . . Real rhetoric and ritual, the pattern and form, heart and soul of Negro expression are largely unknown in white America. Indeed, the words themselves have taken on decidedly negative connotations." Or as Roger D. Abrahams puts it, "One of the aspects of lower class Negro life as an oral culture which is least understood by middle class society is the way in which everyday life is suffused with play. In an environment such as the ghetto's, *gaming* or the art of the *put-on* suffuses interpersonal relations. Thus all public activities have a tendency to gravitate toward performances."[6]

Since Jews come from a preeminently literary culture, one which inculcates reverence for the word, Blacks are often surprised by the seriousness and passion with which Jews respond to Black verbal play. The misunderstanding is enhanced by the two groups' different perceptions of the American Jews' status in American society. Blacks see Jews as having "made it" in American society; Jews see themselves as weak and vulnerable, with their sense of vulnerability having been exacerbated by the precariousness of Israel's political and military position.

How does the Holocaust bear on all this?

For Blacks, it should be clear that anti-Semitism is unacceptable, whether as a political strategy or merely a rhetorical device. If this retrospective view of Auschwitz and the Holocaust does nothing else, it should make clear, beyond any doubt, that anti-Semitism is not simply an expression of prejudice. Because of the millennia of hatred and destructiveness to which anti-Semitism is linked, and because of the results of anti-Semitism in our own time, any use of anti-Semitism goes beyond shouting "Fire" in a crowded theater; it runs the danger of lighting the fire itself.

In this context, therefore, I respectfully request Professor Long to withdraw his assertion that Blacks "will not be silenced by cries of anti-Semitism or Black racism. Such cries are ineffectual, since to make sense, they would have to imply a power that Blacks do not have or have never possessed in modern times." After Auschwitz, powerlessness is no defense against the charge of anti-Semitism; to imply that Black powerlessness justifies Black anti-Semitism after Auschwitz seems to me to deny the lessons of history, and to reject the limitations on human conduct that grow out of the Judeo-Christian tradition.

My main interest, however, is in what the Holocaust teaches Jews, rather than what it teaches Blacks. As Irving Greenberg said in his opening paper at this Conference, "The model of the Holocaust makes a repetition the more likely. A limit was broken, a control is gone." Greenberg went on to urge Christians "to quarrel with the Gospels themselves for being a source of anti-Semitism," or else face "the continual temptation to participate in or pave the way for genocide."

In the time remaining to me, I should like to call upon my fellow Jews to quarrel with the conscious—and equally important, the unconscious—racial prejudice that is within ourselves. It is impossible for anyone with a white skin, Jew or Gentile, to grow up in the United States without absorbing and incorporating a significant residue of prejudice. The test of decency and morality is not whether we are prejudiced, but whether we summon the role and intellect to rise above our prejudices, to act decently and justly despite our prejudices.

In speaking about the Holocaust, moreover, it is important to recognize that if genocide is possible in the United States—the lesson of the Holocaust is that it is always possible—Blacks are as likely as Jews to be the victims.

There is, indeed, a precedent of sorts. For a third of a century after the Civil War, Blacks made substantial progress in the South. Around the turn of the century, Whites committed political and spiritual genocide against Black Americans—and I do not use the term loosely. I do not think such a complete reversal is likely again, but it *is* possible. And a considerable segment of Black opinion feels that it is not only possible, but even likely.[7]

What does this moment require of us? The answer was given eleven years ago by Abraham Joshua Heschel, the man whose presence here we miss most—the man whose untimely death has left an almost unbearable void in Jewish (and indeed Christian) life. "There is a form of oppression which is more painful and more scathing than physical injury or economic privation," Rabbi Heschel told the first—and last— National Conference on Religion and Race. "It is public humiliation . . ."

> The crime of murder is tangible and punishable by law. The sin of insult is imponderable, invisible. . . . In the Hebrew language one word denotes both crimes. Bloodshed is the word that denotes both murder and humiliation. . . . It is better, the Talmud insists, to throw oneself into a burning furnace than to humiliate a human being publicly. . . .
>
> By negligence and silence we have all become accessory before the God of mercy to the injustice committed against Negroes by men of our nation. Our derelictions are many. We have failed to demand, to insist, to challenge, to chastise. . . . Most of us are content to delegate the problem to the courts, as if justice were a matter for professionals or specialists. But to do justice is what God demands of every man: it is the supreme commandment, and one that cannot be fulfilled vicariously. . . .
>
> There is an evil which most of us condone and are even guilty of: indifference to evil. We remain neutral, impartial, and not easily moved by the wrongs done unto other people. Indifference to evil is more insidious than evil itself; it is more universal, more contagious, more dangerous. . . . - The prophets' great contribution to humanity was the discovery of the evil of indifference. One may be decent and sinister, pious and sinful. . . .
>
> We must act even when inclination and vested interest should militate against equality. . . . The plight of the Negro must become our most im-

portant concern. . . . Our concern must be expressed not symbolically, but literally; not only publicly, but also privately; not only occasionally, but also regularly. What we need is the involvement of everyone of us as individuals.[8]

As Abraham Heschel remarked on another occasion, "At this moment we find ourselves in an historic situation which cries for understanding as well as for participation on all levels of existence. There is no excuse for abstention or evasion."

PART X

Art and Culture
after the Holocaust

Introduction

This lecture was given to a capacity audience the opening night of the Symposium. It is placed at the end of the volume, rather than at the beginning, as a reminder to us that the Holocaust ultimately defies all intellectual reflection and analysis. When much has been said, we are still left with the unspeakable.

Elie Wiesel was introduced by Rabbi Balfour Brickner, who said: "In biblical days leaders were sometimes determined by their physical size. Saul, for example, was chosen as leader of Israel because he stood physically head and shoulders above the rest of the community. If today that criterion for leadership still applied, Elie Wiesel would not qualify. He is a man of average height and physical stature. But physical qualifications no longer determine leadership. Rather, it is breadth and reach and mind, the scope of a person's spirit, of one's heart, that count. Measured by such standards, Elie Wiesel is a leader of and a leader for humanity. He has had the courage, and has the courage and the capacity, to share his soul with the world, and in the process to remind the world that it too has a soul. Through his writings, he has made each of us painfully conscious of the depths to which we as individuals and as a society can sink, the hopes to which we can turn. He has shown us our brutality and our possibilities. He has shown us our failures. He has shown us our divine likeness. He has shown us our pain. He has shown us our promise. He has taken us from inner death to life. He has passed through the night of despair and disillusion to the dawn of continuation. He has become a legend in our time. He has stood as a beggar in Jerusalem. He has given voice to the Jews of silence, and he has led one generation after another to a revival of their own faith at a time when the word 'faith' has become almost a snide anachronism. By his pen and by his presence, he has set our souls on fire, even leading some of us to a renewal of the oath of life's affirmation."

Art and Culture after the Holocaust

ELIE WIESEL

Let us tell tales. Let us tell tales—all the rest can wait, all the rest must wait. Let us tell tales—that is our primary obligation. Commentaries will have to come later, lest they replace or becloud what they mean to reveal.

Tales of children so wise and so old. Tales of old men mute with fear. Tales of victims welcoming death as an old acquaintance. Tales that bring man close to the abyss and beyond—and others that lift him up to heaven and beyond. Tales of despair, tales of longing. Tales of immense flames reaching out to the sky, tales of night consuming life and hope and eternity.

Let us tell tales so as to remember how vulnerable man is when faced with overwhelming evil. Let us tell tales so as not to allow the executioner to have the last word. The last word belongs to the victim. It is up to the witness to capture it, shape it, transmit it and still keep it as a secret, and then communicate that secret to others.

The difficulty lies in the transmission. Not all tales can be, should be, communicated in language. Some, according to Rebbe Menachem Mendel of Kotzk, can be transmitted only in silence, and others, more profound, not even in silence. What, then, is one to do? What does one do with one's secret and one's silence? That is the question of questions that most writers had to confront when they decided to turn the fire of the Holocaust into words.

Do you remember the story told by the great Russian poetess Anna Akhmatova? During the Stalin era she came and stood in line day after day at the entrance of the Lublianka prison with a package for her son. Hundreds of women were there waiting their turn. Every one had someone inside: husband, brother, son, father. One morning an old woman turned to Anna Akhmatova and said: "Are you Akhmatova the poetess?" "Yes." "Do you think that one day you will be able to tell *this* story?" Anna Akhmatova remained silent for a moment. Then she mustered her strength and said: "Yes, I will try." The old woman looked at her intensely, as though she weighed the answer, then for the first time a smile appeared on her tired, bloodless face.

After the war, every survivor was asked the same question by the dead: Will you be able to tell *our* tale? Now we know the answer: no. Their tale cannot be told—and never will be. Those who spoke were not heard; the story you heard was not the story they had told.

A certain R. Faurisson, professor of humanities at the Sorbonne, wrote a letter to Dr. Aryeh Kubovy, who years earlier had served as head of the Yad Vashem documentation center in Jerusalem. The letter was dated April 3, 1974—which explains why Dr. Kubovy did not receive it: he had died more than a decade ago. Professor Faurisson did not know that. Nor did he know some other things—which was the reason for his letter in the first place. The letter reads as follows:

> Dear Sir: Would you allow me to ask you to give me your personal feeling regarding a delicate subject; it is related to contemporary history. Do you think that the gas chambers were myth or reality? Could you give me your opinion on the value one should attribute to the Gerstein document, to the Hoess confession, and to the Nyiszly testimony? And in general: how important are all the documents written and published about Auschwitz, the Cyklon-B, night and fog, and the Final Solution? I was unable, until now, to discover reliable photographs of the gas chambers. . . .

Thus, in the year 29 of our era, one generation after the event, there is a professor of humanities who does not know—who wishes to know—who asks for proof . . . that Auschwitz indeed existed, and that the Final Solution was not a madman's dream but official policy enacted and implemented by hundreds of thousands of men and women. . . .

But then—it is not his fault, not entirely. A German publisher recently issued a pamphlet called *The Truth about Auschwitz* written by a former SS officer. He had served in Auschwitz and does not recall having seen gas chambers or mass killings; the chimneys there were those of the bakery, according to him.

On another level a famous playright, Peter Weiss, has written a play about Auschwitz and simply omitted the word "Jew"—as though there had been no Jews in Auschwitz. Auschwitz was *judenrein*.

On the twentieth anniversary of the liberation of the death camp, the Polish government refused Jewish representatives permission to speak and say Kaddish.

In Israel, a young woman wrote an article boasting that she has never read any novels about the Holocaust—and that they are not good literature anyway.

In the United States, an official of a Jewish news agency published an "analysis" that called for putting an end to Holocaust literature.

Among his arguments: Jews were not the only victims—so why speak of Jews? Furthermore, he added: after all, there was music even in Auschwitz. . . . Which means: why complain, why lament?

Recently a novelist suggested to the *New York Times* to do a piece for the anniversary of the Warsaw Ghetto uprising, and was told: no, thank you, we have too many anniversaries on the agenda.

The result: there is a Hitler wave in Germany. Warsaw's city council plans to demolish the remains of the ghetto wall and build a kindergarten in its place. In France, the most popular books and movies are about killers and collaborators—and not about their victims. In Moscow, Tass compares Dayan to Eichmann—not in order to emphasize the magnitude of Dayan's guilt, but to diminish that of Eichmann.

Thus, as one who has tried for some twenty-five years to speak on the subject, I feel I must confess to a sense of defeat. The witness was not heard. The world is world—our testimony has made no difference.

Now, one generation after the event, one can still say—or one can already say—that what is called the literature of the Holocaust does not exist, cannot exist. It is a contradiction in terms, as is the philosophy, the theology, the psychology of the Holocaust. Auschwitz negates all systems, opposes all doctrines. They cannot but diminish the experience which lies beyond our reach. Ask any survivor, he will tell you; he who has not lived the event will never know it. And he who went through it, will not reveal it—not really, not entirely. Between his memory and its reflection there is a wall—and it cannot be pierced. The past belongs to the dead, and the survivor does not recognize himself in the words linking him to them. A novel about Treblinka is either not a novel or not about Treblinka; a novel about Treblinka is about blasphemy—is blasphemy. For Treblinka means death—absolute death—death of language and of the imagination. Its mystery is doomed to remain intact.

Yet the Holocaust has for a time, and in some instances, invaded and/or dominated all areas of literary creativity. There exist dramas and even movies on the subject. Some are good, others are not. All show too much and, as a result, no one sees anything. The experience comes through with stronger impact in documents, eyewitness accounts, and personal memoirs, so let us start with these.

But before doing so, I should like to stop for a brief moment and make a preliminary remark about the Symposium itself. I think that you, Dean Morton, are to be commended. The Symposium is an important occasion, for it brings together scholars, critics, and historians, and moves them to listen to each other's perception of the event common to all of us, though to different degrees and on different levels. And it is important that it is taking place here, in a hall belonging to a church, though—traumatized as I am—I do not feel at ease in a church.

I hope you will forgive my frankness. I believe in the usefulness of dialogues, but they must be preceded by an honest exchange. As a child I was afraid of the church to the point of changing sidewalks. In my town, the fear was justified. Not only because of what I inherited— our collective memory—but also because of the simple fact that twice a year, at Easter and Christmas, Jewish schoolchildren would be beaten up by their Christian neighbors. Yes, as a child I lived in fear. A symbol of compassion and love to Christians, the cross has become an instrument of torment and terror to be used against Jews. I say this with neither hate nor anger. I say this because it is true. Born in suffering, Christianity became a source and pretext of suffering to others.

Furthermore, as most historians have stated, Christianity's role in the Holocaust should not be underrated. The Final Solution was rooted in the centuries-old Christian hatred of the Jews. When the historian Jules Isaac came to see Pope John XXIII to plead with him to remove anti-Semitic passages from Catholic liturgy and textbooks, the pope kept him at the Vatican for three days. They talked and they talked. Finally Jules Isaac asked: "Can I leave with hope?" The pope's reply was: "You are entitled to much more than hope." The pope had understood the guilt of the church—and of Christianity in general. The mass killings had taken place in a Christian setting. Protestant leaders applauded Hitler—as did their Catholic counterparts. Those who killed—particularly those of the infamous *Einsatzkommandos*—felt no tension, no conflict between their Christian faith and their criminal deeds. Twenty-two percent of the SS remained loyal to the church even while murdering Jewish men, women, and children. As for Hitler, he was never excommunicated.

Thus I believe that it is important and even necessary to organize such a Symposium in such a place, so that we should hear certain words and then try to bridge them and see where we can go from here. I hope we shall go away with more understanding and more compassion.

And now let us, once again, try and approach the theme we are supposed to explore tonight.

The most striking images, the most fascinating combinations of events, situations, and human metamorphoses, are to be found not in fiction, but in documents and personal testimonies, some of which read like fantasy or poetry.

Ringelblum and Rabbi Huberband, Masha Rolnik and Anne Frank, Leon Wells and Yankel Wiernik: their writings are those of chroniclers, witnesses. Leon Wells kept his diary while working on the Death Brigade. Wiernik wrote his shortly after his escape from Treblinka. Ringelblum collected his archives while in the Warsaw Ghetto. The desire to bear witness—to inform the civilized world on the other side—was overwhelming and not limited to individuals. "People are writing, writing," notes Ringelblum." Everybody is writing." In Zamosc—where Peretz was born—an anonymous Jew was seen pushing forward, in a crowd, witnessing the beating of an old Jew by a sneering German: "I want to see and remember," the anonymous witness was heard saying. There were historians in every ghetto, chroniclers in every murder factory. Convinced that the outside world was unaware of the mechanized, technological killings, each Jew wanted to help break through the walls and barbed wire. Some gave their lives so as to enable one messenger to carry one sentence—one outcry, to the world. Had they been aware that the outside world knew—and knew everything—many would have wanted to die sooner . . . as several hundred children did after their liberation. They who had managed to resist and survive the wickedness of the executioner, were helpless and desperate when they discovered the truth: the world knew and was indifferent.

There were chroniclers even inside the *Sonderkommandos* who, in Birkenau, were compelled to burn the corpses before being burned themselves. One of their documents was discovered only recently, buried at the site of the gas chambers. Written in Polish, a young Jew describes the arrival of Jews from Bendzin, headed by the rabbi. Entering the gas chambers, the rabbi suddenly began to exhort his faithful not to weep, not to moan, but to pray and sing the glory of God. (For years I had thought that this was but a legend: Jews singing, praying on the threshold of such death? Now the legend has been corroborated. And yet—I still read it with disbelief.) The young chronicler in Birkenau knew that he would die soon, in a few days or weeks; no *Sonderkommando* lived longer than three months. Yet he kept on writing.

Most chroniclers were in similar positions. Hence their particular style: telegraphic, tense, nervous. Words instead of sentences, sentences that contained pages and chapters. There was too much the witnesses had to say, and time was running out. Each sentence had to be considered as the last one, death could appear at any moment. Each image contained the images of a lifetime, of more than one person, of more than one community. But then life itself, inside the Kingdom of Night, followed a different rhythm. People met, fell in love, left one another, despaired and died—all this in one week, one day, one hour. Everything went fast, terribly fast. What would take years and years in a normal society, was reduced to minutes inside ghettos and camps. This had to be—and was—reflected in the chronicles, written during the Holocaust itself.

Each chronicler must have felt that he alone was recording the massacre of his people. Each historian must have thought that he alone had the strength and the means to see and to hear—and to remember. "I don't know whether anyone else is recording the daily events," says Chaim Kaplan. "My powers are insufficient to record all that is worthy of being written. . . . As long as my pulse beats I shall continue my sacred task." On August 4, 1942 he wrote: "If my life ends—what will become of my diary?" His life ended that evening—and his diary survived him. This is true of most chroniclers. Their death becomes part of their testimony.

Then, with the liberation, the survivors themselves entered literature, bringing to it their helplessness, their anger. They too, shared in the need to testify on behalf of their people slaughtered in Europe.

One of the first to do so was a man named Yankel Wiernik, carpenter by profession and hero by choice. He is one of the few who took part in the Treblinka uprising and managed to escape. His personal account was first published by the underground in Poland. Here is his introduction:

> Dear Sir: For your sake and for your sake alone I continue to hang on to my miserable life, though it has lost all attraction for me. How can I breathe freely and enjoy all that which nature has created? Time and again I wake up in the middle of the night moaning pitifully. Ghastly nightmares break up the sleep I so badly need. I see thousands of skeletons extending their bony arms toward me as if begging for mercy and life. But I, drenched with sweat, feel incapable of giving any help. And then I jump up, rub my eyes, and actually rejoice that is is but a dream. My life is embittered. Phantoms of death hound me, specters of children, little children, nothing but children. I sacrificed all those nearest and dearest to me. I myself took them to the place of execution. I built their death chambers for them.
>
> Today I am a homeless old man without a roof over my head, without a family, without any next of kin. I talk to myself. I answer my own questions. I am a wanderer. It is with a sense of fear that I pass through human settlements. I have a feeling that all my experiences have become imprinted on my face. Whenever I look at my reflection in a stream or pool of wa-

ter, or when surprise twists my face into an ugly grimace, do I look like a human being? No, decidedly not. Untidy, ugly, dirty, run-down. It seems as if I were carrying a load of several centuries on my shoulder. The load is wearisome, very wearisome. But I *must* carry it for the time being. I want to and must carry it. I who saw the doom of three generations must keep on living for the sake of the future. The world must be told of the infamy of those barbarians so that centuries and generations to come can execrate them. And it is I who shall cause it to happen. No imagination, no matter how daring, could possibly conceive of anything like that which I have seen and lived through. Nor could any pen, no matter how facile, describe it properly. I intend to present everything accurately so that all the world may know what Western culture was like. . . .

Wiernik, in Treblinka, was forced to build the slaughterhouse and the stake for his people. For in 1943, as the end drew nearer, Himmler and his acolytes decided to destroy the living Jews as well as to kill the dead. Every killer kills twice—the second time when he tries to erase the memory of his crime. This is precisely what Himmler had attempted throughout his black kingdom: orders had been given to burn the corpses and disperse the ashes. The task was entrusted to the victims themselves. Everywhere the killer behaved the same way, uttering the same words and making the same gestures. Everywhere the victims were ordered not to look sad, not to weep. Those who looked unhappy were killed.

As I read such things in Wiernik's or Leon Wells's memoirs, I remembered a talmudic legend. When the Romans destroyed Jerusalem and renamed it Aelia Capitolina, they forbade the Jews to come near Jerusalem, except one day a year—on the ninth day of Av, when we commemorate the fall of Jerusalem. The reason? So they could see the ruins and have better reason to weep.

The German enemy went much farther: he deprived the victim of his sadness. The victims had to laugh and look happy. In Treblinka as well as in Janovska, victims were made to dress like devils so as to amuse their fellow inmates. The killer intended to reduce their tragedy to a farce.

What he did not know, what he could not have known, was that everywhere there were chroniclers whose memory would defeat him. As long as their words are being transmitted, the killer cannot claim victory. Hence we may state our deep conviction that anyone who does not commit himself to active remembering is an accomplice of the executioner, for he betrays the dead by forgetting them and their testimony.

Why is Wiernik's narrative authentic? Because it is meant to be testimony and nothing else. He was neither a professional writer nor a poet—he was not even gifted with words. *Because* he had no imagination, he could tell it as it was. *Because* he had no literary skill, he could
remain truthful. In writing of the Holocaust, imagination became an
obstacle. The best descriptions were given by simple people, or—as we
shall see later—by children. They found the right words, the right tone,
the nakedness, the austerity that are the seal of truth and art alike. They
were not confronted with artistic problems of technique. Their purpose was one and one was their obsession: to bear witness, to transmit
a spark of the flame, a fragment of the tale, a reflection of their truth.

Not all testimonies or testaments were written on paper. Some were
carved into stone, prison walls. One example. In Kovel, where the killers had assembled all the Jews in the synagogue before butchering
them, an inscription was found on the wall: "O earth, do not cover my
blood and let my cry have no resting place." It is from Job. When the
Russian Army liberated Kovel, its Jewish soldiers added the following
sentence: "We have read and understood. Of the 330 Nazis captured
here, all were executed. Signed by Zaslavsky and Farbstein, officers of
the Fourth Guards Regiment of Leningrad, en route to Berlin."

What about the novelists? They considered their mission painful, in-
hibiting, almost paralyzing. How can one write about a situation and
not identify with all its characters? How can one identify with so many
victims? Worse: How can one identify with the executioner? How
could the victim say "I" in place of his killer? Furthermore: How can
one convince oneself—without feeling guilty—that one may "use"
such events for literary purposes? Would that not mean that Treblinka
and Belsen, Ponar and Babi-Yar, all ended in . . . words? That it was
all simply a matter of words?

What kind of words? That, too, became a difficulty the writer had to
solve and overcome. Language had been corrupted to the point that it
had to be invented anew, and purified as well. This time we wrote not
with words, but against them. Often we told less—so as to make the
truth more credible.

Once upon a time, the novelist and the poet were in advance of their
readers. Not now. Once upon a time, the artist could foresee the future.
Not now. Now he had to remember the past—knowing all the while
that what he has to say can never be told; what he hopes to transmit can
never be transmitted. All he could possibly hope to achieve was to
communicate the impossibility of communication.

No wonder, then, that after the war there were poets and novelists who chose to commit suicide: Paul Celan, Beno Werzberger, Tadeusz Borowski, or Josef Wulf. Some succumbed—temporarily—to insanity, as did Nelly Sachs; or turned to science fiction—as did Vercors and Robert Merle; or stopped writing novels—as in the case of Piotr Rawicz.

Just as readers committed suicide in the nineteenth century, writers did in ours. They felt impotent. They realized that once you have penetrated the Kingdom of Night, you have reached the end. There is nothing else to discover. Hence they felt inadequate. And guilty: they thought they had said something. No: they had said nothing.

It was simply too much for the survivor to try and fulfill his mission. He had to invent a new language, compose a new rhythm, a new texture to express the ineffable and uncover arts of the secret so jealously guarded by so many dead.

Most novelists of this category seem to have followed the same pattern. Viewing literature as a way to correct injustices, they wrote their tales so as to protest against what was done to their friends, their people. Theirs was meant to be a powerful protest against society, man, and God. Their aim was not only to describe the massacre—but also to paint what preceded it: the life, the peacefulness of the family—the joy of its holidays, the charm of its fools, and the wisdom of its children. They wrote their memoirs so as to bring back to life people and places destroyed by the executioner. And to prove that Jews can—with words—build upon ruins. That is why the shtetl holds such fascination for them: the shtetl—Jerusalem away from Jerusalem—has survived in words alone.

These innumerable cities and villages where ten generations of Jews had sanctified their exile through study and prayer—they are gone. For good. Erased from geography. The shtetl—this small kingdom of fire, erected and purified in fire—has disappeared. Forever. Nowadays we have Jewish cities, capitals, settlements, suburbs, and even military bases. But we don't have the shtetl—and never will. It is swallowed up by smoke and night, along with its sages and their pupils, its preachers and their followers, its dreamers and their dreams. Here, the hangman's victory seems final. Wiped out for good, the shtetl can be found only in words, in words alone. That is why the teller of its tale does whatever he can to present it in its most glorious aspect: let the executioner know what he has destroyed. What is said of Judaism is true of the shtetl: it must be approached from its most exalted angle.

As a result, survivors wrote magnificently about the shtetl—but not about the Holocaust.

It is simple: one cannot write about the Holocaust—not if you are a writer.

Understandably, the theme evoked some sacred awe in literature. It was considered taboo—for the initiated alone. The great novelists of the time—Malraux and Mauriac, Faulkner and Silone and Thomas Mann and Camus—chose to stay away from it. It was their way of showing respect toward the dead—and the survivors as well. Also, it was their way of admitting their inability to cope with themes where imagination weighed less than experience. They were honest enough to realize that they may not penetrate into a domain haunted by so many dead and buried under so many ashes. They chose not to describe something they could not fathom.

In conclusion, let us turn to poetry—to our children.

The purest writings are those devoted to the suffering, the agony, and the death of our children—and those written by the children themselves.

Their words more than others bring us closer to the experience—their words become experience.

We know that our children were the principal target of the executioner; they always have been. Pharaoh began by killing children. So did Haman. So did Hitler.

Itzchak Katznelson, in his *Song of My Slaughtered People* gives us the following description:

> Do not cry. . . . At this station another girl I saw about five years old. She fed her younger brother, and he cried. He cried, the little one; he was sick. Into a diluted bit of jam she dipped tiny crusts of bread and skillfully inserted them into his mouth. This my eyes were privileged to see, to see this mother, a mother of five years, feeding her child, to hear her soothing words. My own mother, the best in the whole world, had not invented such a ruse. But this one wiped his tears with a smile, injecting joy into his heart, the little girl of Israel. Sholom Aleichem could not have improved upon her. They, the children of Israel, were the first in doom and disaster, most of them without father and mother. They were consumed by frost, starvation, and lice. Holy Messiahs, sanctified in pain. Say, then, how have these lambs sinned? Why in days of doom are they the first victims of wickedness, the first in the trap of evil, the first to be detained for death, the first to be thrown into wagons of slaughter? They were thrown into the wagons, the huge wagons, like heaps of refuse, like the ashes of the earth. And they transported them, killed them, exterminated them, without remnant or remembrance. The best of my children were all wiped out, woe unto me, doom and desolation.

There is, in the encounter between child and executioner, something redeeming. Usually the child manages to change, or at least move, the killer. This did not occur during the Holocaust. More than one million Jewish children prove that it did not.

In some ancient religions primitive people would bring their children as offerings to their gods to appease them; and the gods would be appeased. Not so during the Holocaust. One million offerings did not appease God.

There is a legend in the Midrash that disturbs me. When did God decide to liberate his people from Egyptian bondage? When Pharaoh ordered that living Jewish children be used as bricks for his pyramids, the Angel Michael caught one such child and brought it before God. And when God saw the child—already disfigured—He was overcome by compassion and love and chose to redeem his people.

And often I say to myself: *Ribono shel olam,* Master of the universe, one child was enough to move you—and one million children were not?

One million Jewish children were slaughtered—some of them burned alive. What purpose did the executioner wish to achieve in killing them? What did he hate in them: their innocence? their imagination? their future? He wanted to kill our future—our innocence—and our past as well.

And whenever I read about the massacre of children, I know I will need all the strength in me so as not to let go—so as not to despair. This is even more true when I read what these same children wrote before they went to the flames.

Listen:

One young child named Martha wrote:

> I must be saving these days.
> I have no money to save;
> I must save health and strength,
> Enough to last me for a long while.
> I must save my nerves and my thoughts and my mind
> And the fire of my spirit.
> I must be saving of tears that flow.
> I need them for a long, long while.
> I must save endurance these stormy days.
> There is so much I need in my life:
> Warmth of feeling and a kind heart.
> These things I lack.

> Of these I must be saving.
> All these, the gifts of God, I wish to keep.
> How sad I should be if I lost them quickly.

And shortly after having written this, Martha died.
A young boy named Motel wrote a very short poem:

> A little garden,
> And a little boy walks along it.
> When the blossom comes to bloom,
> The little boy will be no more.

Another little girl, Alena, wrote:

> I'd like to go away alone
> Where there are other, nicer people.
> Somewhere into the far unknown,
> There, where no one kills another.
> Maybe more of us, a thousand strong
> Will reach this goal
> Before too long.

She didn't.
And then one that you surely know, "The Butterfly," by Paul Freedman:

> The last, the very last, so richly, brightly dazzlingly yellow.
> Perhaps if the sun's tears would sing against the white stone
> Such a yellow is carried lightly
> Away up high.
> It went away I am sure
> Because it wished to kiss the world goodbye.
> For seven weeks I have lived in here
> Penned up inside this ghetto
> But I found my people here
> And the butterfly called to me
> And the white chestnut candles in the court.
> Only I never saw another butterfly.
> That butterfly was the last one.
> Butterflies don't live in here.
> In the ghettos.

And the last, written by a young boy named Motele. I do not know

who he was, nor how old. He must have been young, because he died
shortly afterwards.

> From tomorrow on, I shall be sad.
> From tomorrow on.
> Today I will be gay.
> What is the use of sadness,
> Tell me that.
> Because these evil winds begin to blow,
> Why should I grieve for tomorrow, today?
> Tomorrow may be good, so good,
> So sunny.
> Tomorrow the sun may shine for us again.
> We shall no longer need to be sad.
> From tomorrow on I shall be sad.
> From tomorrow on, not today, no,
> Today I will be glad
> And every day
> No matter how bitter it be,
> I will say from tomorrow on
> I shall be sad
> Not today.

Yes, let us read tales, tales that are in poems and tales that are in documents, and all the rest can wait, must wait. All the rest does not exist.
And those who have written other things have lost many things, their
own past, also their own present. They have lost many friends, both
past and present.

Let us tell tales. Tales of fear and tales of night. Tales of demented
old men who danced with their grandchildren while ascending into
heaven, and bringing back the fire, the fire God had given man.

Let us tell tales of times gone mad. Of humanity gone mad. Of man's
ultimate suffering. I speak of Jews who were killed in Auschwitz. But
humanity died in Auschwitz. When humanity kills Jews, humanity
kills itself.

Let us tell tales, therefore, tales of children who, one moment before
they died, still sang to life. Let us tell tales of old wise men, who loved
children, and went on loving them until they died.

Let us tell tales. For children love to listen to tales. But there is one
tale which will never be told. And soon we will not even know its
name. Nor its secret.

A Statement

GABRIEL HABIB

The message below was received by Dean Morton during the Symposium. Its author, the Rev. Gabriel Habib, consultant of the World Council of Churches on the Middle East, had been invited to present a paper, but was unable to come. He expresses his reservations about the nature of the Symposium, and suggests some different types of meetings for the future which would compensate for the lacks he outlines. Some of these lacks were felt and expressed also by a number of participants in the meeting.

With sincere apologies that neither I nor Father Moubarak was able to come at the last minute, we thought that it might be useful to send you the following common reflections on the Symposium, for eventual use on your part.

We send our greetings to Dean James Morton and express our appreciation for the invitation to participate, personally, in the Auschwitz Symposium at the Cathedral of St. John the Divine. Please convey to the participants our best wishes, and our regrets at not being able to take part in the deliberations, due to scheduling and travel difficulties. If Dean Morton thinks it useful, we ask that he convey to the assembly this brief statement of our reactions to the assignment proposed to us.

1. Even had we been able to participate in the Symposium, it would have been difficult to involve ourselves in this meeting as it has been conceived. This Symposium involves solely the Western conscience in its Judeo-Christian aspect, as it has been developed in Europe and North America since the Second World War. We of the East, Christian and Muslim, involved with our Jewish brothers and sisters in moving toward a secular, pluralistic future, are sensitive to their sufferings in the West, but are foreign to this way of posing the problem, and object to it as a just vision of contemporary history.

2. The drama of Auschwitz should not be separated from the drama of World War II. Decisions such as those to bomb Dresden, or the annihilation of Hiroshima, along with the more recent massacre of the Vietnamese, can only be characterized as the same madness on the part of the industrialized nations, which has plunged all humanity into a

417

bath of blood and tears. If religious reflection on such dramas takes Scripture as its point of departure, we propose Isaiah 53, the Suffering Servant, victim and witness to all humankind.

3. The Jews in the West should not be singled out in this tragedy. We Christians of the East refuse to theologize on this subject, or to impose a Christian typology on the present condition of Judaism.

4. We remember with indignation the fate of the Palestinian people through the massive exile of another people at the hands of those who claim a heritage based on racial continuity and fulfillment of divine promises.

5. While refusing to engage in a theological examination of the conflict, since we believe it to be political in nature, we point to the imbalance and division that it produces in Judaism. Spiritual Zionism has been emptied by a temporal Zionism, and the traditional Judaism of the East has been subjugated to the technological Jewish ethos of Europe and America. In the conflict within Judaism, we strongly ally ourselves with those Jews who promote a sense of belonging to a common Judeo-Arab community, free from all discrimination. We are thus in accord with the line of Jewish thinkers and militants reaching from Achad Ha'am to Judah Magnes, Henrietta Szold, and the Ihaud movement, without forgetting Simone Weil (*La Pesanteur et la grace*, chapter on Israel).

6. We deplore the absence of representatives of contemporary Judaism, with the exception of isolated individuals, in the struggle of peoples for their liberation. At the Algiers Congress in 1973, we noted that all Third World peoples were present and all traditions sacred to humanity were heard, with the exception of the Hebrew Bible. This absence was due to the collusion of Anglo-Saxon Judaism with the neocolonialist West and the apartheid regimes of Africa.

7. Under these circumstances, our most sincere wish for the Symposium at St. John the Divine is to contribute to the development of a critical conscience at the center of Judaism, and to correct, if possible, the direction in which Western European and American communities have led the whole of Judaism—away from solidarity with the oppressed.

8. The development of this critical conscience and such a correction can only take place through a serious dialogue with the critical consciences of the West, the Christians of the East, and Islam. A Judeo-Islamic dialogue is, in any case, indispensable to the correction of all Jewish-Christian dialogue. Only by taking the Muslim world into consideration can Jews and Christians in the West break out of their

fallacious, anachronistic, and provincial situation and put an end to the fatal epoch of Auschwitz, opening the way, in Palestine, to a new era. Jerusalem will be the symbol of this new era, for all those who claim it as their Mother—not through blood, but through faith and hope in a just and humane world.

9. In view of such a dialogue, we would like to make the following proposal to the Dean of St. John the Divine:

A. A smaller but more diversified meeting, that could include a reduced number of members of the present Symposium on Auschwitz, as well as Arabs, Muslims, and Christians, together with Oriental Jews and non-Zionist Jews.

B. Another meeting that would include only Christians from the American churches and the churches in the East. The purpose of such an encounter would be the promotion of a common Christian understanding of Judaism, and the present state of Christian-Jewish relations, from a humanistic and historical perspective.

Such meetings would allow the problem presently posed in the shadow of the Cathedral to be seen in a new light.

Poems

POEMS

THE SECOND DAY of the symposium ended with an evening of poetry reading, arranged by Muriel Rukeyser, in the nave of the Cathedral. Some of the poets read not only from their own works, but from the work of other poets. The evening gave an intensely personal and living dimension to the Symposium.

ROBERT PAYNE

Jerusalem

Night falls, Jerusalem sleeps, and the world ends.
And I am standing on Gethsemane amid the shadows
Of a city which is no city, a city drained of corporeal essence
Being more and less than a city, being shrouded in darkness,
A place of darkness, invisible, intangible, a city at the bottom
    of the ocean.
Nevertheless in the darkness the city is there, and the eye grows
    accustomed
Slowly to the glimmering stones, to the faint light on the sharp edges,
To that wild scattering of stones on a hill-top in the midst of a desert.
And I ask myself: Is this darkness Jerusalem? Is this the
    heart of the world?
Stone. Stone. Stone, Stone everywhere. Stone and darkness.

ROBERT PAYNE was born in 1911 and lives in New York. He edited *The White Pony*.

O tiger of stone
O stone of the Annunciation
O stone of the Anointment
O stone of the Holy Sepulchre
O stone of Abraham
O stone of the temple
O stone of the heart
O stone of the rib cage
O stone of our sex
O stone of our brain
Is there no end to stone?

Strange how the worship of stones continued through the ages,
And stranger still the worship of the hollowed out rocks,
Sepulchers and tombs, caves, cairns, hollows, monuments
To the defeat of all life under the sun. Stone innumerable,
Cracked and bleached by the sun, pounded into powder.
Beyond all reckoning or reason we worship the holy stones
Wherefore mortality holds us by a stone throat. On this stone
    Jesus trod.
On this stone Jacob slept, seeing the angels ascending and descending.
On this stone Abraham held the knife at Isaac's throat.
From this stone Mahommed rode his horse into Heaven.
This stone, and no other. This rock of ages.
And any child who plays with any stone
May find he is holding an inch of the Holy Sepulchre.

O tiger of stone
O stone of abasement
O stone of triumph
O stone of illumination
O stone of darkness
O seas of stone
O clouds of stone
O flowers of stone
O trees of stone
O days of stone
O nights of stone

So you may travel across the desert and see here and there
A little heap of stones recording that someone passed before you,
For this is the habit in the desert. The wanderers want to be
    remembered.
They write their names on the stones, they scribble blood
    on the stones, make some mark,
Then stand for a while gazing at their handiwork before passing on
To the liquid mirage of the horizon, knowing they are not
    entirely forgotten.
They have spoken, the stones have mouths, the stones speak for them.
For the stones are hungry to take on the form of human flesh,
Of animals, of tigers, even of birds: they go in search of the living.
Mouths they have, eyes also, they watch the passing of the seasons.
The sun climbs up the stone in the morning and descends
    in the evening,
And the stone is made holy by the shadow of everyone who passes by.

        O stone of God
        O Stone of the Resurrection
        O stone of the wailing wall
        O stone of the Assassination
        O stone of our eyes
        O stone of our mouths
        O stone of our hearts
        O stone of our loves
        O stone of Jerusalem

Poems

MURIEL RUKEYSER

To Be a Jew in the Twentieth Century

To be a Jew in the twentieth century
Is to be offered a gift.   If you refuse,
Wishing to be invisible, you choose
Death of the spirit, the stone insanity.
Accepting, take full life, full agonies:
Your evening deep in labyrinthine blood
Of those who resist, fail and resist; and God
Reduced to a hostage among hostages.

The gift is torment.   Not alone the still
Torture, isolation; or torture of the flesh.
That may come also.   But the accepting wish,
The whole and fertile spirit as guarantee
For every human freedom, suffering to be free,
Daring to live for the impossible.

©

The Writer
for Isaac Bashevis Singer

His tears fell from his veins
They spoke for six million
From his veins all their blood.
He told his stories.
But noone spoke this language
Noone knew this music

MURIEL RUKEYSER, the distinguished poet and translator, taught at Sarah Lawrence College from 1956 to 1967. Among her many books are *The Speed of Darkness* (1968), *Breaking Open* (1971), and *Our Face* (1973).

The music went into all people
not knowing this language
it ran through their bodies
and they began to take his words
Everyone the tears
Everyone the veins
But everyone said
Noone spoke this language

©

Muriel Rukeyser and Robert Payne read from
Simone Weil

Simone Weil, who was a Jew and a Christian, and who was neither, and who was both, wrote these words. I would like to think of them as poetry as well as theology.

Inescapable necessity, anguish, wretchedness, the crushing weight of poverty, work that wears down the spirit, cruelty, torture, violent death, bondage, terror, sickness—all these are God's love.
And she said:

We do not have to search for God. We have only to change the direction in which we are looking. It is for him to search for us. We must be happy in the knowledge that he is infinitely beyond our reach.
And she also said:

All the creatures I love are born by the purest chance, and my meeting with them is also by the purest chance. To know this in one's soul and not to love them less.
And she said:

Lovers or friends desire two things. One is to love each other so much that they enter into one another and make one body. The second is to love each other so much that, with half the world between them, their union will not be diminished in the slightest degree.
And she said:

Bread and stone are love. We must eat the bread and lay ourselves open to the stone, so that it may sink as deeply as possible into the flesh.

Nelly Sachs

Epitaph

for B.N. and J.M.

Once more someone in torment
has found the white entrance

Silence — Silence — Silence —
The inner voice releases
great triumph —

Here we plant humility —

Translated by Muriel Rukeyser and Melvin Elliot

STANLEY KUNITZ

Around Pastor Bonhoeffer

The Plot Against Hitler

Jittery, missing their cues,
Bach's glory jailed in their throats,
they were clustered round the piano
in the Biedermeyer parlor,
sisters and brothers
and their brothers by marriage,
rehearsing a cantata
for Papa's seventy-fifth birthday.
Kyrie eleison: Night
like no other night, plotted
and palmed,
omega of terror,
packed like a bullet
in the triggered chamber.
Surely the men had arrived at their stations.
Through the staves of the music
he saw their target strutting,
baring its malignant heart.
Lord, let the phone ring!
Let the phone ring!

Next to Last Things

Slime, in the grains of the State,
like smut in the corn,
from the top infected.
Hatred made law,
wolves bred out of maggots
rolling in blood,
and the seal of the church ravished
to receive the crooked sign.

STANLEY KUNITZ is currently Consultant in Poetry to the Library of Congress. He is editor of the Yale Series of Younger Poets, and a Pulitzer Prize winner.

All the steeples were burning.
In the chapel of his ear
he had heard the midnight bells
jangling: *if you permit*
this evil, what is the good
of the good of your life?
And he forsook the last things,
the dear inviolable mysteries—
Plato's lamp, passed from the hand
of saint to saint—
that he might risk his soul in the streets,
where the things given
are only next to last;
in God's name cheating, pretending,
playing the double agent,
choosing to trade
the prayer for the deed,
and the deed most vile.
I am a liar and a traitor.

The Extermination Camp

Through the half-open door of the hut
the camp doctor saw him kneeling,
with his hands quietly folded.
"I was most deeply moved by the way
this lovable man prayed,
so devout and so certain
that God heard his prayer."
Round-faced, bespectacled, mild,
candid with costly grace,
he walked towards the gallows
and did not falter.
Oh but he knew the Hangman!
Only a few steps more
and he would enter the arcanum
where the Master
would take him by the shoulder,
as He does at each encounter,
and turn him round
to face his brothers in the world.

The Customs Collector's Report

For the sake of the record:
   on Tuesday, the 19th instant,
the third day of the storm,
   shortly before nightfall,
they swam over the pass together,
   this pair in their battered armor,
first seen in my spyglass;
   stovepipes assisting each other,
cylinders skating the snowcrust,
   comedians sprawling,
now and then dropping
   under the surface,
perceptible only
   as mounds in the driftage.

To whom, in this trial,
   could I turn for instructions?

At the north wall of the gorge,
   where zero poured to its funnel,
in the absence of guidelines
I dared the encounter,
half-digging them out
   from the coils of the blizzard,
half-dying of cold
   as I scratched at the ice-pack.
Then came issue of smothered voices,
   wind rumbling in empty barrels,
the sound of flags flapping
   in a cave of the mountain;
and the words that I heard
   flew by in tatters:
"nothing . . . nothing to declare . . .
   our wounds speak . . . heroes . . .
unfairly ambushed . . . the odds impossible . . .
   let our countrymen know . . . pride . . . honor . . .
how bravely . . . and oh
   what a body-count! . . . "

And the thinner voice cried,
   plaintively winding,
"True, brother, true! but tell me—
   what was the name of our war?"
When I lifted their helmets
   a gas escaped from them,
putrid, as from all battlefields,
   the last breath of the human.
That moment they were lightened.
   It seemed the earth shuddered,
the white tombs opened,
   disgorging their breastplates.
I saw them rise in the wind
   and roll off like ashcans.

Dear sirs, my lords, this
   is a lonely post,
what can I ask but your compassion?
   I petition you for transfer.

✿   ✿   ✿

An Old Cracked Tune

My name is Solomon Levi,
the desert is my home,
my mother's breast was thorny,
and father I had none.

The sands whispered, *Be separate,*
the stones taught me, *Be hard.*
I dance, for the joy of surviving,
on the edge of the road.

M. L. ROSENTHAL

from "Three Conversations"

I was thinking how the hunters will come to the shelters;
They'll have war-heroes' hands, smelling of raw meat.
They'll brain the babies and take the canned salmon.
Then I remembered the smell of strawberries in Jónava.

That's what you told me once—that when you were a girl,
In Jónava, the smell of strawberries filled the countryside.
When you were a girl! O happy Jew wandering
Sober among strawberries, everywhere in Jónava.

from *Blue Boy on Skates:* by M. L. Rosenthal.
With permission of the publisher.
Copyright 1964 by Oxford University Press, Inc.

✿ ✿ ✿

Proverbial

In the country of seeing-eye dogs
The blind man is king.
The one-eyed's prime minister,
The two-eyed's a traitor—
Or a seeing-eye dog.

from *Blue Boy on Skates:* by M. L. Rosenthal.
Copyright © 1964 by Oxford University Press, Inc.

M. L. ROSENTHAL, Professor of English at New York University, has published a number of books of poetry and criticism. The most recent are *The View from the Peacock's Tail: Poems* (1972), and *Poetry and the Common Life* (1974). His poems are reprinted here with permission from Oxford University Press. In addition to his own poems he read a poem by Dan Pagis.

Lord Hee-Haw

Do not speak of Auschwitz, or even Vietnam.
The ass's skull is braying again:
Some day, science will put everything right.

Slam the face shut, quick-freeze the heart;
Our true loves have all died in our arms.
Assassins, executioners, are scouring the pavements.

Napalm-blazing ghosts enkindle "the psychopathology of
    everyday life";
The "human form divine" flops in wrinkling ballons.
Beloved, you have died in my arms.

from *Beyond Power:* by M. L. Rosenthal.
Copyright © 1969 by Oxford University Press, Inc.
Reprinted by permission.

✿   ✿   ✿

Beyond Power: A Sequence

The river of our dreams—time's distillation—
mirrors, contains, purifies each life.

Each life dreams into the crystal river,
but the man of power sees only his own reflection.

He comes down to the river to drink of the common dream.
His ribald dog's-head stares up at him out of the flowing crystal.

Blasted are the meek, for their leaders inherit the earth,
but the river has neither policy nor pride.

Darkness lowers over the great wooded park.
The deer close toward us; the trees heave grim and massive.

Chilled lovers shiver now with the coming of dusk.
The deer and the tree-trunks are drifting nearer.

I put out my hand to you. The darkness touches
upon us. It is too much for us. It is our own reflection.

The river whelms over us. It takes us where we would be—but not
as we have willed, not out of any choice of hatred or of love

from *Beyond Power:* by M. L. Rosenthal.
Copyright © 1969 by Oxford University Press, Inc.
Reprinted by permission.

✿   ✿   ✿

In The Burning Glass—

at the pinpoint of flame, where flesh
concenters all unceasing, hurling, driven spirit
in the marriage bed of our love, there bursts
before our dismayed ecstasy
the terrible human face of need—

the dead face longing to return,
face of the swollen-bellied babe with heavy-drooping eyelids.

from *The View from the Peacock's Tail:* by M. L. Rosenthal.
Copyright © 1972 by M. L. Rosenthal
Reprinted by permission of Oxford University Press, Inc.

Scorpions

My beautiful young friends are aging gracefully now.
Soon they will be twinkling old gentlemen and ladies.
We never shout at each other now when we meet.
We are always delighted with each other now when we meet.

Once we prowled like panthers, or skunks, in each other's lairs.
We laughed too much, or we bristled, under each other's magic.
Sexual heat, tropic steam, misted our vision.
Impaled on our own nobility, we thought our passions depraved.

Sedately at family dinner, we devoured our prettier cousins,
raping them and our younger aunts at half-past soup.
Hard, proud as our bodies, we accepted the bounty
of our elders (their lives) indifferently, after a quarrel.

Some of us actually died, or were actually killed;
some actually did kill.
Blood leaked terror over us, staining our monstrous regiment.
What were we? What are we? Sentimental scorpions?
Yes, just like old Yahweh, in whose image we were cast.

from *The View from the Peacock's Tail:* By M. L. Rosenthal.
Reprinted by permission of Oxford University Press, Inc.

DAN PAGIS

Written in Pencil in the Sealed Railway-Car

here in this carload
i am eve
with abel my son
if you see my other son
cain son of man
tell him i

—translated from the Hebrew by Stephen Mitchell

DAN PAGIS was born in Bukowina in 1930 and was interned in a concentration camp during World War II. In 1946 he went to Israel, where he now teaches medieval Hebrew literature at Hebrew University. His books of poetry include *The Shadow Dial* (1959), *Late Leisure* (1964), *Transformation* (1970), and *Brain* (1975). The poem read by Mr. Rosenthal is from T. Carmi and Dan Pagis, *Selected Poems* (Penguin Books, 1976), p. 93. It is reprinted with permission of the publisher.

Sonia Hanna Pilcer

Your Hair

Thick, shiny like red taffeta
the Sabbath wine father blessed
while the silver candelabra burned.

And shall I forget, little lamb
how they sheared your fleece
red desert hair razed from its root.

Sarah, Rachel, Deborah wept!
Your hair was braided in a crown
they removed the tortoise shell combs
your hair, your hair came tumbling.

. . . I stroke the music in your hair
until the electricity flickers,
dying in its diaphanous strands.

SONIA HANNA PILCER was born in Augsburg, Germany, the child of survivors. She is a freelance writer and poet living in New York. She attended the Symposium, and read three of her poems at the end of the scheduled poetry reading in the Cathedral.

Refugees

We were severed limbs of a tree
Pickup-sticks to pyromaniacs
Roasting our skin like marshmallows.

We were phantom arms and legs
Of an amputee creeping
Out of the smoking heap.

We were fevered by visions
Of roots like fingers
Implanted in the earth's belly.

Two by two, we boarded the boat
Noah's grateful beasts
To salvage what was left.

America! America! America!
We chanted the magic word of passage.
Our daughter sat quiet as baggage.

✿   ✿   ✿

My Mother's Father's Cigarette Case

I haven't seen it yet
but I know
that it is
luminescent
my mother's father's cigarette case

It is luminescent
not like moonlight
but teeth
without gold fillings
and fingernail moons

It was hidden in a hole
in the wall
of their basement
the house lasted the war
my mother's father's cigarette case

My mother returned
to the house, the hole
and found her mother's diamond ring
the family's savings in a cup
and the cigarette case of her father

She spent the silver coins
on a foolish fling
she gave her mother's diamond ring to me
and to her uncle
she gave her father's cigarette case

He stopped smoking in his sixtieth year
and put the cigarette case
in a safe place
his wife wrote it into her will
to be left for her sister's children

My mother heard her father's voice
chiding her, "Lucia,
Leah, my little Lutka,
give, give to yourself
as I wish I could have given to you."

She wrote a letter to her uncle
asking for her father's cigarette case
it arrived soon afterwards
without a fuss
my mother's father's cigarette case

She's crying, I know it
into her father's cigarette case
salt is spilling, spilling, spilling
now they've begun their voyage
back to the sea, back to the sea.

Notes

IRVING GREENBERG

1. Dieter Wisliceny, affidavit dated November 29, 1945, printed in *Nazi Conspiracy and Aggression* (Washington: Government Printing Office, 1946), 8:610; he quotes Eichmann as follows: "I laugh when I jump into the grave because of the feeling I have killed 5,000,000 Jews. That gives me great satisfaction and gratification." Rudolf Hoess, the head of Auschwitz, reports Eichmann's joy grew out of his conviction that he had landed a fatal blow by devastating Jewry's life center. In Hoess's responses to Dr. Jan Sehn, the examining judge, printed as appendix 3 in Hoess's autobiography, *Commandant of Auschwitz* (London: Weidenfeld & Nicolson, 1959), p. 215. The estimate of Jewish scholars, rabbis, and full-time students killed is by Rabbi M. J. Itamar (Wohlgelernter), formerly secretary-general of the Chief Rabbinate of Israel. Heydrich, the original head of the Final Solution project and its driving force until his death by assassination, instructed the Einsatzgruppen that in killing the Jews of Eastern Europe, they would be killing the "intellectual reservoir of the Jews."

2. Simon Herman, *Israelis and Jews: A Study in the Continuity of an Identity* (New York: Random House, 1970), pp. 78–80, 175, 186, 191, 203–4, 211–13; idem, lecture given at the annual meeting of the Memorial Foundation for Jewish Culture in Geneva, July 9, 1974, published in 1975 *Proceedings of the Memorial Foundation for Jewish Culture;* idem, "Ethnic Identity and Historical Time Perspective: An Illustrated Case Study; the Impact of the Holocaust (Destruction of European Jewry) on Jewish Identity," mimeographed (Jerusalem, 1972); idem, research in progress.

3. S. Szmaglewska, in *Trial of the Major War Criminals before the International Military Tribunal* (Nuremberg, 1947–49), 8:319–20, quoted in Erich Kulka and Uta Kraus, *The Death Factory* (Oxford: Pergamon, 1966), p. 114. (In the IMT record she is listed as Shmaglevskaya); cf. also Hoess, *Commandant of Auschwitz*, pp. 149–51.

4. S. Szmaglewska, ibid.

5. Raul Hilberg, *The Destruction of the European Jews* (Chicago: Quadrangle, 1966); Hilberg, ibid., p. 569, fn. 65, cites 5.28 RM per kg. for TESTA's price from DEGESCH before resale to Gerstein, the chief disinfection officer in the office of the hygienic chief of the Waffen-SS, for use in Auschwitz. However, a photograph of an invoice from DEGESCH to Kurt Gerstein dated March 13, 1944, published in *La Deportation* (n.d., n.p., published by Fédération Nationale des Déportés et Internis Resistants et Patriots), p. 138, clearly shows a price of 5 RM per kg. (210 kg. for 1,050 RM).

6. Elie Wiesel, *Night* (New York: Hill & Wang, 1960), pp. 43–44.

7. Michael Dov Weissmandl, *Min Hametzar* (1960; reprint ed., Jerusalem, n.d.) p. 24. See also Weissmandl's report of his conversation with the papal nuncio in 1944. He quotes the nuncio as saying: "There is no innocent blood of Jewish children in the world. All Jewish blood is guilty. You have to die. This is the punishment that has been awaiting you because of that sin [dei-

cide]." Dr. Livia Rotkirchen of Yad Vashem has called my attention to the fact that the papal nuncio tried to help save Jews and used his influence to do so. Weissmandl's quote appears to be incompatible with that image. Dr. Rotkirchen speculates that Weissmandl, in retrospect, attributed the statement to the wrong person. In any event, this judgment that the Jews deserved their fate as punishment for deicide or rejecting Christ is a strong and recurrent phenomenon. On the papal nuncio's work, see Livia Rotkirchen, "Vatican Policy and the Jewish 'Independent' Slovakia (1939–1945)," *Yad Vashem Studies* 6 (1967): 27–54.

8. Pastoral letter of March 25, 1941, A.B. Freiburg, no. 9, March 27, 1941, p. 388; quoted in Günter Lewy, *The Catholic Church and Nazi Germany* (New York: McGraw-Hill, 1964), p. 294.

9. Saul Friedlander, *Pius XII and the Third Reich: A Documentation* (New York: Knopf, 1966), p. 97. Cf. the whole discussion of the decrees by the Vatican, ibid., pp. 92–99.

10. "Ein Wort zur Judenfrage, der Reichsbruderrat der Evangelischen Kirche in Deutschland," issued on April 8, 1948 in Dietrich Goldschmidt and Hans-Joachim Kraus, eds., *Der Ungekundigte Bund: Neue Begegnung von Juden und christlicher* (Stuttgart, 1962), pp. 251–54. The extent to which Vatican circles helped Nazi war criminals escape is only now becoming evident. See on this Gitta Sereny, *Into That Darkness* (London: Andre Deutsch, 1974), pp. 289–323. See also Ladislav Farago, *Aftermath: Martin Bormann and the Fourth Reich* (New York: Simon & Schuster, 1974).

11. Cf. memorandum submitted to Chancellor Hitler, June 4, 1936, in Arthur C. Cochrane, *The Church's Confession Under Hitler* (Philadelphia: Westminster Press, 1962), pp. 268–79; J. S. Conway, *The Nazi Persecution of the Churches* (London: Weidenfeld & Nicolson, 1968), pp. xx, xxiii, 84–85, 261–65.

12. A. Roy Eckardt, *Elder and Younger Brothers* (New York: Scribner's, 1967), p. 107.

13. Raul Hilberg, *Documents of Destruction* (Chicago, 1973), pp. 50–51.

14. A selection of these and other testimonies can be found in Binyamin West, *B'Havlei K'laya* [*In the throes of destruction*] *(Tel Aviv, 1963), pp. 43, 43, 62, 65, 66, 77, 96, 106, 112, 118, 155 ff.*

15. *In the District Court of Jerusalem, criminal case no. 40/61, The Attorney-General of the Government of Israel* v. *Adolf, the son of Adolf Karle, Eichmann.* Minutes of Session no. 30, pp. L1, L2, M1, M2, N1, partially quoted in Hilberg, *Documents of Destruction*, pp. 61–62.

16. The trial record of the Einsatzgruppen leaders shows that of twenty-four defendants, Herren Schubert (p. 97), Lindow (p. 99), Schulz (p. 135), Blume (p. 139), Braune (p. 214), Sandberger (p. 532), Haensch (p. 547), Strauch (p. 563), and Klingelhoefer (p. 564) were lawyers. Other professionals included architect Blobel (p. 211), economist Sieberg (p. 536), professor Six (p. 555), banker Noske (p. 570), secondary-school instructor Steimle (p. 578), economist Ohlendorf (p. 224), dentist Fendler (p. 570), and last but not least, clergyman Biberstein (p. 542).

17. Cf. Hannah Arendt, *The Origins of Totalitarianism* (New York: Harcourt Brace, 1950). Also see Jacob Talmon, *The Rise of Totalitarian Democracy* (Boston: Beacon Press, 1952), and *Political Messianism: The Romantic Phase* (London: Secker & Warburg, 1960).

18. Arnold Toynbee, *A Study of History*, vol. 60, p. 433, quoted in Eliezer Berkovits, *Faith After the Holocaust* (New York: KTAV, 1973), p. 18.

19. Arthur Herzberg, *The French Enlightenment and the Jews* (New York: Columbia University Press, 1968); Uriel Tal, *Yahadut V'Natzrut BaReich Ha-Sheni* [Jews and Christians in the Second Reich], *1870–1914* (Jerusalem: Magnes Press, 1969); and Eleanore Sterling, *Er Ist Wie Du: Fruh Geschichte des Anti Semitismus in Deutschland, 1915–1850* (Munich: Chr. Kaiser, 1956). One should also note Elie Wiesel's biting words on the moral collapse in the camps of "the intellectuals, the liberals, the humanists, the professors of sociology and the like." Elie Wiesel, "Talking and Writing and Keeping Silent," in Franklin H. Littell and Hubert G. Locke, *The German Church Struggle and the Holocaust* (Detroit: Wayne State University Press, 1974), p. 273. It could be that relativism and tolerance, in themselves good or neutral moral qualities, combine with excessive rationalism and functionalism to weaken the capacity to take absolute stands against evil: they rationalize that everything is relative and there is no need to say no! at all costs.

20. Henry Feingold, *The Politics of Rescue* (New Brunswick: Rutgers University Press, 1970), passim and summary, pp. 295–307; David Wyman, *Paper Walls* (Amherst: University of Massachusetts Press, 1968).

21. *Punishment for War Crimes: The Inter-Allied Declaration Signed at St. James's Palace, London on 13th January, 1942 and Relative Documents* (New York: United Nations Information Office, [1943], pp. 5–6. See also U.S. Department of State, *Foreign Relations of the United States: Diplomatic Papers, 1942* (Washington: Government Printing Office, 1960), vol. 1, p. 45, and *Foreign Relations of the United States: Diplomatic Papers, 1941* (Washington, Government Printing Office, 1958), vol. 1, p. 447.

22. Alexander Donat, *The Holocaust Kingdom: A Memoir* (New York: Rinehart, 1965), pp. 100, 103.

23. Chayim Greenberg, "Bankrupt!" in *The Inner Eye*, vol. 2 (New York: Jewish Frontier Association 1964), pp. 193–202. Cf. also Fred Lazin, "American Jewish Organizations' Response to the Holocaust," unpublished MS.

24. Henry Feingold, "Roosevelt and the Holocaust," *Judaism,* Summer 1969, pp. 259–76; idem, *Politics of Rescue,* especially pp. 126–66, 208–47; Wyman, *Paper Walls,* passim. See also Yehuda Bauer, *From Diplomacy to Resistance* (Philadelphia: Jewish Publication Society, 1970); Ovadia Margalit, *Bamaagal HaSatoom* (Tel Aviv: Bronfman, 1974).

25. F. E. Cartus [pseud.], "Vatican II and the Jews," *Commentary,* January 1965, p. 21.

26. Elie Wiesel, *The Accident* (New York: Hill & Wang, 1962), p. 91.

27. Elie Wiesel, "The Death of My Father," in *Legends of our Time* (New York: Holt, Rinehart & Winston, 1968), pp. 2, 4, 5, 6, 7; idem, *The Gates of the Forest* (New York: Holt, Rinehart & Winston, 1966), pp. 194, 196, 197, 198, 224, 225–26.

28. Gershom Scholem, *Sabbatai Sevi: The Mystical Messiah* (Princeton: Princeton University Press, 1973).

29. Jacob Neusner, *A Life of Rabban Yohanan ben Zakkai,* (Leiden: E. J. Brill, 1962); idem, *Fellowship in Judaism in the First Century* (New York, KTAV, 1972). But see also idem, "Judaism in a Time of Crisis: Four Responses to the Destruction of the Temple," *Judaism* 21, no. 3 (Summer 1972): 313–27.

See Peter R. Ackroyd, *Exile and Restoration* (Philadelphia, 1968); and Yehezkel Kaufmann, *The Religion of Israel* (Chicago: University of Chicago Press, 1960), epilogue; see also Salo W. Baron, *Social and Religious History of the Jews* (New York: Columbia University Press, 1952), vol. 1, chaps. 4, 5, on the impact of the destruction of the First Temple.

30. See Irving Greenberg, *Crossroads of Destiny* (New York: United Jewish Appeal [1975]), and any of the standard history books, such as Salo W. Baron, *Social and Religious History*, vol. 2, chaps. 11, 12, et seq.

31. Cf. Maimonides, *Commentary on the Mishnah*, Sanhedrin, chap. 10, mishnah 1.

32. Cf. the moving article by Immanuel Hartom, "Hirhurim al Ha Shoa," *Deot* 18 (Winter 5720 [1961]): 28–31, and the responses of Isachar Jacobson, "HaChashiva HaMikrait V'HaShoah," *Deot* 21 (Spring 5722 [1962]): 26–28, and David Chomsky, "Hirhurim al HaShoah v'al Tekumat Yisrael" ibid., pp. 28–39, and Jacob Rothschild, "Od L'Inyan Darkei HaHashgachah V'HaArachat HaShoah," *Deot* 20 (Summer 5722 [1962]): 39–40. Compare this to the ugly work of R. Joel Teitelbaum, *Al HaGeulah v'al Hatemurah* (Brooklyn: Jerusalem Publishing, 1967).

33. A. Roy Eckardt, "Is the Holocaust Unique?" *Worldview*, September 1974, pp. 21–35. See also idem, "The Devil and the Yom Kippur War," *Midstream*, August–September 1974, pp. 67–74.

34. Teitelbaum, *Al HaGeulah v'al Hatemurah*, pp. 6, 11, 18, 29, 77, 84, 88. This is foreshadowed in Teitelbaum's earlier work, *VaYoel Moshe* (Brooklyn: Jerusalem Publishing, 1962), pp. 6–8, 122–24, 140, and passim. Cf. *New York Times* April 1967, seriatim. A news account in *Ha'aretz*, February 16, 1975, reported that a meeting between Neturei Karta representatives (allied with R. Joel Teitelbaum against Israel) and PLO representatives was held. The Neturei Karta delegates identified with the PLO's commitment to destroy the present state of Israel and replace it with a "secular, democratic" Palestine.

35. Berkovits, *Faith After the Holocaust;* Emil Fackenheim, *God's Presence in History* (New York: New York University Press, 1970); Richard Rubenstein, *After Auschwitz* (Indianapolis: Bobbs-Merrill, 1968), especially pp. 128–29.

36. Richard Rubenstein, "Homeland and Holocaust," in *The Religious Situation 1968* (Boston: Beacon Press, 1969), pp. 39–111.

37. Wiesel, *Night*, p. 71.

38. Wiesel, *The Gates of the Forest*, p. 225–26.

39. Rubenstein, *After Auschwitz*, pp. 9–101.

40. Anthony Flew and Alistair MacIntyre, *New Essays in Philosophical Theology* (London: SCM Press, 1958), pp. 103–5, 109–30.

41. Cf. Hoess, *Commandant of Auschwitz*, pp. 88–91; Saul Friedlander, *Counterfeit Nazi: The Ambiguity of Good*, (London: Weidenfeld & Nicolson, 1969); p. 21–22, 36, 59, 64.

42. Emil Fackenheim, "On the Self-Exposure of Faith to the Modern Secular World," reprinted in *Quest for Past and Future* (Boston: Beacon Press, 1968), pp. 289 ff.

43. Wiesel, *The Accident*, p. 118.

44. Cf. I. Greenberg, *The Rebirth of Israel: Event and Interpretation* (forthcoming).

45. Compare and contrast Marshall Sklare (with Joseph Greenblum), *Jewish*

Identity on the Suburban Frontier (New York: Basic Books, 1967), especially pp. 214–49, 322–26, with T. I. Lenn and Associates, *Rabbi and Synagogue in Reform Judaism* (Hartford: Lenn and Associates, 1972), especially chap. 13, pp. 234–52. Note especially the younger age shift on p. 242. Cf. also how low Israel rates in the "essential" category of being a good Jew, in respondents in Sklare, p. 322.

46. Cf. B.T. Yoma 68b.

47. B.T. Baba Mezia 58b.

48. Jose Faur, "Reflections on Job and Situation Morality," *Judaism* 19, no. 2 (Spring 1970): 219–25, especially p. 220; André Neher, "Job: The Biblical Man," *Judaism* 13, no. 1 (Winter 1964): 37–47; Robert Gordis, "The Lord Out of the Whirlwind," ibid., especially pp. 49–50, 55–58, 62–63. See also Margarethe Susman, *Das Buch Hiob und das Schicksal des jüdischen Volkes* (Zurich: Steinberg, 1946).

49. Joseph B. Soloveichik, "Kol Dodi Dofek," in *Torah U'Meluchah*, ed. Simon Federbush (Jerusalem: Mossad Harav Kook, 1961), pp. 11–44, especially pp. 21–25.

50. Eckardt, *Elder and Younger Brothers*, p. 21.

51. Gunter Lewy, *The Catholic Church and Nazi Germany;* Gordon C. Zahn, *German Catholics and Hitler's Wars: A Study in Social Control* (New York: Sheed & Ward, 1962); idem, *In Solitary Witness: The Life and Death of Franz Jaggerstratter* (London: Chapman, 1966).

52. *Trial of the Major War Criminals before the International Military Tribunal* (Nuremberg, 1947–49), vol. 29, 1919. PS printed in *Nazi Conspiracy and Aggression* vol. 4, pp. 518–72 especially pp. 559, 563–64, 566 ff., quoted in Joachim C. Fest, *The Face of the Third Reich* (London: Weidenfeld & Nicolson, 1970), p. 119.

53. Donat, *Holocaust Kingdom,* p. 91.

54. Wiesel, *Night,* pp. 73–74.

55. Falconi, *The Silence of Pius XII* (Boston: Little Brown, 1970), pp. 74–80; Saul Friedlander, *Pius XII and the Third Reich,* pp. 123, 139 ff.

56. Cf. *Bereshith Raba, Seder VaYera,* parsha 50, par. 16; also ibid., parsha 51, par. 10; B.T. Yevamot 77a; see Z. Y. Lipovitz, *Commentary on the Book of Ruth* (Tel Aviv, 1959).

57. Talmud Yerushalmi, *Berakhot* 15b (chap. 2, halakhah 4); *Aychah Rabba,* parsha 1, sec. 51.

58. Albert Camus, *Resistance, Rebellion and Death* (New York: Knopf, 1961), p. 71.

59. Quoted in Roger Manvell, *S.S. and Gestapo* (New York: Ballantine, 1969), p. 109.

60. J. S. Conway, *The Nazi Persecution of the Churches,* pp. 261–65; Saul Friedlander, *Counterfeit Nazi,* pp. 37, 38, 145–49; Falconi, *Silence of Pius XII,* p. 87; Friedlander, *Pius XII and the Third Reich,* pp. 92–102, but see also pp. 114 ff.; Gitta Sereny, *Into That Darkness,* pp. 276 ff., 292–303. See also Weissmandl, *Min Hametzar,* pp. 21–22, 23–24. Cf. also Karl Barth's mea culpa on the Jewish Issue in a letter to Eberhard Bethge quoted in E. Bethge, "Troubled Self-Interpretation and Uncertain Response in the Church Struggle," in Littell and Locke, *German Church Struggle,* p. 167.

61. Cf. Irving Greenberg, "A Hymn to Secularists" (Dialogue of Irving

Greenberg and Leonard Fein at the General Assembly in Chicago, November 15, 1974 [cassette distributed by Council of Jewish Federations and Welfare Funds, New York, 1975]).

62. Cf. Erich Fromm, *The Fear of Freedom* (American title, *Escape from Freedom*), 1st ed. (London; Routledge & Kegan Paul, 1942). See George Stein, *The Waffen SS* (Ithaca: Cornell University Press, 1970); for Ohlendorf's testimony, see *Trials of War Criminals Before the Nuremberg Military Tribunals Under Control Council Law No. 10, October 1946–April 1949* (Washington: Government Printing Office, 1952), vol. 4; *United States of America v. Otto Ohlendorf et al.*, case No. 9, pp. 384–91.

63. The purported Maimonides ruling is quoted in Rabbi Simon Huberband's essay on Kiddush Hashem (Sanctification of God's name), found in the collection of his Holocaust writings printed under the title *Kiddush Hashem* (Tel Aviv: Zachor 1969), p. 23. Rabbi Menachem Ziemba, the great rabbinical scholar of Warsaw, is quoted as citing the same Maimonides ruling in Hillel Seidman, *Yoman Ghetto Varsha* (New York: Jewish Book, 1959), p. 221. An exhaustive search of Maimonides' work (including consultation with Dr. Haym Soloveichik, who has edited a mimeographed collection of Maimonides' writings on Kiddush Hashem for the Hebrew University) makes clear that there is no such ruling in Maimonides. The acceptance during the Holocaust of the view that Maimonides issued such a ruling—even by scholars of Maimonides such as Ziemba—only shows the urgency of the need for such a ruling. The Rabbis instinctively recognized that every Jew was making a statement when killed in the Holocaust—the very statement that the Nazis were so frantically trying to silence by killing all the Jews. This is contra Richard Rubenstein's comments in "Some Perspectives on Religious Faith After Auschwitz," in Littell and Locke, *German Church Struggle*, p. 263.

64. Franklin H. Littell, *The German Phoenix: Men and Movements in the Church in Germany* (Garden City, N.Y., 1960), p. 217.

65. Tadeusz Borowski, *This Way for the Gas, Ladies and Gentlemen* (New York: Viking, 1967), p. 87.

66. A. Carmi, "The Journey to Eretz Israel," in *Extermination and Resistance* (Kibbutz Lohamei Hagetaot, Israel, 1958), 1:87–101, especially pp. 94–96.

67. Haggadah of Pesach; Exod. 12:13, 20:1–14, 22:21; Lev. 11, esp. v. 45, 19:33–36, 23:42–43, 25:34–55; Deut. 4:30–45, 5:6–18, 15:12–18, 16:1–12, 26:1–11; Josh. 24; Judg. 2:1–5, 11–12; Jer. 2:1–9, 7:22–27, 11:1–8, 16:14–15, 22:7–8, 31:3–33, 32:16–22, 34:8–22; Ezek. 20; Neh. 9.

ALAN T. DAVIES

1. Franklin H. Littell, "Christendom, Holocaust and Israel: The Importance for Christians of Recent Major Events in Jewish History," *Journal of Ecumenical Studies* 10, no. 3 (Summer 1973): 496–97.

2. Emil Fackenheim, "The People Israel Lives," *Christian Century*, May 6, 1970, p. 564.

3. Assuming, of course, that Hitler is speaking the truth about his past. It is

not impossible that his anti-Semitism may have had earlier roots which he does not acknowledge in *Mein Kampf.*

4. Jean-Paul Sartre, *Anti-Semite and Jew,* trans. George J. Becker (New York: Schocken Books, 1948), pp. 40 ff.

5. Alan Bullock, *Hitler: A Study in Tyranny* (London: Pelican Books, 1962), p. 703.

6. Cited in Richard Rubenstein, *After Auschwitz* (New York: Bobbs-Merrill, 1966), p. 53.

7. Walter Eichrodt, *Theology of the Old Testament,* trans. J. A. Baker (Philadelphia: Westminster Press, 1961), 1:260.

8. Eugene Borowitz, *How Can a Jew Speak of Faith Today?* (Philadelphia: Westminster Press, 1969), p. 25.

9. Emil Fackenheim, *God's Presence in History,* (New York: New York University Press, 1970), p. 79. "The unprecedented catastrophe of the Holocaust now discloses for us that the eclipse of God remains a religious possibility within Judaism only if it is not total. If all present access to the God of history is wholly lost, the God of history is Himself lost."

10. Borowitz, pp. 55–56.

11. Reinhold Niebuhr, *Faith and History* (New York: Scribner's, 1949), p. 139.

12. Cf. Jacob Neusner, *A Life of Rabban Yohanan Ben Zakkai* (Leiden: E. J. Brill, 1962), pp. 131 f.

13. In an unpublished paper, "God's Acts in History: Contemporary History and Jewish Response," pp. 9 f.

14. A suggestion once made to me by Prof. Martin Rumscheidt, University of Windsor. Perhaps such a crucifixion would be the only valid crucifixion representation of the twentieth century.

ROSEMARY R. RUETHER

1. See, for example, Edward Flannery, *The Anguish of the Jews* (New York: Macmillan, 1964), pp. 60–61, who declares that the sources of anti-Semitism are either "pagan hate" or a misreading of the "legitimate anti-Judaism of Orthodox Christian doctrine." G. W. Buchanan, *The Consequences of the Covenant* (Leiden: Brill, 1970), is an extreme example of a Christian Old Testament scholarship that regards racism and anti-Semitism as a transfer to the Gentiles of Jewish ethnocentricity.

2. The material in this essay is a summary of an extensive study by this author of the theological roots of anti-Semitism in patristic theology: *Faith and Fratricide: The Christian Theological Roots of Anti-Semitism* (New York: Seabury Press, 1974). [This work had not yet been published at the time of the Symposium.]

3. For a treatment of the Jewish response to Jesus and a critique of the Christian interpretation of the trial of Jesus, see Ben Zion Bokser, *Judaism and the Christian Predicament* (New York: Knopf, 1967). There have been a number of recent critiques of the New Testament account of Jesus' trial, e.g., Paul Winter, *On the Trial of Jesus* (Berlin: Walter de Gruyter, 1961).

4. The *Adversus Judaeos* tradition refers here to writings in various genres: collections of testimonies, sermons, and treatises; also dialogues which have, as their essential theme, the reprobation of the Jews and the rejection of the Law. The standard treatment of these writings from the second century down through the Middle Ages is A. L. Williams, *Adversos Judaeos* (Cambridge, 1935).

5. Detailed references, as well as textual sources and available translations for these doctrines against the Jews in patristic thought, can be found in chap. 3 of *Faith and Fratricide* (see n. 2, above). I have based my study on the following texts: *The Epistle of Barnabas.* Justin Martyr's *Dialogue with Trypho.* Irenaeus, *Against the Heresies* (iii, xxi; iv, iv–xviii). Tertullian, *In Answer to the Jews.* Lactantius, *Divine Institutes* (iv, x–xx). Hippolytus, *Refutation of All Heresies* (ix, xxv) and *Expository Treatise Against the Jews.* Novatian, *On Jewish Meats.* Origen, *Contra Celsus* (esp. bk. ii). Cyprian, *Three Books of Testimonies Against the Jews.* Pseudo-Nyssa, *Selected Testimonies from the Old Testament Against the Jews.* Eusebius, *Demonstrations of the Gospel* and *Ecclesiastical History.* John Chrysostom, *Eight Orations Against the Jews,* and *Demonstration to the Jews and Gentiles That Christ Is God.* Augustine, *Tract Against the Jews* and *The City of God* (xvi–xviii; xx, 29). Pseudo-Augustine, *Against the Jews, Pagans, and Arians,* and *Altercation Between the Church and the Synagogue.* Ephrem the Syrian, *Rhythm Against the Jews.* Sargis d'Aberga, *The Teachings of Jacob.* Pseudo-Athanasius, *Questions to Antiochus Dux.* Aphrahat, *Demonstrations Against the Jews.* Jacob of Serug, *Homilies Against the Jews.* Anonymous, *Trophies Framed Against the Jews at Damascus.* Isidore .32 ,vi ,*htiaF xodohtrO ehT* ni ",sweJ eht tsniagA ,htabbaS eht nO" ,enec 5730 cene, "On the Sabbath, Against the Jews," in *The Orthodox Faith,* iv, 23. *Dialogue of Jason and Papiscus. Dialogue of Timothy and Aquila. Dialogue of Athanasius and Zacchaeus. Dialogue of Papiscus and Philo. Dialogue of Archbishop Gregentius and the Jew Herban. Dialogue on the Law between Simon, a Jew, and Theophilus, a Christian,* attributed to Evagrius. *Discussion of St. Silvester with Jews at Rome.* Pseudo-Cyprian, *On the Mountains of Sinai and Zion.*

6. The laws can be found in Clyde de Pharr, *The Theodosian Code and Novels and the Sirmonian Constitution* (Princeton: Princeton University Press, 1952), esp. sec. 16:8. Detailed analysis of these anti-Judaic laws in their historical context is found in James S. Seaver, *The Persecution of the Jews in the Roman Empire; 300–438 A.D.* (University of Kansas Press, 1952). For a general treatment of this period, see also James Parkes, *The Conflict of the Church and the Synagogue* (London, 1934).

7. Andrew Sharf, *Byzantine Jewry from Justinian to the Fourth Crusade* (London: Routledge & Kegan Paul, 1971), p. 184 and passim.

8. For a general survey, see James Parkes, *The Jew in the Medieval Community* (London: Soncino Press, 1938); also Leon Poliakov, *The History of Anti-Semitism* (New York: Vanguard, 1968), 2 vols.

9. Joshua Trachtenberg, *The Devil and the Jews* (New Haven: Yale University Press, 1932); also Salo Baron, "Demonic Alien," in *Social and Religious History of the Jews* (New York: Columbia University Press, 1958), 9:122 ff.

10. Cecil Roth, *The History of the Marranos* (Philadelphia, 1947), and Yitz-

hak Baer, *The History of the Jews in Christian Spain* (Philadelphia, 1966), 2 vols.

11. For an introduction, see James Parkes, *Antisemitism* (Chicago: Quadrangle, 1963).

12. Laura Benson, *The Negroes and the Jews* (New York: Random House, 1971).

13. Norman Cohn, *Warrant For Genocide: The Myth of the Jewish World Conspiracy and the Protocols of the Elders of Zion* (New York:Harper & Row, 1966).

WALTER J. BURGHARDT

1. See Walter J. Burghardt, "Jewish Christian Dialogue: Early Church versus Contemporary Christianity," in *The Dynamic in Christian Thought,* ed. Joseph Papin (Villanova, Pa.: Villanova University Press, 1970), esp. pp. 200–201.

GREGORY BAUM

1. For various attempts of Christian theologians to make room for a living Judaism, see Alan Davies, *Antisemitism and the Christian Mind* (New York: Herder & Herder, 1969).

2. Newsletter, *The Church and the Jewish People* (World Council of Churches, Geneva).

3. *The Documents of Vatican II,* ed. Walter Abbot (New York: Herder & Herder/Associated Press, 1966). The conciliar documents are quoted according to paragraphs since these are the same in all the editions.

4. See par. 4.

5. See pars. 2 and 5.

6. *Constitution on the Church,* par. 16; *Const. on the Church in the Modern World,* par. 22.

7. See par. 5.

8. It was the great achievement of Emile Durkheim and Max Weber to demonstrate that symbols are co-constitutive of culture and society and hence of people's self-definitions.

9. For a discussion of this understanding of religion, see C. Geertz, "Religion as a Cultural System," in *The Religious Situation: 1968,* ed. D. Cutler (Boston: Beacon Press, 1968), pp. 637–87.

10. This is the thesis of Rosemary Ruether, outlined in her lecture given at this Symposium, and worked out in detail in her *Faith and Fratricide* (New York: Seabury Press, 1974).

11. See the above-mentioned work of Rosemary Ruether.

12. K. Mannheim, *Ideology and Utopia* (1929; reprint ed., New York: Harcourt, Brace & World, 1967), pp. 55–58.

13. For the Hegelian trend in nineteenth-century Protestant theology, see E. Troeltsch, *The Absoluteness of Christianity and the History of Religions* (1901;

reprinted., Richmond, Va.: John Knox Press, 1971). For the crucial influence of Blondel on Catholic theology, see G. Baum, *Man Becoming* (New York: Herder & Herder, 1970), pp. 1–34.

14. See *Hoerer des Wortes* (1941; reprint ed., Freiburg i.Br.: Herder, 1971).

15. See *Constitution on the Church in the Modern World*, Study-Club Edition (New York: Paulist Press, 1967), commentary by G. Baum, pp. 1–35.

16. See H. R. Schlette, *Toward a Theology of Religions* (New York: Herder & Herder, 1965).

17. "Das Christentum und die nichtchristlichen Religionen," *Schriften* 5 (Cologne: Benziger Verlag, 1962).

18. The same eschatological perspective has been adopted in the lectures of Rosemary Ruether and John Pawlikowski given at this Conference.

JOHANNES C. HOEKENDIJK

1. Rosah and David were raised in the Hoekendijk's home until they and the Hoekendijks were betrayed to the Nazis.

2. Richard Rubenstein, *After Auschwitz* (New York: Bobbs-Merrill, 1966).

3. Bernhard Blumenkranz, *Juifs et Chrétiéns dans le Monde Occidental* (1960), chap. on "La Mission Juive," pp. 159–208.

4. Cf. Rom. 1:14.

5. From Eigil's "Life of Sturmi, Abbot of Fulda," translated in J. T. Addison, *The Medieval Missionary* (1936), p. 49.

6. Heinz Robert Schlette, *Towards a Theology of Religions* (New York: Herder & Herder, 1966).

7. Jurgen Moltmann, unpublished address at the Duke University Conference on Hope, 1968 (mimeographed notes of Thomas Herrin, p. 20).

AARNE SIIRALA

1. In *Luther's Works*, vol. 47, *The Christian in Society* (St. Louis, Mo.: Concordia–Fortress Press, 1958).

2. Ibid., p. 123.

3. Marwin Lowenthal, *The Jews in Germany* (New York, 1936), p. 161.

4. Jacob Marcus, *The Jew in the Medieval World* (New York, 1960), p. 165.

5. Arnold Ages, "Luther and the Rabbis," *Jewish Quarterly Review* 58, no. 1 (1967).

6. Hans Preuss, *Von den Katakomben bis zu den Zeichen der Zeit: Der Weg der Kirche durch zwei Jahrthausende* (Martin Luther Verlag, 1960).

7. Wilhelm Maurer, "Die Zeit der Reformation," in K. H. Rengstorf and S. von Kortzfleisch, *Kirche und Synagoge: Handbuch der Geschichte von Christen und Juden*, vol. 2 (Stuttgart, 1968).

8. Ibid., 1:384.

9. *Politics of Hysteria* (New York, 1964).

10. René Dubos, *God Within* (New York, 1972).

11. *Ecumenist* 10, no. 5 (1972).

12. Robert Bellah, *Beyond Belief: Essays in Religion in a Post-Traditional World* (New York, 1970).

13. Cf. Aarne Siirala, *Divine Humanness* (Philadelphia: Fortress Press, 1970), p. 142.

14. Ibid., pp. 93 ff.

15. Ibid., p. 98.

16. Ibid., pp. 50 ff., 151.

17. Ibid., pp. 60. ff.

18. Ibid., pp. 165.

19. Ibid., pp. 75 ff.

JOHN T. PAWLIKOWSKI

1. New York: Holt, Rinehart & Winston, 1964.

2. New Haven: Yale University Press, 1963.

3. New York: American Jewish Committee and National Conference of Christians and Jews, 1972. Also cf. Franklin H. Littell, "The Strober Report," *Journal of Ecumenical Studies* 9, no. 4 (Fall 1972): 860–62.

4. Cf. "Catholic Panel Finds Pejorative Image of Judaism in French Religious Texts," *New York Times,* October 12, 1969.

5. New York: Holt, Rinehart & Winston, 1971.

6. New York: Paulist Press, 1973. Also cf. James W. Arnold, "Religious Textbooks . . . Primers in Bigotry," *Ave Maria,* October 10 and 17, 1964.

7. June 1969, p. 80.

8. Cf. Sister Mary Alice Muir, S.N.D. de Namur, "Catholic-Jewish Team Reviews Textbooks," *Christian Century,* January 15, 1969, p. 99.

9. "A Survey and Evaluation of Christian-Jewish Relationships Since Vatican Council II" (Paper presented by Rabbi Marc H. Tanenbaum, national interreligious office director of the American Jewish Committee, in cooperation with Sister Rose Albert Thering of the Seton Hall Institute of Judaeo-Christian Studies, Mrs. Judith Banki, Rabbi James Rudin, and Dr. Gerald Strober).

10. Cf. "Christian Lessons Lack Information on Jews, Parallel Studies Show," *Catholic Virginian* (Richmond, Va.), May 22, 1970.

11. Ibid.

12. "The Parting of the Ways," in *Face to Face: A Primer in Dialogue,* ed. Lily Edelman (Washington: B'nai B'rith Adult Jewish Education, 1967).

13. "Christian Education and the Jewish People," *Christian Century,* February 8, 1967, p. 168.

14. On Pharisaism cf R. Travers Herford, *The Pharisees* (Boston: Beacon Press, 1962); Ellis Rivkin, "The Internal City," *Journal for the Scientific Study of Religion* 5, no. 2 (Spring 1966): 225–40, and "The Pharisaic Background of Christianity," in *Root and Branch: The Jewish/Christian Dialogue,* ed. Michael Zeik and Martin Siegel (Williston Park, N.Y.: Roth Publishing, 1973); Louis Finkelstein, *The Pharisees,* 2 vols. (Philadelphia: Jewish Publication Society, 1964); Jacob Neusner, *From Politics to Piety: The Emergence of Pharisaic Judaism* (Englewood Cliffs, N.J.: Prentice-Hall, 1973); Asher Finkel, *The Pharisees and the Teacher of Nazareth* (Leiden: E.J. Brill, 1964); J. Massingberd

Ford, "The Christian Debt to Pharisaism," in *Brothers in Hope: The Bridge*, ed. John M. Oesterreicher, vol. 5 (New York: Herder & Herder, 1970), pp. 218–30; Rosemary Ruether, "The Pharisees in First-Century Judaism, *Ecumenist* 11, no. 1 (November–December 1972): 1–7; John T Pawlikowski, "The Minister as Pharisee," *Commonweal* 95, no. 16 (January 21, 1972): 369–73; "Jesus and the Revolutionaries," *Christian Century* 89, no. 44 (December 6, 1972): 1237–41, "On Renewing the Revolution of the Pharisees," *Cross Currents* 20, no. 4 (Fall 1970): 415–34, "The Pharisees and Christianity," *Bible Today*, October 1970, pp. 47–53.

15. New York: Weybright & Talley, 1970.

16. *The Foundations of Judaism and Christianity* (London: Vallentine-Mitchell, 1960); also cf. John T. Pawlikowski, "The Church and Judaism: The Thought of James Parkes," *Journal of Ecumenical Studies* 7, no. 1 (Winter 1970): 37–51, and "Pauline Baptismal Theology and Christian-Jewish Relations," in *Root and Branch*, ed. Zeik and Siegel, pp. 89–110.

17. "The Doctrinal Basis for Jewish-Christian Dialogue," in *Root and Branch*, ed. Zeik and Siegel, pp. 159–74.

18. "Christian Theology and the Covenant of Israel," *Journal of Ecumenical Studies* 9, no. 2 (Spring 1972): 249–70.

19. "An Invitation to Jewish-Christian Dialogue: In What Sense Can We Say That Jesus Was 'the Christ'?" *Ecumenist* 10, no. 2 (January–February 1972): 17–24. Also cf. "Christian-Jewish Dialogue: New Interpretations," *ADL Bulletin* 30, no. 5 (May 1973): 3–4, and "Anti-Judaism Is the Left Hand of Christology," *New Catholic World* 217, no. 1297 (January–February 1974): 12–15.

20. "Christian and Jew Today from a Christian Theological Perspective," *Journal of Ecumenical Studies* 7, no. 4 (Fall 1970): 744–62.

21. "Jewish-Christian Relationship: The Two Covenants and the Dilemmas of Christology," *Journal of Ecumenical Studies* 9, no. 2 (Spring 1972): 249–70.

22. Cf. Bruce Long, ed., *Judaism and the Christian Seminary Curriculum* (New York: Anti-Defamation League, 1967); also Solomon S. Bernards, "Judaic Studies in College and Seminary Classrooms," *Christian Century*, August 19, 1970.

23. Cf. Silvio E Fittipaldi, "Jewish-Christian Relations and the Curriculum," *Journal of Ecumenical Studies* 10, no. 3 (Summer 1973): 651–54.

24. An excellent bibliographical aid in this regard can be found in *The Study of Judaism: Bibliographical Essays* (New York: Anti-Defamation League, 1972).

25. "Anti-Semitism and the Gospel," *Commonweal*, March 24, 1967, pp. 16–18.

26. An example of a Yom HaSho'ah liturgy for Christians can be found in Franklin Littell, *The Crucifixion of the Jews* (New York: Harper & Row, 1975), pp. 141–53. This service, which was first printed in *Christians Concerned for Israel* 10 (October 1972), was originally planned by Dr. Elizabeth Wright and conducted in the chapel at Queens College, Charlotte, N.C., on May 10, 1972.

27. John M. Oesterreicher, *Shalom: The Encounter of Christians and Jews and the Catholic Educator* (South Orange, N.J.: Institute of Judaeo-Christian Studies, 1969).

28. *The Hours of Divine Office in English and Latin* (Collegeville, Minn.: Liturgical Press, 1964), p. 518.

29. Ibid., p. 518.

30. Oesterreicher, *Shalom*, p. 14.

CLAIRE HUCHET-BISHOP

1. Jules Isaac, *Jésus et Israèl* (Paris: Albin Michel, 1948); rev. ed., Paris: Fasquelle, 1959); published in English as *Jesus and Israel,* ed. Claire Huchet-Bishop, trans. Sally Gran (New York: Holt, Rinehart & Winston, 1971).

2. The Ten Points of Seelisberg, based on eighteen points presented in *Jesus et Israèl* (cf. English ed., pp. 401–4) as an "Appendix and Practical Conclusion," formed the basis for the statement issued by the Third Commission of the International Emergency Conference of Christians and Jews at Seelisberg, Switzerland, in August 1947. The conference, noteworthy for its early date, included both Catholic and Protestant Christians.

3. Paul Démann, *La Catéchèse chretienne et le peuple de la Bible: Constatations et perspectives* (Paris: Cahiers Sioniens, 1952).

4. From Professor Isaac's own motto, *pro veritate pugnator.*

5. Claire Huchet-Bishop, *How Catholics Look at Jews: Inquiries into Italian, Spanish, and French Teaching Materials* (New York: Paulist Press, 1974).

6. Jean-Paul Sartre, *Réflexions sur la question juive,* Col. Idées (Paris: Gallimard, 1954), pp. 82–83.

7. Comité Episcopal pour les Relations avec le Judaisme, "Pastoral Orientations with Regard to the Attitudes of Christians toward Judaism," *Catholic Mind* 81, no. 1275 (September 1973): 51–Trans. from *L'Amitié judeochrétienne de France,* supp. no. 2 (April–June 1973).

8. Jules Isaac's succinct term. See his *The Teaching of Contempt,* ed. Claire Huchet-Bishop, trans. Helen Weaver (New York: Holt, Rinehart & Winston, 1964). The French edition is *L'Enseignement du mépris* (Paris: Fasquelle, 1962).

9. Matt. 3:3.

10. Comite Episcopal, "Pastoral Orientations."

11. Elie Wiesel (unpublished talk).

12. Comité Episcopal, "Pastoral Orientations."

13. Jean Aucagne, S.T. "Un geste politiquement inopportun et une théologie irrecevable," *Informations catholiques internationales* (Paris), no. 432 (May 15, 1973): 5–6.

14. Cardinal Jean Daniélou, S.J., "L'Eglise devant le Judaisme," *Le Figaro* (Paris), April 28–29, 1973.

15. Ibid.

16. Aucagne, "Un geste politiquement."

17. François Biot. "La foi au Christ ne suffit-elle plus?" *Témoignage chretien* (Paris), April 26, 1973.

18. Daniélou, "L'Eglise devant le Judaisme."

19. Comité Episcopal, "Pastoral Orientations."

20. Pierre Teilhard de Chardin, *The Divine Milieu* (New York: Harper, 1960).

21. John P. Markham, "Is There Anti-Semitism in New Testament Translations?" (Essay presented to the Steering Committee of the Project on the Jewish-Christian Dimension in the New Testament Translation, National Conference of Christians and Jews, New York, 1972).

22. Rev. D. Peter Burrows. "Palm Sunday: The Christian Feast of Tabernacles," *Christian News from Israel* 24, no. 1(13) (Summer 1973): 16–24.

23. Chaldean rite, quoted in Sister Marie Despina, "Jews in Oriental Literature," *Sidic* (Rome), October–November 1967.

24. Rom. 11:18.

25. John 4:22.

EMIL FACKENHEIM

1. *Sefer Ha-Geulah,* ed. J. Lipschitz (London, 1909), especially pp. 3–16, 29.

2. See, e.g., *Haggadat Pesaḥ Arẓi-Yisraelit,* arranged and edited by Rabbi Menachem M. Kasher (New York, 1950), pp. 132 ff.

3. Maimonides, *Yad, Hilkhot Melakhim,* bk. 14, treatise 5, chaps. 11 and 12.

4. Walter Laqueur, *A History of Zionism* (London: Weidenfeld & Nicholson, 1972), p. 593.

5. Manes Sperber, . . . *Than a Tear in The Sea* (New York: Bergen Belsen Memorial Press, 1967), p. xiv.

6. *Quest For Past and Future* (Boston: Beacon, 1970), chap. 1, and *God's Presence in History* (New York: Harper Torchbooks, 1973), chaps. 1 and 3.

7. Cited in Kasher, p. 137.

8. *Ani Ma'amin,* (Jerusalem: Mossad Harav Kook, 1965), p. 206.

9. "Kiddush Hashem Over the Ages and Its Uniqueness in the Holocaust Period," in *Jewish Resistance During the Holocaust* (Jerusalem: Yad Vashem, 1971), p. 473.

10. *The Fighting Ghettos,* trans. and ed. M. Barkai (New York: Tower, n.d.), pp. 26 ff.

11. Ibid., p. 30.

SEYMOUR SIEGEL

1. *Kiddush Hashem,* ed. S. Niger (New York: Cyco Bicher Farlag, 1948), pp. 27–28. See also Seymour Siegel, "Theological Reflections on the Destruction of European Jewry," *Conservative Judaism* 18, no. 4 (1963–64).

2. Mishnah *Sotah,* end.

3. Gershom Scholem, *The Messianic Idea in Judaism* (New York: Schocken Books, 1971), pp. 1 ff.

4. Ibid. Also, for an interesting analysis of this problem, see Louis Jacobs, *Principles of the Jewish Faith* (New York: Basic Books, 1964), pp. 368–98.

5. See the article by Scholem, "The Messianic Idea in Kabbalism," in Scholem, *Messianic Idea in Judaism,* pp. 37–49.

6. "The expectation of the coming of the Messiah, by which and because of which Judaism lives, would be a meaningless theologumenon, a mere idea in the philosophical sense, empty babble, if the appearance again and again of a false Messiah did not render it reality and unreality, illusion and disillusion. The false Messiah is as old as the hope for the true Messiah. He is the changing form of the changeless hope." Franz Rosenzweig, *The Star of Redemption,* trans. William Hallo (New York: Holt, Rinehart & Winston, 1971), p. 250. See also Z. Werblowsky, "Crisis of Messianism," *Judaism* 7, no. 2 (1958).

7. For a comprehensive analysis of the role of Messianism in Zionist thought, see Arthur Hertzberg, *The Zionist Idea* (Garden City: Doubleday, 1959), especially the introduction, pp. 14 ff.

8. For the text of Pinsker's pamphlet, see ibid., pp. 181 ff.

9. Ibid.

10. For a good example of this, see Waldo Frank, *The Jew in Our Day* (New York: Duell, Sloan, 1944). It is interesting that in his introduction to Frank's book, Reinhold Niebuhr understands the Jewish situation much better than Frank, the Jew.

11. Abraham J. Heschel, *Israel: An Echo of Eternity* (New York: Farrar, Straus & Giroux, 1969).

12. Reinhold Neibuhr, introduction to Frank, *Jew in Our Day,* p. 13.

13. *Israel and the World* (New York: Schocken Books, 1963), pp. 229–30.

14. Heschel, *Israel.*

15. *Commentary* 57, no. 3 (March 1974).

EVA FLEISCHNER

1. Emil Fackenheim, "Jewish Faith and the Holocaust, a Fragment." *Commentary* 64, no. 2 (August 1968): 30–36.

2. Rosemary Ruether, "Theological Anti-Semitism in the New Testament," *Christian Century,* February 14, 1968, p. 193.

3. Gershom Scholem, "The Holiness of Sin," *Commentary* 51, no. 1 (January 1971): 41–70; reprinted in Scholem, *The Messianic Idea In Judaism* (New York: Schocken Books, 1971), pp. 78–141.

4. Ruether, "Theological Anti-Semitism," p. 195.

5. Krister Stendahl, "Judaism and Christianity: A Plea for a New Relationship," *Harvard Divinity Bulletin,* Fall 1967. Reprinted in *Cross Currents* 17 (1967): 445–58.

6. Elie Wiesel, "To a Concerned Friend," in *One Generation After* (New York: Random House, 1970), pp. 146–55.

7. Quoted in H. Berkhof, "Israel as a Theological Problem" *Journal of Ecumenical Studies* 6, no. 3 (Summer 1969): 345.

8. Ibid.

9. *Criterion* 2, no. 1 (Winter 1963): 23 ff.

10. Berkhof, "Israel as a Theological problem," p. 345.

11. Wiesel, "To a Concerned Friend," in *One Generation After,* p. 155.

SHLOMO AVINERI

1. Karl Marx, "On the Jewish Question," in *Early Writings,* trans. T. B. Bottomore (London, 1963), esp. pp. 4–6, 32–33.

2. This has been most persuasively argued recently by Emil L. Fackenheim in his *Encounters between Judaism and Modern Philosophy* (New York, 1973).

3. On this see ibid., pp. 134 ff; also Nathan Rotenstreich, "The Bruno Bauer Controversy," *Leo Baeck Institute Yearbook* (London), 4 (1959).

4. His anonymous tract *Die Posaune des jüngsten Gerichts über Hegel den Atheisten und Antichristen* (Leipzig, 1841) does contain, however, a section on historical Judaism (pp. 107–13).

5. The literature is voluminous. See esp. Horst Stuke, *Philosophie der Tat* (Stuttgart, 1963), pp. 123–87; *Die Hegelsche Linke,* ed. Karl Lowith (Stuttgart, 1962), pp. 75–225; Sidney Hook, *From Hegel to Marx,* new ed. (Ann Arbor, 1962), pp. 98–125.

6. G. W. F. Hegel, *Philosophy of Right,* trans. T. M. Knox (Oxford, 1940), § 270; also § 209, where Hegel says, "a man counts as a man in virtue of his manhood alone, not because he is a Jew, Catholic, Protestant, German, Italian, etc."

7. "Die Fähigkeit," p. 71.

8. *Early Writings,* p. 32. On Marx's support of the spokesmen for Jewish emancipation in their polemic against Bauer, see Shlomo Avineri, "Marx and Jewish Emancipation," *Journal of the History of Ideas* 25 no. 3 (July-September 1964): 445–50.

9. "The Left, The Jews and Israel," in his *Revolution and Counterrevolution,* rev. ed. (Garden City, 1970), p. 375.

10. In this, many socialists followed a lead already to be discerned in some thinkers of the Enlightenment, especially Voltaire. See Arthur Hertzberg, *The French Enlightenment and the Jews* (New York and London, 1968).

11. In Russia, during 1884–90, 13.5 percent of the political prisoners were Jewish; in 1897 the proportion rose to 25 percent and in 1903 to 53 percent! After 1917, the following top officials of the new Soviet regime were Jewish: the head of the Red Army (Trotsky), the first head of the Soviet state (Sverdlov), the head of the Third International (Zinoviev), the head of the Moscow Soviet (Kamenev), the head of the Cheka (Oritzki).

12. Michel Bakounine, "Rapports personels avec Marx," in *Archives Bakounines,* ed. Arthur Lehning (Leiden, 1963), Vol. I/2, pp. 124–25. Trans. by the editor.

13. For similar developments in a slightly later period, see George L. Mosse,"Die Linken in ihrer Stellung zum Nationalsozialismus—das jüdische Problem," in *Zur Geschichte der Juden in Deutschland im 19. u. 20. Jahrhundert* (Jerusalem: 1971), Leo Baeck Institute, pp. 94 ff.

14. Karl Kautsky, *Rasse und Judentum,* 2d ed. (Stuttgart, 1921), p. 93.

15. Ibid., pp. 94–95. For a detailed study of the relationship between Marxism and Zionism, see Walter Laqueur's "Zionism, the Marxist Critique, and the Left," in *Israel, the Arabs and the Middle East,* ed. Irving Howe and Carl Gershman (New York, 1972), pp. 16–44.

16. Published in the *Journal of Palestine Studies* (Beirut) 2, no. 1 (Autumn 1972): 86–110.

17. See my "Political and Social Aspects of Israeli and Arab Nationalism," *Midstream,* January 1973, pp. 41–55.

18. For some of the most representative collections of New Left writings on the Middle East, see the following: Mordechai Chertoff, ed., *The New Left and the Jews* (New York, 1971); Herbert Mason, ed., *Reflections on the Middle East Crisis* (Paris and The Hague, 1970), esp. Noam Chomsky's "Nationalism and Conflict in Palestine," pp. 65–100; Maxime Rodinson, *Israel and the Arabs* (Harmondsworth, 1968); idem, *Israel: A Colonial-Settler State?* (New York, 1973); Gerard Chaliand, *The Palestine Resistance* (Harmondsworth, 1971). For a critique of some of these positions, see Shlomo Avineri, "The New Left and Israel," in *People and Politics in the Middle East,* ed. Michael Curtis (New Brunswick, 1971), pp. 293 ff.

19. Rodinson, *Israel: A Colonial-Settler State?*, p. 91.

20. Rodinson, *Israel and the Arabs,* p. 36.

21. The most interesting attempt in this direction has been Michael Landmann's *Das Israelpseudos der Pseudolinken* (Berlin, 1971).

22. The full text of Daniel Berrigan's remarks appeared in *American Report,* October 29, 1973.

23. For some of the rejoinders, see: Arthur Hertzberg, in *American Report* November 12, 1973; Michael Novak, "The New Antisemitism," *Commonweal,* December 21, 1973; Robert Alter, "Berrigan's Diatribe," *Commentary,* February 1974. See also *Christian Attitudes on Jews and Judaism,* no. 34 (February 1974): 12–13; *The Great Berrigan Debate* (Committee on New Alternatives in the Middle East, 1974); John M. Oesterreicher, "Berrigan's Bankruptcy," *Jewish Frontier,* February 1974, pp. 6–8; Rosemary R. Ruether, "The Suffering Servant Myth," *World View,* March 1974, pp. 45–46; Seymour Cain, "Berrigan, Buber, and the Settler State," *Christian Century* 91 (June 26, 1974).

PAUL JACOBS

1. Harry Fleischman, *Norman Thomas: A Biography* (New York: Norton, 1964), p. 281.

2. Stanley Diamond, "Eruption in the Middle East," *Dissent* 4, no. 1 (Winter 1957): 9.

3. Ibid., p. 10.

4. Paul Jacobs, *Is Curly Jewish?* (New York: Atheneum, 1965; reprint ed., New York: Vintage Books, 1973).

MILTON HIMMELFARB

1. Milton Himmelfarb, in *Commentary,* February 1973, p. 75.

2. "Jews and Judaism as Seen by the English Deists of the Eighteenth Century" (Hebrew, with English abstract), *Zion* 39 (1964).

3. *Zion* 33 (1968).

4. "Judaism and the Jews as Seen by Voltaire" (Hebrew), *Molad,* October–December 1973.

5. *Leo Baeck Institute Yearbook* 16 (1971).

6. *Are the Jews a Race?* (New York: International Publishers, 1926), pp. 246–47.

MICHAEL D. RYAN

1. Blake, *Jerusalem,* chap. 1, in *The Poetry and Prose of William Blake,* ed. David V. Erdman (Garden City, N.Y.: Doubleday, 1970), p. 146.

2. Byron, *Childe Harold's Pilgrimage,* canto 3, in *Lord Byron: Selected Poems and Letters,* ed. William H. Marshall (Boston: Houghton Mifflin, 1968), p. 91.

3. Georg W. F. Hegel, *The Philosophy of History* (New York: Dover Publications, 1956), p. 456.

4. Arthur O. Lovejoy "On the Discrimination of Romanticisms," included as the introductory essay in *English Romantic Poets: Modern Essays in Criticism,* ed. M. H. Abrams (London and New York: Oxford University Press, 1960), pp. 3–24.

5. Ibid., p. 6.

6. Horace L. Friess, introduction to *Schleiermacher's Soliloquies* (Chicago: Open Court, 1957), p. xxiv.

7. See Marshall, *Lord Byron,* pp. 87 f.

8. Friedrich Schleiermacher, *On Religion: Speeches to Its Cultured Despisers,* trans. John Oman (New York: Harper & Row, 1958), p. 36.

9. Ibid., pp. 1 ff.

10. Friedrich Schleiermacher, *The Christian Faith* (New York: Scribner's, 1956), par. 4, p. 12.

11. Ibid., par. 98, p. 413.

12. Friedrich Schleiermacher, *Des Leben Jesu* (Tubingen: C. F. Osiander, 1835), p. 130.

13. Ibid.

14. Ibid, p. 116.

15. *Christian Faith,* par. 106, p. 476.

16. Friedrich Schleiermacher "On the Discrepancy Between the Sabellian and Athanasian Method of Representing the Doctrine of the Trinity," pt. 2, *Biblical Repository and Quarterly Review,* no. 19 (July 1835): 61. Pt. I, found in the same journal, no. 18 (1835): 265–353.

17. Ibid., pt. II, p. 61. The German original is in "Ueber den Gegensatz zwischen der sabellianischen und der athanasianischen Vorstellung von der Trinitaet," Friedrich Schleiermacher's *Sämmtliche Werke,* 1. Abt. zur Theologie, bd. 2 (Berlin: G. Reimer, 1836), p. 555 ff.

18. Schleiermacher, *Speeches,* p. 108.

19. Schleiermacher, "On the Discrepancy," pt. I, p. 331.

20. Ibid.

21. Schleiermacher, *Speeches,* pp. 238 f.

22. As reported by Michael A. Meyer, *The Origins of the Modern Jew: Jewish Identity and European Culture in Germany, 1749–1824.* (Detroit: Wayne State University Press, 1967), p. 70. Meyer's account of the careers of Moses Mendelssohn and David Friedlander, and of the identity struggles of the Jewish intellectuals of Berlin, is most informed and illuminating.

23. Schleiermacher, "Briefe bei Gelegenheit der politischen theologischen Aufgabe und des Sendschreibens judischer Hausvater, Von einem Prediger ausserhalb Berlin, 1799," in *Sämmtliche Werke,* Erste Abteilung. Zur Theologie bd. 5. (Berlin: G. Reimer, 1846), pp. 4–12.

24. Ibid., p. 7.

25. Ibid., p. 8 as translated by Meyer, *Origins of the Modern Jew,* pp. 77 f.

26. Ibid., p. 9.

27. Ibid., p. 10.

28. Ibid., p. 12.

29. The article on Schleiermacher in *The Encyclopaedia Judaica* (1971) suggests that Schleiermacher believed the irrational teaching that he was in fact opposing, for the article says that he advocated "that Jews, as individuals be granted complete emancipation in order to save the Church from contamination by insincere converts seeking equality." Schleiermacher was indeed opposing "quasi-conversion," as he put it, but the language about "contamination" reflects the prejudicial dogma and maxim that he opposed at the end of his letter.

30. Paul Hazard, *The European Mind 1680–1715* (Cleveland and New York: Meridian Books, 1963), pp. 40 f. Hazard describes the significance of Christian chronology within what he called "the old order." This order was still defended by Chateaubriand in his *Genius of Christianity* in 1810.

31. Theodore H. Von Laue, *Leopold Ranke: The Formative Years* (Princeton: Princeton University Press, 1950), pp. 45–47, describes the conception of history shared by the *historische Schule* at the University of Berlin. This "school" included Schleiermacher, but not Hegel.

32. See pp. 000–000 below and William Irwin Thompson *At the Edge of History* (New York: Harper & Row, 1971), chap. I, "Looking for History in L.A.," pp. 3–26, where he takes his own perception of Los Angeles as a clue for the direction of history based on his unprovable assumption that Los Angeles represents what will happen to the rest of the nation and so is the leading edge of history. But why should Los Angeles be considered the sign of the future any more than say Newark—that city lying in rubble as mute testimony to the incapacity of America to solve the terrible and agonizing intrication of the problems of racism and poverty?

33. Robert Jay Lifton, "Protean Man," in *The Religious Situation: 1969,* ed. Donald R. Cutter (Boston: Beacon Press, 1969), pp. 812–28.

34. Ibid., pp. 815 ff.

35. Ibid., p. 818.

36. Ibid., pp. 822 ff.

37. Charles A. Reich, *The Greening of America* (New York: Bantam Books, 1971).

38. Ibid., p. 2.

39. Ibid., p. 3.

40. Ibid., p. 37.

41. Ibid., p. 184.

42. Ibid., p. 176.

43. Ibid., p. 181.

44. Ibid., p. 251.

45. Ibid., p. 16.

46. Dwight Macdonald, *Against the American Grain* (New York: Random House, 1952, 1962), p. 37.

47. Ibid.

48. Theodore Roszak, *The Making of a Counter Culture* (Garden City: Anchor Books, 1969), p. 132.

49. Ibid., p. 267.

50. Theodore Roszak, *Where the Wasteland Ends* (Garden City: Doubleday, 1972), pp. xx ff., where he affirms "The Old Gnosis" against the religion of "Belief and Doctrine."

51. Ibid., p. 127.

52. Ibid., p. 113.

53. Ibid., p. 122.

54. Ibid., p. 135.

55. Erdman, *Poetry and Prose of William Blake,* pp. 198 ff.

56. Roszak, *Where the Wasteland Ends,* p. 135.

57. Thompson, *At the Edge of History,* p. xi.

58. Ibid., p. 58.

59. Ibid., p. 72.

60. Ibid., p. 113.

61. Ibid., p. 117.

62. Ibid., p. 119.

63. Ibid., p. 120.

64. Derek De Solla Price, *Science Since Babylon* (New Haven: Yale University Press, 1961).

65. Ian McHarg, "Man: Planetary Disease," *Vital Speeches* 37, no. 20 (August 1, 1971): 636.

ARTHUR I. WASKOW

1. Soncino Press edition of Midrash Rabbah in English, vol. 7, sec. 2, pp. 43–49.

2. *Franz Rosenzweig: His Life and Thought,* ed. Nahum N. Glatzer (Philadelphia: Jewish Publication Society, 1953), pp. 350–51. Original publication of this note to a poem by Judah ha-Levi, 1924.

3. Martin Buber, *Paths in Utopia* (Boston: Beacon Press, 1958), p. 129. Original publication in Hebrew, 1946.

EDITH WYSCHOGROD

1. G. W. F. Hegel, *Reason in History,* trans. Robert S. Hartman (Indianapolis: Bobbs-Merrill, 1953), p. 22.

2. G. W. F. Hegel, *The Phenomenology of Mind,* trans. J. B. Baillie (London: George Allen & Unwin, 1910), p. 105.

3. *Reason in History,* p. 23.

4. Op. cit.

5. Friedrich Nietzsche, *Twilight of the Idols,* in *The Portable Nietzsche,* trans. Walter Kaufmann (New York: Viking Press, 1954), p. 480.

6. Ibid., p. 542.

7. *Thus Spake Zarathustra*, in Kaufmann, *Portable Nietzsche*, p. 128.

8. My interpretation of "destructuring" reflects the analysis of Jacques Derrida in this connection. Derrida refers to "decentering," to the absence of something transcendental which is signified, thus forcing language to refer to other bits of language rather than to something outside itself, by means of which language "locates" itself as it were. Nietzsche's denunciation of philosophical language is cited as particularly significant in this connection: "I would particularly cite the Nietzschean critique of metaphysics, the critique of the concepts of being and truth, for which were substituted the concepts of play, interpretation, and sign (sign without truth present)," writes Derrida. See "Structure, Sign and Play," in *The Structuralist Controversy*, ed. Richard Macksey and Eugenio Donato (Baltimore: Johns Hopkins Press, 1970), esp. pp. 250 ff.

9. This point is stressed in Arthur C. Danto, *Nietzsche as Philosopher* (New York: Macmillan, 1965).

10. *On Truth and Lie*, in Kaufmann, *Portable Nietzsche*, pp. 46 ff.

11. Norman O. Brown, *Closing Time* (New York: Random House, 1973), p. 80.

12. Ibid., p. 88.

13. Ibid., p. 74.

14. *Thus Spake Zarathustra*, p. 129.

15. *Reason in History*, p. 31.

16. Ibid., p. 29.

17. Lewis Pauwels and Jacques Bergier, *The Morning of the Magician*, trans. Rollo Myers (New York: Avon Books, 1960), p. 218.

18. Robert Lifton, *Boundaries* (New York: Random House, 1967), p. 45.

19. Philip Rieff, *The Triumph of the Therapeutic* (New York: Harper & Row, 1966), p. 93.

20. *Closing Time.*, p. 109.

21. George Steiner, *In Bluebeard's Castle* (New Haven: Yale University Press, 1971), p. 15.

22. Ibid., pp. 54 ff.

23. This claim has been made by analysts of contemporary culture too numerous to mention. Among them might be cited: Marshall McLuhan, Theodore Roszak, Alvin Toffler, William Erwin Thompson.

24. Theodore Roszak, *Where the Wasteland Ends* (Garden City: Doubleday, 1972) p. 421.

25. The humanizing possibilities of technology are also stressed in Willian Irwin Thompson, *At the Edge of History* (New York: Harper & Row, 1971).

26. The term "biblical metaphysics" is used by Claude Tresmontant to indicate the experiential, nonmythological character of biblical thinking. He tends to identify this metaphysics with what is true in the sense of what can be verified by experience. I wish, rather, to emphasize its nonintrospective character, its point of reference being covenantal history rather than personal psychic development. The latter motion is totally foreign not only to ancient Israel but to Greek thought as well, since the idea of freedom upon which it depends appears fully only in the eighteenth century. For Tresmontant's view, see "Biblical Metaphysics," *Cross Currents* 10, no. 3 (Summer 1960): esp. 247 ff.

LIONEL RUBINOFF

1. Goethe, *Faust*, pt. I, "Night."

2. *Reason in History* (New York: Bobbs-Merrill, 1953), pp. 27, 25.

3. "My Negro Problem and Yours," *Commentary*, February 1963, p. 101.

4. Trans. Max Hayward and Manya Harari (London: Collins & Harvill Press, 1958).

5. Ibid., p. 22.

6. Ibid., pp. 117–18. Cf. also, Albert Memni, "Does the Jew Exist?" *Commentary*, November 1966, and *The Liberation of the Jew* (Orion Press, 1966).

7. *God's Presence in History* (New York: New York University Press, 1970).

8. Cf. George Steiner, in *Psychology Today*, February 1973, p. 57.

9. "Jewish Values in the Post-Auschwitz Future," *Judaism*, Summer 1967, p. 278.

10. Dietrich Bonhoeffer, cited by Emil Fackenheim in "Jewish Faith and the Holocaust," *Commentary*, August 1968, p. 34.

11. Cf. Emil Fackenheim, *Quest For Past and Present* (Boston, Beacon Press, 1968), introduction.

12. Ibid., p. 18.

13. Ibid.

14. "Jewish Faith and the Holocaust," p. 31.

15. Ibid., p. 32. *God's Presence in History*, p. 79.

16. "Jewish Faith and the Holocaust," p. 32.

17. For a further discussion of functional rationality, see Karl Mannheim, *Man and Society in an Age of Reconstruction* (London: Routledge & Kegan Paul, 1940), and Lionel Rubinoff, "Technology and the Crisis of Rationality: Reflections on the Death and Rebirth of Dialogue," *Philosophy Forum* 15, no. 3/4 (1976).

18. "Psychological Characteristics of Man Projected in the Image of Satan," *Catholic Psychological Record*, Spring 1967.

19. "For a Sociology of Evil," *Journal of Social Issues* 25 (1969): 115.

20. "Some Conditions of Obedience and Disobedience to Authority," *Human Relations* 18, no. 1 (1965): 57–76. See also *Obedience to Authority* (New York: Harper & Row, 1974).

21. "Obedience and Disobedience to Authority," p. 67.

22. "The Visibility of Evil," *Journal of Social Issues* 25 (1969).

23. "Obedience and Disobedience to Authority," p. 124.

24. *The Shadow of Hitler: A Critique of Political Consciousness* (Chicago: Quadrangle Books, 1967), p. 31.

25. *Critique of Pure Reason*, trans. Norman Kemp Smith (London: Macmillan Co., 1952), p. 20.

26. *Sketch for a Theory of the Emotions*, trans. Philip Mairet (London: Methuen & Co., 1962).

27. *Anti-Semite and Jew*, trans. George J. Becker (New York: Schocken Books, 1948), pp. 18–19, 22.

28. *Mein Kampf*, trans. Ralph Manheim (Boston: Houghton Mifflin Co., 1971), p. 65.

29. Cited by Werner Maserin *Hitler: Legend, Myth and Reality* (New York: Harper & Row, 1974, p. 170)

30. *Anti-Semite and Jew*, pp. 43–45.

31. "Anti-Semitism through Theological Silence": Bonhoeffer and the Nuremberg Laws," in *Muhlenberg Essays* (Allentown, Huckleberry Collage, 1968, p. 202)

CHARLES E. SILBERMAN

1. Ralph Bunche, foreword to *The Reaction of Negro Publications and Organizations to German Anti-Semitism*, by Lunabelle Wedlock (Washington: Howard University Press, 1942).

2. Richard Wright, *Black Boy* (New York: Harper & Row Perennial Classics, 1966), p. 70–71.

3. Jacob R. Marcus, *Early American Jewry* (Philadelphia: Jewish Publication Society, 1961), 1:419.

4. Bertram W. Korn, *American Jewry and the Civil War* (New York and Philadelphia: Meridian Books and Jewish Publication Society, 1961), chap. 2.

5. Robert G. Weisbord and Arthur Stein, *Bittersweet Encounter: The Afro-American and the American Jew*, contributions in Afro-American and African Studies, no. 5 (Westport, Conn.: Negro Universities Press, 1970).

6. Charles Keil, *Urban Blues* (Chicago: University of Chicago Press, 1966), pp. 17–18; Roger D. Abrahams, *Positively Black* (Englewood Cliffs, N. J.: Prentice-Hall, 1970), p. 27. Cf. Roger D. Abrahams, *Deep Down in the Jungle* (Chicago: Aldine, 1970); Lee Rainwater, *Behind Ghetto Walls* (Chicago: Aldine 1970); Eliot Liebow, *Tally's Corner* (Boston: Little, Brown, 1967).

7. Cf. Samuel F. Yette, *The Choice: The Issue of Black Survival in America* (New York: Berkley, 1972).

8. Abraham J. Heschel, "The Religious Basis of Equality of Opportunity: The Segregation of God," in *Race: A Challenge to Religion*, ed. Matthew Ahmann (Chicago: Henry Regnery, 1963).

Contributors

SHLOMO AVINERI is Director General of the Israeli Foreign Ministry. Until 1976 he was Dean of the Faculty of Social Sciences and Professor of Political Science at the Hebrew University of Jerusalem. He has also served as visiting professor at Yale, Wesleyan, Cornell, and the Australian National University in Canberra. His books include *Israel and the Palestinians* (1971) and *Hegel's Theory of the Modern State.* (1972) His articles have appeared in numerous journals.

Gregory BAUM, O.S.A., is Professor of Religious Studies and Theology at St. Michael's, College of the University of Toronto. During Vatican II Baum was a member of the Secretariat for Promoting Christian Unity in Rome. He has been active in the ecumenical movement and Jewish-Christian relations. He has published several books, most recently *Recently and Alienation: A Theological Reading of Sociology* (1975).

WALTER BURGHARDT, S.J., is Professor of Patristic Theology at the Catholic University of America and editor of *Theological Studies.* He has published several books and numerous articles, is a member of the Papal International Theological Commission and the Faith and Order Commission of the World Council of Churches, and has participated in many Lutheran-Catholic and Jewish-Christian conversations.

ALAN T. DAVIES is Professor of Religious Studies at Victoria College, the University of Toronto. He studied at McGill University, received his Ph.D. from Union Theological Seminary, and did postdoctoral studies at Hebrew Union College in Cincinnati. He has seved as a minister of the United Church of Canada. He is the author of many articles and reviews, and of *Anti-Semitism and the Christian Mind* (1969).

EMIL FACKENHEIM is Professor of Philosophy at the University of Toronto. Born in Germany, he was ordained a rabbi in Berlin, and studied at the Universities of Aberdeen and Toronto. He has published numerous articles, mostly on medieval Arabic and Jewish philosophy, German idealism, and Jewish thought. His books include *Metaphysics and Historicity* (1961), *The Religious Dimension in Hegel's Thought* (1967), *God's Presence in History: Jewish Affirmations and Philosophical Reflections* (1970), and *Encounters Between Judaism and Modern Philosophy: A Preface to Future Jewish Thought* (1973).

EVA FLEISCHNER is Professor of Religion at Montclair State College, N.J. Her articles and reviews have appeared in a variety of journals, and she is author of *The View of Judaism in German Christian Theology* (1975). She is a member of the Grail, an international movement for Christian Women.

IRVING GREENBERG is Professor and Chairman of the Department of Jewish Studies at City College of CUNY. He also serves as Director of the National

Jewish Conference Center. His field of special interest is Jewish religious thought. He spent 1974–75 in Jerusalem on a Fellowship from the National Endowment for the Humanities, working on a book dealing with the religious and ethical impact of the Holocaust.

MILTON HIMMELFARB is Director of the Information and Research Services of the American Jewish Committee, editor of the *American Jewish Year Book*, and contributing editor of *Commentary*. He has been visiting professor at the Jewish Theological Seminary, the Reconstructionist Rabbinical College, and Yale. He is the author of *Jews of Modernity* (1973).

JOHANNES HOEKENDIJK was born of Dutch missionary parents in Indonesia. During World War II he was involved in the Dutch resistance struggle through his work as a student pastor. After serving in Indonesia and as Secretary for Evangelism in the World Council of Churches, he became Professor of Church History of the Twentieth Century at Utrecht University. From 1965 until his death in 1975 he was Professor of Mission at Union Theological Seminary. His best-known book in English is entitled *The church Inside out* (1966)

THOMAS HOPKO is Professor of Systematic Theology at St. Vladimir's Orthodox Theological Seminary in Crestwood, N.Y. He is also Vice-Chairman of the Department of Religious Education of the Orthodox Church in America.

CLAIRE HUCHET-BISHOP worked for thirteen years as close collaborator with the historian Jules Isaac, and is responsible for the English editions of *The Teaching of Contempt* (1964) and *Jesus and Israel* (1971). She has lectured widely in the United States and Europe, and is the author of two books for young people dealing with Judaism, as well as of *How Catholics Look at Jews*, (1974). She is on the Board of the Amitie Judeo-Chretienne de France, and chairperson of the International Council of Christians and Jews.

PAUL JACOBS is a writer, television commentator, and social critic, editor of *New Outlook*, and Associate Fellow with the Institute for Policy Studies in Washington, D.C. He has written for a wide variety of magazines and is the author of many books, among them: *To Serve the Devil* (with Saul Landau and Eve Pell, 1971), *Prelude to Riot* (1966), and *The New Radicals* (with Saul Landau, 1966).

ALFRED KAZIN is Distinguished Professor of English at the City University of New York, and has also taught at other universities, both in the United States and in Europe. Among his books are *On Native Grounds* (1942), *A Walker in the City* (1951), *Contemporaries* (1962), and *Bright Book of Life* (1973).

CHARLES H. LONG is the William Rand Kenan, Jr. Professor of the History of Religion at the University of North Carolina, Chapel Hill, and previously was Professor of the History of Religion and Dean of Students at the University of Chicago Divinity School. A past president of the American Academy of Religion and the editor of the *Journal of the History of Religion,* he is the author of *Alpha: The Myths of Creation* (1963) and other works.

JOHN T. PAWLIKOWSKI, O.S.M., is Professor and Acting President of the Catholic Theological Union in Chicago. He is a past chairman of the National Council of Churches' Faith and Order Study Commission on "Israel: Land, People, State." He lectures widely and contributes to many journals. Among his books are *Catechetics and Prejudice* (1973).

PAUL RITTERBAND is Professor at the City College of CUNY, and Director of the Institute for the Study of Modern Jewish Life. He was ordained at the Jewish Theological Seminary, and holds his Ph.D. in sociology from Columbia. He is the author of many papers, and editor of the book *Student Migrants* (1968), a study of Israeli migration to the United States.

LIONEL RUBINOFF has taught at the University of Toronto and York University, and is currently Professor of Philosophy at Trent University. In addition to articles and reviews in scholarly journals, he is the author and editor of several books, including *Faith and Reason: Essays in the Philosophy of Religion by R. G. Collingwood* (1968), *Tradition and Revolution* (1971), and *Lordship and Bondage: The Master-Servant Theme in Hegel and Marx* (with John O'Neill, 1968).

ROSEMARY RADFORD RUETHER holds the Georgia Harkness Chair of Theology at Garrett-Evangelical Seminary in Evanston, Illinois. She has taught at the Howard University School of Religion, and at the Harvard and Yale Divinity Schools. She contributes to many magazines and journals and lectures widely. Among her most recent books are *Faith and Fratricide: The Theological Roots of Anti-Semitism* (1974), *New Woman/New Earth* (1975), and *From Machismo to Mutuality* (with Eugene Bianchi, 1975).

MICHAEL D. RYAN is Professor of Theology at Drew University. He was a Fulbright Fellow at the University of Tuebingen and received his Ph.D. from Drew University, where he studied as a Kent Fellow and Rockefeller Doctoral Fellow. He is a contributor to the volume edited by Littell and Locke, *The German Church Struggle and the Holocaust* (1974), and edited *The Contemporary Explosion of Theology* (1975).

SEYMOUR SIEGEL is Professor of Theology at the Jewish Theological Seminary, and Adjunct Professor of Jewish Studies at the City College of CUNY.

AARNE SIIRALA is Professor of Religion at Wilfrid Laurier University in Waterloo, Ontario, and at the Waterloo Lutheran University. He was born in Finland, was ordained in the Finnish Evangelical Lutheran Church, and served as pastor in Finland for some years. He is affiliated with the Therapeia Foundation, a meeting place for theologians and psychiatrists. He is the author of numerous articles in Finnish, Swedish, German, and American periodicals. Among his books are *Gottes Gebot bei Martin Luther* [The Commandment of God in Martin Luther] (1956), and *The Voice of Illness: A Study in Therapy and Prophecy* (1964).

CHARLES SILBERMAN is Director of the Study of Law and Justice, a research project funded by the Ford Foundation. He has taught at Columbia University, City College of CUNY, and the Training Institute of the International Ladies Garment Workers Union. From 1953 to 1971 he was a member of the editorial staff of *Fortune* magazine. His most recent book, *The Open Classroom Reader* (1973), is a companion volume to the widely acclaimed *Crisis in the Classroom* (1970).

ARTHUR I. WASKOW is Fellow of the Institute of Policy Studies, member of Fabrangen and Tzedek Tzedek in Washington, D.C., on the Advisory Committee of Breira, and author of *The Bush Is Burning* (1971).

ELIE WIESEL is Distinguished Professor of Jewish Studies at the City College of CUNY. A survivor of Auschwitz, he is the author of many books, among them *Night* (1960), *The Jews of Silence* (1966), and *Souls on Fire* (1972). He has written the text for an oratorio, *Ani Maamin,* and a play, *Zalmen; or, The Madness of God.*

EDITH WYSCHOGROD is Professor of Philosophy and Director of the Religious Studies program at Queens College, CUNY. She is the author of *Emannuel Levinas: The Problem of Ethical Metaphysics* (1974), and has written for such journals as the *Thomist, Philosophy East and West, Cross Currents,* and *Judaism.* She has edited *The Phenomenon of Death: Faces of Mortality* (1973).

YOSEF HAYIM YERUSHALMI is Professor of Hebrew and of Jewish history at Harvard. He is the author of *From Spanish Court to Italian Ghetto* (1971) and other works on the history of Sephardic Jewry, the Marranos, and the Inquisition, and of *Haggadah and History* (1975).

Some References to the Symposium in Newspapers and Journals

NEWS COVERAGE

New York Times,	June 4, 1974
	June 5, 1974
	June 6, 1974
	June 9, 1974 (*Sunday Times*)
New York Post,	June 4, 1974
	June 6, 1974
Jerusalem Post,	June 7, 1974
Newsweek	June 17, 1974 (International edition)

A DEBATE

New York Times,	June 25, 1974 (Op Ed page, William Styron)
	July 24, 1974 (A reply to Styron)

REPORTS AND ANALYSES

Gregory Baum, "Theology after Auschwitz: A Conference Report," *Ecumenist* 12, no. 5 (August 1974). The entire issue is devoted to this report, which is the fullest account of the Conference to have appeared.

David Glanz, "The Holocaust As a Question," *Worldview,* September 1974, pp. 36–38. The author looks not only at the content of the Symposium but at the process as well, much of which he criticizes.

Tracy Early, "Jewish-Christian Dialogue: Sorting out the Issues," *Christianity and Crisis,* 34, no. 18 (October 28, 1974): 234–39.